THE GOSPEL OF JOHN

A UNIVERSALISTIC READING

Biblical Hermeneutics Rediscovered

The Series as the name suggests will focus on Biblical Hermeneutics, i.e., literary works concerned with methods of interpreting the Old and New Testaments of the Bible via different stream of topics like Literature and Poetry, Indigenous Philosophizing, Ethical response towards Ecology, Health and Healing, Science and Technology, Feminist Theology, Sociological approach towards Human Rights, Law and Politics, Arts, History of Ideas, Ancient Civilizations, Cultural Contiguity, Religious Cosmologies and Mysticism, Appraisal of various Theologians, World Peace and Harmony, Global Capitalism, Network Marketing, Cybertheology, Population and Demographics, Epigraphic Studies, Contextualized Education, and many others. We welcome a Mss. on any topic/s mentioned, whether they are original works, scholarly monographs, collections of conference papers, revised dissertations, or translations of historical documents. Through the Series we, the Publishers, are striving to put forward published works that may help Institutions, Academic Bodies, Researchers, Scholars and the World at large in furthering their respective knowledge and understanding on the concerned subject. We welcome your comments on our efforts and further suggestions on how we can enshrine new ray of analysing and explaining the written Texts through our upcoming books.

Biblical Hermeneutics Rediscovered - 25

THE GOSPEL OF JOHN

A UNIVERSALISTIC READING

Johnson Thomaskutty

Foreword by
Paul N. Anderson

CWI
Christian World Imprints

First Published in 2020 by

Christian World Imprints
Christian Publishing & Books from India
C-3, Shop No. 14, Ground Floor
Wazirpur Industrial Area, **Delhi-110052**
cwidelhi2017@gmail.com
www.ChristianWorldImprints.com
Phone: +91 11 41526079

ISBN: 978-93-5148-400-4 (HB)
ISBN: 978-93-5148-401-1 (PB)

Printed in India.

Contents

Foreword vii

Acknowledgements ix

Introduction xi

PART I: Universalistic Linguistics and Literary Characteristics of John 1

Chapter 1: Universalistic Language and Literary Style of the Fourth Gospel 3

Chapter 2: Re-reading the Gospel of John in the Light of William Carey's Linguistic Methods 15

Chapter 3: Dialogical Nature of John's Prologue 37

Chapter 4: Dialogue as a Literary Genre in the Book of Signs (John 1:19-12:50) 53

PART II: Universalistic Nature of Themes and Characters in John 75

Chapter 5: Glo[b/c]alization and Mission[s]: Reading John's Gospel 77

Chapter 6: Missional-Pneumatology of the Fourth Gospel 97

Chapter 7: Explorations of *Prosperity* in the Fourth Gospel 111

Chapter 8: Characterization of Thomas in the Fourth Gospel 125

PART III: Dynamic Localization: Johannine Texts and the Contexts 143

Chapter 9: Biblical Interpretation in the Global-Indian Context: Reading John 4:1-42 as a Paradigm 145

Chapter 10: "Religious Freedom and Conversion in India Today": Reading John's Gospel as a Jewish-Christian Conflict Narrative 153

Chapter 11: Johannine Women as Paradigms in the Indian Context 173

Chapter 12: The Event of Foot Washing in John 13:1-20 as a Paradigm for Witnessing Christ in the Indian Context 191

Chapter 13: Faith and Theology in the Johannine Community and in the Reformation: A Paradigm in the Indian Context 209

Chapter 14: Reading John's Gospel in the Nepali Context 229

Chapter 15: Reading John's Gospel in the Bangladeshi Context 245

Bibliography 261

Index of Ancient Sources 289

Index of Authors 297

Foreword

One of the most intriguing features of the Fourth Gospel is its tensive presentation of nearly all of its major theological themes. John's Jesus is presented as the most human and the most divine everywhere in the New Testament; the Son is both equal to the Father and yet subservient; the Spirit proceeds from the Father and is also sent by the Son; miracles are embellished and existentialized—to name a few. Indeed, John's literary and historical riddles abound, but its theological riddles continue to captivate the attention of its readers across the bounds of time and space.[1]

While these truths held in tension precipitated worldwide discussions among Christians of the second to fifth centuries, leading to the classic theological confessions of Christianity from Nicea to Chalcedon (325-451 CE),[2] one of the great theological issues of the modern era pivots on the question of salvation.[3] Put pointedly, how could it be that there is only one way to the Father, Jesus Christ (John 14:6), while the Light of Christ enlighten everyone (John 1:9)? Is salvation exclusively limited to those who get their theology right in confessing Jesus as the Christ and Son of God, or might people responding in faith to God's saving initiative and grace be recipients of that gift, even before they come to appreciate more fully the timeless truth of standard Christian expressions. Along these lines, a more nuanced understanding of the saving-revealing work of Jesus as the Christ in the Gospel of John is required,

---

[1] The origin, character, and meaning of thirty-six of these tensions and perplexities—theological, historical, and literary riddles—are laid out in my text: *The Riddles of the Fourth Gospel: An Introduction to John* (Minneapolis: Fortress, 2011).

[2] Paul N. Anderson, *The Christology of the Fourth Gospel: Its Unity and Disunity in the Light of John 6* (3rd edn. Eugene: Cascade Books, 2010).

[3] See also my treatment of "The Saving/Revealing Work of Christ: Universal or Particular?" in *Riddles*, 34-35, 183-186.

and in the present book, Johnson Thomaskutty has provided helpful treatments of this and other important subjects.

In particular, Thomaskutty here addresses John's literary and theological features in ways that are both globalizing and localizing. John's message speaks to all persons in culture-transcending ways, and yet it also speaks clearly to the local readers within particular cultures. The dialogical character of John's linguistics draws people into transformative dialogues with Jesus, whether it is through an engaging story or a worship hymn at the beginning of the Gospel. In the narrative, characterization also plays a role within John's missional outreach. Indeed, misunderstanding subjects expose the flawed views of this-worldly perspectives, while the teachings and example of Jesus lift the reader's sight to authentic ways forward. In these and other ways, John's story of Jesus also addresses pressing contemporary issues: economic disparity, the role of women, interfaith dialogue, political power, and social concerns. Thus, John's story of Jesus reaches today's audience, offering liberating insights into authentic spirituality and liberating truth.

Just as the Fourth Gospel spoke powerfully across faiths and cultures two millennia ago, it continues to speak to audiences today in globalizing and localizing ways. Along these lines, Johnson Thomaskutty's new book furthers a growing number of internationalizing biblical studies, lifting our understandings of ancient texts beyond their western interpretations, which have all too often missed the sociological and grounded nuance of a passage. Especially within the contexts of India, Bangladesh, and Nepal, as well as other nations, John's cross-cultural and multivalent thrust of Jesus and his ministry is especially welcome. Thus, furthering the good works of Kanagaraj, Ravindra, and others, this new book will speak to modern and postmodern audience powerfully, connecting people with the one claiming to the Way, the Truth, and the Life.

After all, if the Light of Christ is indeed at work—illuminating at least potentially all persons, regardless of culture, faith, gender, age, or status—John's Jesus may yet speak to that which is "of God" among unexpected audiences today, just as he did in ancient times. And, if such be the case, the liberating words of Jesus will certainly ring true for today's readers: "You shall know the truth, and the truth shall set you free" (John 8:32).

Paul N. Anderson
Professor of Biblical and Quaker Studies at George Fox University
Newberg, USA;
Professor of Religion at the North-West University
Potchefstroom, South Africa

Acknowledgements

After the publication of the monographs, like *Dialogue in the Book of Signs: A Polyvalent Analysis of John 1:19-12:50* (Leiden/Boston: E. J. Brill, 2015) and *Saint Thomas the Apostle: New Testament, Apocrypha, and Historical Traditions* (London/New York: Bloomsbury T & T Clark, 2018), the current book is the third major publication of the Center for Biblical Research (CBR). CBR facilitates the study of the Bible for theological education, missional and ministerial advancement, and contextual reflections.

This monograph is a revised version of some of my academic presentations in some of the national and international consultations and seminars. At this moment, I am deeply indebted to some of my teachers and academic colleagues who inspired me to the field of Johannine studies. They include my *Doktorvater* Prof. Dr. Jan G. van der Watt of Radboud Universiteit Nijmegen, Holland; Prof. Dr. James H. Charlesworth of Princeton Theological Seminary, USA; Prof. Dr. Paul N. Anderson of George Fox University, USA; and many others. My one-on-one discussions with them helped me in several ways during the brainstorming, writing and revision processes. I remain thankful to all of them.

Majority of the chapters in this book were presented in different national and international consultations and a few of them were delivered as lectures in some of the prestigious universities, like New Testament Scholars Meet (NTSM) in Bangalore, Centre for Mission Studies (CMS) Consultation in Pune, Radboud Universiteit Nijmegen in Holland: Union Biblical Seminary Faculty Seminar in Pune, Aarhus University in Denmark, Princeton Theological Seminary in USA, Harvard Divinity School in USA, Cambridge University in UK, South Asia Institute of Advanced Christian Studies (SAIACS) in Bangalore, Fuller Theological Seminary in USA, Hindustan Bible Institute in Chennai, Serampore College in West Bengal, Madras Theological Seminary in Chennai, Nepal Theological Forum in Nepal, 500th Anniversary of Reformation in Germany, and Bangladesh Mission Forum in Bangladesh. I remain thankful to all those who involved me in those consultations, seminars and lectures.

Special thanks to Prof. Dr. Paul N. Anderson of George Fox University for writing a Foreword for this book and Prof. Dr. Brian C. Wintle of Asia Theological Association for his meticulous reading of the manuscript and writing an endorsement. I am deeply indebted to my students and colleagues in Union Biblical Seminary, Pune, for your moral and intellectual support. I thank Mr. Sudhanshu Kanda and the entire team of Christian World Imprints, Delhi, for their professional support in publishing this monograph. I thank my wife Shyni, daughter Jemimah, and son Jeremiah for their continuous support. This monograph is dedicated to all my Johannine students who challenged me to take a different path in my academic pursuit.

Johnson Thomaskutty
Pune, India
November 2019

Introduction

The Fourth Gospel functions as a literary masterpiece that facilitates a narrative beyond the time and space aspects. The Gospel's linguistic phenomena and stylistic aspects are peculiar as they attune the attention of the readers toward a dramatic and ideological world that facilitates myriad possibilities of interpretation. The connection between the narrator and the historical/implied/contemporary reader is established from an eternal vantage point as the narrator directs the reader toward atemporal and universal realities. The author as a classicist encompasses the socio-cultural and religio-political realities of the Greco-Roman world, incorporates the hope of the Jewish society, foregrounds the contextual realities and the struggles of the Johannine community, and fulfills the various demands and requirements of the future generations of the readers and the believers. The peculiar linguistic and idiosyncratic techniques of the narrator have the power to absorb the attention of the reader not only from a 'there and then' and 'here and now' senses but also from an 'everywhere and ever' perspective. In that sense, the Fourth Gospel functions as a gnomic and universalistic artistry.

The word *gnome* can mean 'a wise, pithy saying,' 'a maxim,' or 'an aphorism' expressing a general truth or principle.[1] "Gnome" is metaphorically defined as "an ageless and often deformed dwarf of folklore who lives in the earth and usually guards treasure." The symbolical representation of a deformed dwarf conveys a semantic detail that connotes timeless or ageless facts.[2] The adjectival form of the word is *gnomic* that means "consisting of, or using gnomes or aphorisms or sententious."[3] Gnomes are used without the

---

[1] The Greek expression *gnōmē* means an 'opinion.' See A. S. Hornby, *Oxford Advanced Learner's Dictionary*, Sixth Edition (Oxford: University Press, 1948/2000).

[2] It is also connected to *ginōskō* that means 'know.'

[3] Hornby, *Oxford Advanced Learner's Dictionary*.

implication of time to express a general truth. In the process of interpreting the Fourth Gospel, an interpreter can view that John as a classicist expresses his ideas and characters in a gnomic and timeless way in order to sustain its effect atemporally. This peculiar feature of the Gospel has to be analyzed for a renewed interest and for a universalistic interpretation.

John's Gospel can be considered as a commentary in its own terms. The peculiar chronology of the Gospel with its pre-existent Christology (1:1-5), the event of an early temple cleansing (2:13-22), repeated visits of Jesus to the temple at Jerusalem (2:13-22; 7:14; 10:22-23), the focus of Jesus' mission in the Judean, the Galilean, and the Samaritan contexts, the narrations about the feasts and the festivals, and other details demonstrate the idiosyncratic nature of the narrator. The extended episodes of the Fourth Gospel, different from the Synoptic style of pericopes, foreground the ideas of the author through the exchange and episode developments. The Logos-Christology and the poetic demonstration of the coming of Jesus (1:1-18) reveal its universalistic aspects. As Kermode states, the Fourth Gospel as a whole has to be considered as a fusion of poetry and history, that means, a fusion of the universal and the particular.[4] While history is concerned with the contingent, poetry is concerned with the universal.[5] In that sense, John interprets history in the form of a quasi-poem, an interpretation, or ultimately a commentary in its own way. This style of the Gospel is designed with a gnomic perspective.

A week long explanation of the call narratives (1:19-2:12), the dialogue to monologue development of the Nicodemus story (3:1-21), the extended dialogue between Jesus and the Samaritan woman (4:1-42), the story of the invalid and the succeeding theological discourse (5:1-47), the feeding of the five thousand followed by an extended bread discourse (6:1-15, 22-71), the detailed Tabernacles discourse (7:10-8:59), the dramatic development of the story of the man born blind (9:1-41), the Good Shepherd imagery and its detailed explanation (10:1-18), the episode of the raising of Lazarus (11:1-54), the extensive Farewell Discourse (13:1-17:26), the seven-scene development of the trial of Jesus (18:1-19:42), the appearance of Mary Magdalene and Thomas in the climax (20:1-29), the post-resurrection appearance of Jesus (21:1-25) and other events reveal the commentary style of the Fourth Gospel. The narrator has his own order, length, and duration in developing the characterization, plot development, and point of view throughout the Gospel. The literary devices and the figures of thought rhetorize the story with a peculiar punch.

---

[4] See Frank Kermode, "John," *The Literary Guide to Bible* (Harvard: University Press, 1987), 3-16).

[5] See Mark W. G. Stibbe, *John*, Readings: A New Biblical Commentary (Sheffield: JSOT Press, 1993), 19.

The Fourth Gospel's 'vertical' and 'realizing' eschatology and the 'ever-continuing' present aspect support its gnomic and universalistic development. The Gospel's pre-existent Christology and the emphasis on life/eternal life take the reader's attention toward the everlasting perspective. The maxims like "I AM Sayings" and the symbolic presentation of the Signs attune the attention of the readers toward the universal significance of the Gospel. The narrator and the implied reader dynamism of the text enable the modern readers to understand the narrative world of the Gospel. The contemporary readers find this dynamism of the text as an interpretative means to get engaged with the text. The purpose statement of the Gospel (20:30-31; cf. 21:25) makes the implied reader aware of the logic behind all the events and the coherence of the discourse units. The narrator is fully concerned to inspire readers *in/with* the text to believe/continue to believe in Jesus that he is the Messiah and the Son of God and that through believing they may receive 'eternal life' and be saved. Thus, from the soteriological point of view, the Gospel promises eternal guarantee and protection.[6]

The dialogues as active voice and direct speech units influence the reader to be a 'believer' and to be saved. This feature of the dialogue enables it to be a performative act in itself. It provides pleasure to the reader and helps her/him to be persuaded, provoked and transformed. Thus, the text works with all the characteristic features of a rhetorical masterpiece. The text, in that sense, cannot be reckoned as a 'passive' treatise rather as an 'active' counterpart to the reader. It happens only when the narrator takes extra effort to tell the story dramatically through the means of *showing* and *telling* (cf. Quintilian, *Inst* 10.1.19-27, 10.2.1-2, 10.2.27).[7]

The fifteen chapters in this book analyze some of the key ideas and characters with a universal perspective. In that process, the Gospel as a whole is treated as a timeless and space- transcending narrative that encompasses the feelings and aspirations of the people from an eternal and universal perspective. The fifteen chapters of the book arc diveded into three sub-sections, like "Universalistic Linguistics and Literary Characteristics in John," "Universalistic Nature of Themes and Characters in John," and "Dynamic Localization: Johannine Texts and the Contexts." The first four chapters are included under the first sub-section as they focus on the linguistic and literary characteristics of the Fourth Gospel. While the first and the second chapters address the gnomic linguistic pattern of the Gospel, the third and the fourth chapters explore the literary master plan from the narrative pattern of the Gospel.

[6] Johnson Thomaskutty, *Dialogue in the Book of Signs: A Polyvalent Analysis of John 1:19-12:50* (Biblical Interpretation Series 136; Leiden/Boston: E. J. Brill, 2015), 480-481.

[7] Thomaskutty, *Dialogue in the Book of Signs*, 479.

The first chapter entitled *Gnomic Linguistic and Literary Style of the Fourth Gospel* attempts to understand the typical linguistic and literary aspects of the Gospel with an emphasis on its deep structures. Its usage of the present indicatives, aorists, and present participles and the symbolic and metaphorical portrayal of facts and events guide the readers to some of the atemporal and eternal realities. In that sense, the Fourth Evangelist uses language and literary aspects in his own idiom to rhetorize the facts with a universal appeal. This feature of the Gospel persuades the readers to understand the linguistic and literary aspects of the Gospel from a different vantage point.

The second chapter entitled *Re-reading the Gospel of John in the Light of William Carey's Linguistic Methods* further demonstrates the paradigmatic relevance of the Fourth Gospel in the Bengali [and Indian] contexts taking into consideration the linguistic aspects of the Gospel and the sociolinguistic methods of William Carey in the Indian context. Carey's colloquial linguistic phenomena that include dialogic genres, *code switching*, *diglossia*, *Sadhu Bhasha*, *Christian Bengali*, and attention to both the popular and lesser tongues see results in the Indian context. John's usage of language and linguistic phenomena in the Gospel can be understood with the help of William Carey's linguistic methods. The Johannine narrator uses language as a means that connects oral history, social dynamics, linguistic matrix, epistemological details, historical insights, and literary rhetoric to develop an ideological and contextual artistry. In that sense, the Fourth Evangelist is a linguist par-excellence in several ways similar to the linguistic expertise of William Carey.

The third chapter entitled *Dialogical Nature of John's Prologue* takes the attention of the reader toward the Gospel's quasi-poetical and timeless facts. The interactional, intra-textual, and inter-textual relations of the prologue and its poetical and dialogical nature within the text, beyond the text, and between the 'world from below' and the 'world from above' reflect its ideological and phenomenological connections. In the text, the narrator interweaves history with poetry in order to reveal the essential realities with a global punch. This aspect of the Gospel foregrounds its eternal and universal reverberations. As the poetical and rhythmic style is integrally connected to the universalistic function, the Fourth Gospel has to be perceived from the eternal and idealistic standpoint.

The fourth chapter, i.e., *Dialogue as a Literary Genre in the Book of Signs (John 1:19-12:50)*, spearheads the literary genre called dialogue as a means of universalistic element in the Gospel. The narrator uses dialogue at the *micro-*, *meso-*, and *macro-*levels of the Gospel to stitch the story as a unified and complete whole in order to convey the message in a universalistic idiom. Dialogue as the basic unit of communication is employed to develop the human and divine realities. The narrator embeds it within the *intradiegtic* and *metadiegetic* narrative framework.[8] As a universally employed literary genre, dialogue appears as a means to convey the message of divine salvation. As the chapter outlines, the Johannine dialogue has the following peculiarities: first, the Aristotelian style of ordering the story by keeping a *beginning*, a *middle*, and an *ending*; second, the rhetoric of *ethos*, *logos*, and *pathos* in order to attract the attention of the readers; and third, its poetical development with an emphasis beyond the time-and space-boundaries.[9] The semantic, syntactic, and pragmatic aspects of the Johannine dialogues encompass the human feelings and aspirations with a universal and eternal implication.

In the second sub-section of the book, the universalistic nature of the themes and characters is at focus. While the fifth, the sixth, and the seventh chapters deal with several themes of the Gospel, the eighth chapter is an exclusive analysis of the character of Thomas. The fifth chapter entitled *Glo[b/c]alization and Mission[s]: Reading John's Gospel* attempts to see the way Trinitarian mission is outlined in the Fourth Gospel in relation to the global realities. In this chapter, the discussion is all about Johannine community's local struggles and aspirations and their alignment with the universal revelation of the divine reality. The fusion of the *Sitz im Leben Jesu*, *Sitz im Leben Kirche*, and *Sitz im Leben Indien* demonstrates the universalistic and atemporal implications of the Gospel as a gnomic masterpiece. The chapter attempts to delineate the local and global dynamism and the mission of the *God-Father*, *Savior-Son*, and *Spirit-Paraklete* in closer relationship with the day to day struggles of the Johannine community. This is done with a universalistic intent in mind.

The sixth chapter titled as *Missional-Pneumatology of the Fourth Gospel* takes the attention of the reader toward the progressive manifestation of the Holy Spirit: first, Spirit-endowment upon Jesus; second, its promise for the disciples; and third, the Johannine Pentecost as the ultimate fulfillment of all the promises. The Missional-pneumatology of the Fourth Gospel underscores the missional role and status of the Holy Spirit in a comprehensive and universalistic manner. The chapter is an attempt to see the unique features of the Johannine pneumatology and to understand the missional aspects of the Gospel by placing the Holy Spirit at the significant narrative transitions. The personal, communal, missional and gnomic aspects of the Holy Spirit can be understood with a special punch from the narrative annals of the Fourth Gospel.

The seventh chapter entitled *Explorations of Prosperity in the Fourth Gospel* discusses wealth, health, and happiness from a Johannine perspective by critiquing the trends of prosperity interpretations in the contemporary churches. The chapter outlines the way the Fourth Gospel emphasizes certain

---

[8] Thomaskutty, *Dialogue in the Book of Signs*, x.

[9] Thomaskutty, *Dialogue in the Book of Signs*, 470-474.

gnomic maxims to develop the idea of prosperity with the help of a network of ideas and concepts. It also emphasizes how the concept of prosperity develops around the themes such as faith, love, knowledge, and abundant life and how the characters within the Gospel "increase" or "decrease" on the basis of their relationship with Christ. The spiritual growth of the believers and its impact on generations beyond time and space are at focus in the deliberations of the Gospel.

The eighth chapter entitled *Characterization of Thomas in the Fourth Gospel* considers Thomas as a historical and at the same time ideological character who demonstrates a new way forward in faith journey. Thomas appears in the Gospel in some of the significant narrative intervals with a narrative closure to the story (chaps. 20-21). The characterization of Thomas in 20:24-28 and his apex utterance in 20:28 introduce an inclusio with the narrative statement in 1:1. Thomas' appearances in 11:16; 14:5; 20:24-28; and 21:2 add a unique plot structure to the story and a resolution of its own with a universalistic intent. As the character of Thomas appears in the important transitions, the narrator places him as a symbolical figure in order to actualize certain ideological aspects. As a loyal, inquisitive, and developing model, Thomas' character contributes certain levels of narrative impact to the story.

In the third sub-section of the book, the dynamic contextualization of the texts and the contexts is at view. The ninth chapter, titled as *Biblical Interpretation in the Global-Indian Context: Reading John 4:1-42 as a Paradigm*, foregrounds some of the key factors related to Biblical interpretation in a pluralistic context. By outlining four key aspects such as crossing the traditional boundaries in interpreting the text, creating contextual and ideological constellations, building dialogical relationships, and rhetorizing the discourse toward a "third space," the chapter emphasizes a locally-oriented and globally-focused interpretation of the Johannine text. In the chapter, a paradigm is suggested to lead the interpreters moving away from *pure localization* to *dynamic localization* methods in order to brainstorm the text with eternal appeal. In the process of reading the text, the horizons of the text and the interpreter are fused together to form a "third space." Jesus' conversation with the Samaritan woman illustrates such an ideational and universalistic approach.

The tenth chapter entitled *Religious Freedom and Conversion in India Today: Reading John's Gospel as a Jewish-Christian Conflict Narrative* sharpens the conflict between the Johannine community and the Jewish community in alignment with Jesus' conflict with the Jewish leaders of his time. In the chapter, the aspects of religious freedom and conversion in the Jewish society are taken into account to develop a new rhetoric in the Indian context. As the attempt here is to understand John's story as a *tri-level drama* (over against the prevailing notion of a *two-level drama*), the chapter develops as a gnomic masterpiece that can encompass the aspirations and struggles of the persecuted Christian groups. As John is a unique dramatic document, its ideas can be considered as paradigmatic in the contemporary Indian context. This aspect of the Gospel demonstrates its quality as a persuasive artistry that spans beyond the time and space aspects.

The eleventh chapter entitled *Johannine Women as Paradigms in the Indian Context* suggests a new paradigm by bridging between the First Century CE realities and the Twenty-First Century CE realities. The struggles and marginalization of women in the First Century context and their freedom in the Jesus Movement are reconsidered for a renewed interest and a hermeneutical interplay. The characters such as the Mother of Jesus, the Samaritan woman, Martha and Mary of Bethany, and Mary Magdalene are foregrounded as gnomic figures rather than descriptive characters. The metaphorical and symbolical aspects of the Gospel coupled with its ideological framework introduce a new paradigm. The Gospel's contemporaneity is reflected in the process of interpretation. The current chapter also attempts to build the story of the Johannine women in closer relationship with the struggles of the Indian women for liberative action. The historical and symbolical roles of the Johannine women introduce a unique paradigm with a universal appeal.

The twelfth chapter entitled *The Event of Foot Washing in John 13:1-20 as a Paradigm for Witnessing Christ in the Indian Context* describes the *being*, *becoming*, and *doing* aspects pertinent to the mission and ministry of the Johannine community. John's Gospel as a flexible, accommodative, and gnomic literary masterpiece has all the ingredients to stretch its message and bring implications to people from all places without limiting the timeframe. While Jesus' *being* nature as the only begotten and eternal Son of God and his *becoming* nature as one who washes the feet of the disciples are highlighted, the narrator also emphasizes the disciples' *doing* by looking at the universal realities in general terms. The *agape*-centric utterances of Jesus in the Farewell Discourse and their connections with the foot washing event help the reader to connect the universal realities of loving, serving, and having fellowship with one another. In that sense, the event of foot washing foreshadows Jesus' death on the cross and thus its universal significance. The current chapter looks at how the narrative is conducive to the Indian realities and how its reverberations can introduce a new ethics in the contemporary context.

The thirteenth chapter entitled *Faith and Theology in the Johannine Community and in the Reformation: A Paradigm in the Indian Context* attempts to underscore how faith and theology were conceptualized and practiced in the Johannine community and how they were taken into account during the Reformation in the European context. In the chapter, the Johannine community, the Reformation Movement, and the Indian Christian Community are brought into a parallel line in order to fathom faith and theology in a Johannine way. The gnomic hermeneutical and interpretative processes enable us to see how Jesus Movement was a paradigm for the Johannine community and how was it with the Reformation Movement and the Indian Christianity. In that way, the first century realities of the Johannine community, the sixteenth century contexts of the Reformers, and the twenty-first century realities of the Indian Christians are brought into parallel lines to foreground the transformative and paradigmatic role of the Gospel beyond time and space aspects.

The fourteenth and fifteenth chapters such as *Reading John's Gospel in the Nepali Context* and *Reading John's Gospel in the Bangladeshi Context* contextualize the message of John's Gospel with a local impact and a global orientation. The narrative master plan of the Gospel is contextually analyzed through the perspectives of the narrator, the implied reader, and the contemporary reader. In that process, the aspect of discipleship, persecution, mission and eschatology, women and mission, power misuse and corruption, children at risk, and other concerns are looked at from a holistic and gnomic perspective. As the Johannine community situation is analyzed in par with the Nepali and Bangladeshi contextual aspects, a new rhetoric is facilitated to understand the narrative dynamics beyond time and space.

The fifteen chapters of the current book propose a gnomic or universalistic reading strategy. The following aspects of the Fourth Gospel are important in that process: first, the unique linguistic and literary aspects of the Gospel guide the reader toward some of the general and atemporal realities embedded within the narrative framework; second, the quasi-poetical, dialogical, and rhetorical framework of the Gospel invites the reader to be engaged with the text and to fathom its universalistic outlook; third, the historic and at the same time representative role of the characters function as indicatives to the reader for a global outlook; fourth, the figurative, metaphorical, and symbolical expressions of the Gospel invite the attention of the reader to some of the common platforms and universalistic truths; fifth, the universalistic utterances of Jesus (i.e., the "I AM Sayings") and their performative side (i.e., the signs) inspire the reader beyond time and space aspects; sixth, the "direct speech" statements of Jesus within the narrative framework provide a poetical outlook to John's story and that enables the reader to get involved in the narrative world of the Gospel; and seventh, the dualistic framework of the Gospel attunes the attention of the reader toward the eternal and salvific truths from above. Moreover, the Trinitarian outlook, the open-ended and flexible nature, the global missional emphasis, and the vertical and realizing tendency of the Gospel accommodate the aspirations and struggles of the people from a universalistic perspective. These characteristic features of the Gospel call our attention toward its classical and gnomic function.

The pre-existent Christology is engraved within the general, simple and deep structures of the Fourth Gospel with a focus on people's response. The family metaphor of the Gospel portrays the integral connectivity of the Triune God in the affairs of the Johannine community and that in turn enables the reader to associate its story with the contemporary realities. The literary devices and the figures of thought provide an impression and aesthetic to the modern realities of the reader. The Gospel has the power and potential to absorb the local realities (like Indian, Nepali, and Bangladeshi) through its peculiar situational details and characterization. Thus, an interlocking between the narrator and the reader is demonstrated through the narrative annals from a gnomic and universalistic perspective. This tendency of the Gospel is detailed with more clarity in the chapters hereafter.

PART I

Universalistic Linguistics and Literary Characteristics of John

Chapter 1

Universalistic Language and Literary Style of the Fourth Gospel

Introduction

The Fourth Gospel is framed with the help of multiple linguistic and literary features. One of the peculiar aspects of the Gospel is its usage of the universalistic linguistics and literary framework to make its semantic and pragmatic domains beyond the time and space aspects. The narrator's peculiar usage of the present indicatives, aorists, and present participles and other literary features make us to think about its intended readers beyond the First Century CE socio-religious and politico-cultural contexts. In the process of reading the Gospel, a reader can raise the following questions: Can we construe that John uses language in his own idiom? Do we need to think that the Fourth Evangelist frames his language and literary artistry with a universal intent? What are the ways and means through which the Fourth Evangelist takes the attention of the reader toward atemporal aspects? The task of the chapter is threefold: first, analyzing the peculiar linguistic and literary aspects of the Gospel; second, understanding the various elements of the Gospel in relation to the universal linguistic phenomena; and third, interpreting the Gospel with an 'everywhere and ever' perspective.

A Bird's Eye-view of Gnomic or Universalistic Language

Gnomic language is universalistic in scope and *atemporal* in its duration, sense, and meaning contrary to the temporal and descriptive linguistic phenomena found either within an oral discourse or in a literary unit.[10] Although the author/narrator may use a tense in the indicative mood, the time indicated by that tense may be other than or broader than the real time of the event. The text through the context, lexeme, and other grammatical features will normally give sufficient clues to signal for such suggestions.[11] Tsoukas and Knudsen define, "Gnomic utterances are the opposite of narrative ones: they are situated neither in place nor in time."[12] In that sense, gnomic utterances direct the attention of the reader even beyond the space-bound and time-bound facts. Wallace states that,

> The present tense may be used to make a statement of a general, timeless fact. 'It does not say that something *is* happening, but that something *does* happen.' The action or state continues without time limits. The verb is used 'in proverbial statements or general maxims about what occurs at *all* times.'[13]

Wallace distinguishes between two predominant semantic situations in which the gnomic present occurs: first, instances that depict *deity or nature as the subject of the action.*[14] Such gnomic presents are true *all* the time. There is a *second* kind of gnomic, slightly different in definition: the use of the present

---

[10] Daniel B. Wallace, *Greek Grammar Beyond the Basics* (Grand Rapids: Zondervan, 1996), 523.

[11] Wallace states that, "Examples of time *other than* what the tense (in the indicative) signifies include the historical present, futuristic present, proleptic aorist, epistolary aorist." Similarly, "Examples of time *broader than* what the tense (in the indicative) signifies include gnomic present, extension-from-past to present, gnomic aorist, gnomic future." See Wallace, *Greek Grammar*, 498.

[12] Gnomic present "has to do with *ethos*: both Bible and folklore wisdom favor the gnomic present. Partly, it is a matter of special kind of *logos*. There is no base on which to contest a statement in gnomic present. Any sentence situated in a real time and place can be contested as to its validity: there are other witnesses, or at least there are counter-examples from different places and times. Not so with the gnomic present, which is situated no-place in no-time and features abstract protagonists." Haridimos Tsoukas and Christian Knudsen, eds., *The Oxford Handbook of Organizational Theory: Meta-Theoretical Perspectives* (Oxford: University Press, 2003), 243.

[13] See Wallace, *Greek Grammar*, 523. Fogle says, "The gnomic present is actually a sub-group under the aoristic (punctiliar) present. The gnomic present expresses general truth but this does not mean there are no continuing consequences. The gnomic present is timeless in reality, meaning that it is true of all time. It is sometimes called the proverbial present because this use of the present occurs in proverbial statements or general maxims about that which occurs at all times." Joe Fogle, *One Flesh: A Biblical Perspective on the Permanence of Marriage* (Eugene, Oregon: Wipf & Stock, 2007), 85.

[14] For instance, statements such as 'the wind blows' or 'God loves' fit within this category.

in *generic* statements to describe something that is true *any* time.[15] The above description amply explains that gnomic presents function both in *all* and *any* time with a general and universalistic sense.

Gnomic present statements are usually absolute and axiomatic in sense.[16] Many substantial participles in the New Testament are also used in generic utterances. Most of these instances involve the present participle.[17] The *pas hō akouōn* (or *agapōn, poiōn*, and others) formula is always or almost always generic. As such it is expected to involve a *gnomic* idea. In narratives, aorists are also used with a gnomic intent (John 1:12). Gnomic or parabolic rhetoric is one of the peculiar speech-patterns of Jesus within which he uses generic metaphorical/figurative style to convey some universal truths (see John 10:1-21; 15:1-11).[18] Terry comments that, "“Proverbs proper are . . . to be understood as short, pithy sayings, in which a wise counsel, a moral lesson, or a suggestive experience, is expressed in memorable form. Such sayings are often called *gnomic* because of their pointed and sententious form and force."[19] The present indicatives and present participles have their own peculiar functions in the process of interpretation. The universalistic aspect of the speaker or narrator may be understood mostly on the basis of the verbal semantics involved in their speech patterns.

Universalistic Linguistic References in John's Gospel

In gnomic present expressions, the natural realities are usually used to identify and explain some of the divine axioms. In John 1:5, the narrator expresses a universalistic factor that occurs all the time: "The light shines in the darkness,

[15] For instance, these are events or statements that can occur at *any* time rather than a universal statement that is true *all* the time. Wallace says, "This kind of gnomic present is more common. Thus, pragmatically, it is helpful to note a particular grammatical intrusion: *A gnomic verb typically takes a generic subject or object*. Further, the present participle, especially in such formulaic expression as *pas hō + present participle* and the like, routinely belong here." See Wallace, *Greek Grammar*, 523.

[16] Wallace, *Greek Grammar*, 525. Wallace also defines the gnomic aorist in the following way: "The aorist indicative is occasionally used to present a timeless, general fact. When it does so, it does not refer to a particular event that *did* happen, but to a generic event that *does* happen. Normally, it is translated like a simple present tense." See Wallace, *Greek Grammar*, 562.

[17] See Wallace, *Greek Grammar*, 615.

[18] Henderson comments that, "In relation to Jesus, rhetoric assures us of the perspicuity and intentional significance of the repeated pattern; we can know how gnomic or parabolic rhetoric worked in Jesus' speech-world. On the other hand, the same gnomic and intensified (*deinos*) rhetoric advises us to search for the historical meaning, the *logos*, of Jesus' allusive and vehement style precisely in the definition of Jesus' *ethos* and in its summons of an audience to personal adherence (*pathos*)." Ian H. Henderson, *Jesus, Rhetoric and Law*, BINS 20 (Leiden: Brill, 1996), 71.

[19] See Milton S. Terry, *Biblical Hermeneutics* (Eugene: Wipf & Stock, 1999), 239.

and the darkness did not overcome it." The usage of three aspects such as a universal element (i.e., *to phōs* [the light]) in the form of a subject, a present indicative (i.e., *phainei* [shines]) as the verb, and another universal aspect (i.e., *tē skotia* [the darkness]) as the object qualifies the expression all the features of a gnomic utterance.[20] In the first clause, the subject *to phōs* refers to Jesus (v. 4), the present active indicative *phainei* functions as a gnomic verb, and *tē skotia* functions as the opposite to the subject.[21] As the Fourth Evangelist interchanges *Word* (*logos*; John 1:1, 14), *Light* (*phōs*, John 1:4-5; 3:19-20; 8:12; 9:5, 39), and *Life* (*zoē*, John 3:15-16; 6:33, 48; 11:25; 14:6) throughout the Gospel, a reader is able to see the universal significance of the Word at the core of the discussion.[22] The sequence of eternal Word/Light as the subject, a gnomic verb as the guiding semantic element, and a universal object as the opposite reality direct the utterance into a complete circle. It is a unique expression to introduce the universality of Jesus as the light with a gnomic effect. The same is repeated in v. 9 where Jesus is introduced as *to phōs to alēthinon* ('the true light'), his action is stated again in the present indicative format (i.e., *phōtidzei* [enlightens]), and the object is *panta anthrōpon* 'everyone' (yet another general maxim to address the universal effect beyond time and space).[23] As the prologue of the Gospel sets a gnomic framework that integrates both the divine and the natural elements, the rest of the narrative has to be understood within this interpretative principle.

In 1:12, the narrator states that accepting Jesus enables people to get the unique status of 'becoming his children' (*tekna theou genesthai*).[24] Here the narrator uses a gnomic aorist at the heart of the statement. Gnomic aorists are reckoned as punctiliar tenses with generic maxims. Alongside of the present indicatives, aorist tenses also indicate gnomic features. The gnomic aspects of the Fourth Gospel are not restricted to the utterances of Jesus and the narratorial voice. But, some of the truths revealed to the followers are also declared in gnomic present forms. For example, Nathanael declares that "Rabbi, you are

---

[20] Francis J. Moloney, *The Gospel of John*, Sacra Pagina 4 (Collegeville: The Liturgical Press, 1989/1998), 42-43.

[21] Beasley-Murray states that, "The present *phainei* is unexpected; it embraces history and the present time of the Evangelist. The true light of the Logos shone in the primal darkness at creation, and continued amidst the darkness of fallen mankind; it shone with greater brilliance in the glory of the Incarnate One; and it shines on in the era of the Resurrection, which is the time of the Paraclete." See George R. Bearley-Murray, *John*, WBC 36 (Nashville: Thomas Nelson Publishers, 1999), 11.

[22] Beasley-Murray comments that, "The Logos is Mediator not only in the act of creation, but in its continuance. Hence *zoe* (life) and *phōs* (light) include the life and light which come to man in *both* creation *and* new creation." Bearley-Murray, *John*, 11.

[23] Cf. Moloney, *The Gospel of John*, 43-44.

[24] Moloney, *The Gospel of John*, 44.

the Son of God, you are the King of Israel" (*Rabbi, su ei ho huios tou theou, su basileus ei tou Israēl*, v. 49). Nathanael's utterance reveals Jesus' eternal sonship and Kingship to the world.[25] Another example we see in 3:8, where a natural phenomenon (i.e., *to pneuma* [the wind/the spirit]) appears as the subject, the verb *pnei* (blows) is in the present indicative form, and the spatial expression is *hopou thelei* (where it desires).[26] Here the work of the Holy Spirit is explained in gnomic idioms (that is, "The wind [the Spirit] blows where it chooses") that demonstrates the universal work of the Holy Spirit.[27] In most of the cases, the work of the Holy Spirit develops in closer alignment with the work of Jesus. The paradigmatic maxims of the narrator, the parabolic utterances of Jesus the protagonist, and the divine declarations of the interlocutors together foreground the gnomic linguistic phenomena within the Fourth Gospel. This tendency further attributes a universalistic narrative framework for the Gospel as a whole. This is very clear when the divine maxims are explained in relation to the natural phenomena.

The statement of Jesus in 3:16 is both gnomic and continual that explains: "everyone who [continually] *believes* (*pas hō pisteuōn*) in him should not perish."[28] Gnomic aspects are introduced not only through the present indicatives and aorists, but also through the use of the present participle (see 3:16), especially in soteriological contexts in the NT.[29] The obvious symbolic structure and gnomic language of the story of the woman at the well foreground its representative nature. When John uses the expression *pas hō pinōn* ("everyone who drinks" in 4:13), it may be that the evangelist does have a habitual (as well as the gnomic) idea in mind.[30] Similar expressions with universal maxims are expressed also in 1:38; 2:10; 4:14, 24; 14:17, and in other places.[31] The Fourth evangelist employs three methods with prime focus to make the gnomic aspects foregrounded: first, through narrative statements (1:1-18; 3:31-36); second, through the utterance of Jesus the protagonist (3:8; 4:7-26); and third, through the revelatory means as the interlocutors utter about Jesus (1:29, 33, 49; 4:7-26).

Dialogue as a Universalistic Literary Aside

It is not only the linguistic aspects but also the literary asides contributed toward the gnomic/universalistic framework of the Fourth Gospel. A

---

[25] Beasley-Murray, *John*, 27.

[26] Wallace, *Greek Grammar*, 524.

[27] Beasley-Murray, *John*, 49.

[28] See Wallace, *Greek Grammar*, 522.

[29] See Wallace, *Greek Grammar*, 620-621.

[30] Moloney, *The Gospel of John*, 122.

[31] See Wallace, *Greek Grammar*, 621.

paradigmatic reader of the Gospel can perceive that the exchanges and episodes are rhetorical to form a dramatic plot within the extended narrative master plan (see 1:19-2:12; 2:13-22; 3:1-21; 3:22-36; 4:1-42; 4:43-54; 5:1-47; 6:1-71; and others).[32] Within the gospel, the dialogues are foregrounded as the major component of the narrative sections. It helps the narrator to tell the story artfully and also to communicate it performatively.[33] In order to achieve his goal, the implied reader functions as a narrative clue to the historical as well as the contemporary readers. The narrative technique of showing and telling provides interpretative avenues within the Gospel as it inspires the historical and contemporary readers to see the chances of contexualization of the story.[34]

The narrator engages the modern readers through the means of dialogues with contemporaneity. The first and second person language of the dialogues sustains the dramatic and *live* demonstration of the events. The character dialogue in the Gospel functions as a major narrative link to facilitate a wider dialogue between the narrator and the modern reader.[35] Though dialogue is a distinguishable literary category, its interaction with the narratives is strong within the Gospel. Klink says, "the dialogues cannot be divorced from the narrative movement and emplotment of the gospel as a whole."[36] In most of the cases, dialogue remains cryptic if not linked to the narrative expositions. Similarly, the narratives themselves are incomprehensible apart from the dialogue. This mode of interlocking of the narratives and the dialogue is a conspicuous phenomenon within the text.[37] This mode of transaction facilitates a dialogue between the narrator and the modern readers through the means of character dialogue embedded within the text.

The reader of the text can configure its fullest meaning only through adopting interactive reading techniques. The Johannine phenomenon of placing the dialogue within the narrative framework prompts the reader to associate these two component parts in an integrated way. Witherington says that, "There are narratives, discourses, and dialogues between 1:19 and 12:50, meant to reveal something about Jesus' ministry."[38] This nature of the text suggests that the readers (i.e., both *inside the text* and *with the text*) should be watchful not only of the interlocutors within the story but also of what the narrator suggests,

---

[32] See the exchanges and episodes in the Gospel of John. Thomaskutty, *Dialogue in the Book of Signs:* 461.

[33] See Thomaskutty, *Dialogue in the Book of Signs*, 466.

[34] Thomaskutty, *Dialogue in the Book of Signs*, 466.

[35] See Thomaskutty, *Dialogue in the Book of Signs*, 474.

[36] https://www.biola.edu/blogs/good-book-blog/2011/dialogues-in-the-gospel-of-john.

[37] Thomaskutty, *Dialogue in the Book of Signs*, 477.

[38] See Ben Witherington, *John's Wisdom: A Commentary on the Fourth Gospel* (Louisville: Westminster John Knox, 1995), 41.

where he guides, and how he makes movements. There develops a dialogue between the narrator and the readers *inside* and *with* the text.[39] This double-layered nature of the dialogue is exposed in an inseparable way through the reading of the text.[40] This peculiarity of John's text is globalistic in style with an 'everywhere and ever' effect in the interpretative processes.[41]

The Usage of Universalistic Metaphors

The usage of metaphors, imageries, and figurative language, and their symbolical application provides the readers a universal effect in the initiative of reading the text.[42] Even the type scenes John uses (for example, John 4:7-26 is usually considered as a type scene of Gen 24:34-67) enable the readers to relate the narrative with their own thought-world.[43] A similar story of a high-caste man asking water to a lower-caste woman is narrated in the Buddhist traditions.[44] The metaphors in John represent one of the most significant elements in the totality of the communication process.[45] Metaphors are used to produce new meanings in new contexts. They transfer the semantic and pragmatic aspects of the text to new situations. The metaphorical expressions and their symbolical meanings take semantic shapes into the emerging life situations. John makes use of imageries in 10:1-11 and 15:1-15 in order to convey the divine truths in worldly idioms. He often uses events and objects from everyday life to communicate a message in natural ways.[46] Moreover, the metaphors and imageries he uses are mostly familiar to the universal audience and they can create a gnomic effect in the *Sitz im Leben* of the contemporary reader.

---

[39] See Thomaskutty, *Dialogue in the Book of Signs*, 24-25.

[40] Thomaskutty, *Dialogue in the Book of Signs*, 478.

[41] In John, dialogue is used as a linguistic and literary means that "connects oral reality, social dynamics, linguistic matrix, epistemological details, historical insights, and literary rhetoric to develop a contextual and ideological artistry." For more details read, Johnson Thomaskutty, "Re-reading the Gospel of John in the light of William Carey's Linguistic Methods," *Serampore Mission: Perspectives in Contexts* (Delhi: ISPCK, 2019), 109, 94-122.

[42] See Jan G. van der Watt, *Family of the King: Dynamics of Metaphor in the Gospel according to John* (Boston: Brill, 2000), 8.

[43] See Paul N. Anderson, *The Riddles of the Fourth Gospel: An Introduction to John* (Minneapolis: Fortress Press, 2011), 84.

[44] José Ignacio Cabezón, *Sexuality in Classical South Asian Buddhism*, Studies in Indian and Tibetan Buddhism (Somerville: Wisdom Publications, 2017), 468-469.

[45] Van Den Heever, "Theological Metaphors and the Metaphors of John's Gospel," *Neotestamentica* 26/1 (1992), 89. Jan G. van der Watt defines metaphor as "giving the thing a name that belongs to someone else." See Van der Watt, *Family of the King*, 8.

[46] Craig Koester, *Symbolism in the Fourth Gospel: Meaning, Mystery, Community* (Minneapolis: Fortress Press, 1995), 2.

John begins his Gospel as a whole with a Christological metaphor, *Logos* (*Word*) in 1:1-5. He uses *Logos* not only as a title for Jesus but also as a metaphor to denote the pre-existent nature and incarnation of the Son.[47] The Word eternally existed with God, both in close communion and oneness with Him (1:1).[48] The temple of Jesus' body in 2:21 is a genitive metaphor that states that the body (of Jesus) is the Temple.[49] The theme of water appears continually throughout the Gospel (see 1:26; 2:1-11; 3:5; 4:7-15; 5:1-9; 6:16-21; 7:37-38; 9:1-12; 13:1-20; 19:34; 21:1-3). This universal metaphor is mostly used to refer regeneration and transformation in human life.[50] Similarly, the usage of 'food' as a metaphor in 4:31-34 and 6:41-59 is obvious.[51] As Jan G. van der Watt considers 'the family of God' (God as Father; Jesus as Son of God; and believers as children) is a metaphor to be considered with universal effects.[52] The expressions like "Son of God" (1:14, 18; 3:16, 18), "Eternal life" (1:4; 3:15; 4:10; 7:38; 11:25), "water" (4:14-15, 26, 39, 42), "bread" (6:27, 33, 35, 51), "light" (8:12; 9:5; 12:46), "darkness/night" (1:4-5, 9-11; 8:44) and others are universally significant metaphors in order to decipher divine realities. As Loader says, "The God of Jesus is the God who offers bread and light and life in whatever guise, language, culture or religion."[53] The narrator's attempt to catch the attention of the universal audience and to interlock the message with 'everywhere and ever' situations is obvious in the text.

The Universalistic Aspect of the "I AM" Sayings

The Greek formula *egō eimi* or *ego* (*I am* or *I*) exhibit a unique authority and identity of Jesus. His self-revelatory aspects are potentially reflected through his "I AM" sayings (see 6:35, 48; 8:12; 9:5; 10:7, 9, 11; 11:25; 14:6; 15:1, 5).[54] His saying "I am the bread of life" (6:35, 48) is stated after giving thanks and distributing the bread, and feeding the five thousand people (6:1-15).[55] While

---

[47] Beasley-Murray, *John*, 10-11.

[48] Jey J. Kanagaraj, "Use of New Testament Metaphors in Mission," *Transformation* 23/2 (April 2006), 122.

[49] Moloney, *The Gospel of John*, 82-83.

[50] Stephen D. Renn, *Expository Dictionary of Bible Words* (Peabody: Hendrickson Publishers, 2005), 1031.

[51] Renn, *Expository Dictionary of Bible Words*, 400.

[52] Van der Watt, *Family of the King*, 161-393.

[53] William Loader, "Competing Spiritualities: Reflections on John 6 in Global Perspective," *Matthew, Paul and Others: Asian Perspectives on New Testament Themes* (Innsbruck: University Press, 2019), 287-288.

[54] Anderson, *The Riddles of the Fourth Gospel*, 14-16.

[55] A comparison is made between the manna of the Law and Jesus, the true bread from heaven. In that way, while the manna of the Law of Moses was effective in the past, Jesus is the bread of life with everlasting effect. See Moloney, *The Gospel of John*, 218.

he utters that he is the "light of the world" in 8:12, he appears as the fulfiller of the festival of lights (or the festival of Tabernacles) described in chapters seven and eight.[56] His second usage of the expression in 9:5 is described in the context of giving sight to a blind person (9:1-41). The utterances "I am the gate for the sheep" (10:7, 9) and "I am the good shepherd" (10:11, 14) are expressed immediately after the expulsion of the man born blind from the synagogue (9:34). In his response, Jesus implies that while the Jews expel people from their assemblies on account of him, he is right there to accept them as a "gate for the sheep."[57] While the Jews are unable to solve the lifelong problems of the man who was closely associated with them in their assemblies, they are reduced to "hired hands." Jesus' significance as the "good shepherd" through his involvement in the life of the person is brought to the notice of the reader.[58] While the dialogues/discourses are presented in relation to some significant local events, Jesus' self-revelatory aspect is the highlight through these "I AM" Sayings."[59] The "I AM" Sayings in all these cases appear as indicative utterances with universal significance.

Jesus' self-revelatory statement that he is the "resurrection and life" (11:25) appears in the context of Lazarus' raising from his death. In all cases, his utterances are supplemented with complementary actions. In 14:6, Jesus' revelation that "I am the way, the truth, and the life" is expressed in a local situation when the disciples are perplexed. The one who was able to turn water into wine (2:1-11) appears in 15:1-5 as the "True Vine." The Father appears as the gardener and the followers appear as branches.[60] In John, Jesus' utterances go beyond their literal meanings and actually *do* something. A paradigmatic reader can create a world of his/her own in the process of reading the text. In the language of Warren and Wellek, every reading is a performance.[61] John develops his narratives and discourses in his own idiom and persuades the reader with a personal punch. This narrator-and-reader interaction is poignantly presented through the medium of Jesus' "I AM" statements. Jesus' utterances in John enable us to derive the following semantic situations in the process of interpretation: first, Jesus' utterances, mostly the "I AM" Sayings, function as universalistic or atemporal in sense over against the particularistic

---

[56] Anderson, *The Riddles of the Fourth Gospel*, 14-15.

[57] Thomaskutty, *Dialogue in the Book of Signs*, 450-451.

[58] Koester, *Symbolism in the Fourth Gospel*, 17.

[59] Schneiders states that, "The sēmeia he [Jesus] performs and the words he speaks, are his own self-symbolization. The Gospel text is the literary resymbolization of Jesus for successive generations." See Sandra M. Schneiders, *Written That You May Believe: Encountering Jesus in the Fourth Gospel* (New York: A Herder & Herder Book, 1999), 74.

[60] See Thomaskutty, *Dialogue in the Book of Signs*, 452.

[61] Austin Warren and René Wellek, *Theory of Literature* (London: Jonathan Cape, 1955), 181.

and temporal senses; second, the narrator and the implied reader interaction is designed through the means of character dialogues and that further facilitates dialogues between the protagonists/narrator with the historical and the contemporary readers; and third, the metaphors attached to the statements of Jesus demonstrate their significance beyond the time-and space-realities.

Characters as Universalistic Figures

It is important to look at how the characters of the Gospel are perceived. There is a growing consensus among the Johannine scholars that the characters of the Gospel represent some ideologies and thus they are figurative within the narrative framework. Raymond F. Collins published two essays in 1976 indicating that Johannine characters as symbolic or representative types rather than historical persons.[62] While the mother of Jesus (2:1-11; 19:25-27) is introduced as a type of the Church,[63] the Beloved Disciple (13:18-30; 18:15-18; 20:3-10; 21:20-23) represented either the disciple *par excellence* or an ideal response of faith to Jesus.[64] The characters such as Nicodemus, the Samaritan woman, the invalid person by the pool, Nathanael, Thomas, the man born blind, and others were perceived from this perspective.[65] Collins argues that:

> [W]ithin the life-situation of the Johannine church we ought to envision a series of homilies directed to enkindling faith in Jesus. In the development of these homilies, various persons were chosen from the common gospel tradition or selected from his own tradition by the homilist in order to illustrate some point about the nature of faith, or lack of it, in Jesus Christ . . . [T] hey have been selected from the homiletic tradition of the Johannine tradition to teach the evangelist's readers something about that faith in Jesus Christ which is life-giving.[66]

According to Collins, major Johannine characters embody a dominant trait that is intended by the evangelist to represent a certain type of faith response to

---

[62] See Raymond F. Collins, "Representative Figures in the Fourth Gospel, I and II," *The Downside Review* 94 (1976), 26-46, 118-132. Cf. Christopher W. Skinner, "Introduction," *Characters and Characterization in the Gospel of John* (London: Bloomsbury T & T Clark, 2012), xix-xxii.

[63] The mother of Jesus is symbolized as a model of faith or an eschatological presentation of 'woman.' See Raymond F. Collins, *These Things Have Been Written: Studies on the Fourth Gospel*, LTPM 2 (Louvain: Peeters Press, 1990), 30-33; cf. Skinner, *Characters and Characterization in the Gospel of John*, xix.

[64] Collins, *These Things Have Been Written*, 42-45.

[65] Collins, *These Things Have Been Written*, 11-38.

[66] Collins, "Representative Figures," 7-8.

Jesus.[67] Similarly, Pamment's discussion also relies heavily on a representative understanding of character. She notes that Nicodemus represents the secret admirer rather than the open advocate. In her view, calling him 'the Pharisee who came to Jesus by night' would have emphasized his representative character.[68] Culpepper also states that, "They [characters] exist to serve specific plot functions, often revealing the protagonist, and may carry a great deal of representative or symbolic value."[69] Based on the textual clues in John and other NT writings, it is not feasible to consider the characters as merely representative figures. Rather it is more convenient to argue that the narrator of John uses history symbolically. The readers of the Johannine story can identify with the characters either positively or negatively, and thus enters into the symbolic portrayal of the history in a deeply personal way.[70] We can even consider some of the characters as prototypes of identity for Christ-followers.[71] In that sense, it is more viable to understand Johannine characterization as a merge of symbolism with historicity. This feature of the Gospel makes it gnomic in its narrative master plan.

The indications within John's narrative framework, such as "the true light, which enlightens *everyone*" (1:9), "*all* who received him, who believed in his name" (1:12), "*no one* has ever seen God" (1:18), "*no one* can see the Kingdom of God" (3:3), "*no one* can enter the Kingdom of God" (3:5), "*everyone* who believes in him" (3:16), "*everyone* who drinks" (4:13) and others, give us obvious clues of universalism. Such clues within John's narrative framework cannot be considered in local terms, but as universal realities.

Conclusion

As symbolism is the hermeneutical key of the Fourth Gospel, the events and utterances are recorded to address readers of/beyond the time and space realities. As John employs language in an idiosyncratic way, he attempts to describe history symbolically. John's peculiar linguistic and literary aspects attune the modern readers toward gnomic and atemporal maxims. As Jesus is

---

[67] See Skinner, *Characters and Characterization in the Gospel of John*, xx. Also see Margaret Pamment, "The Fourth Gospel's Beloved Disciple," *ExpTim* 94 (1983), 363-367.

[68] Pamment, "The Fourth Gospel's Beloved Disciple," 364. Also see W. R. Domeris, "The Johannine Drama," *Journal of Theology for Southern Africa* 42 (1983), 29-35; R. Alan Culpepper, *Anatomy of the Fourth Gospel* (Philadelphia: Fortress Press, 1983), 104; contra. Fred W. Burnett, "Characterization and Reader Construction of Characters in the Gospels," *Semeia* 63 (1993), 3-28; Cornelis Bennema, *Encountering Jesus: Character Studies in the Gospel of John* (Milton Keynes: Paternoster, 2009), 12-15.

[69] Culpepper, *Anatomy of the Fourth Gospel*, 104.

[70] Schneiders, *Written That You May Believe*, 75.

[71] See Philip F. Esler and Roland A. Piper, *Lazarus, Mary and Martha: Social-Scientific Approaches to the Gospel of John* (Minneapolis: Fortress Press, 2006), 17.

the self-symbolization of God in the Word became flesh,[72] the contemporary readers of the Gospel are expected to derive new semantics in the pragmatic domains of their time and space. In sum, the Gospel features some of the following interpretative principles: first, the present indicatives, the aorists, and the present participles of the Gospel have the potential to point us toward general maxims; second, the narrative statements, the utterances of Jesus the protagonist, and a large number of the revelatory utterances of the followers of Jesus usually point the reader toward universal truths; third, through the means of dialogue the narrator facilitates a narrator-and-reader interaction based on gnomic principles; fourth, through the means of metaphorical, figurative, and symbolical-linguistic framework, the story world of the gospel absorbs the realities of the modern reader; and fifth, as the narrator encodes the historical realities through the means of symbolism, the modern readers of the story can decode the message into their own *Sitz im Leben*. Thus, the narrative master plan and literary artistry of the Gospel attune the attention of the readers toward 'everywhere and ever' realities.

[72] See Schneiders, *Written That You May Believe*, 76-77.

Chapter 2

Re-reading the Gospel of John in the Light of William Carey's Linguistic Methods

Introduction

Here I attempt to understand William Carey's linguistic methods in the Bengali context in particular and the Indian context in general. Though Carey, with the help of several Indian *pundits*, initiated to bring transformative attempts in the Indian context, his contributions did not receive due attention from the academic communities in Indian and elsewhere. As Carey endeavored for the linguistic renaissance in the Bengali/Indian context, his achievements and contributions should be acknowledged and be given due attention. In this essay, I attempt to understand the linguistic contributions of Carey and also explore how his linguistic methods can bc cxpounded for interpreting the biblical documents in their own sociolinguistic contexts. With that aim in mind, I will implement some of the linguistic methods of Carey into the narrative framework of the Fourth Gospel and will explore the sociolinguistic matrix of the Gospel for interpretative avenues.

Answering the following questions might be significant in our investigation: How did Carey develop his linguistic methods in the Bengali/Indian context? Was Carey able to implement his linguistic methods effectively in the Bengali context? Can we use Carey's linguistic methods for interpreting the scriptures? How do Carey's linguistic methods help us to understand the sociolinguistic matrix of the Fourth Gospel? How is such a hermeneutical method useful for understanding the scriptures in the contemporary context?

My attempt here is to answer these and many other questions. The task of this study is threefold: understanding the linguistic contributions and methods of William Carey in the Indian context; implementing the methods in interpreting the sociolinguistic and communitarian dynamics of the Fourth Gospel; and developing a new hermeneutic for understanding the scriptures in the contemporary context.

William Carey's Linguistic Methods

In the following section, we attempt to analyze Carey's linguistic methods in the Bengali context in particular and the Indian context in general. That will bring a broader outlook of Carey's linguistic methods to see their possible avenues in the NT interpretation.

Grammar and Linguistics: A General Understanding

Linguistics is understood as a science devoted to the study of language in all its aspects such as structure, interrelationship with the rest of human activity, history and mutual relations.[73] Walter R. Bodine comments that, it is "the study of language as language, in contrast to the study of any specific language."[74] Linguistics as a discipline evaluates human language capability and other cognitive abilities.[75] Kutscher and Werning state that, "The current state of knowledge suggests that on the basis of common biological sensory systems, the human perception of space is driven by universally-applicable principles of signal processing and interpretation. This leads one to hypothesize that universal special concepts are to be found in human language."[76] In that sense, human language perceives the universals in particularistic contexts. It is mostly understood through the process of grammar and its syntactic connections.

It is believed that the Greeks were indeed greatly interested in the grammar of their language and that Plato is one of the first to speculate on it.[77] But, what is most admirable in the Greek conception of the business of grammar is that it includes rhetoric, prosody, and literary criticism.[78] The section on diction in Aristotle's *Poetics* is an early extant treatment of grammar in Greek and it is significant that the parts of speech are here examined as a part of critical

[73] See "Linguistics," *Encyclopaedia Britannica*, 162.

[74] See Bodine, "Linguistics and Biblical Studies," 327.

[75] See Kutscher and Werning, *On Ancient Grammars of Space*, vii.

[76] See Kutscher and Werning, *On Ancient Grammars of Space*, vii.

[77] Law comments, "In a series of dialogues Plato depicts Socrates deep in debate, showing how, through a careful process of questioning, it is possible to elicit knowledge that a person has never been taught." See Law, *The History of Linguistics in Europe*, 18.

[78] See Gupta, "William Carey and Bengali Grammar," 189-190.

activity.[79] In Latin too grammar includes everything that relates to the making and understanding of literature.[80] Quintilian of the first century CE divides grammar into two parts, the science of correct speech and the interpretation of poets.[81] In the Middle Ages, grammar was the most important branch of learning and the first of the seven arts.[82] Leonard Bloomfield considers Pānini's grammar that "it is one of the greatest monuments of human intelligence."[83] And those who know about the great Tamil grammar in *Tolkappiyam*, a work belonging to the Third Sangham, that is, the early centuries of the Christian era, would know how grammar in Dravidian letters was as comprehensible a literary discipline as it was in ancient Greece.[84] Thus, grammar as a discipline within the study of language was well-explored in the Western and in the South Indian contexts.

William Carey's Linguistic Initiatives

It is impossible to imagine life without the influence of language. The nation of India is popularly known for its plurality of languages and dialects. The term 'Indian' is perceived as a blend of all kinds of pluralities based on languages, socio-cultural ethos, religions, customs, beliefs, ethnicity, color, caste and creed. During the Enlightenment, in the eighteenth century, there was a renewed interest in grammar emerged in Europe.[85] This was the period in which the educated middle classes had assumed leadership in society and the vernaculars had become an effective instrument of communication for social change and intellectual progress.[86] When William Carey landed in Calcutta on 11th November 1793, the European Enlightenment was at its height and its manifestation in the study of language is to be found in great achievements

---

[79] See Modrak, *Aristotle's Theory of Language and Meaning*, 1-9.

[80] See Oniga, *Latin a Linguistic Introduction*, 1-8.

[81] See Chakkuvarackal, "Serampore Mission and the Linguistic Renaissance in India," 124-125; also see Law, *History of Linguistics in Europe*, 62.

[82] See Gupta, "William Carey and Bengali Grammar," 189-190.

[83] See Bloomfield, *Language*, 11; also see Gupta, "William Carey and Bengali Grammar," 191. Kapoor's text describes: "It [Panini's *Ashtadhyayi*] is a complete, explicit and comprehensive grammar of both spoken and textual (compositional) Sanskrit." See Kapoor, *Dimensions of Pānini Grammar*.

[84] See Athithan, *Linguistic Structures in Tamil*, 1-30.

[85] The period of Enlightenment in the 18th century was marked by the intellectual and philosophical conviction that truth could only be obtained through the powers of human reason, observation, and experiment. See McKim, *Westminster Dictionary of Theological Terms*, 90.

[86] Delon comments that, "European Enlightenment thinkers were interested in diverse aspects of language and languages: their structure, their historical relationships, their 'moral' and philosophical qualities, the methods used to teach languages, their function in society, and their role in science and literature." See Delon, *Encyclopedia of the Enlightenment*, 617.

in lexicography and grammar.[87] As a product of Enlightenment, Carey transformed many of the Indian vernaculars from their debased condition.[88]

Carey's Bengali Grammar published in 1801 reflects the new urge for a scientific study of living languages.[89] It appeared at a time when the Brahmin scholars of Bengal thought that the language was not respectable enough to deserve the attention of qualified grammarians.[90] As Gupta comments, "A society that values grammar values propriety in expression and when that society has no sense of propriety about anything it must not be expected to care for propriety in the use of language. Rule of law in language is guaranteed only by rule of law in public life."[91] As a youth, Carey learned Greek, Latin, and Hebrew. Moreover, he acquired substantial knowledge in Sanskrit, Oriya, Marathi, Punjabi, and Bengali languages. Bengali was his first-love apart from his deep love and attachment for Sanskrit.[92] The learned people of Bengal were not willing to dissociate themselves from the orthodox conventional style, largely derived from and shaped by classical Sanskrit language and literature.[93] William Carey and his Serampore associates started to advocate strongly for development and improvement of all the popular Indian languages.[94]

Carey's Linguistic Blend

Many held the view that William Carey's uncommon genius was best manifested in his linguistic works.[95] If he could concentrate his labor in this field only he undoubtedly would have been regarded as one of the greatest

---

[87] See Gupta, "William Carey and Bengali Grammar," 188.

[88] Mangalwadis say, "Carey transformed Bengali, previously considered 'fit only for demons and women' into the foremost literary language of India." See Mangalwadi, *The Legacy of William Carey*, 20.

[89] See Gupta, "William Carey and Bengali Grammar," 188.

[90] See Gupta, "William Carey and Bengali Grammar," 188. Bengali was called by those who speak it, *Banla* or *Bangla-bhasha*, the language of *Benga* or *Vanga* (in Sanskrit, the word 'Vanga' meant Eastern and central Bengal). See Chakkuvarackal, "The Serampore Mission and the Linguistic Renaissance in India," 126.

[91] See Gupta, "William Carey and Bengali Grammar," 188.

[92] See Mangalwadi, *The Legacy of William Carey*, 20.

[93] See Ray, "William Carey—Linguist with a Difference," 157.

[94] See Chatterjee, "William Carey and the Linguistic Renaissance in India," 159.

[95] Recognizing Carey's courageous missionary works and remarkable success in Bible translation into Oriental languages, Carey was awarded the Diploma of Doctor of Divinity by the Brown University of America on 8th March 1807. See Ray, "William Carey—Linguist with a Difference," 155-158; also see Mukhopadhyaya, "William Carey's Contribution for the Promotion of Sanskritic Studies," 194.

linguistic scholars of the world.[96] Though he emphasized on the vernacular school of thought, he also attempted to link the *Vernacularist* school with the *Orientalist*[97] and *Anglicist* schools of thought.[98] He was able to achieve greater heights in the fields of translation works, vernacular grammar, creating dictionaries and polyglots, and building vocabularies.[99] He developed his love toward Sanskrit language alongside of his special interest in Bengali.[100] Carey believed that the development of vernaculars would lead to a country's quick modernization.[101] With that aim in mind, he worked for the development of Bengali language and literature.

In a context in which Bengali was mostly used as a spoken language and rarely used as a written language, Carey attempted to develop the language through various means.[102] Ray comments that, "Carey was the first among the scholars and authors to have felt the need of recording the colloquial language with its own diction and distinctive style."[103] Though he was considered as a missionary, his attempts helped to promote the Indian languages in the educational, commercial, administrative and cultural activities. Carey's attachment to Serampore College and Fort William College enabled him to foster the vernaculars with focus. He worked, on the one hand, as a professor of Bengali and Sanskrit in Fort William College and, on the other hand,

---

[96] See Chakkuvarackal, "The Serampore Mission and the Linguistic Renaissance in India," 123-140.

[97] Thomas says that, "Orientalism, a Western scholarly discipline of the 18th and 19th centuries that encompassed the study of the languages, literatures, religions, philosophies, histories, art, and laws of Asian societies, especially ancient ones." See Thomas, "Orientalism," 1.

[98] See Chakkuvarackal, "The Serampore Mission and the Linguistic Renaissance in India," 124.

[99] The following are some of Carey's works on language: (1) *Grammar*: Bengali, Marathi, Sanskrit, Punjabi, Telugu, Bhotani, and Kurnataka; (2) *Dictionaries*: Bengali, Marathi, Bhotani, and Sanskrit; and (3) *Polyglot*: 13 Indian languages and 4 hilly languages. See Chakkuvarackal, "The Serampore Mission and the Linguistic Renaissance in India," 129.

[100] See Mukhopadhayay, "William Carey's Contributions for the Promotion of Sanskritic Studies," 193-202; also see Chakkuvarackal, "The Serampore Mission and the Linguistic Renaissance in India," 128.

[101] See Chakkuvarackal, "The Serampore Mission and the Linguistic Renaissance in India," 127.

[102] Carey considered Bengali as one of the most expressive and elegant languages of the East. Bengali of Iswarachandra, Bankim, Rabindranath, and others is now honored as a world language. Carey's endeavors behind such a development cannot be ignored. See Tapan Banerjee, "Growth and Development of Bengali Literature from Serampore"; also see Murshid, *Kalantare Bangla Gadya*, 184; Sen, "Bengali Language, Literature and William Carey," 4.

[103] See Ray, "William Carey—Linguist with a Difference," 157.

as a Baptist missionary in Serampore.[104] In 1921, Rabindranath Tagore observed that, "Carey was a pioneer of revived interest in the vernaculars."[105] Carey realized the complexity of India's socio-cultural problems due to its multilingual character. He strongly felt that the people should be made aware of their mother tongues and should be conversant in some languages other than their mother tongues.[106] The missionaries must know several Indian languages to work in this country. In order to facilitate this purpose, he envisaged to develop a language study center in Serampore.[107] One of the objects of this center would be to help the European missionaries, coming to work in India, to learn quickly some Indian languages so that they could come closer to the common people.[108] Through all these attempts, Carey was able to give the Bengalis several linguistic and grammatical tools to work with.[109]

Carey and His Colloquialism

Carey wrote two books in lucid and colloquial Bengali prose style: *Kathopākathan* and *Ithihāsamālā*.[110] He used some natives to complete

---

[104] See Gupta, "William Carey and Bengali Grammar," 187; also see Chakkuvarackal, "The Serampore Mission and the Linguistic Renaissance in India," 128.

[105] See Carey, *Life of William Carey*, 209.

[106] See Bhattacharya, *Ravindranath Tagore: Adventure of Ideas and Innovative Practices in Education*, 16-17.

[107] See Ray, "William Carey—Linguist with a Difference," 155-158.

[108] See details about Carey's translations: Christopher Arangadan, "Carey's Legacy of Bible Translation," 177-186. Carey's Bible translations include: (1) *The whole Bible*: Bengali, Oriya, Hindi, Marathi, Sanskrit, and Assamese (6 languages); (2) *New Testament and Old Testament up to Ezekiel 26*: Punjabi (1 language); (3) *New Testament and Old Testament up to 2 Kings*: Pashtoo and Kashmiri (2 languages); (4) *New Testament and Pentateuch*: Telugu and Konkani (2 languages); (5) *New Testament*: Lahnda, Gujarati, Rajastani, Bikaneri, Pahari, Nepali, Hindi, Bangheli, Hindi Kanouji, Rajastani Marwari, Rajastani Harauti, Kanarese, Bhatneri, Hindi Braj Bhasha, Pahari Dogri, Bihari Maghadi, Rajastani Malvi, Pahari Garhwali, Manipuri, Pahari Palpa, Khasi, and Pahari Kumaoni up to Colossians (19 languages); and (6) *One or more Gospels*: Balochi (Matthew, Mark, and Luke), Rajastani Jaipuri (Matthew), Rajastani Mewari (Matthew), Hindi Awadhi (Matthew and Mark), and Sindhi (Matthew; 5 languages). Also he translated Sanskrit works to English, such as *Mahabharata* (1795), *Ramayana* (1806) and philosophical treatises like *Samkhya*. For more details, see Chakkuvarackal, "The Serampore Mission and the Linguistic Renaissance in India," 129-130, 135-136; also see Mangalwadi, *The Legacy of William Carey*, 20; Chatterjee, "William Carey and the Linguistic Renaissance in India," 161.

[109] H. H. Wilson of Oxford University would say of Carey's 80,000-words Bengali dictionary that "it was unique in those days for its erudite and minute philological exactness." See Arangadan, "Carey's Legacy of Bible Translation," 148-150. Similarly, from 1794 to 1810 Carey collected more than 40,000 Sanskrit words with synonyms in twelve different languages. See Urmi Gangopadhyay, "Carey's Contributions to Linguistics."

[110] See George, *Modern Indian Literature and Anthology*, 74.

Kathopākathan or *Dialogues*.[111] As an important contribution demonstrating human life as it is, this work was intended to facilitate Bengali language.[112] The text relates encounters experienced in recruitment of domestic hands, conversation between Sahib and his Moonshi, between money-lender and the debtor, gentry and gentry, between women and women, clergy and the parishioner, zemindar and the riot, besides market scene and the style of speech current among laborers, quarrelling people, and gesticulating women.[113] Ray says that, "The dialogues were meant to serve as a lingual bridge between the Englishmen and the so-called lower ranks of the Bengali people."[114] The text was mainly intended to flourish the colloquial words and to communicate human life in day-to-day affairs.[115] Chatterjee says that, "*Kathopākathan* using the dialect of the common people also established that Bengali, unaided by Sanskrit, could be developed as a powerful expressive language."[116] The text uses common phrases and idioms to express ideas in colloquial terms. This book has thrown much light on the manners, customs, social ideas, daily dialogues and the like.[117] Some even argue that the simple language of the book clearly established that it had not come all on a sudden, but it existed in unwritten or manuscript form before the final compilation of it.[118]

Colloquial expressions of different districts of Bengal are presented in it because the compilers came from different parts of Bengal.[119] De wrote in 1919: "It (*Kathopākathan*) had still not lost all the force and precision of realism and was a rich source for the literary historians of the idioms and slangs spoken in Bengali. Reflecting the results of Carey's minute and sympathetic observation and familiarity with the people, it proved that he had a thorough acquaintance with the resources of the language in all odds and different colloquial forms."[120] Through all these means, Bengali literature progressed astonishingly between 1800 and 1830. If Carey with the help of Serampore Mission and Fort William College had not come forward to enrich Bengali literature giving it due recognition, the elite society of Calcutta including Ram Mohan Roy would not have started writing in Bengali but rather preferred Persian or Sanskrit.[121]

---

[111] See Mukherjee, *A Dictionary of Indian Literature*, 174.

[112] See Ray, "William Carey—Linguist with a Difference," 157.

[113] See Ray, "William Carey—Linguist with a Difference," 158.

[114] See Ray, "William Carey—Linguist with a Difference," 158.

[115] See Ray, "William Carey—Linguist with a Difference," 158.

[116] See Chatterjee, "William Carey and the Linguistic Renaissance in India," 169.

[117] See Das Sajanikanto, *Sahilya Sadak Charitmala* 15, 54.

[118] See Chatterjee, "William Carey and the Linguistic Renaissance in India," 170.

[119] See Chatterjee, "William Carey and the Linguistic Renaissance in India," 170.

[120] See De, *History of Bengali Literature*, 136-137.

[121] See Chatterjee, "William Carey and the Linguistic Renaissance in India," 168.

Similarly, *Ithihāsamālā* is a collection of various types of fictitious stories of earlier period. The language of the book is more lucid and simple than that of the earlier publications of Serampore Mission.[122] These writings under the initiative of Carey demonstrate how Bengali as a language developed from its oral and colloquial form to its elegant and flourishing literary style.

Other Linguistic Methods

Through the establishment of a Language Study Center in Serampore, Carey initiated to build a cultural bridge between the East and the West.[123] That introduced a new style of a linguistic mix in the society. Carey's approach to language can be best explained through the following points. First, he developed a socio-linguistic approach to understand the language system of Bengal.[124] The *code switching* and *diglossia* of language systems in which a classical form of language ('H' form) exists alongside of another form or forms of the same language ('L' form).[125] When we consider the Indian languages in general, all other languages including Bengali are rooted in Sanskrit and that can be counted as the 'H' form. It was again true in the case of Bengali, that is, the elegant Bengali (the classical 'H' form) which was distinct but at the same time related to the colloquial ('L') forms of the same language.[126] Carey's understanding of the language system of Bengal enabled him to foster the language from multiple angles. In Carey's assessment, Sanskrit was at the center of Indian languages. Therefore, he approached other languages ('L' forms) through the means of Sanskrit.[127]

Second, Carey pioneered a style of Bengali language called *sadhu bhasha*. This style made use of loan words from Sanskrit, a natural course to follow where the sanskritic overlay of religious terms was manifested even in some languages belonging to other linguistic families such as the Dravidian.[128] Third, Carey was known for his style of language called *Christian Bengali*, a form that developed through the interaction of colloquial Bengali under the

---

[122] See Chatterjee, "William Carey and the Linguistic Renaissance in India," 170.

[123] See Chatterjee, "William Carey and the Linguistic Renaissance in India," 159.

[124] For more details about socio-linguistics, see Jaffe, *Stance: Sociolinguistic Perspectives*.

[125] See Gangopadhyay, "Carey's Contribution to Linguistics"; also see Gardner-Chloros, *Code-Switching*, 1-19.

[126] See Chakkuvarackal, "The Serampore Mission and the Linguistic Renaissance in India," 131-132.

[127] See Chakkuvarackal, "The Serampore Mission and the Linguistic Renaissance in India," 131-132.

[128] See Arangadan, "Carey's Legacy of Bible Translation," 176-177. Mangalwadis say, "The Bengali songs of Tagore's Gitanjali display both on the influence on the language of Carey as well as the worldview of the Bible, which Carey translated." See Mangalwadi, *The Legacy of William Carey*, 93-94; Carey, *William Carey*, 209.

western influence.[129] As a result, the biblical text and its contents continued to remain under the domain of western thinking and the language of the Bengali Bible continued to exist as *Christian Bengali*.[130] Thus, there was a prevailing 'European-Indian mixed culture' in the colonial India, especially in the context of Bengal.[131] Fourth, Carey spent a considerable time in translating the New Testament into a multitude of minor Indian tongues. The names of these languages were at that time scarcely known to the linguists of Europe.[132] Carey did not remain content with his intimate acquaintance with numerous languages; he also tirelessly utilized his knowledge in undertaking publications.[133] These and other linguistic methods of Carey made profound influence in the Indian context.

The above discussion enables us to understand some of the linguistic methods developed by Carey and the Serampore mission. Those linguistic methods were instrumental for the advancement of colloquial languages in the Indian context. Some of them are important to be restated here: first, development of a descriptive and scientific approach to the languages that emphasized vocabulary, grammar, and structure to translate them from their oral traditions to the written form; second, advancement of a Vernacular linguistic style in closer relationship with the Oriental and Anglicist styles; third, composition of a colloquial dialogic style that facilitates a linguistic bridge between the natives and the foreigners; fourth, perceiving the colloquial languages through the means of *code switching* and *diglossia*, that means, understanding 'L' forms of language in relation to their 'H' forms;[134] fifth, facilitating a style of *sadhu bhasha* to accommodate the lower strata of the society; sixth, formation of a new style of language called *Christian Bengali*; and seventh, paying attention on both the popular and lesser tongues of the society. These linguistic methods of Carey are significant in

---

[129] See Chakkuvarackal, "The Serampore Mission and the Linguistic Renaissance in India," 132-133.

[130] See Gine, *'Nomos' in Context*, 184-185.

[131] See Chakkuvarackal, "The Serampore Mission and the Linguistic Renaissance in India," 133.

[132] See Chakkuvarackal, "The Serampore Mission and the Linguistic Renaissance in India," 133.

[133] Several of these languages were vernaculars of only a few hundreds of thousands. Yet they had been distinct languages from time immemorial, and some had substantial literary traditions (i.e., Awadhi, Braj Bhasha, Kanouji, Malvi and others). See Chakkuvarackal, "The Serampore Mission and the Linguistic Renaissance in India," 133.

[134] Carey's approach to the study of languages was in a sense sociolinguistic, because he studied and analyzed languages in their social contexts and the study of social life through linguistics. See Chakkuvarackal, "The Serampore Mission and the Linguistic Renaissance in India," 136.

today's interpretative contexts. In his study of languages, Carey attempted to understand the following aspects: the forms of speech and patterns of communication; community differences in the 'ways of speaking' they have adopted; typical patterns in multilingual people's use of languages; and involvement of language in social transformation.[135] In the following section, we will examine how the above stated linguistic methods are significant to understand the narrative framework of John's Gospel.

Re-Reading John's Gospel in the Light of Carey's Linguistic Methods

William Carey's implementation of his linguistic methods introduced some of the transformative measures in the sociolinguistic context of India.[136] Some of his linguistic methods can be used as hypothetical tools to throw more light on the understanding of the New Testament. In the current study, we attempt to apply some of his linguistic methods in the sociolinguistic context of the Johannine community. Carey's linguistic methods can be used as hermeneutical tools for understanding the core realities of John's community.[137] The seven methods recapitulated in the previous section can be used to demonstrate their reverberations in the Johannine community situation. In that process, the Johannine implied author is considered as a linguist who communicates his message to the implied reader with rhetorical punch and narrative efficacy. The principles of language adopted by Carey in the Indian context and their interpretative significance can be introduced as innovative methods for developing contextual hermeneutics pertinent to the Johannine community.

Carey developed a descriptive and scientific approach to the languages that emphasized vocabulary, grammar, and narrative structure to translate the oral traditions to their written form. At the semiotic level of the Fourth Gospel, the semantic domains, the narrative syntactic, and the pragmatic interplay reveal the author's idiosyncrasies.[138] A simple impressiveness of presentation and repetition of words and phrases enable the Gospel elegant in appearance.[139] Abbott understands that the authors of the New Testament,

---

[135] See Chakkuvarackal, "The Serampore Mission and the Linguistic Renaissance in India," 136.

[136] See Chakkuvarackal, "The Serampore Mission and the Linguistic Renaissance in India," 131.

[137] For more details about Carey's linguistic principles, see the previous section.

[138] See Blomberg, *A Handbook of NT Exegesis*, 117-142.

[139] See Guthrie, *NT Introduction*, 335. In the words of Petersen, "One of the most distinctive features of the Gospel of John is its blatantly self-conscious use of language. Everyone in the narrative, including the narrator, speaks everyday language, but the narrator and Jesus also speak what we will call a special language, one that employs the grammar and vocabulary of the everyday but uses the vocabulary in a different way, leading to misunderstanding on the

especially the Evangelist John, "knew Greek more from hearing others speak it than from reading authors."[140] Barrett says that, "It [the Greek of John] is neither bad Greek nor (according to classical standards) good Greek."[141] The narrator builds an "insider" linguistic dynamics through the repetitive use of love, truth, life, light, witness, and abide over against the "outsider" linguistic pattern.[142] Through all these means, the Johannine community developed its own sociolinguistics and semantic domains. Though the range of vocabulary in John is comparatively less, the range of meaning appears profound.[143] For John words are signs of communication that build the semantic domains.[144] He uses words both as denotative and connotative vehicles to convey the message in his own idiom.[145]

John's style of *relexicalization*[146] and *overlexicalization*[147] of words is demonstrated as follows: the expressions such as *following*, *abiding*, *loving*, *keeping the word*, *receiving*, *having*, and *seeing* are used to describe "believing in Jesus," and *spirit*, *above*, *life*, *light*, *not of the/this world*, *freedom*, *truth*, and *love* are used to describe "the realm of God."[148] Similarly, he uses two sets of words that are variants to describe contrasting spheres of existence, opposing

---

part of those who only speak the everyday language." See Petersen, *The Gospel of John and the Sociology of Light*, 1; cf. Grelot, *The Language of Symbolism*, 7-24.

[140] See Abbott, *Johannine Vocabulary*. Stanton states that, "John's Gospel is like a stream in which children can wade and elephants swim. For many readers the gospel's main themes are simple and clear, and the evangelist's dramatic presentation of the story of Jesus compelling." See Stanton, *The Gospels and Jesus*, 97.

[141] See Barrett, *Gospel according to St. John*, 5-6. W. F. Howard considered that the author "was a man who, while cultured to the last degree, wrote Greek after the fashion of men of quite elementary attainment." See Moulton and Howard, *A Grammar of New Testament Greek*, 33.

[142] Guthrie says, "in the reverse direction, many of the expressions used frequently in the synoptics are little used, or do not occur at all, in John (e.g., kingdom, people [*laos*], call, pray or prayer)." See Guthrie, *NT Introduction*, 336.

[143] For more details about repetition as a style in John, see Van der Watt, "Repetition and Functionality in the Gospel according to John," 87-108.

[144] See Van der Watt, "Ethics through the Power of Language," 139-167.

[145] *Denotation* is the meaning that words have for most everyone who hears them in most contexts. *Connotation* is the special meaning that a word has for a particular person or group of people, perhaps only in certain contexts. See Cotterell and Turner, *Linguistics and Biblical Interpretation*, 45-47; Blomberg, *A Handbook of NT Exegesis*, 121.

[146] Malina and Rohrbaugh define, "Relexicalization refers to the practice of using new words for some reality that is not ordinarily referred to with those words." See Malina and Rohrbaugh, *Social-Science Commentary on the Gospel of John*, 4.

[147] Malina and Rohrbaugh define, "To overlexicalize is to have many words for the central area of concern." See Malina and Rohrbaugh, *Social-Science Commentary on the Gospel of John*, 5.

[148] See Malina and Rohrbaugh, *Social-Science Commentary on the Gospel of John*, 4.

modes of living and being; there is a contrast between *spirit*, *above*, *life*, *light*, *not of the/this world*, *freedom*, *truth*, and *love*, and their opposites, *flesh*, *below*, *death*, *darkness*, *the/this world*, *slavery*, *lie*, and *hate*.[149] Moreover, his repetitive uses of the *hour*, *lifting up*, and *glorification* of the Son of Man direct the attention of the reader toward the death of Jesus.[150] Abbott makes much of the fact that in the Fourth Gospel, often within the limits of one verse, words of different root are used to express the idea of *seeing*.[151] Some of John's vocabularies like *agapē/agapaō* (44 times), *alētheia* and its cognates (46 times), *ginōskein* (56/57 times), and *kosmos* (78 times) make a noticeable distinction in comparison to other gospels.[152] When we observe Carey's method of emphasizing vocabulary, grammar, and narrative structure in the Bengali context, we can also see how the Johannine narrator picks up words and other linguistic elements with focus and community consciousness. Analyzing Johannine words, phrases, clauses, sentences and micro-sections, and their interplay within the macro-structure of the Gospel provides us new insights for a Johannine hermeneutics.[153] The language of John and its community dynamics enable the reader to develop a Johannine contextual hermeneutics.

Not only relexicalization and overlexicalization of words, but also John constructs grammar in his own way. The author conveys his message with the help of a widespread use of *kai* as a parataxis to join words, phrases, clauses, and sentences together to build his semantic domains (1:19-21; 2:9).[154] Alongside of that, John prefers his peculiar style of using the conjunctions *oun* (2:16-18; 3:23-25; 4:8-9; 6:3-5; 9:4-6; 11:12-14; 11:57-12:1; 18:1-3, 5-6) and *de* (2:8; 6:71; 11:45-46, 54-55), and asyndeton (1:17, 39; 2:6-7, 17; 4:22; 6:59; 9:9; 12:12, 22).[155] Grammarians point out that colloquial Greek as a source for asyndeton in John.[156] Within the literary Aramaic and the Mishnaic Hebrew, asyndeton becomes a frequent feature.[157] Buth comments that, "It appears that

---

[149] See Malina and Rohrbaugh, *Social-Science Commentary on the Gospel of John*, 5.

[150] See Van der Watt, "Repetition and Functionality in the Gospel according to John," 87-108.

[151] See Nicklin, *Aboott's Johannine Vocabulary*, 172-175.

[152] See Martin, *NT Foundations*, 271-272.

[153] See Martin, *NT Foundations*, 271-272.

[154] Guthrie comments that, "Perhaps the most characteristic feature of John's style is the widespread use of *kai*, instead of subordinating clauses, in joining sentences (*parataxis*). It is this feature more than any other which creates such an impression of simplicity in Greek. The author is clearly more intent on imparting a message than on stylistic niceties." See Guthrie, *NT Introduction*, 336.

[155] See Buth, "Oun, De, Kai, and asyndeton in John's Gospel," 144-161.

[156] For more details about Johannine grammar, refer Abbott, *Johannine Grammar*; also see Fitzmyer, *The Semitic Background of the New Testament*, 3-186.

[157] See Turner, *A Grammar of New Testament Greek*, 1963: 340-341.

a colloquial substratum in Hebrew, and probably Aramaic and Greek, could all have influenced John in the direction of a 'normal' narrative function for asyndeton."[158] John orchestrates a distinctive grammatical structure in the Gospel through the means of a cluster of words and their semantic integration.

Carey was concerned of developing vocabulary, grammar, and structure in the Bengali context to develop the language from the oral tradition to the literary form. Carey's sociolinguistic approach was demonstrable when he considered the Bengali socio-cultural and linguistic dynamics together into account.[159] Once when we apply this method into the Johannine narrative framework for interpretative purposes, we can perceive that the Johannine vocabulary and language lie much closer to the core realities of the community life.[160] In that sense, it appears as if it was closer to the oral level of the community language. A serious question to be posed from the hermeneutical point of view is: "How did John build his own lexicon and his own grammar based on the community demands or the *Sitz im Leben Kirche*?" An interpreter of John's Gospel has to respond to this question before s/he addresses any other questions derived out of the text.

As Carey emphasized a Vernacular linguistic style in relationship with the Oriental and Anglicist styles, an analysis of John's sociolinguistic interplay shall enable us to throw light on its semantic underpinnings.[161] Christianity began in a Jewish cultural environment, with a Hebrew or Aramaic vocabulary and a background of Semitic hopes and longings.[162] At the time of Jesus, Hebrew was the language which had been in use among the Jews of Palestine for the longest time.[163] Moreover, there had come to be a standard Literary Aramaic and its various spoken dialects.[164] At the time of Jesus most educated Palestinian Jews of the upper classes knew at least some Greek.[165] In that sense, John's Gospel integrates literary styles from the Hebrew, Aramaic, Greek, and Latin linguistic thought-worlds.[166] As John demonstrates the Johannine

---

[158] See Buth, "Oun, De, Kai, and asyndeton in John's Gospel," 159.

[159] See Chakkuvarackal, "The Serampore Mission and the Linguistic Renaissance in India," 131-132.

[160] Cf. Blomberg, *A Handbook of NT Exegesis*, 117-142.

[161] See Barr, *The Semantics of Biblical Language*, 1-30.

[162] The author's knowledge of Jewish customs, Jewish history, and Palestinian geography reveal the Palestinian background of the Gospel. See Guthrie, *NT Introduction*, 261-263; also see Chakkuvarackal, "Important Issues in the Translation of the Bible in the Indian Context," 165; Thompson, "John, Gospel of," 371-372.

[163] See Wise, "Languages of Palestine," 435.

[164] See Wise, "Languages of Palestine," 437.

[165] See Wise, "Languages of Palestine," 439; also see Guthrie, *NT Introduction*, 266-267.

[166] See Wise, "Languages of Palestine," 434-444. Robertson considers John's Gospel as a "Jewish Gospel." See Robertson, *John: The Jewish Gospel*, 1-4. The crime of Jesus, written as a

community's idiomatic style, he accommodates the linguistic and literary features of the Greco-Roman and Jewish worlds. Brown comments that, "The community or part of it may have moved from Palestine to the Diaspora to teach the Greeks (7:35), perhaps to the Ephesus area—a move that would cast more light on the Hellenistic atmosphere of the Gospel and on the need to explain Aramaic names and titles (e.g., rabbi, Messiah)."[167] As the Johannine community was formed as a sect within the Synagogue set-up and later on excommunicated (9:22, 34; 12:42; 16:2), the Johannine Christians would have developed a different rhetoric.[168]

The colloquial styles of Hebrew, Aramaic, Greek, and Latin and their integration would have given birth to a new style in the community of John.[169] As scholars had identified, John also had influences from the Old Testament,[170] Qumran, Platonic,[171] Hermetic, Mystery religious, Philonic, Gnostic, Mandaean,[172] and Samaritan backgrounds.[173] Furthermore, John also would have developed his own linguistic and ideological style to make his community identity distinct from the Synoptic and Pauline communities.[174] In that way, John's method of *evaluation* and *acceptance* of ideas enabled him

superscription over His head, was inscribed in three languages: Hebrew, Latin, and Greek (John 19:20). See Gromacki, *NT Survey*, 23. Gromacki states that, "Since there was such a language mix, public documents had to be written in several languages in order to reach all of the people. This is why the crime of Jesus, written as a superscription over His head, was inscribed in three languages (John 19:20)." Latin was spoken only by native Romans and key political subjects. The language most spoken and read throughout the Mediterranean area was Greek. In Palestine and throughout the Near East, Aramaic was very popular. Hebrew was no longer spoken and read by the average Jew; the orthodox, including the rabbis of the Pharisaic order, still embraced its usage.

[167] See Brown, *An Introduction to the New Testament*, 375.

[168] See Lamb, *Text, Context, and the Johannine Community*, 1-35.

[169] See Brown, *The Community of the Beloved Disciple*; Martyn, *History and Theology of the Fourth Gospel*.

[170] For more details about OT influence in John, see Guthrie, *NT Introduction*, 248-249; Thomaskutty, *Dialogue in the Book of Signs*, 34-36.

[171] See Thomaskutty, *Dialogue in the Book of Signs*, 443-444.

[172] See Dodd, *The Interpretation of the Fourth Gospel*, 9; also see Brown, *The Gospel according to John*, 1:lii-lxiv.

[173] Brown states that, "much of the Qumran-like vocabulary appears in the speeches of Jesus in John (to a much greater extent than in the Synoptics) need not lead us to conclude hastily that the raw materials in those speeches were the artificial compositions of the evangelist. If Qumran exemplifies a wider range of thought, Jesus could well have been familiar with its vocabulary and ideas; for the Word-made-flesh spoke the language of his time." See Brown, *An Introduction to the New Testament*, 373; also see Dodd, *The Interpretation of the Fourth Gospel*, 9; Guthrie, *NT Introduction*, 291; Thomaskutty, *Dialogue in the Book of Signs*, 3-4.

[174] See Thompson, "John, Gospel of," 375; Thomaskutty, *Dialogue in the Book of Signs*, 36-39; Beasley-Murray, "Synoptics and John," 792-795.

to build a distinctive identity in semiotic terms.[175] As Carey emphasized the Vernacular linguistic style in relationship with the Orientalist and Anglicist styles, John's mixed phenomenon provides an amalgam of linguistic and literary interaction.[176] In the hermeneutical procedures, a reader who neglects this important aspect of the Fourth Gospel may miss its linguistic, stylistic, and ideological flavor.

Carey's composition of a colloquial dialogic style through *Kathopākathan* facilitated a linguistic bridge between the Bengali nationals and the missionaries who came to India. The Johannine dialogues show how the narrator makes use of this literary category to dramatize the *Sitz-im-Leben Jesu* in the *Sitz-im-Leben Kirche* context.[177] A genre analysis of the Johannine dialogues, which takes into consideration the content, form, and function, helps us to understand the semantic, syntactic, and pragmatic aspects of the Fourth Gospel.[178] We are informed that dialogue is a recognizable and established literary category which is spread throughout John.[179] In John's narrative, a reader can recognize several common conventions of dialogue that form the text into a specific literary category.[180] John's narrative develops with a focus on the characters and their verbal exchanges.[181] Some narrative similarities between the Platonic and the Johannine dialogues are conspicuous to the reader.[182] Plato's literary style transformed the real-life conversations of Socrates with his friends and students into creative 'inventions' which incorporated various dramatic elements for the purpose of progressing toward a philosophical truth.[183] Similarly, in John, the narrator attempts to imitate the real life conversations of Jesus with his interlocutors.[184]

---

[175] John's ideas would have developed from various other sources. But, the evangelist would have used them with a scrutiny. Thus, he clustered his ideas with that of the ideas from the surroundings.

[176] See Fitzmyer, *The Semitic Background of the New Testament*, 3-186.

[177] Martyn considers the John as a *two-level drama.* See Martyn, *History and Theology of the Fourth Gospel.*

[178] Van Aarde comments that, "The tern *genre* refers to the *generic* characteristics of a specific literary form, which differ from the characteristics of other forms, and which enable us to identify a specific *literary type.*" See Van Aarde, "Narrative Criticism," 381; cf. Thomaskutty, *Dialogue in the Book of Signs*, 433-474.

[179] See Stibbe, *John's Gospel*, 54.

[180] See Greimas and Courtés, *Semiotics and Language*, 78.

[181] See Thomaskutty, *Dialogue in the Book of Signs*, 476-477.

[182] See Van Kooten, *The Creation of Heaven and Earth*, 168; Thomaskutty, *Dialogue in the Book of Signs*, 444.

[183] See Denning-Bolle, *Wisdom in Akkadian Literature*, 72 and 76.

[184] See Brant, *Dialogue and Drama*, 13; Thomaskutty, *Dialogue in the Book of Signs*, 444-445.

The synagogue and church dialogue in the Johannine community context is well connected to other layers of dialogues. While the community was in constant conflict with the world and their existence was under threat, 'eternal life' was the key concept introduced to them.[185] The evangelist reinterprets the 'divine'/'transcendental' story (at the rear of stage) and the story of the earthly Jesus to the community (at the front of stage) in his own idiom.[186] Thus, a reader of the dialogue can notice the way linguistic, literary, historical, and theological aspects blend together within the text.[187] As *Kathopākathan* demonstrates the day-to-day affairs of the common people in colloquial language, John's dialogues reveal how God in flesh reveals himself to humanity. In that way, the socio-religious, socio-cultural, and sociolinguistic conventions of the community are at view. Carey and his colleagues foster a linguistic category through *Kathopākathan* to redeem the language from its oral condition to a literary form. Considering the dialogues in John as a literary category and recognizing their proximity to the oral pre-condition, a reader of the text can reconstruct a new hermeneutics that take into consideration the sociolinguistic and literary roots of the Fourth Gospel.[188]

Carey perceived the colloquial languages through the means of *code switching* and *diglossia*, that means, identifying the 'L' forms of the dialects and their geographical concentration distinct from their 'H' forms. As Jesus' character in John demonstrates his knowledge in the Pentateuch (Exo 16:4 in 6:31; Num 21:9 in 3:14; 35:30 in 8:17), the Prophetical writings (Isa 6:10 in 12:40; 40:3 in 1:23; 53:1 in 12:38; 54:13 in 6:45; Zech 13:7 in 16:32; 12:10 in 19:37) and in the Wisdom literature (Psa 22:18 in 19:24; 35:19 in 15:25; 41:9 in 13:18; 69:9 in 2:17; 69:21 in 19:28; 82:6 in 10:34; 118:26 in 12:13), a reader gets the impression that Jesus was knowledgeable in the 'H' form of the Hebrew language.[189] At the oral level of communication, Jesus, his disciples, and the Johannine community exercised their scriptural knowledge in the oral (or 'L') forms of the languages. This is the nature of the linguistic attitudes at the heart of code switching.[190] Wise says that, "in ancient Palestine, Jesus' Aramaic sayings, if they were such, might well come down in writing in an 'H' form of the language rather than the actual 'L' form in which they were

---

[185] See Thomaskutty, *Dialogue in the Book of Signs*, 480.

[186] See Thomaskutty, *Dialogue in the Book of Signs*, 480.

[187] See how John's dialogues are framed as follows: 1:19-2:12; 2:13-22; 3:1-21; 3:22-36; 4:1-42; 4:43-54; 5:1-47; 6:1-71; 7:1-52/8:12-59; 9:1-10:21; 10:22-42; 11:1-53; 11:54-12:50; and the like. See Thomaskutty, *Dialogue in the Book of Signs*, 480.

[188] See Martin, *NT Foundations*, 272.

[189] See Fitzmyer, *The Semitic Background of the New Testament*, 3-186.

[190] Cf. Wise, "Languages of Palestine," 444.

spoken."[191] The Johannine community, emerged in Jerusalem and flourished in the Ephesian context, was exposed to various linguistic, cultural, and ideological phenomena.[192] In that sense, the Aramaisms, Hebraisms, and Semitisms (i.e., constructions abnormal in Greek, but normal in Aramaic, in Hebrew, or both in these Semitic languages) paved way to the distinctive Greek structure of the Gospel.[193]

The poetic format of John reveals his literary style and that led Burney and Torrey to suggest a theory of an Aramaic origin of John.[194] Based on all these available information, we come to a point that Jesus might have been a multilingual or at least a bilingual. Recent discoveries of ossuary inscriptions in Judea have revealed that the inhabitants of first century Palestine were trilingual, speaking Hebrew, Aramaic, and Greek.[195] Jesus the Galilean and the apostles, who were predominantly if not exclusively Galilean, might have used Greek in addition to the Semitic tongues.[196] Carey distinguished the 'L' level of the Bengali language from its 'H' level and from other elegant 'H' (i.e., Sanskrit) forms and made all efforts to translate the colloquial language to the literary level. When Fourth Gospel is placed in its own sociolinguistic context, we might notice that the 'L' forms of languages might have converted into 'H' forms in his writing.[197] In that sense, Jesus' 'L' forms of communication might have received an *inferior* 'H' form in the Johannine community context and later on into a *superior* 'H' form in the literary composition of John.

Carey facilitated a style popularly known as *sadhu bhasha* to accommodate society's lower strata of people. Let us see how John has to be perceived from this perspective. Jesus spoke both in Aramaic and in Hebrew; similarly, the Johannine community shared their concerns in Aramaic and in Hebrew.[198]

---

[191] See Wise, "Languages of Palestine," 444.

[192] See Gromacki, *NT Survey*, 23.

[193] Brown says that, "Still another factor is that the Christian message in the Greek world was first preached in the diaspora synagogues and consequently was phrased in the religious vocabulary of Greek-speaking Judaism—a Greek which was influenced by the Semitized style of the LXX, the Greek OT." Brown continues saying that, "Personally, we tend to agree with the majority of scholars who do not find adequate evidence that a complete edition of the Gospel according to John ever existed in Aramaic. It is possible, however, that bits of the historical tradition underlying John were written in Aramaic, especially if the source of this tradition was John son of Zebedee." See Brown, *The Gospel according to John*, CXXIX.

[194] See Burney, *The Poetry of the Lord*; cf. Burney, *The Aramaic Origin of the Four Gospels*; Torrey, *The Four Gospels*; Torrey, "The Aramaic Origin of the Gospel of St. John," 305-344.

[195] See Hiebert, *An Introduction to the NT*, 29; Ong, *The Multilingual Jesus*, 32-37.

[196] See Gundry, "The Language Milieu of First-Century Palestine," 407.

[197] See Porter, *Linguistic Analysis of the Greek New Testament*, 113-132.

[198] Porter says, "Jesus was born to a Palestinian Jewish family and was apparently well versed in the institutions of the Jewish people, including the use of Aramaic, the language of

Jesus' use of Greek or a varied dialect of Aramaic or even an 'L' form of Latin can be perceived at least in the following occasions: first, Matthew 8:5-13 par. John 4:46-54: Jesus' conversation with the centurion or commander (probably in Greek); second, John 4:4-26: Jesus' conversation with the Samaritan woman (either in Greek or in Samaritan Hebrew/Aramaic); and third, Mark 15:2-5 par. Matthew 27:11-14; Luke 23:2-4; John 18:29-38: Jesus' trial before Pilate (dialect of either Greek or Latin).[199] Jesus and, later on, the Johannine community developed their rhetoric based on the linguistic codes available to them from Aramaic, Hebrew, Greek, and Latin thought-worlds.[200] That further means, the *ipsissima verba Jesu*[201] or at least his *ipsissima vox*[202] developed from an amalgam of Aramaic, Hebrew, Greek, and Latin dialects.[203] John's message with *extra-linguistic*,[204] *para-linguistic*,[205] and *linguistic*[206] aspects reveals this unique and multifaceted semiotics.[207]

The above details enable us to systematize a multi-lingual rhetoric that absorbs multifaceted social reactions.[208] Just as Carey developed his own peculiar style that bridges the gap between the literate and illiterate and

---

the Jews since their return under the Persians from exile in Babylon." See Porter, "Greek of the New Testament," 433.

[199] See Porter, "Greek of the New Testament," 433-434.

[200] Malina and Rohrbaugh comment that, "John indeed highlights the interpersonal and textual functions of language. The linguistic dimensions of how Jesus speaks (textual component) and with whom he speaks (interpersonal component) come through in a way not found in the Synoptic narratives." See Malina and Rohrbaugh, *Social-Science Commentary on the Gospel of John*, 6; also see Halliday, *Language as Social Semiotic*, 8-36.

[201] Jesus' own very exact words.

[202] Jesus' own very exact voice.

[203] While the Synoptics and Paul emphasize new structures to replace old ones (i.e., Kingdom of God/Heaven, Church, Body of Christ, those "in Christ," and the like), John and his group seek the implementation of new values, not new structures, in place of old ones.

[204] Such as time and place, typography, format, medium of presentation, and background and history of a text. See Louw, "Reading a Text as Discourse," 18.

[205] Such as punctuation, intonation, pause, speech acts, genre (e.g., epic, lyric, drama, conversation, parable). See Louw, "Reading a Text as Discourse," 18.

[206] Such as word order, embedding, nominalization, levels of language, style, and, in particular, the discrepancy between syntax and semantics. Louw, "Reading a Text as Discourse," 18.

[207] Malina and Rohrbaugh state that, "In the Gospel of John . . . who is involved and how things are said are everything." See Malina and Rohrbaugh, *Social-Science Commentary on the Gospel of John*, 6; also see Louw, "Reading a Text as Discourse," 18.

[208] John's language and literary artistry are informative, cognitive, performative, expressive, and cohesive in nature. See Caird, *The Language and Imagery of the Bible*, 7-36; also see Malina and Rohrbaugh, *Social-Science Commentary on the Gospel of John*, 7; also see Halliday, *Language as Social Semiotic*, 8-36; Barrett, *The Gospel according to St. John*, 70-72.

adopting loan words from Sanskrit,[209] Jesus and the Johannine community at the 'L' level and the literary Gospel at the 'H' level reflect a flexible dialect that incorporates loan words from other dialects.[210] This peculiar style of John is persuasive to attract people from varied backgrounds.[211]

Carey approached the Bengali language in a different way and that resulted into the formation of a new style called *Christian Bengali.* This hybrid style of language in the Bengali context can be used as a model to ponder deep into the realities of the Johannine community.[212] The 'L' style of language(s) at the *Sitz im Leben Jesu*, the *Sitz im Leben Kirche*, and the *Sitz im Leben* of the evangelist himself reflect the multilingual and multicultural hybridity of the oral reflections around Jesus.[213] When the language received its 'H' status through the written composition(s), many of those hybrid aspects also might have survived.[214] In that sense, through the oral ('L') level and written ('H') level communications, the community of John developed its own peculiar linguistic style. John's in-group dynamism of language over against the out-group dimensions is expressed through its peculiar dualistic framework: light (vs. darkness, 1:5), born of water/spirit (vs. born of blood/flesh/humans, 1:13), above (vs. below, 8:23), spirit (vs. flesh, 3:6), life (vs. death, 3:36), truth (vs. lie, 8:44-45), sky (vs. land [earth], 3:31), God (vs. Satan, 13:27), Israel (vs. Judeans (1:19, 47), and not of this world (vs. this world = Israelite society, 17:1). This phenomenon reveals the community's style of antilanguage (1:19-28).[215]

---

[209] See Chakkuvarackal, "The Serampore Mission and the Linguistic Renaissance in India," 132.

[210] See Stambaugh and Balch, *The NT in Its Social Environment*, 87-88.

[211] See Fitzmyer, *The Semitic Background of the New Testament*, 3-186.

[212] See Torrey, *The Four Gospels*.

[213] Aune discusses about the nature of the Gospels as a "Nonliterary" Genre. See Aune, *The NT in Its Literary Environment*, 23-25.

[214] See Guthrie, *NT Introduction*, 337. In the classical period different dialects, such as Attic, Ionic, and Doric, existed side by side. Of these, the Attic became the foremost literary dialect, and it was adopted as the official language of the Macedonian Empire after the conquests of Alexander the Great. Wenham comments that, "Alexander himself ardently desired to propagate Hellenistic culture throughout his domains, and in time Greek became the *lingua franca* of the civilized world." "This 'common' language" Wenham says, "the so-called Koine or Hellenistic Greek, developed somewhat simpler (and sometimes less precise) forms than the present Attic Greek and it incorporated some forms from other dialects." See Wenham, *The Elements of NT Greek*, 17.

[215] Malina and Rohrbaugh comment that, "'Antilanguage' is the language of an 'antisociety,' that is 'a society that is set up within another society as a conscious alternative to it. It is a mode of resistance, resistance which may take the form either of passive symbiosis or of active hostility and even destruction." See Malina and Rohrbaugh, *Social-Science Commentary on the Gospel of John*, 7; Halliday, *Language as Social Semiotics*, 164-182.

John's characterization develops based on its dualistic framework and linguistic phenomena that results into a series of conflicts between the protagonist and the antagonists.[216] Within the literary and narrative framework of the Fourth Gospel, John develops a peculiar Greek style that is Greco-Roman in dialect, Hebraic/Semitic in rhythm, Syrian and Antiochene in influences, and Aramaic in proximity.[217] Semitic literary parallelisms are obvious in John's passages like 3:11, 18, 20-21, 31-32, and others.[218] This style of John can be considered as a hybrid form called *Christian Greek* in particular and *Semitic Greek* in general.[219] When John develops his language, he adopts several linguistic and ideological aspects from the Greco-Roman and Jewish thought-worlds and that helped him to develop a purely Johannine sociolinguistics and narrative rhetoric.[220] Carey paid attention on both the popular and lesser tongues of the society.[221] As Carey developed a peculiar style emerged out of his sociolinguistic context, in John a reader can notice a rhetoric that reflects the in-group dynamism of his community. That means, the social and religious matrix of the Jesus movement was emerged out of a multilinguistic context.[222]

Conclusion

In recapitulation, William Carey's linguistic methods were instrumental for the linguistic and literary renaissance in the Indian context and that further contributed to several areas of human life in Bengal. He spearheaded a new movement in India with intellectual insights from the European Enlightenment. In his nativistic and vernacular emphasis on linguistics, Carey brought into focus a dynamic interwovenness between vocabulary and social ethos, a cultural interlocking of grammar, and a colloquial dialogic style. His interest in a scientific approach to language that emphasizes development of vocabulary,

---

[216] See Petersen, *The Gospel of John and the Sociology of Light*, 23-79.

[217] Porter says, "The New Testament, apart from a few Aramaic and/or Hebrew words and phrases, is written in a form of ancient Greek. This Greek, however, is not the Greek of the classical writers, such as Plato, Thucydides or the tragedians, but is that of the Greek of the Greco-Roman world of the first century." See Porter, "Greek of the New Testament," 426-427. Eusebius quoted Papias as saying that Matthew composed his logia in the Hebrew (Aramaic). See Hiebert, *An Introduction to the NT*, 31; Martin, *NT Foundations*, 281-282.

[218] See Martin, *NT Foundations*, 272.

[219] See White, "Ancient Greek Letters," 85-105; Fitzmyer, *The Semitic Background of the New Testament*, 3-186.

[220] More details about language during NT times: Stambaugh and Balch, *The NT in Its Social Environment*, 87-88.

[221] See Gromacki, *NT Survey*, 23.

[222] Hezser says that, "Jews who lived in Roman Palestine were Roman subjects who reacted to the experience of Roman imperialism in different ways, depending on their socio-economic status, geographical location and religious persuasion." See Hezser, "The Torah Versus Homer," 5.

grammar, and literary structure, and the advancement of vernacular linguistic style in relation to the Orientalist and Anglicist methods was well-placed in sociolinguistic terms. Carey's involvement in the composition of colloquial dialogic genres, usage of linguistic methods such as *code switching* and *diglossia*, facilitation of the literary and linguistic phenomenon called *sadhu bhasha*, formation of the sub-dialect called *Christian Bengali*, and attention to both the popular and lesser tongues reveals his sociolinguistic approach in the advancement of languages.

As his linguistic methods were taking into consideration the socio-cultural realities of the Bengali community, they can be explored as hermeneutical tools to understand the matrix behind the biblical documents. In our analysis of the Gospel of John, we found that John's relexicalization and overlexicalization, simple grammatical and literary structures, Semitic linguistic styles (Aramaism and Hebraism), Greco-Roman influences, dialogic and monologic language, continuous asyndeton and parataxis, *code switching* and *diglossia* from oral communications to written language, the usage of antilanguage through the means of dualistic narrative framework and other phenomena together demonstrate the linguistic matrix of the literary masterpiece. John's linguistic matrix takes our attention to the life situations of Jesus and the Johannine community and also invites our acumen to the final written composition of the Gospel. Thus, we understand how a linguistic configuration developed from the 'L' level in Jesus' and the community's life situations to the 'H' level in the written framework of the Gospel. A reader of the Fourth Gospel can go closer to the linguistic framework that is derived out of a multilinguistic and pluralistic socio-cultural reality of the Johannine community.

As John's literary composition, historical underpinnings, and theological insights are integrally connected to the sociolinguistic and communitarian dynamics, it is important to understand the linkage between the community existence and the usage of language in the process of textual interpretation. Porter comments that, "Interpretation of the Bible should rightly involve a significant linguistic component, since biblical studies, regardless of whatever else it may be, is a textually based discipline."[223] As Porter says, the role of sociolinguistic analysis of the scripture should be emphasized in the exegetical and hermeneutical explanations of the Fourth Gospel.

With the above stated standpoint in mind, the current study challenges the readers to consider the following aspects in the process of interpreting the scripture in the contemporary context: first, integrating the dynamics of sociolinguistics both within the biblical traditions and within the contemporary socio-political and religio-cultural realities of the reader; second, applying the sociolinguistic methods enables us to fathom deep into the matrix of the text

---

[223] See Porter, *Linguistic Analysis of the Greek New Testament*, 83.

and to explore the social dynamics closer to the message; third, understanding the language dynamics of the scriptures and the contextual dynamics of the interpreter in relation to the semiotic aspects (i.e., semantics, syntactic, and pragmatics) and assimilating them for a dialogue between the narrator of the text and the contemporary reader; fourth, evaluating the way *code switching* and *diglossia* occurs as the language(s) alter(s) from its/their 'L' levels to the 'H' levels to enable a linguistic transition from the communitarian (i.e., oral) traditions to the literary (i.e., written) traditions; and fifth, demonstrating how language can be used as an unavoidable means to derive community dynamics and contextual underpinnings from the textual framework. In short, language is used as a powerful means that connects oral reality, social dynamics, linguistic matrix, epistemological details, historical insights, and literary rhetoric to develop a contextual and ideological artistry.

Chapter 3

Dialogical Nature of John's Prologue

Introduction

It is widely recognized that Early Christianity had developed its theological motifs and literary features with influences from traditional Judaism in particular and Greco-Roman culture in general.[224] Johannine dialogues as a literary genre are not an exception for this fact. In recent years, there has been a growing perception that the Gospel writers were strongly influenced by the literary models and conventions of their day.[225] George A. Kennedy states that, "The New Testament lies on the cusp between Jewish and Greek culture; the life and religious traditions it depict are Jewish, its language is Greek."[226] Everything in the NT assumes and interprets the master narrative, the defining story of Jesus, sent by God, crucified and raised.

The four evangelists have narrated the story of Jesus according to their own theological and literary concerns and in light of how they perceived the need of their readers. We might even say that the four Gospels are four "contextualizations" of the same story.[227] "The Gospels," as Dean Flemming

[224] David E. Aune, ed., "Introduction," *Greco-Roman Literature and the New Testament*, Society of Biblical Literature (Atlanta: Scholars Press, 1988), 1.

[225] See Richard A. Burridge, *Where are the Gospels?: a Comparison with Greco-Roman Biography* (Cambridge: University Press, 1992).

[226] George A. Kennedy, *New Testament Interpretation through Rhetorical Interpretation* (Chapel Hill: The University of North Carolina Press, 1984), 8.

[227] Dean Flemming, *Contextualization in the New Testament: Patterns for Theology and Mission* (Illinois: InterVarsity Press, 2005), 234.

says, "form an important piece of the total picture of how the Christian message is re-expressed for new audiences in the New Testament."[228] The principle that NT writings are with influence from its surroundings has to be taken seriously when we deal with the dialogical structure of John's Gospel. This feature of the Gospel demonstrates its atemporal and gnomic function as the content of it reflects proximity to the surrounding realities. Scholars continue to debate the extent to which John's Gospel reflects the specific historical situation and needs of its readers.[229] A specific treatment of the Johannine dialogues will provide us with greater insights of the overall content of the Gospel and will generate alacrity of the literary features that are embedded therein.

Johannine dialogues conspicuously speak of the point of view of the author.[230] Literary genres and forms are not simply neutral containers used as convenient ways to package various types of written communication. They are social conventions that provide contextual meaning for the smaller units of language and text they enclose.[231] David E. Aune says that, "The original significance that a literary text had for both author and reader is tied to the genre of that text, so that the meaning of the part is dependent upon the meaning of the whole."[232] Early sayings of Jesus seem especially to have been the nuclei of the development of literary genres like discourses and dialogues.[233]

A new paradigm of communication emerges in John, "a form of dialogue in which God speaks anew to 'his people,' initially to the ethnic Israel he had called into being in the Hebrew Bible, but then beyond Israel to the larger humanity of the Gentiles. And in this new form of dialogue God speaks

---

[228] Flemming, *Contextualization in the New Testament*, 234. Also see Richard Bauckham, "For Whom Were the Gospels Written?" *The Gospel for All Christians: Rethinking the Gospel Audience* (Grand Rapids: Eerdmans, 1998).

[229] Cf. R. E. Brown, *The Community of the Beloved Disciple* (New York: Paulist, 1979); J. Louis Martyn, *History and Theology in the Fourth Gospel*, 2nd ed. (Nashville: Abingdon, 1979); R. A. Culpepper, *The Gospel and Letters of John* (Nashville: Abingdon, 1998), 42-61.

[230] Wead states, "since Henry James laid the foundation for twentieth century literary criticism, the point of view has become one of the most discussed areas of literary analysis." David W. Wead, *The Literary Devices in John's Gospel* (Basel: Friedrich Reinhardt Kommissionsverlag, 1970), 1. Also see Percy Lubbock, *The Craft of Fiction* (1926), 59-91. Point of view shows the position where the author stands in relation to the events to his readers.

[231] David E. Aune, *The New Testament in its Literary Environment*, ed. Wayne A. Meeks (Philadelphia: The Westminster Press, 1987), 13.

[232] Aune, *The NT in Its Literary Environment*, 13.

[233] Helmut Koester, *Introduction to the New Testament: History and Literature of Early Christianity*, Vol. 2 (Philadelphia: Fortress Press, 1980), 179. Cf. Alan Millard, *Reading and Writing in the Time of Jesus*, The Biblical Seminar 69 (Sheffield: Sheffield Academic Press, 2000/2001).

almost exclusively through the unique figure of 'a Son.'"[234] Reed shows how the dialogues of the NT engage both the NT canon and the Hebrew Bible, particularly in the "internal echoes or dialogic answering" within a book and between books and with the OT.[235] In the case of John, the dialogic engagements of the Gospel within itself, with other NT and OT books and with the surroundings and ideologies is more obvious. The reverberating nature of the Fourth Gospel makes it universalistic in its nature and function. In the succeeding analysis, we will see how dialogue both as a literary piece and as a communication device is used in the larger framework of the Gospel of John.

The Prologue of John's Gospel (1:1-18)

According to Mikhail Bakhtin, "Life by its very nature is dialogic. To live means to participate in dialogue: to ask questions, to heed, to respond, to agree, and so forth."[236] Within this theory of dialogue, Bakhtin declares that the word or utterance is integrally dialogical in nature. Each word or utterance responds in one form or another to utterances that precede it. Moreover, the word or utterance is related also to subsequent responses. He further argues that the speaker is constructing an utterance in anticipation of possible responses, something he calls the "act of responsive understanding."[237] Thus, no word or utterance or text is ever spoken in isolation. It always calls to mind other words, utterances, or texts pertaining to the same theme. The dialogical character of the word or utterance has a profound effect on the discourses involved in the interaction. This basic argumentation helps us to view the entire Gospel of John from a dialogical perspective. A careful examination of the various functions of dialogues as a literary genre in John will enable the reader to see the point of view of the author with specificity. The prologue of John is not an exception in maintaining the dialogical character of the Gospel; it remains as an excellent threshold for the succeeding chapters. The prologue maintains several layers

---

[234] Walter L. Reed, *Dialogues of the Word: The Bible as Literature According to Bakhtin* (Oxford/New York: Oxford University Press, 1993), 87-89.

[235] Reed, *Dialogues of the Word*, 99.

[236] Quoted in L. Juliana M. Claassens, "Biblical Theology as Dialogue: Continuing the Conversation on Mikhail Bakhtin and Biblical Theology," *JBL* 122/1 (2003), 127-44, 129. Cf. Mikhail M. Bakhtin, "Toward a Reworking of the Destoevsky's Book," *Problems of Dostoevsky's Poetics*, Theory and History of Literature 8 (Minneapolis: University of Minnesota Press, 1984), 293. Michael Holquist, *Dialogism: Bakhtin and His World* (London: Routledge, 1990).

[237] Mikhail M. Bakhtin, *Speech Genres and Other Late Essays*, Theory and History of Literature 8 (Minneapolis: University of Minnesota Press, 1984), 94. Bakhtin employs the terms "word," "discourse," and "utterance" interchangeably. For Bakhtin, the utterance is the real unit in speech communication. The utterance, which might be represented by a word, discourse, or text, is marked by a change of speaking subjects.

of dialogic characteristics in its overall function within the body of the larger biblical text. Some of them are identified in the following discussion.

Jesus, "the Dialogue in Flesh"

The prologue introduces Jesus as the incarnation of the divine logos which was active in creation. His mission is to reveal the Father.[238] This very idea or imagery makes the Johannine message universal and atemporal. According to Brown, "If John has been described as the pearl of great price among the New Testament writings, then one may say that the prologue is the pearl within this Gospel."[239] It also establishes the antithetical norms which will be in conflict throughout the narrative: light and darkness, belief and unbelief, grace and truth and the law.[240] In John, as D. H. Johnson says, "Every occurrence of *logos* occurs in some syntactical sequence with Jesus or God."[241] *Logos* is a verbal noun from the Greek verb *legō*. The three basic meanings of the verb are: first, *objective meaning*: the rational ground or basis for something;[242] second, *subjective meaning*: the power or faculty of reasoning or thought; and third, *impressive meaning*: thought or reason as expressed in speech or in writing.[243]

In his dialogues, Plato saw an association of *logos* with discourses or rational explanation. He generally identified thinking (*dianoia*) and rational discourse (*logos*); *logos* was the inward dialogue of the mind as it flowed from the mind through the lips.[244] Depending on the context, *logos* has a wide variety of meanings: explanation, argument, theory, law or rule of conduct, hypothesis, formula or definition, narrative, oration, communication, conversation, dialogue, oracle, proverb or saying. The context here enables us to see in Jesus the internal dialogue of God which later developed as a dialogue of God with the world. Hence Jesus is God's dialogue in flesh. The usage of the expression *logos* to introduce the "Savior of the world" (4:42) makes the Fourth Gospel a globalized narrative masterpiece.

---

[238] See Culpepper, *Anatomy of the Fourth Gospel*, 89.

[239] Raymond E. Brown, *The Gospel According to John i-xii: Introduction, Translation, and Notes*, The Anchor Bible (New York: Doubleday, 1966), 18.

[240] Culpepper, *Anatomy of the Fourth Gospel*, 89.

[241] D. H. Johnson, "Logos," *Dictionary of Jesus and the Gospels*, eds. Joel B. Green and Scot McKnight (Illinois: IVP, 1992), 481-484, 481.

[242] This is often of a numerical or logical nature and functions as a principle of explanation. Jean Pepin, "Logos," *The Encyclopedia of Religion*, Vol. 9, ed. Mircea Eliade (New York: McMillan Publishing Company, 1987), 9-15, 9.

[243] The "speech" may be either vocalized or purely cerebral.

[244] Thomas H. Tobin, "Logos," *The Anchor Bible Dictionary*, Vol. 4, ed. David Noel Freedman (New York: Doubleday, 1992), 348-356, 348. *Logos* is something said (including the thought); by implication (the mental faculty) or motive; by extension a computation; specifically (with the article in John) the Divine expression (Christ).

"This Logos," as Kanagaraj says, "is the embodiment of God's life, light, creative power, and glory, which is communicated to human beings."[245] Instead of using the term 'Christ,' which would have aroused suspicion or a political understanding in the minds of his Jewish readers, John chose a familiar term that conveyed clearly God's dialogue from within to the people of all religions and streams of philosophy.[246] Jesus, the dialogue of God in flesh, became the core subject-matter for the narrator to describe various aspects like God's dialogue within, its outward expression through sending the Son to the world, and human response to it through the expression of faith in Jesus. Thus, John's idea of *logos* absorbs the extended story-world unto itself.

Rhythmical Responsive Style

The Prologue maintains a *rhythmical responsive style* that is characteristic to the dialogic nature of the Gospel. "One of the most puzzling of the Fourth Gospel's many puzzles," as Frank Thielman observes, "is its peculiar style."[247] All through the prologue, the narrator is not trying to present a text for a *single reading*; rather a *rhythmical reading* where at least two participants are involved. As a responsive reading, the author maintains features of the rhetoric called *sayings chreia*.[248] It is viewed that parts of the prologue appear to come from an early Christian hymn, or at least from a creedal or confessional material of the church. Carson says, "The term 'poem' can be applied to the

---

[245] Jey J. Kanagaraj, *The Gospel of John: A Commentary with Elements of Comparison to Indian Religious Thoughts and Cultural Practices* (Secunderabad: OM Books, 2005), 38.

[246] Kanagaraj, *The Gospel of John*, 38.

[247] Frank Thielman, "The Style of the Fourth Gospel and Ancient Literary Critical Concepts of Religious Discourse," *Persuasive Artistry: Studies in New Testament Rhetoric in Honor of George A. Kennedy: Journal for the Study of the New Testament Supplement Series 50*, ed. Duane F. Watson (Sheffield: JSOT Press, 1991), 169.

[248] Vernon K. Robbins, "The Chreia," *Greco-Roman Literature and the NT*, ed. David E. Aune (Atlanta, Georgia: Scholars Press/SBL, 1988), 2-7. A *chreia* is a particular type of reminiscence. Rhetoricians distinguish between *sayings chreiai* and *action chreiai*. A saying chreia may belong to the "response" species rather than the "statement" species. There are at least four kinds of response species: first, some contains a question in the situation which may be answered simply by 'yes' or 'no'; second, some contains an inquiry in the situation which requires the speaker to provide some kind of information beyond 'yes' or 'no'; third, another kind includes an explanation, advice, or some such thing in addition to the answer to the question; and fourth, still another kind of "response" chreia contains simply a remark in the situation rather than a simple question or inquiry to which the response is made. Also see, Ronald F. Hock and Edward N. O'Neil, eds., *The Chreia in Ancient Rhetoric*, Vol. 1: The Progymnasmata, Text and Translations 27 (Atlanta: Scholars Press, 1986); D. F. Watson, "Chreia/Aphorism," *Dictionary of Jesus and the Gospels*, eds. Joel B. Green, Scot McKnight and I. Howard Marshall (Illinois: InterVarsity Press, 1992), 104-106.

Prologue only with hesitation."[249] According to him, "The most that can be concluded is that the frequency of such features in 1:1-18 enables us to speak of 'rhythmical prose.'"[250] When we analyze the structure of John 1:1-5, there are multiple *dialogical-responses*. Whereas all the four 'A sayings' exist by themselves, the 'B sayings' are adjoined to the 'A sayings' with the help of the conjunction *kai*.[251] In all these instances, a reader may be brought to the thinking about a 'second reader' behind the narrative. When the 'A readings' are combined together, that presents a thorough-going flow of the mind of the narrator. It is this rhythmical-responsive style that invites the readers for participation in the act of reading.

In a responsive-reading,[252] the latter reading can be seen as a 'response' to the previous. This basic aspect is well-maintained in the prologue of John. If we consider the prologue as a responsive reading between A and B, the following format shall explain the structure of the pericope.

A. In the beginning was the Word
B. And the Word was with God, and the Word was God. He was in the beginning with God

A. All things came into being through him
B. And without him not one thing came into being

A. What has come into being in him was life
B. And the life was the light of all people

A. The light shines in the darkness
B. And the darkness did not overcome it

[249] D. A. Carson, *The Gospel According to John* (Leicester: InterVarsity Press, 1991), 112. It is important to ascertain whether the Prologue of John is a "poem" or a "prose," a "rhythmic prose" or a "responsive dialogical literary piece." Jacobus says, "the Prologue is a poem with a forward movement building up tension toward a climax at the end: 'the-grace-and truth emerged through Jesus Christ.'" Also see, Frank Kermode, "St. John as Poet," *Journal for the Study of the New Testament* 28 (1986), 3-16; Jacobus Schoneveld, "Torah in the Flesh: A New Reading of the Prologue of the Gospel of John as a Contribution to a Christology without Anti-Judaism," *The New Testament and Christian-Jewish Dialogue: Studies in Honor of Daniel Flusser, Immanuel* 24/25 (1990), 81.

[250] Carson, *The Gospel According to John*, 112.

[251] The Prologue is arranged in a responsive-style below. It is arranged in the fashion of an 'A-B Dialogue.'

[252] A 'Responsive Rhetoric' can be a stylistic feature adopted by the author to incorporate the community's interactive features. It is a kind of 'responsive reading' that maintains the dialogical nature of a literary piece. The author of the Gospel of John attempts to sustain the dialogical feature of the entire document right from the beginning.

A. There was a man sent from God
B. Whose name was John

A He came as a witness to testify to the light
B. So that all might believe through him

A. He himself was not the light
B. But he came to testify to the light

A The true light... was coming into the world
B. Which enlightens everyone

A. He was in the world, and the world came into being through him
B. Yet the world did not know him

A. He came to what was his own
B. And his own people did not accept him

A. But to all who received him, who believed in his name, he gave power to become children of God
B. Who were born, not of blood or of the will of the flesh or of the will of man, but of God

A. And the Word became flesh and lived among us
B. And we have seen his glory, the glory as of a father's only son, full of grace and truth

A. John testified to him and cried out
B. 'This was he of whom I said, "He who comes after me ranks ahead of me because he was before me"'

A. From his fullness we have all received
B. Grace upon grace

A The law indeed was given through Moses
B. Grace and truth came through Jesus

A. No one has ever seen God
B. It is God the only Son, who is close to the Father's heart, who has made him know.

The A readings are simple statements, and the B readings are embellishments upon A readings. An orderly arrangement of the 'A readings' together will give the reader a nutshell of the message of the prologue; but the 'B readings' add further information to get a detailed grasp of it. The A sections are the real content of the prologue, and the B sections are qualifications upon the A sections. The author of the Gospel, as a profound composer of dialogues, employs his artistic skills innovatively right from the beginning. This poetic style of the prologue is universalistic in nature.

A *Chiastic* Communication

The prologue is not only responsive in style; but it also can be read as a *chiasm*.[253] As Neyrey comments this chiasm is not merely ornamental but structures the communication.[254] A chiasm places parallel words or phrases at the top and bottom of the passage (A and A') and also includes subsequent parallels (B and B', C and C', and the like), thus signaling beginnings and endings, which frame the intervening communication. Scholars mark the parallels by labeling them as A, B; C and C', B', A', which often draws attention to a central passage, "D," which serves as the focus or climax of the rhetoric.[255] The seven pairs of parallel narratives in the chiastic rearrangement of the prologue provide a dialogic structure. There are at least two levels of parallelism, namely *synonymous* and *antithetical*.[256] Synonymous Parallelism, where the second line supports the idea of the first is exemplified in 1:1-2 and 18 (A and A'), 1:3-5 and 16 (C and C'), 1:6-8 and 15 (D and D'), 1:9-10 and 14 (E and E'), 1:11 and 13 (F and F') and 1:12 and 12c (G and G'). Antithetical Parallelism, where the second line offers a contrast with the first, is found in 1:3 and 17 (B and B'). The pivotal point of the chiastic dialogue is found in 1:12b (i. e., H). John's usage of the device *chiasm* helps the reader to analyze the internal communication of the narrative in a symmetrical fashion. The internal communication of Johannine prologue through the way of a chiasm is not without an intention. It has the power of interaction not only within the pericope, but also with the entire Gospel. The poetical and chiastic style of the Fourth Gospel calls the attention of the readers from all the places and at all times.

---

[253] A "chiasm" describes the conscious shaping of a passage according to an "X" shape (the Greek letter "chi" is X-shaped, *chiasm*). By providing clarity and focus, a chiastic structure draws an audience's attention to significant materials both by means of repetitive parallels and by highlighting the centre of the figure, presumably the major thrust of the passage. This common form, moreover, was anticipated by audiences to aid in following the argument or narrative. Jerome H. Neyrey, *The Gospel of John*, The New Cambridge Bible Commentary (New York: Cambridge University Press, 2007), 38. The pioneering work on the chiastic interpretation was done by M.-E Boismard in *St. John's Prologue* (London: Blackfriars, 1957), 76-81; see also R. A. Culpepper, "The Pivot of John's Prologue," *NTS 27* (1980), 2-7.

[254] Jerome H. Neyrey, *The Gospel of John* (Cambridge: University Press, 2007), 39.

[255] Neyrey, *The Gospel of John*, 38. Also see Stibbe, *Mark*, 30. Neyrey arranges John 1:1-18 by employing the style of chiasm: A and A' (1:1-2 and 18); B and B' (1:3 and 17); C and C' (1:3-5 and 16); D and D' (1:6-8 and 15); E and E' (1:9-10 and 14); F and F' (1:11 and 13); G and G' (1:12a and c); and H (1:12b).

[256] Raymond E. Brown, *The Gospel According to John 1-12: Introduction, Translation and Notes*, The Anchor Bible (New York: Doubleday, 1966), cxxxii.

Tri-level Dialogical Functions

John's dialogues have multifarious layers which reflect through the interaction of the primitive Greco-Roman socio-historical backgrounds. The Gospel facilitates dialogues with the narrator, the narrator with his own community, internal structures, characters, themes and meanings in the text, and the narrator with the current readers. All these together present a *live* representation of the content of the prologue to every reader within a principle of 'everywhere and ever.' This character of the book is eternal in duration and universal in application. Stibbe comments that, "this magnificent overture has three functions: *interactional, intra-textual* and *inter-textual*."[257] All these functions are basically dialogical in nature. The *interactional* function is basically between the narrator and the reader in an eternal point of view. In interaction with the reader, the narrator views Jesus the Word from an omniscient perspective. Stibbe says, "The reader is given the impression from the start that the story is being told by one who views events from a transcendent and eternal vantage point."[258] The prologue is framed by employing rhetorical devices like inclusion, dualism, symbolism, irony, chiasmus and multivalence.[259] These various linguistic components decide the polyphonic[260] character of the prologuc.

The text also reveals its function of *intra-textuality*,[261] which means, within the Gospel itself. When scholars argued that the prologue was a wisdom hymn stitched by the author to the front of the Gospel to make it more acceptable to Hellenistic readers, it was judged to have little relationship

---

[257] Mark W. G. Stibbe, *John*, Readings: A New Biblical Commentary (Sheffield: Sheffield Academic Press, 1993), 22. Also see E. S. Malbon, "Ending at the Beginning," *Semeia 52* (1991), 177. The interactional function concerns the communication between the narrator and the reader. The inter-textual function has to do with the relationship of John 1:1-18 with other literary texts. The intra-textual function of the Prologue is to introduce the reader to certain narrative qualities which will be ubiquitous in the Gospel.

[258] Stibbe, *John*, 22-23. The narrator seems to speak on behalf of a group or a community of people. The narrator employs more of a We-Thou than an I-Thou form of address.

[259] Stibbe, *John*, 29-31.

[260] On one level, Bakhtin observes the "heteroglossic" character of language. On another level, Bakhtin suggests that discourse is always "polyphonic." Because meaning reverberate with and against each other upon their utterance, transmission, and reception, the making of meaning is itself a dialogical reality. See Paul N. Anderson, "Bakhtin's Dialogism and the Corrective Rhetoric of the Johannine Misunderstanding Dialogue: Exposing Seven Crises in the Johannine Situation," *Bakhtin and Genre Theory in Biblical Studies 63*, ed. Roland Boer (Atlanta: SBL, 2007), 133.

[261] It is specifically dealt with in the seventh section, titled "Prologue in Dialogue with the rest of the Book."

to the rest of the Gospel.[262] Now scholars stress the extensive relationship between the prologue and the Gospel, such that one might say that the prologue is a topic sentence, an overture, a summary of what is subsequently developed.[263] Many of the central, thematic words of this Gospel are first introduced in these verses: life, light (1:4), witness (1:7), true (in the sense of 'genuine' or 'ultimate,' 1:9), world (1:10), glory, and truth (1:14). But supremely, the prologue summarizes how the 'Word' which was with God in the beginning came into the sphere of time, history, tangibility—in other words, how the Son of God was sent into the world to become the Jesus of history, so that the glory and grace of God might be uniquely and perfectly disclosed. In essence, this snippet is in dialogue with the rest of the book.[264] The significance of the prologue, therefore, is that it determines how the entire Gospel should be read and understood.[265] The prologue is a work of immense assurance and literary power. It moves with measured steps from the creation to the climactic moment of the incarnation (vs. 14), and then indicates the fullness of revelation which results from it.[266]

Opening with an echo of Genesis 1:1, the prologue goes on to identify its protagonist as the "Logos," the Word of God, and thus places the drama in a cosmic setting and against an OT background. The narrator also sets up an *inter-textual* relationship between the story of Jesus and the story of Moses. Comparison between Jesus and Moses, and between Jesus' death and the Exodus, recur throughout John.[267] Stibbe says, "This network of Moses symbolism is initiated in the Prologue."[268] Moreover, the text interacts within itself. The interrelationship of Jesus, the Word with God (vv. 1-2), creation (vv. 3-5), John the Baptist (vv. 6-9), his enemies (vv. 10-11) and the community

---

[262] Neyrey, *The Gospel of John*, 41. Cf. J. A. T. Robinson, "The Relation of the Prologue to the Gospel of St. John," *NTS 9* (1962), 120-29; Warren Carter, "The Prologue and John's Gospel: Function, Symbol and Definitive Word," *JSNT 39* (1990), 35-58; and Elizabeth Harris, *Prologue and Gospel: The Theology of the Fourth Evangelist* (Sheffield: Sheffield Academic Press, 1994), 1-25.

[263] Neyrey, *The Gospel of John*, 41-43. Also see George R. Beasley-Murray, *John*, Word Biblical Commentary, Vol. 36 (Waco, Texas: Word Books Publisher, 1987), 3. The Prologue is considered as a foyer to the rest of the Fourth Gospel, simultaneously drawing the reader in and introducing the major themes. Carson, *The Gospel According to John*, 111.

[264] Cf. Carson, *The Gospel According to John*, 111.

[265] Cornelis Bennema, *Excavating John's Gospel: A Commentary for Today* (Delhi: ISPCK, 2005), 22.

[266] Lindars, *The Gospel of John,* 77.

[267] Stibbe, *John*, 23.

[268] Stibbe, *John*, 23. The narrator not only establishes an inter-textual relationship between this story and the stories of Wisdom and of Moses, the same thing is also done with the opening of the book of Genesis. There is hardly a work of literature with more of a sense of a beginning than John's Gospel.

(vv. 12-16) is conspicuously narrated in succinct form. These diverse functions of the prologue exemplify the multifarious dialogues of the text 'within,' 'between' and 'among' an array of concepts, figures and texts. This character evidently projects the dialogic and at the same time universalistic intention of the opening snippet of the Gospel.

Conflict and Characterization

The author uses various episodes skillfully to enrich the texture of the whole. While the dialogues slow down the action, they intensify *conflict and characterization* and provide space for *thematic development*.[269] The effect of the narrative structure, with its prologue followed by episodic repetition of the conflict between belief and unbelief, is to enclose the reader in the company of faith. The gospel's plot, therefore, is controlled by thematic development and a strategy for wooing readers to accept its interpretation of Jesus.[270] The plot of the Gospel cannot be determined unless the readers comprehend the dialectical stature. In John's Gospel, God incarnate in Jesus has a controversy with the world, and the Jewish leaders who epitomize the world in its opposition to the Gospel (John 5:16, 18; 6:41; 7:1; 10:31; 11:8). This tension is the real thrust of the Gospel, a dialogue between belief and unbelief, and the prologue establishes this fact right at the beginning itself. John 1:1-18 foreshadows the division between belief and unbelief so characteristic of the rest of the Gospel (1:10-11).[271] By means of the prologue the author attempts to help Jews, Greeks, and other religious philosophers to understand God in His relationship with human beings.[272] The Gospel is framed in a fashion in which the dialectical role of belief and unbelief moves antithetically. Mostly the discourse sections are fashioned by strategically inserting the 'belief-unbelief conflict.' This hidden agenda of the story is the pavement of the Gospel's dialogic structure. By foregrounding the ideological conflict between 'belief' and 'unbelief,' the narrator introduces a globalized conflict at the centreplace of the discussion.

In the Gospel of John, the reader is alerted at the outset that the story of Jesus is the crucial manifestation of a cosmic struggle between light and darkness or belief and unbelief (1:5). The historic circumstances of Jesus in his time are the stage on which the ultimate cosmic drama is played out. Jesus' victory (16:33) is not just a personal triumph, but the act in which the light finally overcomes the darkness and God's plan of salvation for all humanity

---

[269] Culpepper, *Anatomy of the Fourth Gospel*, 97.

[270] Culpepper, *Anatomy of the Fourth Gospel*, 98.

[271] M. M. Thompson, "John, Gospel of," *Dictionary of Jesus and the Gospels*, eds. Joel B. Green, Scot McKnight and I Howard Marshall (Illinois: InterVarsity Press, 1992), 373.

[272] Jey J. Kanagaraj, *The Gospel of John: A Commentary with Elements of Comparison to Indian Religious Thoughts and Cultural Practices* (Secunderabad: OM Books, 2005), 34.

is achieved. The Gospel is carefully planned with a series of set pieces, each leading up to a dramatic climax. The presentation is controlled by the skilful use of dialogue, or dramatic monologue, to engage the readers on the side of Jesus and to confront them personally with the decision which is set before Jesus' audience in the play. John's writing has perennial power and challenges the modern reader still.[273] .

A Vertical Dialogic Drama

The Prologue is an abstract form in which the *Heaven-Earth Drama* is initiated. We notice that John is an artist with a strong feeling of drama. Barnabas Lindars rightly points out that "In fact the form and structure of the Prologue are in conformity with John's discourse style."[274] This is not a fresh discovery, since many studies of the Fourth Gospel have drawn attention to its dramatic elements.[275] Smalley says, "By considering the Fourth Gospel as a highly-wrought drama, moreover, we can determine John's distinctive presentation of the gospel tradition, centered in Jesus, and appreciate further the evangelist's theological understanding."[276] In the prologue it is conspicuous that the heavens come in dialogue with the earth. The scene is set in heaven (vv. 1-13), but moves swiftly to earth (v. 14), with heaven in mind. In prologue, we encounter John's principal theological themes, and the chief characters in the drama: Jesus, John the Baptist, the disciples, and the world.[277]

Scholars like Brant and Parsenios have proposed that the Fourth Evangelist modeled his Gospel on Greek drama, especially tragedy.[278] The Gospels are, however, too long for dramas, which maintained a particular

---

[273] Barnabas Lindars, Ruth B. Edwards and John M. Court, *The Johannine Literature: With an Introduction by R. Alan Culpepper* (Sheffield: Sheffield Academic Press, 2000), 35.

[274] Barnabas Lindars, *The Gospel of John*, New Century Bible (London: Oliphants, 1972), 82.

[275] Stephen Smalley, *John: Evangelist & Interpreter*, Second Edition (Carlisle: Paternoster Press, 1998), 141. George Mlakuzhyil describes Johannine Gospel in its totality as a five-act theological drama, and identifies some of the dramatic techniques used in its composition: such as change of scenes, change of characters and double-stage action. Similarly, Ben Witherington believes that John has drawn on the conventions of Graeco-Roman drama to present the story of Jesus 'in a dramatic mode.' See G. Mlakuzhyil, *The Christocentric Literary Structure of the Fourth Gospel*, AnBib 117 (Rome: Pontificio Instituto Biblico, 1987); Ben Witherington, *John's Wisdom: A commentary on the Fourth Gospel* (Cambridge: Lutterworth Press, 1995).

[276] Smalley, *John: Evangelist and Interpreter*, 142.

[277] Smalley, *John*: *Evangelist and Interpreter*, 142.

[278] Jo-Ann A. Brant, *Dialogue and Drama: Elements of Greek Tragedy in the Fourth Gospel* (Peabody: Hendrickson, 2004); George L. Parsenios, *Departure and Consolation: The Johannine Farewell Discourses in Light of Greco-Roman Literature* (Leiden/Boston: Brill, 2005).

length in Mediterranean antiquity.[279] They also include far too much prose narrative for ancient drama. Despite its inadequacy as a full-fledged generic category, however, the proposal has some merit in that it at least invites us to investigate elements of Mediterranean storytelling from this period that were borrowed from Greek drama. Some scholars pointed out that John generally has only two or at most three active (speaking) characters at a time, which fits rules for staging in Greek drama, and he divides scenes in a manner similar to such works.[280] Paul Duke regards John's "dramatic style" as so similar to classical Greek drama that he believes the author shows some acquaintance with Greek drama.[281]

In the prologue, John introduces the most important themes that he will develop in the rest of the work.[282] The evangelist shows the progression from pre-existence (1:1-2) to creation (1:3), the time subsequent to creation but prior to the incarnation (1:4-5), the Baptist (1:6-8), and the incarnation and its results and benefits (1:9-18).[283] The framework John wants us to adopt is as follows: this world is a world enveloped in spiritual darkness; it does not know God; but by divine initiative, God came to this world as a human being—Jesus.[284] Thus the 'world from above' is in a dialogue with the 'world from below.' More briefly it should be noted the way in which the gospel moves back and forth between narratives and discourses. The interrelationship between narratives and discourses is a feature of the literary skill of the author.[285] The reader has been told *who* Jesus is and *what* he has done, but an important question remains

---

[279] Craig S. Keener, *The Gospel of John: A Commentary*, Vol. 1 (Peabody: Hendrickson, 2003), 10. Also see Burridge, *Gospels*, 225; Robert A. Spivey and D. Moody Smith, *Anatomy of the New Testament: A Guide to Its Structure and Meaning* (London: The Macmillan Company, 1969).

[280] Keener, *The Gospel of John*, 10; also see Koester, *Symbolism*, 36; Ellis, *Genius*, 8.

[281] Duke, *Irony,* 141.

[282] Andreas J. Köstenberger, *John*, BECNT (Grand Rapids, Michigan: Baker Academic, 2004). This is why the prologue has also been called the "Proleptic Quintessence" (Harnack, A. von, "Ubes das Verhaltnis des Prologs des Vierten Evangeliums," *Zeitschrift fur Theologie und Kirche* 2, 1982, 189-231); a "Microcosm" (Valentine, S. R., "The Johannine Prologue—a Microcosm of the Gospel," *Evangelical Quarterly* 68, 1996, 291-304); and an "Adumbration" (Booser, K. D., "The Literary Structure of John 1:1-18: An Examination of Its Theological Implications concerning God's Saving Plan through Jesus Christ," *Evangelical Journal* 16, 1993, 13-29) of the entire Gospel.

[283] J. G. Van der Watt, "The Composition of the Prologue of John's Gospel: The Historical Jesus Introducing Divine Grace," *Westminster Theological Journal* 57 (1995), 311-32; Lindars, *The Gospel of John*, 77.

[284] Bennema, *Excavating John's Gospel,* 27.

[285] Kysar, "John, the Gospel of," *ABD*, 916.

unanswered: *how* did this action of God in the human story take place? Only a Johannine story of Jesus can answer that question.[286]

Prologue in Dialogue with the Rest of the Book[287]

In Greek rhetoric, the introduction and statement of facts must come first in a speech. In the introduction to a forensic speech, one should state facts concisely so the jury will understand them, including arguments which anticipate the main arguments of speech. Yet such an introduction does not expound the main points; it merely introduces them; its "sole purpose" is to dispose the audience favorably to the rest of the speech or work. A prologue could not expound at any length, since it was to be kept short. As a formal preface, John's prologue is thus "likely to reveal something of the author's purpose, intentions and interest."[288] The narratives of the gospel are often told in a dramatic style. They progress in deliberate stages which constitute scenes and evoke a sense of suspense as the narrative moves forward. Such a dramatic structure is typical of a series of longer narratives within the gospel. Among these are 4:1-42; 6:1-71; 9:1-41; 11:1-44; and 18:28-19:16. The narratives, however, are not exclusively of this longer variety. Punctuating the story are much shorter tales told with economy and clarity (see 2:1-11; 2:12-25; 4:43-54; 12:1-11; 13:1-30).[289] John 1:1-18 informs the reader that Jesus Christ is the incarnation of the pre-existent Word and that life, light, and divine filiations flow from an acceptance of the story of the unseen God revealed by the incarnate Word. This story perfects the former gift of the Law given through Moses.[290] The failure to link the prologue with the literary and socio-historical contexts of the Gospel is evident in a brief examination of several significant contributions from previous scholarship.[291]

---

[286] Moloney, *The Gospel of John*, 34.

[287] It is an extension of the arguments of the *intra-textual* connections of the Gospel.

[288] Keener, *The Gospel of John*, 338. Cf. Dionysius of Halicarnassus, *Lysias* 24. Rhetorical handbooks already insisted that the introduction should summarize the arguments the speech would use (Dionysius of Halicarnassus, *Thucyd.* 19), though there were some exceptions in spoken rhetoric.

[289] Robert Kysar, "John, the Gospel of," *ABD*, ed. David Noel Freedman, Vol. 3 (New York: Doubleday, 1992), 916.

[290] Francis J. Moloney, *The Gospel of John*, Sacra Pagina Series, ed. Daniel J. Harrington, Vol. 4 (Collegeville, Minnesota: The Liturgical Press, 1998), 34.

[291] Warren Carter, "The Prologue and John's Gospel: Function, Symbol and the Definitive Word," *Journal for the Study of the New Testament* 39 (1990), 35. Harnack concluded that the Prologue was a secondary addition. The exchange between Bultmann and Kasemann which has dominated the discussion of the prologue since Harnack, was concerned primarily with its original form and provenance. J. A. T. Robinson similarly overlooked the literary and socio-historical context of the Gospel in arguing that the Prologue was a later addition to a Gospel. Cf. Harnack, "Ubes das Varhaltnis des Prologs," *ZTK* 2, 189-231; E. Käsemann, "The Structure and

In John, the *Logos* is narrated as a divine emissary in conflict with the world throughout the Gospel. Jesus, the emissary from above, has come into this world (1:9-10; 3:16-17, 19; 6:14; 10:36; 11:27; 12:46; 16:28; 17:18, 21, 23; 18:37). His mission was an expression of God's love for the world (3:16). The coming of *Logos* is expressed in terms of the coming of the light into the world and as the light of the world (3:19; 8:12; 9:5; 12:46).[292] J. Painter observes, "Only those who believe perceive the light of the world which has the power to transform those who belong to the world so that their lives are shaped by the light from above."[293] John's *Logos*, thus, permeates all through the Gospel as a focused theme. The coming of the *Logos* is delineated as the coming of the 'World from Above' in dialogue with the 'World from Below.' These features of Johannine duality in both synonymous and antithetical format enable the readers to look into the entire Gospel from a dialogical and gnomic perspective.

Conclusion

The above details reveal that the Prologue in particular and the Gospel of John as a whole develop *interactional*, *intra-textual* and *inter-textual* relations. It happens· through the ideological resonances that John sharc with the surrounding literary, religio-political, and socio-cultural backgrounds. The dialogic nature of the prologue reveals its reverberating nature. This particular nature of the prologue is gnomic as it reflects universal maxims and thus makes the message of incarnation is known. And that is done through a deeply rooted concept like *Logos*. This piece of writing demonstrates its power to encompass and absorb other ideas and other contextual underpinnings into its own semantic and pragmatic domains. In that way, a series of dialogues take place: within the text, beyond the text, and between the 'world from above' and the 'world from below.' This aspect of the gospel is presented with an eternal and universal perspective. Thus, dialogue as a literary genre is dynamically and creatively used by the narrator with an 'everywhere and ever' perspective. This characteristic of John 1:1-18 is rhetorical in its delineation and articulation.

Purpose of the Prologue to John's Gospel," *New Testament Questions of Today* (Philadelphia: Fortress, 1969), 138-67; and J. A. T. Robinson, "The Relation of the Prologue to the Gospel of St. John," *NTS* 9 (1962-63), 120-29.

[292] J. Painter, "World," *Dictionary of Jesus and the Gospels*, 890.

[293] J. Painter, "World," *Dictionary of Jesus and the Gospels*, 890.

In the Fourth Gospel, Jesus is the *Logos* who was with God and yet was God (1:1) and was the source of all creation (1:2). This idea is further expressed through the presence of Jesus as the divine 'I am' (8:58) who can be called 'Lord and God' (20:28). On the other hand, he is also presented as a real human being in the localized situation. These aspects reflect both the globalizing and localizing natures of Johannine Jesus. The narrator foregrounds all these aspects through the means of poetical and prose structures.[294]

---

[294] See Gregory MacDonald, *The Evangelical Universalist*, Second Edition (Eugene, Oregon: Cascade Books, 2012), 39.

Chapter 4

Dialogue as a Literary Genre in the Book of Signs (John 1:19-12:50)

Introduction

The dialogue of the Gospel of John remains as one of the most significant literary genres yet to be adequately explored by scholars. It is one of the oral or literary genres universally used to promote human interaction and communication. The Book of Signs (1:19-12:50)[295] in the gospel comprises of several dialogue

[295] According to classical Johannine scholarship, the Gospel of John is mainly divided into four parts: two small parts (i.e., 1:1-18 as the 'prologue' and 21:1-25 as the 'epilogue') and two larger parts (i.e., 1:19-12:50 as the 'Book of Signs' and 13:1-20:31 as the 'Book of Glory'; cf. Moloney, *The Gospel of John*. Brown, similarly, divides the gospel into four parts (the Prologue [1:1-18]; the Book of Signs [1:19-12:50]; the Book of Glory [13:1-20:31]; and the Epilogue [21:1-25]) and he discusses the Sēmeia-Quelle or *Sign Source* in detail. See Brown, *The Gospel according to John*, xxviii-xxxix. Van Belle describes in detail the origin and development of the "Sēmeia Hypothesis." See Gilbert Van Belle, *The Signs Source in the Fourth Gospel: Historical Survey and Critical Evaluation of the Semeia Hypothesis*, Bibliotheca Ephemeridum Theologicarum Lovaniensium CXVI (Leuven: University Press, 1994), 1; cf. Albert Schweizer, *Das Evangelium Johannes nach seinem innern Werthe und seiner Bedeutung für das Leben Jesu kritisch untersucht* (Leipzig, 1841); Rudolf Bultmann, *The History of the Synoptic Tradition*, tran. Marsh, J (Oxford, 1963/1968); Rudolf Bultmann, *The Gospel of John: A Commentary*, ed. Beasley-Murray, G. R (Oxford: B. Blackwell/ Philadelphia: Westminster, 1971). For Dodd, the Book of Signs begins with 2:1 and ends with 12:50, with at least seven episodes (2:1-4:42; 4:46-5:47; 6; 7-8; 9:1-10-21 [with appendix, 10:22-39]; 11:1-53; and 12:1-36) and an 'Epilogue to the Book of Signs' (12:37-50). See C. H. Dodd, *The Interpretation of the Fourth Gospel* (Cambridge: University Press, 1953/1960).

texts.[296] This large block of the gospel appears to be a major dialogue portion in the NT connected to the life and ministry of Jesus of Nazareth. Dodd rightly points out that, "Among the various forms in which the church's witness and saving work of Christ is presented in the gospels, the one most characteristic of the Fourth Gospel is the elaborately wrought dramatic dialogue."[297] In view of Dodd's statement, the central question to be addressed here is: 'How does John use the literary genre called dialogue within the gospel?' Though Dodd is one of the pioneers in dealing with the dialogue of the gospel, a concentrated study of the subject matter is scarce even in his writings.

Along with the central question posed above, a few other questions also have to be dealt with, such as 'How does John use dialogue as a means to promote the universality of the Gospel?' 'How does John structure dialogue as a literary genre?' 'What are the ways exchanges and episodes function within the narrative framework?' 'How do the content, form, and function contribute to the semantic, syntactic, and pragmatic levels of the dialogue?' 'How are dialogues involved in expressing the aspects of the Johannine community?' 'What are the peculiar literary characteristics of his dialogue?' and 'What is the theological/rhetorical function of the Johannine dialogue?' These questions have to be adequately dealt with in the process of exploring the dialogue of the gospel. The task of this study will be threefold: to explore the gnomic significance of the Johannine dialogues; to investigate the development of the dialogue within the narrative framework of John; and to understand the peculiar approaches and methodologies of the author/narrator for framing the dialogue.

The Exchange Development

The nature and function of the dialogue at the *macro*-level can be comprehended through the means of its development at the exchange and episode (i.e., *micro*-and *meso*-) levels. A careful analysis of the Book of Signs confirms that the narrative comments and the utterance units function contributively

---

Barrett broadly structures 1:19-12:50 as a separate section that deals with "Narratives, Conversations, and Discourses." See C. K. Barrett, *The Gospel according to St. John: An Introduction with Commentary and Notes on the Greek Text* (London: SPCK, 1978), 11; cf. Thomaskutty, *Dialogue in the Book of Signs*. Similarly, Brodie divides the book into two, as 'Book One' (chaps. 1-12) and 'Book Two' (chaps. 13-21). See T. L. Brodie, *The Gospel According to John: A Literary and Theological Commentary* (New York: Oxford University Press, 1993). The above descriptions give a detailed picture of the scholarly views with regard to the Book of Signs. In the present study, we will consider the section 1:1-18 as an appropriate introduction to the entire gospel and the section 1:19-12:50 as the Book of Signs and analyze the dialogues of the latter section.

[296] See Barrett, *The Gospel according to St. John*, 11; Moloney, *The Gospel of John*, 1998.

[297] See C. H. Dodd, *Historical Tradition in the Fourth Gospel* (Cambridge: University Press, 1963), 41.

to one another.[298] Herman rightly states that, "Utterances do not stand alone. They are generally issued and exchanged in specific contexts, and form complex units, within wider units like *speech events*."[299] What Herman says is proved in the Johannine utterances as they are attached to their contexts. The interactive nature of the utterances with the pure and formula narratives provide the reader important insights concerning the two major dialogue tenets of the Book of Signs, i.e., dialogues between the characters and between the narrator and the reader.[300] The utterance units of the dialogue are rhetorical as they work efficaciously within the narrative framework.[301] In the process of reading, a paradigmatic reader realizes the interactive nature of the dialogue and the narrative within the exchange structures.[302] This interaction of the utterances/dialogues and the narratives within the exchanges at the micro-level dynamically works for the development of the episodes.[303]

A careful analysis of the Book of Signs helps us to identify some of the major dialogue trends at the micro-level.[304] The narrator uses *question-and-answer* (1:19-28; 6:1-15;[305] 6:22-59, 67-71; 9:1-7, 8-12, 13-17, 18-23; 10:22-39; 11:30-37, 54-57; 12:1-11),[306] *request-rebuke-response* (2:1-11; 4:43-

---

[298] R. W. Funk, *The Poetics of Biblical Narrative* (Sonoma, California: Polebridge Press, 1988), 2; also see Derek Tovey, *Jesus: Story of God, John's Story of Jesus* (Adelaide: ATF Press, 2007), 42-48.

[299] V. Herman, *Dramatic Discourse: Dialogue as Interaction in Plays* (London/New York: Routledge, 1995), 13; cf. M. M. Bakhtin, *Speech Genres and Other Late Essays*, tran. McGee, V (Austin: University of Texas Press, 1986/1998), 62.

[300] D. F. Tolmie, *Narratology and Biblical Narratives: A Practical Guide* (San Francisco/London: International Scholars Publications, 1999), 13; See T. J. Martin, *Living Words: Studies in Dialogues about* Religion (Atlanta, Georgia: Scholars Press/Oxford: Oxford University Press, 1976/1988), 27; cf. M. J. Buss, "Dialogue in and among Genres," *Bakhtin and Genre Theory in Biblical Studies*, ed. Boer, R (Atlanta: SBL, 2007), 9-18; P. N. Anderson, "From One Dialogue to Another: Johannine Polyvalence from Origins to Receptions," *Anatomies of Narrative Criticism: The Past, Present and Future of the Fourth Gospel as Literature* (Leiden/Boston: Brill, 2008), 93-120.

[301] See H. Lausberg, *Handbook of Literary Rhetoric: A Foundation for Literary Study* (Leiden/Boston/Köln: Brill, 1998), 2-37; S. Chatman, *Story and Discourse: Narrative Structure in Fiction and Film* (Ithaca: Cornell University Press, 1978), 176.

[302] See T. Maranhão, *The Interpretation of Dialogue* (Chicago: University of Chicago, 1990), 14.

[303] Herman, *Dramatic Discourse*, 13.

[304] G. A. Press, *Plato: A Guide for the Perplexed* (London: Continuum, 2007), 57.

[305] Here it is in a *question of test-answer of impossibility-action of possibility* sequence.

[306] D. E. Aune, "Dialogue," *The Westminster Dictionary of New Testament and Early Christian Literature and Rhetoric* (Louisville/London: Westminster John Knox Press, 2003), 126.

54),[307] *challenge-and-riposte* (2:13-22; 4:16-26; 6:67-71; 7:14-36; 8:12-20; 9:1-7; 10:22-39; 12:1-11),[308] *report-and-defense* (3:22-36), and other forms of dialogues at the *micro*-level in order to present the story of Jesus to the reader. Other formats of dialogues such as *double meaning-misunderstanding-clarification* (3:1-10; 4:7-15; 4:31-38; 8:12-20, 21-30; 9:39-41; 11:7-16, 17-27; 12:12-36a),[309] *dialogue leading to monologue* (1:19-34; 3:1-21; 5:10-47; 12:36b-50),[310] *dialogue to action* (2:1-11; 6:5-14; 9:1-7; 11:38-44),[311] and *action to dialogue* (2:13-22; 5:[9]10-13; 6:16-21;[312] 12:1-11) are also used within the exchange structures of the Book of Signs.[313] The dialogues at the exchange level are grouped together to form the dialogues at the episodic level.[314] As dialogue is a common means of communication used in all places and at all times, a reader of the story can easily relate her/himself with the settings and the characters of the Gospel. This characteristic of the Gospel reveals its gnomic nature.

The Episode Development

At the meso-level, the narrator places two glory-focused revelatory dialogues at the beginning (1:19-2:12) and towards the end (11:1-54) of the Book of Signs. If we consider John 1:1-18 as the introduction and 11:55-12:50 as the conclusion,[315] then the *glory-focused revelatory dialogues* (1:19-2:12 and 11:1-54) form a thematic inclusion within the Book of Signs.[316] While the episode in 1:19-2:12 sets a strong foundation for the gospel through the transfer of role from John the Witness to Jesus the Word and his ministry, the episode in 11:1-54 inaugurates the passion and leads toward the end of his ministry.[317] In both cases, dialogues are used as an important literary phenomenon. Also in

---

[307] A. J. Köstenberger, *Encountering John: The Gospel in Historical, Literary, and Theological Perspective* (Grand Rapids, Michigan: Baker Book House, 1999), 72-74.

[308] Neyrey, *The Gospel of John,* 71-72, 79, 93, 100.

[309] P. F. Ellis, *The Genius of John: A Composition Critical Commentary on the Fourth Gospel* (Collegeville, Minnesota: Liturgical Press, 1984), 7; also see Neyrey, *The Gospel of John*, 12-3, 78, 90-1, 195-6.

[310] In 12:36b-50, it is in the form of a *soliloquy*.

[311] In 2:1-11 and 6:5-14, the narratives develop in a *dialogue-action-dialogue* sequence.

[312] In 6:16-21, the pericope is in the form of an *action-dialogues-action-dialogue* narrative.

[313] See Press, Plato: *A Guide for the Perplexed*, 66.

[314] J. A. Brant, *Dialogue and Drama: Elements of Greek Tragedy in the Fourth Gospel* (Peabody: Hendrickson, 2004), 27.

[315] C. H. Talbert, *Reading John: A Literary and Theological Commentary on the Fourth Gospel and the Johannine Epistles* (New York: Crossroad, 1992), 179-188.

[316] M. De Jonge, and H. M. J. Van Duyne, *Taal en Teken: Ontmoetingen met Jezus in het Evangelie van Johannes* (Nijkerk: Uitgeverij G. F. Callenbach b. v, 1978).

[317] See Dodd, *The Interpretation of the Fourth Gospel*, 292-296.

both cases the dialogues are leading to/centered on signs performed by Jesus. While in the first case the miracle is performed in a context of a wedding, in the second case it is done in a context of death and bereavement. All other episodes within the Book of Signs are framed within this inclusion, except for the concluding episode in 11:55-12:50 that accelerates toward the climax and is structured as a *conflict-centered* one.

The second episode (2:13-25) maintains a *challenge-and-riposte* format. Though the challenge-and-riposte format is a continuous trend in the Book of Signs (cf. 4:16-26; 6:67-71; 7:14-36; 8:12-20; 9:1-7; 10:22-39; 12:1-11), it is used to develop an independent episode only in 2:13-22.[318] In 2:13-25, through a dialogue-centered action, Jesus reveals his authority at the religio-political headquarter of Judaism, i.e., the temple at Jerusalem.[319] The *pedagogical dialogue* at 3:1-10, as the third episode, reveals Jesus' authority as a teacher from above. While Jesus' role as a teacher is explicit in the other dialogues in the Book of Signs (cf. 4:1-42; 6:1-71; 7:1-8:59), 3:1-21 is significant as he was placed over against a leading teacher of Israel called Nicodemus.[320] At the meso-level, the trend of dialogue leading to monologue begins here.[321] The framework of the episode as one beginning in the form of a dialogue (vv. 1-10) and ending as a monologue (vv. 11-21) is onc of the characteristics of the gospel. The *report-and-defense dialogue* in 3:22-36, as the fourth, is the only episode in which Jesus does not have a direct involvement. But, the discussion within the dialogue is close-knit to the role of Jesus within the narrative framework of the gospel.[322]

---

[318] The *challenge-and-riposte* format is used in several episodes in the Book of Signs.

[319] A. Barus, "John 2:12-25: A Narrative Reading," *New Currents through John: A Global Perspective* (Leiden/Boston: Brill, 2006), 123-40.

[320] Cf. S. M. Schneiders, *Written That You May Believe: Encountering Jesus in the Fourth Gospel* (New York: A Herder and Herder Book/The Crossroad Publishing Company, 1999/2003), 117-125.

[321] The trend of dialogue leading to monologue in two consequent days is introduced in 1:19-34 (and again to a dialogue, 1:35-42). But, it was done at the micro-level.

[322] See Dodd, *The Interpretation of the Fourth Gospel,* 384.

Figure 1: Thirteen episodes of the Book of Signs
(i.e., dialogues at the *meso*-level)

Episode #	Texts	Episode Title (at the Meso-lével)
1	1:19-2:12	A *Glory-focused Revelatory* Dialogue
2	2:13-22	A *Challenge and Riposte* Dialogue
3	3:1-21	A *Pedagogical* Dialogue Leading to a Monologue
4	3:22-36	A *Report-and-Defense* Dialogue to a *Narratorial Commentary*
5	4:1-42	An *Inter-Religious* Dialogue
6	4:43-54	A *Request-Rebuke-Response* Dialogue
7	5:1-47	A Sign and a *Controversy* Dialogue Leading to a Monologue
8	6:1-71	From *Sign-centered* Dialogues to *Question-and-Answer* Dialogues
9	7:1-52; 8:12-59	A *Religious-Theological* Dialogue
10	9:1-10:21	A *Dramatic dialogue* leading to a monologue and a community dialogue
11	10:22-42	A *Forensic dialogue*
12	11:1-54	A *Glory-focused Revelatory Dialogue*
13	11:55-12:50	A *Conflict-centered Dialogue*

The fifth dialogue at 4:1-42 is *inter-religious* in nature.[323] While Jesus confronts the Samaritan woman and directs her to eternal life perspectives, she accepts the new religiosity that is introduced by Jesus.[324] This is different from the *religious-theological dialogue* of 7:1-52/8:12-59 (i.e., the ninth episode), where Jesus confronts the religious leaders of Israel.[325] In both the cases, Jesus introduces his "from above" ideology over against the "from below"

[323] K. Elam, *The Semiotics of Theatre and Drama* (London/New York: Methuen, 1980), 19, 54, 91, 135-136.

[324] D. R. Sadananda, *The Johannine Exegesis of God: An Exploration into the Johannine Understanding of God* (Berlin/New York: Walter de Gruyter, 2004), 254.

[325] As religious complaints against Socrates form the substance of Platonic *Euthyphro*, in John religious complaints against Jesus form the central stuff of the dialogues.

ideologies of his interlocutors.[326] In the case of the dialogue between Jesus and the Samaritan woman, a cordial relationship between the interlocutors is established. While Jesus reveals his identity to her progressively (4:10, 13-14, 17b-18, 21-24, 26), she advances in her understanding about Jesus and her faith in him (4:9, 11-12, 15, 19-20, 25).[327] The dialogue between Jesus and the woman results in the conversion of many in the city of Sychar (4:39-42).[328] But, the dialogue between Jesus and the Jews in 7:1-8:59 develops in antagonistic terms as the brothers of Jesus did not believe in him (7:1-9) and the Jews attempted to arrest him (7:30, 44) and stone him (8:59).[329] The *request-rebuke-response dialogue* in 4:43-54, as the sixth episode, introduces the theme that Jesus is the giver of life.[330] While the first *request-rebuke-response* dialogue in 2:1-12 appears as the final slot of the first episode (i.e., 1:19-2:12), the dialogue in 4:43-54 is introduced as an independent episode.[331]

In 5:1-47, the seventh episode, the narrator presents a sign and a *controversy dialogue* leading to a monologue.[332] As in the case of the third episode (3:1-21), the narrator here introduces the pattern of a dialogue followed by a monologue. While the pattern is used in 3:1-21 in relation to a pedagogical dialogue, in 5:1-47 the pattern is used in relation to a sign and a controversy dialogue.[333] This pattern is used yet another time in the tenth episode (9:1-10:21), where a *dramatic dialogue* leads to a monologue and further to a community dialogue.[334] This trend of dialogue leading to monologue (i.e., 3:1-21; 5:1-47; 9:1-10:21) is one of the characteristic features of the Johannine

---

[326] G. H. Van Kooten, *The Creation of Heaven and Earth: Re-Interpretations of Genesis 1 in the Context of Judaism, Ancient Philosophy, Christianity, and Modern Physics* (Leiden/ Boston: Brill, 2005), 149-94.

[327] E. Leidig, *Jesu Gespräch mit der Samaritanerin und Weitere Gespräche im Johannesevangelium*, Band XV der Theologischen Dissertationen, herausgegeben von Bo Reicke (Basel: Friedrich Reinhardt Kommissionsverlag, 1979).

[328] G. R. O'Day, *Irony and the Johannine Theology of Revelation: An Investigation of John 4* (Ann Arbor, Michigan: University Microfilms International, 1986), 130.

[329] Brown, *The Gospel according to St. John*, 1:305-68.

[330] J. P. Louw, "Reading a Text as Discourse," *Linguistics and New Testament Interpretation: Essays on Discourse Analysis* (Nashville, Tennessee: Broadman Press, 1992), 17-30.

[331] Moloney, *The Gospel of John*, 150-63.

[332] Dodd, *Historical Tradition in the Fourth Gospel*, 177.

[333] In Plato's *Euthyphro* and *Crito*, while Socrates' speech is increasing, Euthyphro's and Crito's speeches are decreasing. This method is also seen in John's dialogues.

[334] Schneiders says that, "John 9 is related by the evangelist backward to the story of the healed paralysed man at the pool of Bethzatha in 5:1-18 and forward to the story of the raising of Lazarus in 11:1-57." See S. M. Schneiders, "To See or Not to See: John 9 as a Synthesis of the Theology and Spirituality of Discipleship," *Word, Theology and Community in John* (St. Louise, Missouri: Chalice Press, 2002), 191.

narrative.[335] As in 10:19-21, the community dialogues are also used in other narrative segments such as 7:40-44; 9:8-12; and 11:54-57. While in 7:40-44 and 9:8-12, the community dialogues develop at the intervals of the episodes, in 10:19-21 and 11:54-57, they develop at the close of the episodes. From this detail we understand that the tenth episode has two community dialogues, one at the interval (9:8-12) and one at the end (10:19-21).

The eighth episode in 6:1-71 has a sequence that moves from a *sign-centered dialogue* to *question-and-answer dialogues*. While in vv. 1-21 two signs of Jesus are narrated with the help of both explicit and implicit dialogues, in vv. 22-71 we see an explicit dialogue in *question-and-answer* format. In chap. 6, Jesus' performance of feeding the five thousand (vv. 1-15) and the subsequent bread discourse (vv. 22-71) are presented progressively within the narrative framework.[336] Though *forensic* nature is part of several exchanges (i.e., 7:45-52; 8:31-59; 9:8-12, 13-17, 18-23, 24-34, 39-41), in 10:22-42, the eleventh episode, the narrator introduces an episode with forensic aspects as the leading trend.[337] The feature of the development of action and dramatic climax is obvious in the first half of the Gospel of John. In the Book of Signs, the narrator weaves several dialogic episodes sequentially. This sequence of the Book of Signs informs the reader about the discourse pattern (*sjuzet*) of the story (*fabula*) persuasively.[338] A reader of the Gospel can place her/himself at several settings, exchanges, and episodes of the *macro*-story, identify her/himself with one or multiple characher/s, and develop a new point of view according to the changing situations. In that sense, a careful reading of the Gospel opens up polyvalent opportunities and global possibilities.

Some Significant Narrative Features

The dialogue of the Fourth Gospel is imitation of the real situation of Jesus' life and ministry. The *mimetic* function of the dialogue is obvious especially in the Book of Signs. As Van der Watt says, "Mimesis, copying Jesus, becomes a central theme in the Johannine literature."[339] Some narrative

---

[335] Martyn calls the story of the blind man as a "synagogue-church drama." See J. L. Martyn, *History and Theology in the Fourth Gospel* (Nashville: Abingdon, 1968/1979), 23-36.

[336] Refer to Dodd, *The Interpretation of the Fourth Gospel*, 333-45.

[337] P. F. Bartholomä, *The Johannine Discourses and the Teaching of Jesus in the Synoptics: A Comparative Approach to the Authenticity of Jesus' Words in the Fourth Gospel*, A PhD Dissertation (Heverlee: The Evangelical Theological Faculty, 2010), 75-292.

[338] For details about Saussure's structuralism and discourse analysis, refer to D. Howarth, *Discourse*, Concepts in Social Sciences (Buckingham/Philadelphia: Open University Press, 2000), 16-66.

[339] Jan van der Watt, "Narrative Analysis and Ethics," *Unpublished Document* (Nijmegen: Radboud Universiteit, 2012), 1-13; M. A. Powell, *What Is Narrative Criticism?* (Minneapolis: Fortress Press, 1990), 11.

similarities between the Platonic and the Johannine dialogues are conspicuous to the reader.[340] Plato's literary style transformed the real-life conversations of Socrates with his friends and students into creative 'inventions' which incorporated various dramatic elements for the purpose of progressing toward a philosophical truth.[341] Similarly, in John, the narrator attempts to imitate the real-life conversations of Jesus with his interlocutors and incorporates the philosophical, theological, and community aspects.[342]

Just as Socratic *elenchus*,[343] in John, Jesus is continually in dialogue with his interlocutors and brings them to the knowledge that they are "not in the know." Their "not in the know" is brought in sharp contrast with Jesus' "in the know" for the progression of the dialogue. As the Platonic protagonist uses the method of *epagoge* (induction),[344] in the Book of Signs, Jesus emphasizes the 'from above' aspects as requirements for his interlocutors. As universalism is one of the significant tenets of Johannine theology, the particulars are viewed with an intention of universal expansion. This aspect of development from the particular to the universal provides an eternal effect for the message of John. As in the case of Socratic *definition*,[345] in the Book of Signs, Jesus is portrayed as the authentic interpreter and the one who can define things. Denning-Bolle states that, "these three 'elements' [i.e., elenchus, epagoge, and definition] are not to be sharply differentiated from one another; they intertwine constantly and do not stand by themselves."[346] Though there are several stylistic similarities between Plato and John, one difference is compelling. While Plato attempts to describe the truth that is remote, in John, the truth himself appears in flesh and in constant dialogue with his interlocutors.

John uses a dialectic sort of argumentation[347] to lead the reader toward a certain point.[348] In the Book of Signs, this characteristic tenet is developed from

---

340 Van Kooten, *The Creation of Heaven and Earth*, 168.

341 Van Kooten, *The Creation of Heaven and Earth*, 168-177. Denning-Bolle states that, "In Plato, the dialogue presented the best form in which to encapsulate the lively sort of exchange of which Socrates was a master. The written form of the dialogue was to act simply as an aid to memory but was never meant to take the place of verbal debate." S. Denning-Bolle, *Wisdom in Akkadian Literature: Expression, Instruction, Dialogue* (Leiden: Ex Oriente Lux, 1992), 72, 76.

342 See *Inst.* 10.2.18 and *Inst.* 10.2.27.

343 Denning-Bolle, *Wisdom in Akkadian Literature*, 72.

344 Denning-Bolle, *Wisdom in Akkadian Literature*, 72.

345 Denning-Bolle, *Wisdom in Akkadian Literature*, 72.

346 Denning-Bolle says that, "Socrates tried to arrive at a definition of something through the use of elenchus but also through induction (particulars to universals)." See Denning-Bolle, *Wisdom in Akkadian Literature*, 72-73.

347 Denning-Bolle, *Wisdom in Akkadian Literature*, 72.

348 Press, *Plato: A Guide for the Perplexed,* 82.

a dualistic point of view.[349] Anderson makes mention about the development of the human-divine dialogue in John's Gospel through the means of dialectical thinking of the evangelist and of the agency schema.[350] The narrative support for the dialogue is continually stated all through the Book of Signs. Guthrie observes that, "Since in discussions of his [i.e., Plato's] work so much is made of dialectic as a technical or semi-technical term, it is worth noticing this general use to stand for any philosophical discussion carried out in a spirit not of competition (as by the Sophists) but of cooperation, not for personal prestige but solely to reach the truth."[351] This principle of the Platonic dialogues can be noticed in the Johannine dialogues.[352]

In John's dialogue, Jesus the protagonist is in constant dialogue with his interlocutors in order to reveal his Messiahship and to lead them toward eternal life perspectives. The interlocutors come up with intriguing questions and later on turn out to be either in the category of believing or unbelieving. On several occasions, the narrator employs the *question-and-answer*, *request-rebuke-response*, and *challenge-and-riposte* methods in order to maintain the dialectical nature of the dialogues. The dialectical aspects of John develop as the *thesis* and the *antithesis* are united through a higher *synthesis*. The characters like Nicodemus, the Samaritan woman, the man born blind, and others engage in a dialectical duel with Jesus and realize the truth claims of the protagonist.[353] In this sense, Jesus' interlocutors are transferred to a different (higher) level. While the Platonic dialogues truth is discussed in abstract terms, in John truth is manifested in concrete form through the person of Jesus. John uses some of the universally accepted styles and methods in order to develop his exchanges and episodes, and the author takes the attention of the reader toward a higher level with a universalistic intent.

---

[349] Denning-Bolle mentions that, "The use of the dialogue form is a *literary* device. Plato's famous dialectical method, on the other hand, is a *philosophical* phenomenon. *Dialektikè technè* is the art of using dialogue; dialectic literally means the 'conversational method' (e.g., *Phaedrus* 276e)." Denning-Bolle, *Wisdom in Akkadian Literature*, 73.

[350] P. N. Anderson, "From One Dialogue to Another: Johannine Polyvalence from Origins to Receptions," *Anatomies of Narrative Criticism: The Past, Present and Future of the Fourth Gospel as Literature* (Leiden/Boston: Brill, 2008), 109-111.

[351] W. K. C. Guthrie, *A History of Greek Philosophy*, Vol. 4 (Cambridge: University Press, 1975), 1.

[352] For more details about the connection between Plato and John, refer to Van Kooten, *The Creation of Heaven and Earth*, 168-77.

[353] Kennedy says that, "a dialectical dispute is cast as a *question-and-answer* dialogue." G. A. Kennedy, *New Testament Interpretation through Rhetorical Criticism* (Chapel Hill/London: The University of North Carolina Press, 1984), 9.

Signs and the Dialogue

The signs and dialogues are integrally connected in the Book of Signs and together they help the protagonist to reveal himself.[354] While Platonic dialogues concentrate mostly on arguments,[355] John's dialogues develop in association with actions and movements of the characters.[356] In John, the protagonist appears not simply as one who argues his cause but rather as one who proves his arguments through the means of signs.[357] Keener (cf. Aristotle, *Rhet.* 1.2.18, 1357b) states that, "A 'sign' signified something beyond itself, and functioned as a proof or attestation; thus the term appears in rhetoric as well as in the context in which we employ it."[358] This tendency of the connection between the utterances and the actions of the protagonist dynamically works within the narrative framework (2:1-12; 4:46-54; 5:1-18; 6:1-15, 16-21; 9:1-10:21; 11:1-54).[359] The interconnection between the speech and the action of the protagonist facilitates a universalized reading of the Gospel.

Jesus' first sign of turning water into wine appears as the last exchange of the first episode (1:19-2:12). Though he does not make a glory proposal anywhere in 1:19-2:12, the revelation of his glory is presented through a sign toward the climax of the episode (2:11). The story of Jesus' turning of water into wine proleptically works with his discourse in 15:1-11. Jesus, the one who turns water into wine, is revealed as the 'I AM' and the 'True Vine' (15:1-11). The entire episode in 1:19-2:12 maintains a typical sequence, i.e., a series of dialogue leading to a sign and the glorification of the protagonist. This format is different from that of the seventh sign in 11:1-54, where the protagonist proposes the glory at the beginning (11:4) and fulfills it toward the end (11:43-53). The common factor in both the episodes is the use of dialogue as

---

[354] Chatman states that, "It has been argued, since Aristotle, that events in narratives are radically correlative, enchaining, entailing. Their sequence, runs the traditional argument, is not simply linear but causative. The causation may be overt, that is, explicit, or covert, implicit." Chatman, *Story and Discourse*, 45.

[355] Press states that, "Certainly one of the most striking features of Plato's dialogues is that they are full of opinions being stated by interlocutors, reason's being given, and then opinions and reasons subjected to criticism and refutation." Press, *Plato*, 75.

[356] J. G. Barry, *Dramatic Structure: The Shaping of Experience* (Berkeley, Los Angeles: University of California Press, 1970), 51.

[357] Kennedy, *New Testament Interpretation through Rhetorical Criticism*, 15.

[358] C. S. Keener, *The Gospel of John: A Commentary* (Peabody, Massachusetts: Hendrickson, 2003), 1:251; cf. L. Morris, *The Gospel According to John*, NICNT, Revised (Grand Rapids, Michigan: Eerdmans, 1995).

[359] Köstenberger says that, "The first half of John's narrative sets forth evidence for Jesus' messiahship by way of seven selected signs (1:19-12:50)." A. J. Köstenberger, *Studies on John and Gender: A Decade of Scholarship*, Studies in Biblical Literature 38 (New York/Oxford: Peter Lang, 2001), 8.

a rhetorical means to actualize the sign and vice versa. Dodd rightly says that, "Word and action form an indivisible whole, to a degree unique in the Book of Signs."[360] In both 1:19-2:12 and 11:1-54, the signs are performed, after a series of dialogues, as a matter of glorification. But in 11:1-54, an antithetical dialogue develops after the performance of the sign (vv. 47-50).[361] In that sense, though both the episodes are thematically well-connected, the narrator employs other literary features to present them distinctively to the reader. The narrator's multiple styles in developing dialogues in closer relationship with people's life situations strengthen the possibilities of reading the Gospel in cross-cultural terms.

While the first Cana incident in 2:1-12 follows a 'dialogue-sign-dialogue' pattern, the second Cana sign in 4:43-54 follows a unique pattern in which 'the time of dialogue is the time of healing.'[362] The third sign in 5:1-9 also has a pattern of 'the time of dialogue is the time of healing.' But differently from the two Cana miracles, the larger framework of chap. 5 maintains a 'dialogue-sign-dialogue-monologue' sequence (5:1-47). While the fourth sign story (6:1-15) has a 'dialogue-action-dialogue' format, the fifth one (6:16-21) has an 'action-dialogue-action' format. The feeding of the five thousand (vv. 1-15), followed by the discourse of the bread of life that is maintained in a question and answer format (vv. 22-71), is one of the striking features of the chapter. In the episode, the action of feeding the five thousand is symbolically connected to the revelation of Jesus as the "bread of life." Thus the entire chapter follows a symbolical action followed by a metaphorical speech.[363] The story of healing the man born blind follows a 'dialogue-sign-dialogue-monologue-community dialogue' format.[364] Though the format of the sixth sign is similar with the third sign (i.e., 5:1-47), there are noticeable differences between them. While in 5:1-47 the healed man's role as a believer is not clear, in 9:1-41 the healed man's progress in faith is recorded through his exchange with his interlocutors. The above evidences convincingly show how the narrator employs different patterns to incorporate dialogues and signs as interactive elements within

---

[360] Dodd, *The Interpretation of the Fourth Gospel*, 363.

[361] R. Schnackenburg, *The Gospel according to St. John* (London: Burns and Oates, 1980), 1:112.

[362] Beets attempts to look at the symbolic significance of Johannine events. See M. G. J. Beets, *The Voice of Reason: a Philosopher's Approach to St. John's Gospel* (Amsterdam: Hilversum, 1995).

[363] Keener, *The Gospel of John*, 1:251.

[364] Maniparampil says that, "The lengthy discourses that are glued to the signs are Johannine meditations on the identity of the person of Jesus and his unique assignment." J. Maniparampil, *Reading the Fourth Gospel: A Text Book for Students of Gospel according to John* (Bangalore: Claretian Publications, 2004), 77.

the narrative framework.[365] Moreover, the dialogues of John demonstrate the usefulness of both the synthesized and antithetical dialogue forms to attune readers' attention beyond time and space.

'I AM Sayings' and the Dialogue

Jesus' self revelatory[366] aspects are potentially reflected through his "I AM" sayings (see 6:35, 48; 8:12; 9:5; 10:7, 9, 11; 11:25; cf. 14:6; 15:1, 5).[367] His saying, "I am the bread of life" (6:35, 48), is stated after giving thanks and distributing the bread, and feeding the five thousand (6:1-15). While he utters that he is the "light of the world" in 8:12, he appears as the fulfiller of the festival of the lights (or the festival of Dedication) described in chapters seven and eight. His second usage of the expression in 9:5 is described in the context of giving sight to a blind person (9:1-41). The utterances "I AM the gate for the sheep" (10:7, 9) and "I AM the good shepherd" (10:11, 14) are expressed immediately after the expulsion of the healed man from the synagogue (9:34). In his response, Jesus implies that while the Jews expel people from their assemblies on account of him, he is right there to accept them as a "gate for the sheep." While the Jews are unable to solve the lifelong problems of the man who was closely associated with them in their assemblies, they are reduced to "hired hands." Jesus' significance as the "good shepherd" through his involvement in the life of the person (10:1-18) is brought to the notice of the reader.[368] While the dialogues/discourses are presented in relation to some significant events, Jesus' self-revelatory aspect is the highlight through these "I AM" sayings.[369]

Moreover, Jesus' self-revelatory statement that he is the "resurrection and life" (11:25) appears in the context of Lazarus' resurrection from his death.[370] In all these occurrences, his self-revelatory utterances are always supplemented with complimentary actions.[371] The aspect of dialogues centered on signs and revelatory "I AM" sayings is one of the peculiar features of

---

[365] J. C. De Klerk and S. W. Schnell, *A New Look at Jesus: Literary and Sociological-Historical Interpretations of Mark and John* (Pretoria: J. L. van Schaik, 1987), 15.

[366] The dialogues of the BS are revelatory as they reveal several important aspects with regard to the life and ministry of Jesus. See W. Carter, *John and Empire: Initial Explorations* (New York/London: T & T Clark, 2008), 123-129.

[367] Köstenberger, *Studies on John and Gender*, 8.

[368] For details about the discourses of John, refer Maniparampil, *Reading the Fourth Gospel*, 77-78.

[369] Earlier, Aristotle in his *Poetics* referred to the *Sōkratikoi logoi* ("Socratic discourses," or "conversations with Socrates") as an established literary genre.

[370] Schnackenburg, *The Gospel according to St. John*, 2:331.

[371] For more details about the linguistic character of John, refer Schnackenburg, *The Gospel according to St. John*, 1:105-118.

the Book of Signs.[372] This feature is rhetorical as the narrator persuades the reader through the character of Jesus. In John, Jesus' utterances go beyond their literal meanings and actually *do* something.[373] A paradigmatic reader can create a world of her/his own in the process of reading the gospel. In the language of Warren and Wellek (1955: 181), every reading is a performance.[374] John develops his narratives and discourses in his own idiom and persuades the reader with a personal punch. This narrator-and-reader interaction is poignantly presented through the medium of Jesus' "I AM" sayings.[375] The universal metaphors used in the "I AM" statements can easily relate to all places and at all times.

Content, Form, and Function of the Dialogue

The 'content,' 'form' and 'function' of dialogues[376] help us to understand the characteristic features of that literary genre.[377] The dialogues are the major semantic units within the narrative framework.[378] But, the meaning of the utterance units and their function within the exchanges/episodes cannot be deciphered apart from the narratives.[379] In the Book of Signs, the dialogues convey the theological meaning of the text in association with the narratives.[380] The dynamic interlocking between the narratives and the dialogues/discourses is one of the primary features within the first half of the gospel.[381] The meaning of the dialogue can be understood primarily on the basis of the themes that are held together. The message (or the aspect of the 'what' of the text) is

---

[372] John builds the narratives around the sayings and actions of Jesus. This is also a proven factor in the synoptic evangelists. But the question is how far the evangelists were able to sustain the originality of the sayings of Jesus. This was same with the *Sōkratikoi logoi.*

[373] Press calls such utterances *performatives*. See Press, *Plato*, 60.

[374] A. Warren and R. Wellek, *Theory of Literature* (London: Jonathan Cape, 1955), 181; also see M. Stockhammer, ed., *Plato Dictionary* (London: Vision Press, 1963), 224.

[375] J. G. Van der Watt, *An Introduction to the Johannine Gospel and Letters*, T & T Clark Approaches to Biblical Studies (New York: T & T Clark, 2007), 49.

[376] D. Hellholm, "The Problem of Apocalyptic Genre and the Apocalypse of John," *Semeia 36: 'Early Christian Apocalypticism, Genre and Social Setting'* (Decatur, Georgia: SBL/ Scholars Press, 1986), 13.

[377] Press, *Plato*, 55.

[378] E. Garver, *Aristotle's Rhetoric: An Art of Character* (Chicago/London: The University of Chicago Press, 1994), 53.

[379] Literary critics like Warren and Wellek say that the total meaning of a work of art cannot be defined. See Warren and Wellek, *Theory of Literature*, 34.

[380] Just as a typical Platonic dialogue, in John, "the conversation topics themselves are historically contextualised rather than abstract perennial questions." See Press, *Plato*, 57.

[381] For more details about the narrative dynamics, refer to F. Kermode, *The Genesis of Secrecy: On the Interpretation of Narrative*, The Charles Eliot Norton Lectures, 1977-1978 (Cambridge, Massachusetts: Harvard University Press, 1979).

expressed through the utterance units and their function within the dialogues, the actions and movements of the characters, and the narrative asides.[382] Jesus' revelation of his identity, in relation to his Father, his disciples, and the Jews, is highlighted through the dialogue sections. One of the most prevalent themes is Jesus' identity as he is the fulfiller of the Jewish messianic hopes. It is God who fulfills his work of love in the world through the agency of Jesus. This aspect of the fulfillment theme is expressed through several direct quotations from/allusions to the OT passages (1:23, 45; 2:6, 16-17; 3:28; 4:19-26; 6:30-33; 7:19-24; 8:33-58; 11:21-27; 12:13-15). It is mostly through the dialogues that the fulfillment language comes out in its full potential.[383] At the beginning of the gospel, the narrator introduces a transfer of role from John the Baptist, the witness, to Jesus, the Word, through a fulfillment formula (1:23). Jesus' role as the revealer of God's plan and his mission and glory is a running theme throughout the Book of Signs.

The dialogues, coupled with the actions, in the Book of Signs usher in a new order through Jesus' life and ministry, as he is introduced as the bringer of a new temple (2:19), the one who demands new birth (3:3), and the provider of new water and new life (4:13, 14; 4:46-54; 7:37-38).[384] Through dialogues the narrator also introduces the aspect of believing in Jesus and the resultant experience of eternal life (2:11, 22; 4:41, 53; 6:14; 7:31; 8:30; 10:19-21, 42; 11:27, 45). By contrary, unbelief and the resultant judgment are brought together (6:64; 7:1-9, 30-1, 43-4; 8:59; 9:18; 10:19-21, 39; 11:57; 12:36b-41). The themes such as discipleship (1:19-51), missional harvest (4:7-38), and Jesus' universal significance (4:39-42) are leading aspects in the Johannine dialogues.

The self-revelatory aspects are climax with the "I AM" sayings of Jesus and their integral connection with the actions (6:35, 41, 48, 51; 8:12; 9:5; 10:7, 9, 11, 14; 11; 25 [also 14:6; 15:1, 5]). The dialogues also reveal the dualistic contrast between belief and unbelief, truth and untruth, and the 'from above' and the 'from below.' It is ironic that Jesus risks his life due to his life-giving and eternal life-centered performances (11: 1-12:50).[385] Proleptic themes that take the attention of the reader are the 'hour' of Jesus (2:4; 4:21; 7:6, 30; 12:23, 27) and the 'lifting up of the Son of Man' (3:14; 8:28; 12:32). The union and relationship between Jesus and his Father and the role of Jesus as the

---

382 Vanhoozer, *Is There a Meaning in this Text? The Bible, the Reader and the Morality of Literary Knowledge* (Leicester: Apollos, 1998), 26.

383 J. D. Schaeffer, "Dialogue," *Dictionary of Literary Themes and Motifs, A-J* (New York: Greenwood Press, 1988), 387-395.

384 Keener, *The Gospel of John*, 1:54.

385 J. L. Resseguie, *Narrative Criticism of the New Testament: An Introduction* (Grand Rapids: Baker Academic, 2005), 67-75.

emissary of God have important implications all throughout the discourses and dialogues. The theology of the dialogue is centered on the person and work of Jesus.[386] At the semantic level, the universality of Jesus' message, the vertical and horizontal levels of eschatology, the newness motif, and the experience of everlasing life align well with all other themes and they together express the gnomic intent of the Gospel.

At the syntactic level, we view 'how' the dialogue texts are structured. The 'what' (or *content*) of the dialogue is structured in specific formats and the plot-structure provides special force to the content.[387] Hence, the 'how' (or *form*) of the text is significant in the process of interpretation.[388] The Book of Signs has its own syntactics that is organized by the help of literary conventions and devices, especially by the help of narratives, dialogues, and monologues. The dialogues primarily develop at two levels: between the narrator and the reader and between the interlocutors of the story. At the structural level, the dialogues develop from micro-units to meso-units and from meso-units to the macro-unit. This *micro*-, *meso*-, and *macro*-dynamism of the dialogue within the Book of Signs convey the content efficaciously to the reader.[389] As Chatman distinguishes 'story' from 'discourse,' the 'content' and 'form' are distinct entities.[390] But, they dynamically merge together in the literary composition. The story of the Book of Signs is presented through appropriate transitions between the episodes, sequence of the events, and dramatic effects. The Book of Signs as a whole is framed with the help of speech units, exchanges (and sub-exchanges), and episodes. This analysis informs the reader how the *macro*-dialogue of the Book of Signs is formed with the help of several layers of *micro*-and *meso*-dialogues.

In the Book of Signs, the narrator's potentiality is proved through the usage of literary figures of speech/thought. The reader of the story experiences new emotions in the process of reading. The message is the vehicle that connects the sender and the receiver. This connectivity is established through the dialogue between the narrator and the reader (Aristotle 1.2.1356a). The development of the 'story' and the 'discourse' has striking similarity with the Greek tragedies. In the Book of Signs, the protagonist undergoes a situation

---

[386] Anderson, "From One Dialogue to Another," 109.

[387] M. M. Bakhtin, *Speech Genres and Other Late Essays*, tran. McGee, V (Austin: University of Texas Press, 1986/1998), 60.

[388] Schaeffer, "Dialogue," 389.

[389] For more details on the rhetorical and literary structural patterns of the fourth gospel, refer G. Østenstad, *Patterns of Redemption in the Fourth Gospel*, Studies in the Bible and Early Christianity, Vol. 38 (Lewiston/Queenston/Lampeter: The Edwin Mellen Press, 1998).

[390] See Chatman, *Story and Discourse*.

of conflict (*agōn*) with the values, goals, and norms of other characters.[391] This is ideological dimension as it develops in the form of a conflict between his values ("from above") and the dominant culture ("from below") of the day. The conflict of the story is well established with the help of verbal abuse (*flyting*) between the characters.[392] The controversial dialogues in John 5-10 make use of this dramatic element as a significant phenomenon. In the narrative, the crisis or reversal (*peripeteia*) happens when the interlocutors continue in their unbelief and when they reject Jesus' messiahship (5:18; 7:1-9, 45-52; 8:57-59; 9:35-41; 10:19-42; 11:45-53; 12:36-43).[393] As in the case of the Platonic dialogues, in the Book of Signs, the use of reversal within the storyline provides additional punch for the development of the narrative (cf. Aristotle, *Poet.* 11).[394] The *pathos*[395] of the protagonist begins in the gospel when the antagonists attempt to stone him and even to kill him (5:18; 7:45-52; 8:59; 10:39; 11:45-53; 12:27-36).[396] Jesus recognizes (*anagnōrisis*) that the hour has come and his time of being lifted up (12:23).[397] This opens up the unraveling or resolution (*dénouement* [*lusis*])[398] of the plot in the rest of the gospel story (i.e., the Book of Glory).[399] In this structure, the Book of Signs comprises of almost all the major plot elements except the dénouement.

The larger story of the Book of Signs has unity of action: a beginning (John 1-4), middle (5-10), and end (11-12). As Stibbe observes a tri-tiered development, a paradigmatic reader of the Book of Signs can see a plot of its own.[400] The coming of the Word from the eternal world (i.e., "from above") to a world that marks the 'hour' of Jesus (i.e., "from below") is narrated in John 1:1-51. His hour of glorification is expected from 2:4 (cf. 4:21; 7:6, 30) and the

[391] C. Baldick, *The Concise Oxford Dictionary of Literary Terms* (Oxford/New York: Oxford University Press, 1990), 3.

[392] Brant, *Dialogue and Drama,* 123-139.

[393] See Brant, *Dialogue and Drama*, 43-50. Also see *Poet.* 1450a.34-35; 1452b.8.

[394] Resseguie, *Narrative Criticism of the NT*, 205.

[395] Baldick says that, "*pathos*, the emotionally moving quality or power of a literary work or of particular passages within it, appealing especially to our feelings of sorrow, pity, and compassionate sympathy." Baldick, *The Concise Oxford Dictionary of Literary Terms*, 163.

[396] Cf. Aristotle, *Poet.* 1425b.13-14.

[397] K. B. Larsen, *Recognizing the Stranger: Recognition Scenes in the Gospel of John*, Vol. 93 (Leiden/Boston: Brill, 2008), 26.

[398] Baldick says, "*Dénouement*, the clearing up or 'untying' of the complications of the plot in a play or story; usually a final scene or chapter in which mysteries, confusions, and doubtful destinies are clarified." See Baldick, *The Concise Oxford Dictionary of Literary Terms*, 55.

[399] J. L. Bailey and L. D. Vander Broek, *Literary Forms in the New Testament: A Handbook* (Louisville, Kentucky: Westminster John Knox Press, 1992), 130.

[400] M. W. G. Stibbe, *John's Gospel*, New Testament Readings (London/New York: Routledge, 1994), 35.

protagonist realizes that the 'hour' of the Son of Man has come in 12:23. This sequence creates an analeptic and proleptic balance in the narrative framework of the Book of Signs. While the first major section (chaps. 1-4) establishes the character and mission of Jesus in the mind of the reader, the second major section (chaps. 5-10) introduces the conflict in which the *theomachus* or 'enemy of God' comes to the fore.[401] In the words of Stibbe, John 11-12 is a significant section. He says that, "It is this event [John 11:1-54] which precipitates Jesus' downfall (11:45-53). It is from this point that the Sanhedrin '*plotted* to take his life' (11:53)."[402] The plot of the Book of Signs is built by the help of transitions and by cause and effect.[403] This careful construction of the Book of Signs forms a *plot within the plot* of the gospel. The above details enable the reader to understand that the plot-structure of the Book of Signs is correlated through the method of *stichomythia*.[404] From these, a paradigmatic reader can understand that the exchanges/episodes of the Book of Signs are rhetorical to form a dramatic plot within the narrative framework of the gospel. From the above discussion of the plot-development, a reader can understand that John uses a universally accepted and paradigmatic style that can have significance at all times.

The function of the dialogue is another significant area that contributes to understanding the development of the genre. While semantics deals with the question of 'what' and syntactics with the question of 'how' of the text, pragmatics deals with the question of 'why' of the text.[405] Why is dialogue a significant aspect within the text and how does that rhetorize the message of it in relation to the paradigmatic reader?[406] Moreover, at the secondary level, it looks at 'how the dialogue invites the attention of the reader?'[407] In the Book of Signs, the dialogue between the narrator and the reader happens by means of the character interactions. The narrator dramatically portrays the story through performative language and especially through the medium of dialogue.[408] Davies says that, "The attribution of direct speech makes a formal distinction between the narrator and the character, and creates a more

---

[401] Stibbe, *John's Gospel*, 35.

[402] Stibbe, *John's Gospel*, 36.

[403] Culpepper, *Anatomy of the Fourth Gospel*, 97.

[404] Baldick, *The Concise Oxford Dictionary of Literary Terms*, 211.

[405] Powell, *What is Narrative Criticism?* 11.

[406] P. Ricoeur, *Interpretation Theory: Discourse and the Surplus of Meaning* (Fort Worth: Texas Christian University Press, 1976).

[407] R. A. Culpepper, *The Gospel and Letters of John*, Interpreting Biblical Texts (Nashville: Abingdon, 1998), 15.

[408] P. Ricoeur, *Time and Narrative* (Chicago/London: The University of Chicago Press, 1988), 3:173.

immediate and mimetic effect, but characters in the Fourth Gospel do not use their own peculiar vocabulary or style of speech."[409] Hence, the double-layered dialogue (i.e., between the narrator and the reader and between the characters) functions in an interconnected way. The double-layered dialogue of the Book of Signs develops in a *narrator*, *dialogue of the characters within the text*, and *reader* sequence.[410]

The narrator progressively shows how the innocent redeemer is under trial. A dualistic contrast between 'belief' and 'unbelief' and 'from above' and 'from below' lies underneath the narratorial framework.[411] The reader develops (and poses) questions one after another on the basis of the movements, acts, and utterances of the characters.[412] The narrator, in return, uses the narrative elements to respond back to the reader. The central theme of the text that the identity of Jesus as the agent of God who comes to introduce himself as the *light-logos-life* (i.e., *licht-liebe-leben*) is convincingly explained to the reader through the medium of dialogue.[413] The dialogue informs the reader that Jesus is the Savior of the world and the light that shines in the darkness.

The above analysis helps us to understand the dynamic interaction of the 'content,' 'form,' and 'function' within the dialogue text. The plot structure of the entire Book of Signs informs us that the narrator arranges the story in exchange and episodic fashion in order to sustain dramatic features and to develop suspense and surprise in the reader. The dialogue as a peculiar genre is explored in the story of John by means of the available rhetorical devices of that time.[414] While the form of the genre sets a framework for the content, the form and content together help the genre function in relation to the reader.[415] Here, the semiotic components, i.e., semantics, syntactics, and

---

[409] M. Davies, *Rhetoric and Reference in the Fourth Gospel*, JSNT Supplement Series 69 (Sheffield: JSOT Press, 1992), 25.

[410] Warren and Wellek, *Theory of Literature*, 34; M. L. Coloe, *Dwelling in the Household of God: Johannine Ecclesiology and Spirituality* (Collegeville, Minnesota: Liturgical Press, 1989/2007), 6.

[411] P. F. Ellis, *The Genius of John: A Composition Critical Commentary on the Fourth Gospel* (Collegeville, Minnesota: Liturgical Press, 1984), 8.

[412] In the language of Eco (1979: 7), the "text creates the competence of its Model Reader." U. Eco, *The Role of the Reader: Explorations in the Semiotics of Texts* (Bloomington/London: Indiana University Press, 1979), 7.

[413] Cf. G. Voigt, *Licht-Liebe-Leben: Das Evangelicum nach Johannes* (Gottingen: Vandenhoeck & Ruprecht, 1991).

[414] Dodd attempts to see the Johannine dialogues in connection with other philosophical and religious dialogues, especially of Plato, Cicero, Plutarch, and Lucian. See Dodd, *Historical Tradition in the Fourth Gospel*, 319.

[415] For more details about semantics, syntactics, and pragmatics, refer A. J. Greimas and J. Courtés, *Semiotics and Language: An Analytical Dictionary* (Bloomington: Indiana University Press, 1979/1982), 272-277, 328-334.

pragmatics, come together to expose the nature and function of the dialogue to the maximum. Eco rightly says that, "An open text is a paramount instance of a syntactic-semantico-pragmatic device whose foreseen interpretation is a part of its generative process."[416] What Eco says here is substantiated through the analysis of John's dialogue at the *micro*-, *meso*-, and *macro*-levels.

Conclusion

A genre analysis of the Johannine dialogues which into consideration the content, form, and function[417] helps us to understand the semantic, syntactic, and pragmatic aspects. Our study informed us that dialogue is a recognizable and established category which is spread throughout the Book of Signs. In the Book of Signs, a reader can recognize several common conventions of dialogue that form it as a specific literary category.[418] Though dialogue is a distinguishable literary category, its interaction with the narratives is strong within the Book of Signs.[419] As dialogue is part and parcel of the narrative framework, it does not make full sense apart from the narrative asides. In most of the cases, dialogue remains cryptic if not linked to the narrative expositions.[420] Similarly, the narratives themselves are meaningless apart from the dialogue. This mode of interlocking of the narratives and the dialogue is a conspicuous phenomenon within the text. The *micro*-, *meso*-, and *macro*-level analyses of the dialogue help the reader to understand this subject matter. This dynamism of the micro-, meso-, and macro-development of the dialogue enables the reader to be interactive with the text of John.[421] Thus, the exchange, episodic,[422] and the *macro*-structure of the Book of Signs develop in a rhythmical way. This phenomenon of the Gospel further helps the historical/implied/contemporary reader to contextualize its message.

The characterization of the story is expressed primarily through dialogues (cf. Aristotle, *Poet.* 6.24). The dualistic framework of the narrative divides

---

[416] Eco, *The Role of the Reader*, 3.

[417] A. G. Van Aarde, "Narrative Criticism," *Focusing on the Message: New Testament Hermeneutics, Exegesis, and Methods* (Pretoria: Protea, 2009), 381.

[418] See more details in the *micro*-, *meso*-, and *macro*-analyses of the Book of Signs.

[419] Beasley-Murray, *John*, xc-xci.

[420] Baldick says that, "In a dramatic work, a narrator is a performer who recounts directly to the audience a summary of events preceding or during a scene or art." See Baldick, *The Concise Oxford Dictionary of Literary Terms*, 146.

[421] Kermode, *The Genesis of Secrecy*, 162.

[422] Baldick defines 'episodic' as "constructed as a narrative by a succession of loosely connected incidents rather than by an integrated plot." See Baldick, *The Concise Oxford Dictionary of Literary Terms*, 72.

the characters either to the side of light or to the side of darkness.[423] The point of view of the narrator is introduced to the reader through the dynamic interlocking of the dialogue and the narrative.[424] The narrator uses the aspects of 'showing' (*mimesis*) and 'telling' (*diegesis*) to integrate the two levels of the story (i.e., the story of Jesus and the story of the Johannine community) as a single whole.[425] This narrative pattern communicates directly to the reader through the medium of the verbal exchanges between Jesus and his interlocutors. The plot structure (*mythos*, in Greek)[426] of the dialogue develops as the exchanges/episodes develop in an interconnected way.[427] The Johannine narrator maintains all the important elements of a plot, such as sequence, causality, unity of action, conflict, suspense and surprise, and effective power (Aristotle, *Poet.* 1450b-1451b).[428] As the Johannine narrator aligns the story of Jesus into her/his new situation, a reader of the story can realign the story into her/his life situation. As the Gospel is known for its accommodative nature, classical plot structure, and the universality of the message, they reveal its gnomic nature.

The order of the Book of Signs reveals the master plan of the narrator: a *beginning* (chaps. 1-4), a *middle* (chaps. 5-10), and an *ending* (chaps. 11-12).[429] As in Plato, in John the "dialogues include lively passages of stichomythia (speeches, stitched together), line-for-line dialogue that sharpen the issue, followed by more relaxed and reflective passages." The plot development of the Book of Signs thus gives strength to the story (cf. Aristotle, *Poet.* 1449b).[430] The thematic development of the story can be understood mostly on the basis of the dialogic progression. The characters' speech and the interaction 'for' and 'against' provide insights for the development of the themes. In the Book of Signs, dialogue contributes largely to the development of theology. In recapitulation, the above mentioned episodic and dialogical framework and the characteristic literary features provide a special appeal for

---

[423] For more details about characterisation, refer B. Hochman, *Character in Literature* (Ithaca: Cornell University Press, 1985).

[424] Culpepper sees the relationship that is established within the gospel of John. See Culpepper, *Anatomy of the Fourth Gospel*, 34-49.

[425] Also refer to Quintilian, *Inst.* 10.2.1-2.

[426] Resseguie sees 'unity of action,' 'causation,' 'conflict,' and 'suspense and surprise' are the important elements of a plot. See Resseguie, *Narrative Criticism of the NT*, 198-203.

[427] Cf. S. D. Moore, *Literary Criticism and the Gospels: The Theoretical Challenge* (New Haven/London: Yale University Press, 1989), 14-15.

[428] In the Book of Signs, the plot develops also through the essential characteristics such as 'order,' 'amplitude,' and 'probable and necessary connection.'

[429] Brant, *Dialogue and Drama*, 42-73.

[430] Russian formalists differentiate between *fabula* (story) and *sjuzet* (plot or discourse; cf. Resseguie, *Narrative Criticism of the NT*, 208-9).

the reader.[431] Any reading that neglects the dialogues and discourses, exchange and episodic sequence, and the dramatic and rhetorical features of the Book of Signs overlooks some of its significant semantic, syntactic, and pragmatic aspects.[432] As a universally accepted genre, John's dialogue influences people towards divine discourse beyond time-and space-boundaries. Above all, the divine truths in the form of God-Father, Savior-Son, and Spirit-Praclete and the interaction between the heavenly and the earthly make it even more gnomic in relation to the reader. In that process, the dialogue of John plays a dynamic role.

The dialogical character and the readability of the Fourth Gospel across the borders demonstrate its inclusive and encompassing nature. This peculiar aspect of the Johannine narrative calls the reader's attention beyond all human-made boundaries. In that sense, John's Gospel has the characteristics of a universalistic Gospel.[433]

---

[431] Brant, *Dialogue and Drama*, 28.

[432] F. T. Gench, *Encounters with Jesus: Studies in the Gospel of John* (Louisville/London: Westminster John Knox Press, 2007).

[433] Robert Kysar, *John the Maverick Gospel*, Third Edition (Louisville/London: Westminster John Knox Press, 2007), 163.

PART II

Universalistic Nature of Themes and Characters in John

Chapter 5

Glo[b/c]alization and Mission[s]: Reading John's Gospel

Introduction

In a world in which a growing sense of integration and convergence is obvious, the scripture has to be interpreted from an entirely different point of view.[434] The contemporary globalizing culture[435] fosters liquid social functionalism and trans-nationalism in a higher proportion.[436] As Christian theologians of the contemporary world, how do we prioritize the gospel message? When describing the genre of the gospels, Burridge considers them as documents "about people, by people, for people."[437] With insights from this important caption of Burridge, we here attempt to explore the gnomic significance of the Fourth Gospel. The present paper attempts to answer the following questions: Does John's Gospel bridge the gap between the 'local' and the 'global'? How

[434] The word used to capture this new phase is 'globalization.' Cf. Neil J. Ormerod and Shane Clifton, *Globalization and the Mission of the Church: Ecclesiastical Investigations* 6 (England: T & T Clark, 2009), 3.

[435] Walters defines "Globalization as a concept refers to both the compression of the world and the intensification of consciousness of the world as a whole . . . both concrete global interdependence and consciousness of the global whole." Malcolm Walters, *Globalization* (UK: Routledge, 1995), 1.

[436] See George Ritzer, *Globalization: The Essentials* (UK: Wiley-Blackwell, 2010).

[437] Richard Burridge, *What are the Gospels? A Comparison with Greco-Roman Biography* (Cambridge: University Press, 1992), 13.

does John attempt to present his theology with a gnomic intent? Does John contribute something significant to the contextual realities of the postmodern world? And how does John's theology function at the *micro-*, *meso-*, and *macro-*levels of his narrative framework? Analyzing the entire gospel verse-by-verse is not the concern of this chapter. Rather we will consider three important aspects seriously: first, the 'global' aspects of the gospel in relation to the 'local' concerns; second, the Trinitarian nature of John's theology and its significance in a *glocalized* cultural context; and third, the mission theology of John in relation to a globalized cosmic order. The task of the chapter is not analyzing the gospel as a whole. It is rather to develop an interpretative frame for the gospel in a globalized social context.

The Phenomenon of *Global* in John and in the Rest of the Bible

The Hebrew noun *tēbēl* appears nearly forty occurrences, with a variety of connotations: first, "world" in the sense of the "created universe" (1 Sam 2:8; Job 18:18; Psa 18:15; 24:1; 50:12; Pro 8:31; Jer 10:12); second, in the sense of universal population of the earth (Psa 9:8; 33:8; Lam 4:12);[438] and third, as an entity that includes both people and other created phenomena (Isa 24:4; 27:6; Nah 1:5).[439] In the NT, *kosmos*, the dynamic equivalent of *tēbēl*, denotes variety of meanings, as follows: first, the realm of humankind inhabited by various kingdoms and nations; second, the universal community of humankind;[440] third, the universe at the point of creation; and fourth, in the figurative sense, the sum total of one's realized ambition for wealth, power, and prestige.[441]

While the synoptic evangelists show a preference for the use of *gē* rather than *kosmos*, John shows a reverse tendency.[442] Painter says that, "Concentrated use of *kosmos* is matched by the distinctly dualistic framework in which it is set with references to 'this world' (planet earth) and 'the judgment of the prince of this world' (12:31; 14:30; 16:11). This world is not contrasted with some future world. Rather, the world below is contrasted with the world above, the world of darkness with the world of light."[443] While employing the word *kosmos*, the narrator uses it as an inclusive terminology. Through the voices of

---

[438] *Expository Dictionary of Bible Words* (EDBW [2005: 1065]) describes further, "The 'world' in this sense is explicitly declared to be judged by God (Psa 96:13; Isa 13:11)."

[439] *EDBW* adds further that, "*ḥeled* is a rare noun denoting 'world' in the quasi-philosophical sense of 'the age (or spirit) of the world' (cf. Psa 17:14). It also refers to the 'world' generally as the 'dwelling place' of human beings (cf. Psa 49:1)." See *EDBW* (2005), 1065; cf. John Painter, *The Quest for the Messiah: The History, Literature and Theology of the Johannine Community*, Second edition (Nashville: Abingdon, 1992/1993) 887.

[440] Cf. Matthew 18:7; John 3:19; 12:31; 14:27; 16:8; Heb 11:7; 1 John 2:2.

[441] Matthew 16:26; Mark 8:36; cf. John 12:19; 18:20.

[442] Painter, *The Quest for the Messiah*, 887.

[443] Painter, *The Quest for the Messiah*, 890.

the narrator, Jesus the protagonist, and the witnesses, a consistent view of the world, its predicament, and its salvation are portrayed.[444]

While the synoptic evangelists portray a horizontal eschatological phenomenon as their major trend (i.e., 'this *aeon*' and 'the coming *aeon*'),[445] John orchestrates a vertical eschatological phenomenon (i.e., 'the world from above' and 'the world from below') as his major thinking pattern.[446] Thus, the author creates more space for a realized eschatological outlook. He uses the word "world" (*kosmos*) more often in a contrasting way: first, Jesus says that: "you are of this world, I am not of this world" (8:23);[447] second, Jesus comes 'from above' to judge 'this world,' i.e., this world is subject to judgment (9:39); third, after Jesus' arrival, 'this world' is divided between "those who gone after him (believing)" and those who are not believing (12:19);[448] fourth, the believing are persecuted by the unbelieving in 'this world,' but Jesus conquers 'this world' (16:33);[449] fifth, the believing (also Jesus), though in this world, do not belong to this world (17:14); and sixth, a mystical union is developed between Father, Son, Spirit-Paraclete, and the believing over against the unbelieving world (17:21).

Three things are noticeable in the above proceedings: first, a *macro-division* between the world 'from above' and the world 'from below'; second, a *meso-division* between the believing and the unbelieving in the global level; and third, a *micro-division* between the believing and the unbelieving at the local levels. While the synoptic evangelists present the story from a historical point of view, John is both a gospel of *reference* (history) and a gospel of *mimesis* (poetic).[450] Aristotle wrote of poetry that it was more valuable than history because history is concerned with the contingent while poetry is concerned with the universal.[451] Aristotle proposed that it is mimesis,

---

[444] Cf. J. L. Resseguie, *The Strange Gospel: Narrative Design and Point of View in John* (Leiden: Brill. 2001), 130-131.

[445] Painter, *The Quest for the Messiah*, 887.

[446] Bennema addresses the world as a character within John's story, calling it "enveloped in darkness but loved by God." C. Bennema, *Encountering Jesus: Character Studies in the Gospel of John* (Bangalore, India: Primalogue, 2009), 31-37; also see John 8:23; 9:39; 12:25, 31; 13:1; 14:30; 16:11; 18:36.

[447] Bennema, *Encountering Jesus*, 31.

[448] D. M. Smith, *John*, Abingdon New Testament Commentary (Nashville: Abingdon Press, 1999), 43.

[449] Cf. J. L. Resseguie, *Narrative Criticism of the New Testament: An Introduction* (Grand Rapids: Baker Academic, 2005), 121.

[450] For details about John's differences from the Synoptics, refer Bartholoma, *The Johannine Discourses and the Teaching of Jesus in the Synoptics.*

[451] See M. W. G. Stibbe, *John*, Readings: A New Biblical Commentary (Sheffield: JSOT Press, 1993).

the universalization of actions, which accounts for the greater value of the poetic over the historical.[452] Stibbe makes it clear that, "What is remarkable about John's story is its fusion of poetry and history, of the universal and the particular."[453] If we consider John narrowly as a historical document, we may miss its real purpose.

The *Global God-Father* in the Gospel

The Greek name *theos* is the dynamic equivalent of Hebrew terms such as *'elōhim* and *YHWH*.[454] The God of the Book of Genesis can be well paralleled with the God of John's Gospel, who was in the beginning, was with the Word, and was the *patēr* of the earthly Jesus.[455] John's considerably more frequent use of *patēr* can be reckoned as a title of God.[456] In the Fourth Gospel, God is portrayed as the creator and giver of life (1:1; 6:57),[457] the loving Father (1:14, 18; 3:16, 18, 35), the righteous judge (3:17-21; 5:19-29; 8:31-38), the sovereign and powerful God (17:1-13), and the only true God (17:3). Hurtado says that, "The God of Jesus' religious experience was 'Father' in an unusually intense manner that involved a powerful sense of personal and special mission. And the mission to which God called Jesus apparently included extending an unusually intimate relationship to God as 'Father' among those who accepted Jesus' proclamation of God's kingdom."[458] While Christopher Wright calls this Father "the God of Mission,"[459] David Bosch addresses the Father's mission as *Missio Dei* ("Mission of God").[460] The God of Israel is deciphered as the only true God (3:33; 5:44; 8:26; 17:3) whom only the Son has seen (1:18; 5:37; 1 John 4:12, 20). The God-Father is the source of life (2:22; 5:26; 6:57; 11:41), of truth (8:40), of protection (10:29; 17:15) as well as the source of, and power

---

[452] For more details about history and theology in the Fourth Gospel, See Martyn, *History and Theology of the Fourth Gospel*.

[453] Stibbe, *John*, 19.

[454] EDBW (2005: 441) rightly mentions that, "The former denotes the general expression for God as Creator and omnipotent deity, the latter constitutes the covenant name 'Lord,' the divine suzerain, initiator of the intimate bond with his people Israel."

[455] J. G. Van der Watt, *An Introduction to the Johannine Gospel and Letters*, T & T Clark Approaches to Biblical Studies (New York: T & T Clark, 2007), 34-35.

[456] It is used 109 times, more than twice the number for any other Evangelist.

[457] For more details about the idea of life in the Fourth Gospel, see R. Schnackenburg, *The Gospel according to St. John* (London: Burns & Oates, 1980), 2:352-361.

[458] L. W. Hurtado, "God," *Dictionary of Jesus and the Gospels* (Downers Grove: InterVarsity Press, 1992), 276.

[459] C. J. H. Wright, *The Mission of God: Unlocking the Bible's Grand Narrative* (Downers Grove: InterVarsity Press, 2006), 71-188.

[460] David J. Bosch, *Transforming Mission: Paradigm Shifts in Theology of Mission* (Maryknoll: Orbis Books, 1991/2006), 488.

behind, all good [things] (9:31-33; see 19:11; 3 John 11) in the universe.[461] This God-Father reveals his glory in the local Israeli context to extend it to the global realms.

The Father reveals himself through his Son.[462] That means, the mission of God (through his Son) is revelatory in character. This special and unique relationship is evident through the *pre-existence* of Jesus (as the *Logos*). A world that was under the power of the 'ruler of this world' (12:31; 14:30; 1 John 5:19), a world that was characterized by the presence of darkness, death, and lies, was/is the arena of God's mission.[463]

The mission of the Father was transformation of human beings, and along with them, the entire cosmic order. Transformation of the world 'from below,' in harmony with the world 'from above,' is the essence of God's mission. In this mission of the *sender-God*, Jesus functions as the 'agent,' initiator to fill the 'gap,' giver of life, judge, authoritative figure, and ultimately the fulfiller of his plan and purpose. The mission of God in John is fulfilling the hour (*hōra*), lifting up of the Son of Man, driving out the ruler of this world, extending the love of God, and glorification of the Father/Son. Whereas the resurrection is the crucial point in the Synoptic Gospels, in John the death of Jesus takes up the prominence.[464] In John, Jesus' death is depicted as a "cosmic battle" in order to drive out the ruler of the world (12:20-36; 14:30-31; 16:8-11). This battle initiated by the Father, through his Son, is the paradigm of the mission of God. In the Fourth Gospel, this cosmic battle is portrayed with the help of dualistic terms and dialectic means.

The *Global Saviour-Son* in the Gospel

While the synoptic evangelists present their stories from a "once upon a time" perspective, John presents his story from a "once before the time" perspective.[465] The incarnation of the *logos*, the beginning of the cosmic order and the pre-existent Christology are significant aspects in John.[466] John's

---

[461] Refer to Van der Watt, *An Introduction to the Johannine Gospel and Letters*, 35.

[462] Culpepper simply states that "God is characterized by Jesus." Culpepper, *Anatomy of the Fourth Gospel*, 113.

[463] God sends his 'only begotten Son' as the agent 'from above' to witnessing the truth in this world.

[464] Brant entitles the section John 12:12-19:42 as "Jesus' Triumphant Hour." J. A. Brant, *John: Paideia Commentaries on the New Testament* (Grand Rapids, Michigan: Baker Academic, 2011), 187-262.

[465] This is the main reason why Johannine narrator does not give any significance for the genealogy and the infancy narratives as it is in Matthew and Luke. But, the global Jesus' speeches and actions are depicted with the help of local settings and characters.

[466] See how Christology, Soteriology, and Eschatology are merged together in John, Beasley-Murray, *John*, lxxxi.

presentation of the cosmic order in a *vertical* 'from above' versus 'from below' fashion recapitulates the global outlook of the story world.[467] Painter says that, "John's prologue (1:1-18) provides a detailed reinterpretation of the Genesis creation story. A Jewish understanding of creation is daringly reinterpreted in the light of faith in Jesus as the savior of the world."[468] Jesus is presented as *light* of the world, *logos* of the cosmic order, and the source of *life* (light-logos-life // *licht-liebe-leben*).[469] He is *begotten Son* (*monogenēs*) of the Father and co-creator with God and through whom "all things came into being" (1:3).[470] The ironical expression "he came to what was *his own* and *his own* [people] did not accept him" (1:11) reveals his possessive relationship with the created world.[471] It also emphasises his 'everywhere' and 'ever' relationship with the global order.

The expression "God's *logos* became flesh and lived among us" literally means that God's logos appeared in anthropomorphic fashion (v. 14). The idea "full of grace and truth" means that he came with the full measure of God's grace and truth before humanity. While Adam lost his glory in the Garden of Eden, Jesus reveals the glory of God in its "fullness." Toward the end of the prologue, the narrator explicitly brings out a contrast between Moses and Jesus.[472] While Moses reveals his potential as a 'local' leader to the people of Israel, Jesus manifests his glory as the 'global' Savior by extending the aspects of grace and truth to humanity. But, the significant thing here is that Jesus extends his global significance through a local historical act. Hence, in Jesus, we see the extension from 'local' to 'global.' That means, Jesus is the *glocal* figure of salvation.

The global phenomenon of Jesus is once again brought to the attention of the reader toward the end of the prologue. The narrator arrays three significant things here: first, God is an unseen reality; second, Jesus has seen God and "is close to the Father's heart"; and third, seeing Jesus is seeing God (v. 18). John is witnessing the "God of the beginning" through the historical revelation of Jesus 'here' and 'now.' Thus, the prologue of the Gospel of John provides several inferences with regard to the global phenomenon of Jesus. Jesus, here, is pictured as the eternal and global figure, agent of God 'from above,'

---

[467] For more details about irony and dualism, refer P. Duke, *Irony in the Fourth Gospel* (Atlanta: John Knox, 1985).

[468] Painter, *The Quest for the Messiah*, 890.

[469] Cf. Voigt, *Licht-Liebe-Leben*.

[470] See 1:10; cf. Painter, *The Quest for the Messiah*, 65-84.

[471] For more details about the logos Christology, refer F. T. Gench, *Encounters with Jesus: Studies in the Gospel of John* (Louisville/London: Westminster John Knox Press, 2007), 1-9.

[472] He says: "the Law was given through Moses; grace and truth came through Jesus Christ" (v. 17).

co-creator (with God) of the world 'from below,' and the reconciler of the transcendent with the imminent.

The body of the gospel extends the above ideas profoundly. The "I am" sayings of Jesus reveal that Jesus is in equal status with the Father.[473] He is "the bread from heaven to earth," "the light of the world," "the good shepherd," "the gate for the sheep," "the resurrection and life," "the way, truth and life," and "the true vine." The universalistic significance of these metaphors is obvious through their global nature. The signs of Jesus are used as self-revelatory means. Jesus is introduced as a sign-performer in a Galilean wedding context (2:1-11), in the life of a royal man's (possibly a Gentile) family (4:46-54), an invalid's life (5:1-18), among a large crowd (6:1-15), on the natural realms (6:16-21), a blind man's life (9:1-41), and in a bereaved family setting (as a concerned person toward Mary and Martha; 11:1-44).[474] Here Jesus involves in the lives of diverse walks of people and natural situations.

While the synoptic miracles usually show tenets of a 'faith + miracle' formula and remain in a *closed-end* fashion, John's signs mostly follow a 'sign + faith' formula and remain *open-ended* to the universal community. Bauckham says that, "In fact, no other figure has so extensively crossed the cultural divisions of humanity and found a place in so many diverse cultural contexts. ... . The search for an African Jesus, an Indian Jesus, a Japanese Jesus goes on, while people inspired by Jesus continue to find him in the poor, the sick, and the dying, wherever and whoever they are."[475] In that sense, he considers Jesus as "a universal icon."[476] In a personified sense, Jesus himself is God's story to the world. This is the Johannine narrative stature typified through a Christo-centric literary structure.

The Son obediently executes the Father's mission to please and glorify him (8:29; cf. 4:34; 17:4) and he does that with a knowledge that the Father is always with him (8:16; 16:32). The Son of God with authority "from above" comes to perform his mission and after completing it he returns to the Father. This descending-and-ascending redeemer motif creates a 'U-shaped plot' for the entire story of John.[477] In the high priestly prayer, Jesus reports back to the Father the outcome of his mission, i.e., establishment of the family of God (17:1-8). Jesus' confrontations with the Jews make the local arena for the mission. His global agenda is explicit through the conversion of the Samaritan woman and the people of Sychar in chap. 4. Here, Jesus trespasses the Jewish

---

[473] See 6:35, 41, 48, 51; 8:12; 9:5; 10:7, 9, 11, 14; 11:25; 14:6; 15:1, 5; cf. Exo 3:14.

[474] Refer to Brown, *The Gospel according to St. John*, 1:xxviii-xxxix.

[475] R. Bauckham, *Jesus: A Very Short Introduction* (Oxford: University Press, 2011), 1-2.

[476] Bauckham sees the death of Jesus as a new beginning. See Bauckham, *Jesus*, 95-109.

[477] M. W. G. Stibbe, *John's Gospel*, New Testament Readings (London/New York: Routledge, 1994), 35-36.

territory and dialogues with the Samaritans.[478] The acceptance of Jesus as a prophet (4:19) and as the Messiah (4:25-26) by the Samaritan woman, and as the Savior of the world (4:42)[479] by the Samaritans reveal the acceptance of his messiahship beyond the Jewish circles.[480] Koester says that, "The title 'Saviour of the world' included and surpassed the previous expressions of Jesus' identity. By calling Jesus 'saviour' (*sōtēr*), the towns-people recognized that 'salvation' (*sōtēria*) is from the Jews but is for all people."[481] It is further strengthened by the quest for the Messiah by the Greeks and Jesus' proclamation about the coming of the awaited time (12:20-22).

The Acts 1:8 pattern of mission development is obvious in the plot development of the Johannine story. The Jerusalem-and-Judean-centric mission at the beginning (chaps. 1-3), the Samaritan mission in chap. 4, and the emphasis on the Gentile mission in chap. 12 follow this pattern. Jesus' mission in John is ushering salvation in a world that is controlled by darkness. In this way John introduces the aspect of *inclusive discipleship* and global mission. Salvation in John means bringing people to the family of God, introducing eternal life, and leading them into faith in Jesus and to spiritual birth. In the Fourth Gospel, believing means living or experiencing the life in its abundance. In that sense, faith is used as a means to attain salvation. Salvation is accessible without any restrictions. It is accessible irrespective of caste, class, race, color, and gender.[482] Here salvation means having faith in the Father and in the Son, being born into the family of God, and be children of light.[483]

The *Global Spirit-Paraclete* in the Gospel

John has a well-developed pneumatology in comparison to the rest of the NT writings. While in chaps. 1-12 he presents the Holy Spirit in synonymous terms with the synoptics, in chaps. 13-17 a personified form of the Holy Spirit is brought to the foreground. In the Farewell Discourse (chaps. 13-17), the identity formation of the disciples is emphasized. And the aspects

[478] R. Irudaya, "Attitudes and Approaches Employed in the Dialogue of Jesus with the Samaritan Woman II: Their Relevance to Interreligious Dialogue Today," *VJTR 67* (August/ September 2003), 707-716.

[479] C. R. Koester, "The Savior of the World (John 4:42)," *JBL* 109/4 (1990), 665-680.

[480] S. M. Schneiders, *Written That You May Believe: Encountering Jesus in the Fourth Gospel* (New York: A Herder and Herder Book/The Crossroad Publishing Company, 1999/2003), 126-148.

[481] Koester, "The Savior of the World (John 4:42)," 1990: 668.

[482] A. Reinhartz, "Women in the Johannine Community: An Exercise in Historical Imagination," *A Feminist Companion to John*, Vol. 2 (London/New York: Sheffield Academic Press, 2003), 14-33.

[483] M. Vellanickal, *The Divine Sonship of Christians in the Johannine Writings* (Rome: Biblical Institute Press, 1977), 89-104.

such as individuals in relation to the church and in relation to the world are highlighted. The Paraclete[484] assures God's continuing presence within the community of faith and that remains as a source of the wisdom of God (cf. 14:15-17, 26; 15:26-27; 16:7-11, 12-14; 1 John 2:1).[485] Richard B. Hays states that, "Though Jesus must go away, returning to heaven to be with the Father, he will send the Paraclete to 'abide' in the midst of the community."[486] It was to the disciples as Jesus was to them—the comforter, the guide, the teacher, the helper and the advocate.[487] The continuing presence of Jesus through the Paraclete as an *Alter Ego* functions well within the dualistic framework of the gospel (14:16).[488] Maniparampil says that, "Jesus is the first Paraclete; the Holy Spirit is 'another' counselor . . . . The Spirit-Paraclete is a specific way of the presence in the believer and action of the Holy Spirit in the believer."[489] The Paraclete is "the Spirit of Truth" from the presence of God the Father (i.e., "from above"). If "God is Spirit" (4:24), then "Spirit is God."[490] Hence it is the Spirit of God "from above." Now, it works in the world "from below" in order to guide the community of God.

The aspect of 'presence while absent' is made obvious in John. The Father is present through the Son even when the Father is physically absent. Similarly, the Son is present through the Paraclete even when he is physically absent. As Van der Watt says, "The *modus* of his [Jesus'] presence is not physical, but *cognitive* and *functional*."[491] The Paraclete guarantees an intimate relationship between the Father, Son and the believer. In that sense, the "from above" extends its power and authority in the "from below" realm.[492] Turner says that, ". . . the disciples are now 'sent' as Jesus was 'sent' (20:21; cf.

---

[484] Paraclete is a combined word in Greek, *para* + *clētos*. Literally, it means "one who is called to one's side." It may mean "comforter," "defender," "mediator," or "helper." Cf. Maniparampil, *Reading the Fourth Gospel*, 319.

[485] Turner describes the following things: *first*, the Paraclete is modeled on Jesus; *second*, the Paraclete will mediate the presence of the Father and the glorified Son; *third*, the Paraclete as teacher and revealer; and *fourth*, the Paraclete as advocate in the Christian Mission. See M. M. B. Turner, "Holy Spirit," *Dictionary of Jesus and the Gospels*, 349.

[486] R. B. Hays, *The Moral Vision of the New Testament: Community, Cross, New Creation: A Contemporary Introduction to NT Ethics* (New York: Harper Collins, 1996), 151.

[487] Also refer Brown, *The Gospel according to St. John*, 2:1135.

[488] Maniparampil, *Reading the Fourth Gospel*, 319.

[489] He is Jesus' successor, which Tertullian expressed when he used the term *vacarius Christi* for the Paraclete. See Maniparampil, *Reading the Fourth Gospel*, 319.

[490] Paraclete is also referred as the "Spirit of Truth."

[491] Van der Watt, *An Introduction to the Johannine Gospel and the Letters*, 69.

[492] J. Joubert, "Johannine Metaphors/Symbols Linked to the Paraclete-Spirit and Their Theological Implications," *Acta Theologica* 27/1 (South Africa: The University of the Free State, 2007), 98.

17:17-18), and the Spirit from the heavenly Lord is given to them to take over the earthly Jesus' advocacy of the case (15:26-27; 16:7b-11)."[493] The post-ascension gift of the Spirit "constitutes the witness to Christ and so is 'the Spirit of mission.'"[494] The role of the Paraclete in the post-Easter Christian community is efficaciously brought to the notice of the reader. Its function is not merely pictured as a local manifestation. Rather, it is universal and it functions as an inspiring spirit to the communities of God.

Johannine community is just a representative community, not the ultimate one, in this ever-continuing process. The same Paraclete was working within the Markan, Matthean, Lukan, and the Pauline communities. The work of the Paraclete is not merely a time-bound ministry within the first century context. Its involvement is universal in space and eternal in duration. As Johnson Chakkuvarackal says, "The centrality of the Holy Spirit provides theological stimulus for interpretation and has more relevance in the present day global context."[495] What Chakkuvarackal says is tantamount to the Johannine presentation of the Paraclete.

The *Global Mission* of the Triune God

The relationship among the Father, the Son, and human beings is outlined in the following fashion: first, the Father knows the Son (10:15), the Son knows the Father (10:15), the Son knows human beings (10:14), human beings know the Son (10:14), and human beings know Father and Son (14:7-8; and second, the Son is in the Father (14:10-11, 20; 17:21), the Father is in the Son (14:10-11, 17:21, 23), human beings are in the Son (14:20; 17:23, 26), and human beings are in Father and Son (17:21).[496] The union of the Father and the Son is universal and is revealed in relation to human beings.[497] The so-called *Immanenzformeln* = formulas of immanence (8:42; 10:38; 14:20; 17:21-23) show the relationship between the Father and the Son in emphatic terms.[498] In his mission to the world, Father not only *functionally equipped* his Son, but was also *actively involved* in the execution and *outcome* of the mission.[499]

---

[493] Turner, "Holy Spirit," 350.

[494] Joubert, "Johannine Metaphors," 2007: 99.

[495] J. Chakkuvarackal, "Toward a Spirit-centered Biblical Theology: The 'From Below' Aspects of the Holy Spirit," *Bangalore Theological Forum*, 35/1 (2003), 23; Maniparampil, *Reading the Fourth Gospel*, 323.

[496] A Father/Son system is undercurrent in the gospel. See N. R. Petersen, *The Gospel of John and the Sociology of Light: Language and Characterization in the Fourth Gospel* (Eugene, Oregon: Wipf & Stock, 1993), 66-69.

[497] The arena of God's mission is the "from below" world.

[498] Moloney, *The Gospel of John*, 21-22.

[499] Refer C. K. Barrett, *Essays on John* (London: SPCK, 1982), 19-36.

Jesus is God as the Father is God (1:1, 18; 20:28; 1 John 5:20), who was/is *homoousios* (same substance) with the Father.[500] Though functionally different, substantially they are one. Jesus' identification as a human being was 'temporary,' missional and functional.[501] His mission in the world involves his incarnation in the human form (in a *physical human body* of flesh and blood, 6:51, 55; 19:34; 1 John 5:8; in a *physical human family* with a mother, father and brothers, 1:45; 2:1, 3, 12; 6:42; 7:3, 10; 19:26).[502] Jesus belongs to the heavenly Father as he is the only begotten Son, and at the same time he has 'this worldly' family relations.[503] This dynamic phenomenon reveals both the 'local' and the 'global' allies of the Father and the Son.[504]

The Trinitarian mission theology of John is at the foreground through the very statement of Jesus that "As the Father has sent me, so I am sending you."[505] John uses the verbs *apostellein* and *pempein* in the gospel frequently (i.e., more than 50 times). These verbs are used to indicate the mission of Jesus (3:17, 34; 4:43; 5:23, 24, 36, 38; 6:38, 44, 57; 7:29), the mission of the disciples (4:38; 13:16; 17:18; 20:21), and the mission of the Holy Spirit (14:26; 15:26; 16:7, 13, 14).[506] Köstenberger states that, "While there are important personal differences in the roles of the Triune God along salvation-historical lines (the Father sends, the Son is sent and sends, the Spirit is sent) the *missio Dei* is characterized by a deep underlying unity among the participants in this mission."[507] John's presentation of the Father, the Son and the Spirit demonstrates his globally-oriented mission theology.[508] Turner states that, "In the Fourth Gospel the Spirit is to be understood primarily as a development of the Jewish understanding of the 'Spirit of prophesy,' redefined christologically and developed in Trinitarian direction."[509] The shape of Jesus' mission determines the shape of the Church's mission and the Church's mission is guided and powered by the Paraclete. The aspects such as theo-centricism,

---

[500] In Greek, *homos* means "same" and *ousios* means "substance."

[501] Painter states, "The world in view is humanity. The coming of the emissary was to save, not to condemn the world (3:17; 4:42; 6:33, 51; 12:47), but condemnation is inevitable where the saving mission is rejected (9:39)." See Painter, *The Quest for the Messiah*, 890.

[502] Painter, *The Quest for the Messiah*, 890.

[503] Dodd, *The Interpretation of the Fourth Gospel*, 194.

[504] Bennema, *Encountering Jesus*, 33.

[505] For more details about the relationship between Father, Son, and Spirit, refer to A. J. Köstenberger and S. R. Swain, *Father, Son, and Spirit: The Trinity and John's Gospel*, New Studies in Biblical Theology (Downers Grove: InterVarsity Press, 2008).

[506] Cf. R. J. Painter, *The Gospel of John: A Thematic Approach* (Eugene: Wipf & Stock, 2011), 61-70.

[507] Köstenberger, *Father, Son, and Spirit*, 19.

[508] Köstenberger and Swain, *Father, Son, and Spirit*, 158-164.

[509] Turner, "Holy Spirit," 347.

christo-centricism and pneumato-centricism are at the core of the Johannine theology.[510] And it is supplemented by cosmo-centricism. Thus, Johannine theology is Trinitarian in nature, global in focus, and missional in outcome.[511]

The *Local-and-Global Dynamism* in Christian Mission

In its mission(s) the Church becomes a truly transnational and transcultural community. Within this community, diversity is not abolished but placed within the higher integration of a common faith. In that way, the Church is dynamically caught between the dialectic poles of particularity and universality, between apostolic rootedness and culture-transcending catholicity.[512] This is true with the missional tenets of the Johannine community. The Johannine community does not adopt a "rhetoric of distance" as the Qumran sectarians do, rather it introduces a "rhetoric of difference." John's community lived alongside of the mainstream Jewish community.[513] But, it adopted its own ethics and ethos as an inclusive community even when they were suffering oppression from their rivals. Bultmann saw 'the Jews' as theological symbols, representing the unbelieving world in general in its hostility towards Jesus and his followers.[514] The conflict that develops between Jesus and 'the Jews' is in essence the conflict between the world "from above" and the world "from below."[515] The characterization of the world "from below" is drastically developed through the medium of the Jews in sharp conflict/contrast with Jesus' "from above" character.[516]

The emerging oppositions in Jerusalem (chap. 5), in Galilee (chap. 6), the domination of the Pharisees (chaps. 7-10), the domination of the chief priests (chap. 11), and Jesus' trial and death (chap. 18-19) are the local manifestations of the plot of this world against Jesus.[517] In John, the narrator uses certain narrative techniques to globalize the stories, as in the case of chaps. 5 and 9. Schneiders says that, "Both the blind man [chap. 9] and the paralyzed man

---

[510] Kelly and Moloney suggest a Theo-centric Christology at the core of Johannine theology. See A. J. Kelly and F. J. Moloney, *Experiencing God in the Gospel of John* (New York/Mahwah: Paulist Press, 2003), 18-20.

[511] H. Windisch, *The Spirit-Paraclete in the Fourth Gospel* (Minneapolis: Fortress Press, 1968), 1-38.

[512] Ormerod and Clifton, *Globalization and the Mission of the Church*, 18.

[513] Stibbe, *John's Gospel*, 5-31.

[514] Bultmann, *The Gospel of John*, 86-87; Bennema, *Encountering Jesus*, 31.

[515] Also refer to S. Motyer, *Your Father the Devil? A New Approach to John and 'the Jews,'* Paternoster Biblical and Theological Studies (UK: Paternoster Press, 1997).

[516] C. Bennema, *Excavating John's Gospel: A Commentary for Today* (Delhi: ISPCK, 2005), 14.

[517] S. H. Ringe, *Wisdom's Friends: Community and Christology in the Fourth Gospel* (Louisville, Kentucky: Westminster John Knox Press, 1999), 10-28.

[chap. 5] are 'nameless,' suggesting that they are Johannine representative figures. Both characters are *anthrōpos*, theologically 'everyperson.'"[518] In the process of reading the Johannine text, a reader has to consider a fusion of at least three horizons: first, the horizon of the pre-Easter Jesus; second, the horizon of the post-Easter Johannine community; and third, the horizon of the 'ever present' reading community.[519] Thus, the Johannine story does not simply remain as a descriptive history, rather a gnomic narrative to influence the paradigmatic reader eternally and universally.

The earliest manuscripts of John 20:30-31 use both present subjunctive (*pisteuēte*) and aorist subjunctive (*pisteusēte*) to refer the expression "that you may believe." If we consider the present subjunctive, the meaning can be "you may continue to believe" (*pisteuēte*). Then it has a pastoral target. But, if we consider the aorist subjunctive, the meaning can be "that you may come to believe" (*pisteusēte*).[520] Then it has a missionary objective. The purpose statement of the gospel in 20:30-31 (as the first conclusion) and 21:24-25 (as the second conclusion) firmly affirm the careful choice of the narrator and the representative nature of the Johannine characters. John's intention of writing this masterpiece is to address both the 'insiders' and the 'outsiders.'

John introduces marginalized characters such as the Samaritan woman (4:1-42), the man born blind (9:1-41), and Mary Magdalene (20:1-2, 11-18), and dominant characters such as the Jews and Judas Iscariot (6:64, 70-71; 12:1-8; 13:2, 10-11, 18-19, 21, 26-30; 18:1-8) in order to make his global point of view clear to the reader. Kobus Kok states that, ". . . those who seek to speak of moral language in John should probably also include the reality of a missional-incarnational ethos that will transcend all boundaries (cultural, social, economical, and racial) to show love and be accepting of everyone."[521] The categorization of the characters into two such as good and evil or saved and damned will help us to reinterpret the story of John both at the local settings and at the universal realms.

The narrator dualistically categorizes men and women, Jews and non-Jews, and lowly and elite at the *micro*-level, believing and unbelieving (at a broader "from below" perspective) at the *meso*-level, and the world "from

---

[518] Schneiders, *Written That You May Believe*, 152-153.

[519] J. G. Van der Watt, "Eschatology in John: A Continuous Process of Realizing Events," *Eschatology of the New Testament and Some Related Documents* (Tübingen: Mohr Siebeck, 2011), 110.

[520] J. G. Van der Watt, *Ethics through the Power of Language: Some Explorations in the Gospel according to John*, Moral Language in the New Testament: The Interrelatedness of Language and Ethics in Early Christian Writings, Vol. 2 (Tübingen: Mohr Siebeck, 2010), 141.

[521] K. Kok, "As the Father has sent me, I send you: Towards a missional-incarnational ethos in John 4," *Moral Language in the New Testament: The Interrelatedness of Language and Ethics in Early Christian Writings* (Tübingen: Mohr Siebeck, 2010), 192.

above" and the world "from below" at the *macro*-level.[522] Köstenberger suggests that "John's narrative focuses on Jesus and his messianic mission."[523] This mission became a paradigm for the mission of the Messianic [Johannine] Community.[524] The missional ethos of the Johannine community persuades a paradigmatic reader to transform her/his existential context(s) to an esteemed level.

The revelation/manifestation of Jesus' glory at the local Jewish context and its extension to post-Easter Johannine community can be viewed as follows. Martyn maintains that the Gospel of John is made up of two stories, namely, the story of Jesus and the story of the Johannine congregation who selected events from the life of Jesus to apply to their own situation, thus interweaving their own situation with the story of Jesus.[525] This resulted in a *two level story/drama*.[526] Van der Watt builds upon Martyn's position and argues in favour of a *third level*.[527] He says that, "There is a (divine) story behind the (earthly) story, which also serves as interpretative frame for the earthly story of Jesus." In my observation, I see significant features in the interpretative frame of Van der Watt. The transcendental (universal) God takes initiative in redeeming the world "from below" through the local manifestation of Jesus. This local manifestation was further localized in the Johannine community. And that became an influential phenomenon for the universal communities forever. Thus, John provides a universal [the transcendental Father and Son realm] – local [the realm of Jesus' ministry] – local [the realm of the Johannine community] – universal [contemporary glocal context] formula. This formula informs us that 'local' and 'global' realms are part and parcel of God's mission.

In their social-scientific commentary on John, Malina and Rohrbaugh merge the first century Johannine Christian *local* context with the situations

---

[522] For more details about Johannine characterization and point of view, see Resseguie, *Narrative Criticism of the NT*, 121-196.

[523] Köstenberger, *John*, 13.

[524] Refer to Köstenberger, *John*, 13-16.

[525] Cf. Martyn, *History and Theology in the Fourth Gospel*, 24-184.

[526] Martyn, *History and Theology in the Fourth Gospel*, 37.

[527] Visotzky (2005: 104) says that, "J. Louis Martyn and Raymond Brown were correct; there is a two-level drama in John: that of Jesus and that of the Johannine community. Yet it is sensitivity to levels three and four—the long history of (mis)interpretation of the Fourth Gospel and our own current biases—that allows us to fully understand those earlier levels of drama and suggest new ways for understanding their historic setting." See B. L. Visotzky, "Methodological Considerations in the Study of John's Interaction with First Century Judaism," *Life in Abundance: Studies of John's Gospel in Tribute to Raymond E. Brown, S. S* (Collegeville, Minnesota: Liturgical Press, 2005), 91-107.

of the modern world.[528] Christopher Wright shapes a *missional hermeneutic* by bridging the OT and the NT.[529] Wright considers the Bible as the product of God's mission, in which the indicatives are present for the imperatives of mission.[530] As biblical God is a mission-oriented God, as Jesus is the fulfiller of God's mission, and as Jesus continues his mission through the Spirit-Paraclete, humanity (the church) is sent for a mission.[531]

Jongeneel comes up with the 'local' and 'global' manifestations of philosophy and science of mission. In his book, he explains in detail how the philosophy of mission (*Missionsphilosophie*) functions in its own right and in relation to the philosophy of religion (*Religionsphilosophie*).[532] Then he argues about the theology of mission (*Missionstheologie*).[533] Jongeneel is truly concerned of bridging the gap between the first century mission theology of the apostolic church and the twenty-first century mission theology of the global Christianity. Ferdinand Hahn says that, "in the view of the fourth gospel mission can only be realized where the disciples are conscious of their contrast with the world; their message in the world is a message of 'salvation universalism' (*Heilsuniversalismus*)."[534] Thus, mission theologians attempt to fill the gap between the 'local' and the 'global' manifestations of Christian mission. Toward that direction John's Trinitarian mission theology contributes significantly. In that sense, the *descriptive* but *gnomic* relevance of John's mission theology requires adequate attention.

Conclusion

Today, one of the largest challenges a biblical scholar faces is to interpret the scripture trans-culturally and trans-nationally. The contemporary culture demands new approaches and methods for interpretation to meet

---

528 Malina and Rohrbaugh (1998) comment that, ". . . both ends of the interpretive chain are of decisive importance." See B. J. Malina and R. L. Rohrbaugh, *Social-Science Commentary on the Gospel of John* (Minneapolis: Fortress Press, 1998).

529 Wright, *The Mission of God*, 48-70.

530 Wright, *The Mission of God*, 48-51.

531 Bosch sees *mission as disciple-making* in Matthew (pp. 69-103), *practicing forgiveness and solidarity with the poor* in Luke-Acts, and invitation to join the eschatological community in Paul. See Bosch, *Transforming Mission*, 104-152, 153-224.

532 [J. A. B. Jongeneel, *Philosophy, Science, and Theology of Mission in the 19th and 20th Centuries: A Missiological Encyclopedia I: Philosophy and Science of Mission* (Frankfurt: Peter Lang,1995/2006), 84-89, 91-99] also does the same with the science of mission (*Missionswissenschaft*) and the science of religion (*Religionswissenschaft*).

533 Jongeneel also takes the biblical theology of mission into serious consideration. See Jongeneel, *Philosophy, Science, and Theology*, 1:113-155, 102-198.

534 F. Hahn, *Theologie Des Neuen Testaments: Band I* (Tübingen: Mohr Siebeck, 1963), 136, 142; quoted in Jongeneel, *Philosophy, Science, and Theology*, 1:144.

the philosophical requirements of the "global village." This new situation influences us to view the Johannine text with a view of integration and convergence.[535] Its message cannot simply be viewed from a 'there and then' perspective. Rather from the point of view of a 'here and now' and 'everywhere and ever' perspective. John contains a mission agenda that is characterized as an *all-inclusive* and *gnomic* entity.

We must consider John the narrator and must engage with him in a relationship. A rhetorically-inclined reading of the text prompts the reader to be engaged. The deep structure of the text has potential and has a performative message to converse with the reader. This very nature of the text provokes the reader to engage with the text pragmatically and to attune its message to her/his local context.[536.] In a globalized culture, a reader's local interpretation/mission has potential to transform the universal. Umbrella expressions such as "family of the King"[537] and "household of God" are integrative in several respects.[538] Barus says that, "... Fourth Gospel is composed both to initiate faith in Jesus (*Missionsschrift*) and to deepen the faith of the believing community (*Gemeindeschrift*). The characters embedded in the narrative world dramatize the evangelistic and edificatory aspects of faith."[539] The pastoral/missional intent of the Johannine text challenges the faith community to witness the truth *glocally*.

While Rensberger reads the gospel from the point of view of the marginalized, he recognizes a message that affirms solidarity with the oppressed (pp. 113-116) and a Jesus who stands firm for the downtrodden (pp. 118-124). He (pp. 124-130) states that Johannine 'love ethic' provides kernel for liberation.[540] The reading tenet of Rensberger has the credentials to guide a modern reader to interlock the local and the universal mission initiatives within the text. Johannine 'love ethic' has the potential to transcend the cultural barriers and to transform communities trans-nationally and trans-culturally. Thus, John remains as a flexible poetic to visualize the globe gnomically.

While the diachronic approaches mostly encourage the reader to look at the text from a local and fixed point of view, the synchronic approaches open

---

[535] Stibbe, *John*, 15-16.

[536] Schneiders, *Written That You May Believe*, 148.

[537] Van der Watt, *An Introduction to the Johannine Gospel and Letters*, 67.

[538] As Ihenacho calls it, it is "the community of eternal life." D. A. Ihenacho, *The Community of Eternal Life: The Study of the Meaning of Life for the Johannine Community* (Lanham/New York/Oxford: University Press of America, 2001).

[539] A. Barus, "John 2:12-25: A Narrative Reading," *New Currents through John: A Global Perspective*, eds. Lozada, F., and Thatcher, T (Leiden/Boston: Brill, 2006), 140.

[540] D. K. Rensberger, *Johannine Faith and Liberating Community* (Philadelphia: Westminster, 1988).

avenues for trans-national and trans-cultural reading practices.[541] Gutiérrez considers humanity as the temple of God (pp. 106-109) and understands that knowing God is to do justice (pp. 110-115). He attempted to experience God, Christ, and the temple of God in the local Latin American context(s).[542] James Cone defends and argues for the cause of the Black experience from the scriptural references and with an understanding of Jesus as an agent of liberation (pp. 16-35). Cone acclaims that God of the Bible is "God of the oppressed."[543] Nirmal and other Dalit theologians attempted to localize the same Christ and the same Bible in the struggles of the Dalits.[544] In his book entitled *Jesus and Culture* Kappen attempts to see Jesus on the crossroads of cultures.[545] The same is true with the Indian Christian theologians who see Christ as the *Crown of Hinduism* (cf. Panikkar)[546] and *Christ of the Indian Renaissance* (cf. M. M. Thomas).[547] Vashum and other tribal theologians from the North-Eastern Indian context search for the relevance of the Bible and its protagonist Jesus.[548] Samartha outlines the way Christian mission has to be done by accepting Christ as the agent of liberation in a multi-religious context.[549]

---

[541] Bultmann [quoted in B. K. Blount, *Cultural Interpretation: Reorienting NT Criticism* (Minneapolis: Fortress Press, 1995), 28] argues that "language cannot be applied effectively if its symbols and terminology are foreign; it must first be interpreted, translated into an understandable idiom." See R. Bultmann, *Jesus Christ and Mythology* (New York: Charles Scribner's Sons, 1958), 19.

[542] G. Gutiérrez, *A Theology of Liberation: History, Politics, and Salvation* (Maryknoll: Orbis Press, 1988).

[543] Refer J. Cone, *Speaking the Truth: Ecumenism, Liberation, and Black Theology*, Second Edition (Maryknoll: Orbis Books, 1975/1997).

[544] Cf. V. Devasahayam, ed., *Dalit Theology* (Chennai: Gurukul Lutheral Theological College, 1997); J. Massey, *Roots of Dalit History, Christianity, Theology, and Spirituality* (Delhi: ISPCK, 1996).

[545] S. Kappen, *Jesus and Culture* (Delhi: ISPCK, 2002); S. Kappen, *Jesus and Society* (Delhi: ISPCK, 2002).

[546] Samartha states that, "The distinctiveness of Christian mission lies precisely in its being *Christian*, that is, in its being rooted in God through Jesus Christ and in being active in the world in the power of the Spirit, without denying, however, that neighbours of other faiths too have *their* 'missions' in the global community." See S. J. Samartha, *One Christ, Many Religions* (Maryknoll: Orbis Books, 1991), 171.

[547] For more details about the Indian Christian reflections, refer to Boyd, 2000.

[548] Y. Vashum, *Tribal Theology and the Bible: A Search for Contextual Relevance* (Jorhat: Tribal Study Center/Eastern Theological College, 2011).

[549] In his book *The Gagging of God*, Carson delineates how Christianity confronts pluralism. See Samartha, *One Christ, Many Religions*, 162-175; D. A. Carson, *The Gagging of God: Christianity Confronts Pluralism* (Grand Rapids: Zondervan Academics, 1996).

The Johannine Jesus who is localized in the above stated contexts is the universal figure of salvation. Catholic Church from its very beginning maintains the qualities of becoming both the local and the global at the same time.[550] Similarly, Pentecostalism "has the unique capacity to take on a shape that aligns to both global and local social realities."[551] A dynamic interlocking of the local and the global is at the root of the Johannine theology. The Trinitarian mission agenda of John's Gospel has rhetorical power to foster a theology of integration. As the universal gospel was localized in the *Sitz im Leben Jesu* and in the *Sitz im Leben kirche* (Johannine community), the localized Palestinian mission-theology was universalized in the subsequent initiatives of the church. Furthermore, the universalized mission of Jesus was/is further localized by the mission practitioners and theologians of our time. In that sense, Christian mission is *glocal* in its very essence.

Our reading experience of John informs us that the gospel is not simply a "museum product." Rather it is a "pragmatic guide" or a "dialoguing character" for equipping the faith communities with an eternal and universal intent. Chow and Berheide argue that, ". . . the perennial popularity of John's Gospel indicates that many readers do find it to be an engaging and meaningful text." This aspect of the Gospel is important to reckon with.[552]

While Matthew extends his mission theology from particularism to universalism, John dynamically intertwines both the particular and the universal right from the beginning. The God of the universe comes to a local context and his own (creation) does not recognize him (1:10-11). The mission theology of John takes heed from this central irony. Jesus fulfills his mission and continues (through the Paraclete) to be with the faith community. As the Father has sent him, he continues to send the transformed to expand the ministry of witnessing (17:18). An exposition of John that combines theology proper, Christology, and pneumatology coupled with cosmology guides our attention toward the Trinitarian missiology of the gospel, both in hypothesis and in praxis.

Understanding John from a gnomic point of view enables the reader to comprehend its universalistic nature. A reading that moves away from the rigid and monotonous dogmatization to a flexible and integrative contextualization will guide us to comprehend the holistic and all-inclusive nature of the Johannine missiology. The holistic presentation of John's missiology is

---

[550] Ormerod and Clifton emphasize that, "The very word 'catholic' mean universal, so that a globalizing thrust has been symbolically captured in its very self-designation." Ormerod and Clifton, *Globalization and the Mission*, 12.

[551] Refer Ormerod and Clifton, *Globalization and the Mission*, 17.

[552] Esther Ngan-ling Chow and Catherine White Berheide, eds., *Women, the Family, and Policy: A Global Perspective* (Atlanta, Georgia: Scholars Press, 1996), 5.

discernible through the integration of the physical, psychological, spiritual, familial, and communitarian emotions of diverse people groups and their life situations. John emphasizes the aspect of witnessing the truth that is salvific in essence. Thus, John's missiology is a *missiology par-excellence*.

Chapter 6

Missional-Pneumatology of the Fourth Gospel

Introduction

The present chapter is an attempt to understand the way the Holy Spirit appears within the narrative framework of the Fourth Gospel. The narrator attempts to provide a distinctive emphasis in presenting the role of the Holy Spirit and thus s/he foregrounds its function with a missional emphasis. The following questions are important to pose at the outset of the essay: How is Holy Spirit narrated within the framework of the Fourth Gospel? Is there a progression happening in its portrayal? What are the characteristic features of the Johannine pneumatology? How the narrative framework of John helps us in understanding the missional role of the Holy Spirit? The Fourth Gospel foregrounds the Holy Spirit as a gnomic and divine force that leads people to missions, inspires them for ministry, and teaches them the realities of the world from above. This unique status of the Holy Spirit persuades the reader for a renewed interest in the third person of the Trinity. The task of the paper is threefold: first, investigating the unique features of the Johannine pneumatology; second, understanding the framework of the Fourth Gospel by placing the Holy Spirit at significant narrative intervals; and third, analyzing the missional role of the Holy Spirit within the Fourth Gospel. The expression "Missional-Pneumatology" is used to underscore the role and status of the Holy Spirit as an agent of global mission. In the following sections we will investigate the Missional-Pneumatology of the Fourth Gospel with an emphasis on its progressive nature within the macro-narrative framework.

Spirit-endowment in the Mission of Jesus

The Fourth Gospel introduces the role and function of the Holy Spirit in relation to the mission and ministry of Jesus. In 1:32-35, John the Baptizer, as a first hand witness, informs his disciples concerning the endowment of the Holy Spirit upon Jesus. As Jesus is introduced to the world, the people are informed about the coming of the Holy Spirit upon him as the initiator of the mission of God. In John, the Mission of God involves several movements and many things. Köstenberger defines it in the following way:

> Mission is the specific *task* or purpose which a person or group seeks to accomplish, *involving various modes of movement*, be it sending or being sent, coming and going, ascending and descending, gathering by calling others to follow, or following.[553]

Here the movements of God, Jesus, Holy Spirit, John the Baptizer, and the disciples are to be understood in terms of the mission of God. The Fourth Evangelist underscores the mission of Jesus in association with the works of the Holy Spirit.[554] The expressions such as *heōraka* (seeing) and *memarturēka* (valid testimony) are used to introduce the person of Jesus and to sum up everything concerning the mission of "the Son of God" (1:34).[555] The coming of the Holy Spirit in the form of a dove and resting upon Jesus associates the works of the Holy Spirit in the world from below.[556] Jesus' coming with full and permanent possession of the Holy Spirit enables him to fulfill the Messianic role among the people (cf. Isa 9:2; 61:1).[557] In that sense, the coming of the Holy Spirit to the world and resting upon Jesus guarantees its association with Jesus' mission and ministry.[558]

The mission of Jesus in the world begins with Spirit-empowerment. The metaphor of dove is used to describe the coming of the Holy Spirit with divine attributes like holiness, gentleness, and genuineness.[559] While John baptizes

---

[553] Andreas J. Köstenberger, *The Mission of Jesus and the Disciples according to the Fourth Gospel* (Grand Rapids: Eerdmans, 1998), 41.

[554] M. M. B. Turner, "Holy Spirit," *DJG*, 347.

[555] See Rudolf Schnackenburg, *The Gospel according to St. John*, Vol. 1 (Kent: Burns & Oates, 1980), 305.

[556] See Raymond E. Brown, *The Gospel according to John (i-xii)*, Vol. 1 (Garden City: Doubleday, 1966), 66.

[557] See Schnackenburg, *The Gospel according to St. John*, 1:303-304.

[558] See Brown, *The Gospel according to John (i-xii)*, 1:62-68.

[559] See Isa 32:15-18; 44:3-5; Eze 36:25-27; Jubilees 1:23; 4 Esdras 6:26; Testament of Judah 24:3; 1QS 4:20-22. Brant says that, "The comparison to a dove may simply point to a slow circling descent or to the role that Noah's dove plays as a sign of new life (Gen 8:8-12)." See Jo-Ann A. Brant, *John*, Paideia Commentaries on the New Testament (Grand Rapids: Baker Academic, 2011), 49-50.

in the water, Jesus' baptism in the Holy Spirit demonstrates a higher form of baptism.[560] The experience of the Trinitarian witness (Father's witness to John the Baptizer and to the world; Son's baptism in water and in the Holy Spirit; and the coming of the Holy Spirit as a dove; 1:33) enabled John to introduce Jesus to the world as the Son of God (1:34).[561] Jesus is presented as the eschatological agent who brings the anticipated eschatological gift (Joel 2:28-32; Isa 44:3-5; Eze 36:26-27; Zech 12:10).[562] This gift is at work in his mission through the endowment of the Holy Spirit.

Jesus' Spirit-endowment is manifested through his various activities within the Gospel. His interlocutors understand him as the Lamb of God and the Son of God (1:29, 34, 49), the Messiah (1:41), the "one Moses wrote about" (1:45), and the King of Israel (1:49).[563] Through the usage of these Messianic titles, Jesus' dialogue partners affirm that he is the anointed one of God. Jesus as the empowered Son of God brings new joy in the wedding place at Cana in Galilee (2:1-11) and initiates for a new worship in Spirit and in truth with a focus on a new temple (2:13-22).[564] His mission was to lead people to a new birth experience (3:3). In 3:5, he says that, "I tell you the truth, no one can enter the kingdom of God unless he is born of water and the Spirit. Flesh gives birth to flesh, but the Spirit gives birth to Spirit." Witherington states that, "Water and Spirit are seen as the mediums or agencies through which birth comes out."[565] The water experience that John initiates and the Spirit experience that Jesus promotes are important levels in the spiritual journey. Jesus proves them true as he was baptized in water under John the Baptizer (1:31) and the Baptizer witnesses that he was endowed by the Holy Spirit (1:32).[566] The physical and spiritual regenerations are emphasized through the symbolic usage of the birth by water and the metaphorical demonstration of the birth through the Spirit.[567]

---

[560] Schnackenburg says that, "John goes on to distinguish still more sharply between his own baptism and that of Jesus; his own is but a shadow of the Messianic baptism with the Spirit." See Schnackenburg, *The Gospel according to St. John*, 1:304.

[561] Turner states that, "In the Fourth Gospel the Spirit is to be understood primarily as a development of the Jewish understanding of the 'Spirit of prophesy,' redefined christologically and developed in a Trinitarian direction." See Turner, "Holy Spirit," 347; Brown, *The Gospel according to John (i-xii)*, 1:66-67.

[562] See Brant, *John*, 50.

[563] See Brown, *The Gospel according to John (i-xii)*, 1:42-91.

[564] See J. Ramsey Michaels, *The Gospel of John*, NICNT (Grand Rapids: Eerdmans, 2010), 139-175.

[565] Ben Witherington, *John's Wisdom: A Commentary on the Fourth Gospel* (Louisville: Westminster John Knox Press, 1995), 97. Also see Pro 5:15-18; Song of Songs 4:12-15; *m. Abot* 3:1; 3 Enoch 6:3; 1QH 3:9-10.

[566] See Neyrey, *The Gospel of John*, 52-54.

[567] Cf. Turner, "Holy Spirit," 347-348.

Through the water and Spirit experiences, Jesus proves that he is indeed the representative of the Kingdom of God (3:3-5). Within the dualistic framework of the Fourth Gospel, the expression "birth in the Spirit" is contrasted with "birth in the flesh" (3:6).[568] A spiritual birth is at the core of the discussion here. The gnomic significance of the Holy Spirit is emphasized through the usage of a universal metaphor 'wind': "The wind blows wherever it pleases" (3:8).[569] Jesus' identity as the prophet of the divine message is emphasized through the declaration "You hear its sound, but you cannot tell where it comes from or where it is going."[570] The Holy Spirit as the universal agent of God and Jesus as one empowered for a mission beyond time and space are at focus through the expression "so it is with everyone born of the Spirit."[571] Jesus' engagement in mission as an eschatological agent of God is foregrounded through the narrative annals of the Fourth Gospel. The narrator is much concerned of introducing Jesus as a charismatic figure with a missional emphasis.[572]

In 4:23, Jesus weighs down both the worship "on this mountain" (i.e., Gerizim) and "in Jerusalem." He states to the Samaritan woman that "true worshippers will worship the Father in Spirit and truth." He further states that, "God is spirit, and his worshippers must worship in spirit and truth" (4:24). In that sense, the woman is brought to a "third space," a new mode of/identity in worship.[573] While the "first space" of Gerizim and the "second space" of Jerusalem are used to create a "third space" of the eternal life experience, Jesus was ushering a new mode of worship in Spirit and truth. The "true worshippers" are introduced as those who "born of the Spirit."[574] By describing that "God is Spirit," God of the heavens is distinguished from all that is earthly and human.[575] God is not described as a physical being but rather a universal being that inspires people beyond all human-made limitations.[576] That further means

---

[568] Schnackenburg says that, "Jesus' words to Nicodemus are not concerned directly with baptism, but with the new creation by the Holy Spirit." See Schnackenburg, *The Gospel according to St. John*, 1:370; Witherington, *John's Wisdom*, 97.

[569] According to ancient understanding, wind did not die down but rather it retreated to an unseen location for a time. Brant, *John*, 75-76.

[570] Michaels, *The Gospel of John*, 187-190.

[571] Witherington, *John's Wisdom*, 97-98.

[572] Turner, "Holy Spirit," 341-351.

[573] See Michaels, *The Gospel of John*, 252-255,

[574] Schnackenburg says, "Jesus describes true (*alēthinos*) adoration as that which is performed in 'Spirit and truth.'" See Schnackenburg, *The Gospel according to St. John*, 1:439; cf. Michaels, *The Gospel of John*, 252-255.

[575] Schnackenburg says, "It is not a definition of God's essence, but it expresses the transcendence and holiness of God." See Schnackenburg, *The Gospel according to St. John*, 1:439.

[576] While Spirit is described as the motivator of speaking in tongues, their interpretation, prayers, blessings (1 Cor 12:7-11; 14:14-16), and singing of "spiritual songs" (Eph 5:19-20; Col

that a worship in Spirit and truth trespasses all the time, space, and personal boundaries. The salvation and the privilege of worship are for all including the Samaritan woman.[577] As Christ is the universal and eschatological figure of salvation, the Holy Spirit is the universal and eschatological force behind Jesus' mission and ministry.

In 6:63, Jesus speaks to his disciples toward the close of a series of instructions. He reveals his identity as the bread of life in the synagogue setup in Capernaum and continues his speech to the next level. Jesus' speech about eating the flesh and drinking the blood of the Son of Man offended his disciples as they were unable to comprehend its metaphorical intent (6:53-58).[578] The speech here is dualistic as he brings a contrast between the Spirit and the flesh. Accepting the way of Jesus (and the word of Jesus) is indeed the way of the Spirit (6:63).[579] Jesus says, "The Spirit gives life, the flesh counts for nothing. The words I have spoken to you are spirit and they are life" (6:63). Schnackenburg comments that, "it is not the flesh and the blood of the earthly Jesus, but that of the heavenly Son of Man, who, filled with the Spirit, possesses a new mode of existence."[580] While the Spirit is referred as the source of life, Jesus introduces its role as the giver of eternal life. On the contrary, the flesh does not count for anything. The coming of the Holy Spirit upon Jesus marks the beginning of the mission of God to bifurcate between those who are born of the spirit and those who are born of the flesh. In that sense, Johannine pneumatology cannot be understood without having a reference to Christology.

Jesus deliberates that the words he has spoken as spirit and life. What he speaks gives an assurance to the reader that his words as well as the deeds are endowed by the Spirit. Witherington comments that, "One of the keys to the whole discourse is mentioned in v. 63b—that which gives spirit and life is Jesus' *words* . . . The issue here is salvation through revelation and the transformation it brings."[581] The two phrases in v. 63 describe two modes of Spirit existence: first, the earthly Jesus gives Spirit and life through his words; and second, the ascending Son of Man sends the life-giving Spirit.[582] In Jesus' mission the

---

3:16), the same spirit is portrayed as motivator in John 14:16, 26; 15:26. See Brant, *John*, 86.

[577] Witherington, *John's Wisdom*, 121.

[578] See Brant, *John*, 124-126.

[579] Gerald L. Borchert, *John 1-11*, The New American Commentary (Nashville: B & H Publishing Company, 1996), 1:275. Neyrey says that, "only 'spirit gives life,' which is a gift from heaven bestowed by God on select people (see 6:37, 44-46). This 'spirit,' moreover, is not attached to any rite but linked with special knowledge and teaching: 'The words that I have spoken to you are spirit and life' (6:63)." Neyrey, *The Gospel of John*, 132.

[580] Schnackenburg, *The Gospel according to St. John*, 2:72.

[581] See Witherington, *John's Wisdom*, 160.

[582] Schnackenburg, *The Gospel according to St. John*, 2:73.

endowment of the Holy Spirit is adhered as a motivating force. The following things are important to make note at this section: first, Jesus' mission was started with the initiation of the Holy Spirit; second, Jesus' words are inspired by the Spirit; third, his deeds are motivated by the Spirit; fourth, as Holy Spirit is the provider of life, Jesus came to give life in abundance; and fifth, both the Son and the Spirit proceed from the Father. This Trinitarian connection is at the center of Jesus' mission within the narrative framework of the Fourth Gospel. In that sense, John's portrayal of the missional-pneumatology is well-attached to Christology. As Holy Spirit is a divine reality that is well attached to the reality of God and Jesus, a reader of the Gospel can witness the gnomic and universalistic function of the triune God.[583]

Transition from Jesus' Mission to that of the Disciples

There is a shift of emphasis happens between the public mission of Jesus narrated in 1:19-12:50 and the private mission among the disciples narrated in 13:1-17:26. While in 1:19-12:50 the emphasis is upon the endowment of the Spirit in Jesus' involvements in mission, in 13:1-17:26 the emphasis is laid on the promise of the coming of the Spirit upon the disciples. In 7:37-39, the promise of the Holy Spirit is analeptically narrated. The metaphors like thirst and water in 7:37-39 are brought to the foreground in order to introduce the coming of the Holy Spirit in relation to the future mission of the disciples.[584] After the use of the metaphor of water and the themes such as worship and Spirit in 4:21-24, the narrator once again uses them in the context of the Feast of Tabernacles. It is on the last and greatest of the day of the feast, Jesus inspires his interlocutors that if they are thirsty come and drink from him. As a fulfillment of the Scripture he offers them streams of living water flow from himself.[585]

The metaphorical expressions such as "thirsty," "drink," "streams," "water," and "flowing" attune the readers' attention toward the overflowing of the Holy Spirit (v. 39).[586] Jesus' statements are analeptic to the promises in the Farewell Discourse (chaps. 14, 15, and 16) as well as the post-resurrection

---

[583] Johnson Thomaskutty, "The Spirit's Witness in John and the Apocalypse," *Mission After Pentecost: The Witness of the Spirit from Genesis to Revelation,* Ed. Amos Yong (Grand Rapids: Baker Academic Press, 2019), 251.

[584] See Borchert, *John 1-11*, 289-291.

[585] See Psa 77:16, 20 LXX (= 78:16, 20 Eng.); Zech 14:8. Schnackenburg says, "In Jesus Christ the hopes of Israel are fulfilled: he is the holy rock from which anyone who thirsts can drink 'living water' and quench his thirst forever (cf. 4:14; 6:35), a spring from which flows a richer, more lasting, more uncheckable river than the rivers of paradise, or even those streams which burst forth in the eschatological temple; rivers of life and salvation (cf. 19:34), an image of the Holy Spirit." See Schnackenburg, *The Gospel according to St. John*, 2:156.

[586] Borchert, *John 1-11*, 291.

experience narrated in 20:21-23. The expression "those who believed in him were later to receive" restricts the endowment of the Holy Spirit to the believing community.[587] Holy Spirit is promised as a sign and a thumbing expression for the believers. The narrator clearly states that the Spirit was not yet given to the community as it was always associated with the mission of Jesus. As the Spirit's coming upon the community is associated with Jesus' glorification, the accomplishment of the mission of Jesus and the ushering of the Spirit upon the believing community are in focus (v. 39). Schnackenburg says that, "The gift of life, which he promises immediately to those who believe in him, will only really be conferred upon those whom the Father has given him when he has returned to his Father and been glorified by him (17:1-2)."[588] In that sense, the coming of the Holy Spirit upon the disciples marks the beginning of the Johannine Pentecost and the direct involvement of the disciples in the mission of God.[589]

The analepsis in 7:37-39 comes to an extended prolepsis and a greater promise in chaps. 14, 15, and 16.[590] In John 14, 15 and 16, Jesus speaks about the Holy Spirit in the context of his private conversations with the disciples (14:15-17, 26; 15:26-27; 16:12-15).[591] While the presence of the Holy Spirit is obvious in the ministry of Jesus in the Book of Signs (1:19-12:50) and he assures the endowment of the Holy Spirit upon the disciples in 7:37-39, in the Farewell Discourse Jesus promises the coming of the Comforter/the Spirit of Truth in more concrete terms.[592] As the glorification of the Son of Man is approaching, Jesus promises the endowment of the Holy Spirit upon the disciples. As the Farewell Discourse emphasizes the theme and the commandment of love, which is the context where he offers the disciples the gift of the Holy Spirit. The love of Jesus seeks responsible love from the disciples.[593] Witherington states that, "In 14:15-16 we have a conditional statement, in which all depends on the believers' loving Jesus. Notice the juxtaposition of loving and keeping Jesus' commandments, which

---

[587] See Borchert, *John 1-11*, 291.

[588] Schnackenburg, *The Gospel according to St. John*, 2:157.

[589] Brant says, "For those who familiar with the book of Acts, John seems to refer to the gift of the Spirit at Pentecost, but John will confute Luke's timeline by narrating the receipt of the Spirit in a resurrection appearance scene (20:22)." See Brant, *John*, 140; cf. Schnackenburg, *The Gospel according to St. John*, 2:157.

[590] More understanding about the term parakletos, refer to Behm, "Parakletos," *Theological Dictionary of the New Testament*, ed. and tran. Geoffrey W. Bromiley (Grand Rapids: Eerdmans, 1967), 801.

[591] Jerald L. Borchert, *John 12-21*, The New American Commentary (Nashville: B & H Publishers, 2002), 120-126.

[592] See Neyrey, *The Gospel of John*, 147-148.

[593] See Neyrey, *The Gospel of John*, 244-245, 249.

leads to his sending the Paraklete."[594] The Comforter comes to the disciples only when Jesus asks the Father (14:15-17). The Father is promising the disciples another Comforter. Though the concept *Parakletos* is adopted from the Greco-Roman legal context, John gives a new meaning to it. While in the Greco-Roman context *parakletos* was considered as a "helper in court" or "one who is summoned" as part of the judiciary system, in John the "indwelling" of the *Parakletos* is at view.[595]

The *Paraklete* shall represent and function like Jesus. Hence the disciples need not be paralyzed by sadness as *Paraklete* would help them to constantly realize the presence of Christ.[596] The word used with *Parakletos* is not *heteron* but *allon* (14:16).[597] The 'another' should not be taken as different but of same kind.[598] That shows that Holy Spirit proceeds not as a different entity; but as a person of the trinity with the same substance.[599] Turner says that:

> (1) both "come forth"/are "sent" from the Father into the world (3:16-17; 5:43; 16:27-28; 18:37 par. 14:26; 15:26; 16:7-8, 13); (2) both are called "holy" (6:39 par. 14:26) and are characterized by "the truth" (14:6 par. 14:17; 15:26; 16:13); (3) if Jesus is the great teacher (cf. 13:13-14), the Paraklete will "teach you . . . all things" (14:26); and (4) just as the Messiah bears witness to God and reveals all things (4:25-26; cf. 1:18; 3:34-36; etc.)—supremely himself and the Father—so too the Paraklete will witness to and reveal especially the glorified Son (15:26-27; 16:13-14).[600]

Here the *Parakletos* is offered in the context of Jesus' glorification. F. F. Bruce calls this "another Paraklete" as Jesus' *Alter Ego* who is to be with the disciples permanently.[601] Parakletos comes as the *Alter Ego* of Jesus in order to continue the mission among the disciples in particular and the world in general. The title given to the *Parakletos*, the Spirit of Truth, goes well with Jesus' own

---

[594] The fulfilment of commandments as an expression of love evokes the Shema (Deut 6:4-9). See Brant, *John*, 214; Witherington, *John's Wisdom*, 250.

[595] John Ashton, "Paraklete," *The Anchor Bible Dictionary*, ed. David Noel Freedman (New York: Doubleday, 1992), 5:152.

[596] Schnackenburg, *The Gospel according to St. John*, 3:126.

[597] Cf. *Jub* 25:14; *T. Jud* 20:1-5; 1QS 3:18-25.

[598] D. A. Carson, *The Farewell Discourse and Final Prayer of Jesus: As Exposition of John 14-17* (Grand Rapids: Baker Book House, 1980), 50.

[599] Witherington states that, "Jesus promises to send to his disciples one called in the Greek *parakletos*, and more to the point is said to be *another parakletos*, which intimates that Jesus was the first one." See Witherington, *John's Wisdom*, 251.

[600] Turner, "Holy Spirit," 349.

[601] F. F. Bruce, *The Gospel of John: Introduction, Exposition, and Notes* (Grand Rapids: Eerdmans, 1983), 302.

identity as the Truth of God (1:17; 14:6). As the Holy Spirit is introduced as the Parakletos, its role and function can be understood as a teacher/counselor/advocate/comforter in relation to the disciples.[602] Moreover, the Paraklete is also considered as *Christomorph*, a person who perpetuates Jesus' mission on earth.[603] In other words, Paraklete mirrors Jesus' earthly mission by guiding the disciples in the way of truth in a hostile situation.

In Jesus' promise concerning the coming of the Holy Spirit upon the disciples, he stresses the fact that the world cannot accept him because they can neither see him nor know him. In that sense, the Holy Spirit functions in an entirely different way in comparison to the work of Jesus.[604] The Holy Spirit lives with the believers and will be in them (v. 17). That means, the function of the Holy Spirit is more personal to the believers and the world can understand its functions only through the believing community. As the community of the believers is possessed with the Holy Spirit, their function shall be different from that of the rest of the humanity. The appearance and disappearance mode of the Holy Spirit is made obvious to the community of the believers. Jesus comforts the community of believers by stating that he won't leave them orphans but he will come with them (v. 18).[605] Thus the Parakletos functions as the presence of Jesus to the community while he is absent. Holy Spirit's function of indwelling, teaching, and enabling in relation to the believer is emphasized in the Farewell Discourse.

In 14:26, Jesus declares that the Counselor is going to be sent by the Father in his name. The function of the Holy Spirit as a teacher who reminds the disciples everything that Jesus said is promised here. The following things are important to note in the text: first, the Holy Spirit proceeds from the Father; second, the Father sends the Spirit in Jesus' name; third, the Spirit functions in the role of a teacher; and fourth, it reminds of everything that Jesus spoke.[606] The phrase 'in my name' refers to unity with Christ.[607] The Trinitarian aspects of the divine realities are informed here. The believers are assured that the presence of Jesus is going to be continued even when he is absent. In that

---

[602] Witherington states that, "the term 'Paraklete' should be translated 'Advocate' and it connotes someone's agent in a judicial situation." See Witherington, *John's Wisdom*, 250.

[603] See Andreas Hoeck, "The Johannine Paraklete: Herald of the Eschaton," *J. Biblic. Pneumatological Res. 4* (2012), 27-28.

[604] See Brant, *John*, 215.

[605] See Brant, *John*, 215.

[606] Borchert, *John 12-21*, 132-133.

[607] V. George Shillington, "The Spirit-Paraclete as Jesus' Alter Ego in the Fourth Gospel (John 14-16)," *Vis. Winn. Man 13.1* (2012), 36.

sense, the mission of God is going to be flourished through the agency of the Holy Spirit during the post-resurrection period.[608] Witherington states that,

> If we examine all the passages in the farewell discourses in which the Spirit is referred to, we see that the Spirit has in the main a threefold task: (1) to indwell the believer and convey the divine presence and peace, including Jesus' presence to the believer (14:17-20, 27); (2) to teach the believer and to guide the believer into all truth and to testify to the believer about and on behalf of Jesus (14:26; 15:26); (3) to enable the disciples to testify about Jesus to the world and by means of the Spirit's guidance and power convict the world about sin, righteousness, and judgment (15:26-27; 16:8-11).[609]

Further in 15:26-27, the function of the *Parakletos* is described in the following way: first, Jesus will send the Parakletos from the presence of the Father; second, it is the Spirit of Truth that goes out from the Father; third, it testifies about Jesus; and fourth, as the Son testifies about the Father and the Spirit testifies about the Son, the disciples are commanded to testify concerning the Son.[610] The phrase "bear witness" has forensic connotations. So, as a witness Paraklete represents the disciples there by vindicating their case while refuting the opponents' accusations.[611] In that sense, Paraklete can be viewed as a "defense attorney."[612] The identification of the Son with the Father makes it obvious that when someone testifies the Son it also includes the testimony of the Father. In that sense, the Trinitarian understanding of the Fourth Gospel comes to a full circle in its *Parakletos* passages.

In 16:12-15, Jesus further speaks about the mission of the Holy Spirit. The following things are made obvious in the passage: first, Jesus has much more to say to the disciples, even things that they cannot bear; second, what is left by Jesus is going to be filled by the Spirit of Truth as s/he is going to guide the disciples in all truth; third, s/he will not speak on her/his own, but tell only what s/he hears from above; fourth, s/he will speak what is yet to come; fifth, the goal of the Holy Spirit is giving glory to the Son; sixth, s/he takes from Jesus and makes things known to the disciples (vv. 14, 15); and seventh, all that belongs to the Father is of the Son, that is what the Spirit is aware of and makes that known. From the above points one can understand that the Spirit

---

[608] Brant says that, "the Paraklete serves as a comforter and a reminder to do God's work just as Jesus has done the Father's work." See Brant, *John*, 216.

[609] Witherington, *John's Wisdom*, 251.

[610] Borchert, *John 12-21*, 159-160.

[611] See Jey J. Kanagaraj, *The Gospel of John: A Commentary*, First Edition (Secunderabad: OM Books, 2005), 515-516.

[612] Shillington, "The Spirit-Paraklete as Jesus' Alter Ego in the Fourth Gospel," 36.

proceeds from above, knows the mysteries of the Father and the Son, stays with the disciples in the absence of the Son, and reveals the heavenly truths in order to guide the disciples in the world from below. While in the Book of Signs the endowment of the Spirit upon Jesus was at focus, in the Farewell Discourse the promise of the endowment of the Holy Spirit upon the disciples is at the core of the discussion.

Johannine Pentecost and the Preparations for World Mission

In 20:21-23, the narrator demonstrates the Johannine Pentecost. While in the Book of Acts the experience of the Holy Spirit was made explicit after the ascension of Jesus (Acts 2:1-4; cf. 1:8), in John it happens as an expansion of Jesus' post-resurrection ministry.[613] While the public mission of Jesus explicitly manifests the Spirit-endowment upon Jesus, the Farewell Discourse demonstrates the promise of the Holy Spirit as another Comforter. In the context of the post-resurrection, the disciples are endowed with the Holy Spirit. In that way, the narrator speaks coherently about the pattern of the Johannine pneumatology. Jesus' wish of peace is repeated in vv. 19b, 21, and 26b. The tripartite repetitive use of the expression "Peace be with you" emphasizes the following aspects: first, Jesus is indeed the resurrected Lord and his presence and wish is revealed to the disciples; second, the peace of Jesus and the mission of the Holy Spirit are integrally connected; and third, the resurrected Lord passes the peace of God and the endowment of the Holy Spirit upon the disciples.[614] The resurrected Lord equips the disciples to receive the peace of God so that they may carry the mission of God. This preparatory aspect is obvious in the text as the involvement of the disciples in general and Mary Magdalene, Thomas, Peter, and the Beloved Disciple in particular are brought to the resurrection and post-resurrection contexts. Hereafter the disciples move away from the background to the foreground as they are the active protagonists of the story.

One of the most significant mission statements of the Fourth Gospel is presented here: "As the Father has sent me, I am sending you." The mission formula used so far is that the Father is the sender, the truth of salvation is the message, Jesus is the messenger, and the world is the receiver. Hereafter the formula is changed to the following sequence: Jesus is the sender, the truth of salvation and the power of resurrection as the message, the disciples are the messengers, and the world is the receiver. In both the cases, the endowment of the Holy Spirit is the marking point. Moloney comments that,

---

[613] Borchert, *John 12-21*, 306-311.

[614] Francis J. Moloney, *The Gospel of John*, Sacra Pagina 4 (Collegeville: The Liturgical Press, 1989/1998), 529-536.

> The reader is aware that the Spirit is *with* the community and *in* the community and will remain with the community forever (cf. 14:16-17), but the community must reach beyond its own borders to continue the mission of Jesus, so that the world might know and believe that he is the Sent One of the Father (cf. 17:21, 23). The Spirit will bear witness to Jesus in his absence so that the disciples, who have been with him from the beginning, might also be witnesses (cf. 15:26-27).[615]

As the Father has sent the Son and the Spirit has endowed him, now the Son sends the disciples and the same Holy Spirit overshadows their mission. As the *sent* one of God became the *sender*, the disciples are expected to be *senders* for the future mission.[616] Thus, the continued mission of the Holy Spirit is brought to the foreground through the narrative dynamism of the Fourth Gospel.

Jesus' breathing on the disciples is in several ways reminiscent to the act of God in Gen 2:7. But, there is a significant difference between the Genesis narrative and the narrative in John. In Genesis, God breathed into the nostrils of the man "the breath of life." Through God's activity of breathing, the man became a living being. This is told in the context of creating the human being from the dust of the ground. In the Fourth Gospel, Jesus breathes on the disciples the Holy Spirit that empowers them for mission. Even though there are terminological similarities and contextual resemblances, the semantic differences are conspicuous. Jesus' action of breathing makes him on par with the God of the Old Testament. In that sense, the following Trinitarian formula can be derived: first, the Father as one breathes [the breath of life] sends the Son in order to fulfill the heavenly mission on earth and the same Father sends the Holy Spirit in the name of Jesus; second, the Son as the one breathes the Holy Spirit upon the disciples and sends them for the mission of the Father/Son; and the Holy Spirit proceeds from the presence of the Father and comes upon the disciples in the name of the Son. The mission of the Father-Son-Spirit flourishes in relation to the disciples. This Trinitarian formula is at the heart of the Fourth Gospel.

As the Johannine Pentecost is introduced, the disciples are prepared for the mission of God and also they are brought to new convictions. Jesus' imperative to receive the Holy Spirit inaugurates a new phase of mission within the narrative framework of John. Until now the disciples were more dependent of Jesus and independent of the Holy Spirit; but from hereafter they are more dependent of the Holy Spirit and independent of the presence of the earthly Jesus. Under the guidance of the Holy Spirit, they involve in the mission of God more convincingly. If they forgive people's sins, they are forgiven; if

---

615 Moloney, *The Gospel of John*, 532.

616 See Moloney, *The Gospel of John*, 530-533.

they do not forgive them, they are not forgiven. The mission of forgiveness of sins is at the center of divine mission and the disciples are made qualified for that. They are given full power to execute the mission of Jesus through the initiatives of the Holy Spirit. Through the above details a reader of the Fourth Gospel can understand that John's pneumatology is well developed and orienting the disciples toward the mission of God. Thus, John's pneumatology is gnomic and universalistic in its essence.[617]

Conclusion

The Gospel of John presents the role and function of the Holy Spirit in more convincing terms in comparison to the Old Testament and the rest of the New Testament. In the Fourth Gospel, we see a development as the narrative framework progresses in pneumatological terms. In the first half of the Gospel (1:19-12:50), the Holy Spirit appears as a motivating force in the mission and ministry of Jesus. The narrator describes how Jesus was endowed by the Spirit during his public mission. Here the role of the Spirit is explained as one who indwells in Jesus for speaking the words of eternal truth and acting the works of God. A transition is clear when he promises the overflow of the Spirit among the disciples in 7:37-39. The promise statement in 7:37-39 can be considered as an analepsis to the utterances of Jesus in the Farewell Discourse (chaps. 14-16). In the Farewell Discourse (chaps. 14-16), Jesus promises the coming of the Parakletos in a detailed description. Thus a transfer of the Spirit of God from Jesus' mission to the mission of the disciples is emphasized. The promise of the coming of the Parakletos reaches into fulfillment when Jesus breathes on the disciples during his post-resurrection appearance (20:21-23). In that sense, the manifestation of the Holy Spirit is unique, developmental, and missional within the narrative framework of the Fourth Gospel.

The Johannine pneumatology outlines the following missional aspects: first, the Spirit of God empowers Jesus, the disciples, and the future generation of believers for missional tasks. The context of the Parakletos passages in John is Jesus' trial and the upcoming persecution. John explains here how God helps his disciples once when they "indwell" in the Holy Spirit; second, the role and function of the Parakletos as a teacher/comforter is introduced to foreground and reaffirm the continued presence of Jesus and the continuance of the mission of God in this world; and third, in the 'vertical' and at the same time 'horizontal' eschatological perspective, eternal life is accessible to people through establishing a closer relationship with the world 'from above' and continuing to 'indwell' in the Holy Spirit to achieve the future glorious reign of God. The personal, communal, missional, and gnomic

[617] Thomaskutty, "The Spirit's Witness in John and the Apocalypse," 251.

aspects of the Holy Spirit can be attuned to the people of God beyond time and space aspects. In that sense, the Fourth Evangelist develops a missional-pneumatological framework that persuades the reader with gnomic and atemporal perspectives.

Chapter 7

Explorations of *Prosperity* in the Fourth Gospel

Introduction

The Gospel of John presents the aspects of wealth, health, and happiness from an entirely different standpoint. The prologue of the Gospel (1:1-18) emphasizes that prosperity is possible only through Jesus Christ. The aspect of prosperity is described in terms of holistic development of human beings rather than mere material improvements. In 1:1-3, the narrator introduces Jesus the Word and states that "All things came into being through him, and without him not one thing came into being" (v. 3). This narratorial statement makes the reader aware that the entire created world is the handiwork of Jesus/God and that everything belongs to and flourishes from Him. It goes well with Paul's statement in Col 1:16: "All things have been created through him and for him." John the Baptist testifies about the incarnation of Jesus as follows: "The true light, which enlightens everyone, was coming into the world" (1:9). His utterance here gives a clear indication that through Jesus all can be enlightened. The narrator further makes it clear that, "He [Jesus] came to his own, and his own people did not accept him. But to all who received him, who believed in his name, he gave power to become children of God" (v. 12). Being part of the family of God is emphasized as one of the highest priorities of human life. Receiving the Son as the greatest gift and accepting grace and truth are emphasized in 1:16-17. Thus, the prologue puts a way forward for John's distinctive and Christ-centered understanding of prosperity.

The prologue narrates that prosperity in John cannot be viewed from a materialistic perspective. Rather it is rooted in Christ and at the same time distinct from the contemporary understanding of the term. The following questions are significant in the process of exploring the concept of prosperity and its related aspects such as health, wealth and happiness in John: How the network of themes and the development of characterization facilitate the understanding of prosperity in John? How John's Gospel is a corrective to the postmodern understanding of prosperity? What are the ways and means through which the narrator rhetorizes the concept of prosperity? How the aspects of prosperity enable the narrator to develop a gnomic maxim within the Gospel?

Prospering in Faith

The Fourth Gospel emphasizes the aspect of believing in Jesus with priority and significance.[618] The ministry of John the Baptist was intended to lead people to believing in Jesus (1:7).[619] Believing in Jesus means accepting his name and thus becoming the children of God (1:12).[620] The belief of the disciples is not merely based on their witness about Jesus' public ministry; but it is also rooted in his resurrection.[621] The disciples believed the words of Jesus, his demonstration of words through action, and in the rootedness of his utterances and actions in the Scripture.[622] All of these aspects together contributed to the increase of their faith in Jesus (2:22). The narrator states that believing in Jesus enables people to be relieved from all sorts of condemnation. That further means that people's belief in the name of Jesus saves them from eternal punishment (3:18).[623] In that sense, the Fourth Evangelist orchestrates believing as a soteriological terminology. John 4:41-42 outlines three aspects to increase people's faith: first, what others say about Jesus; second, hearing what Jesus himself says; and third, come to the knowledge that Jesus is truly the Savior of the World.[624] The Samaritans flourished in their faith through all these processes.[625]

The Fourth Gospel reiterates that believing in the Father enables people to increase their faith and knowledge in Jesus (5:37; 6:29; 12:44-46; 14:10-11;

---

[618] See France, "Faith," 224-225.

[619] *Expository Dictionary of the Bible* defines that, "*Pisteuō* most commonly means 'believe' in reference to saving faith in Christ." See John 1:7; 3:15-16, 36; 4:39-42; 6:29-30; 7:38-39; 11:25-26; 16:27-28. See Stephen D. Renn, ed., *Expository Dictionary of the Bible* (Peabody: Hendrickson Publishers, 2010), 106.

[620] See Beasley-Murray, *John*, 13.

[621] Schnackenburg, *The Gospel according to St. John*, 1:353.

[622] See Beasley-Murray, *John*, 41.

[623] See Renn, *Expository Dictionary of the Bible*, 106.

[624] Beasley-Murray, *John*, 65.

[625] See Schnackenburg, *The Gospel according to St. John*, 1:456-458.

16:30-31).[626] In the story of the Royal official, believing is demonstrated in a progressive manner and also it is integrally connected to knowledge (4:43-54).[627] As a person of honor and status, the Royal man increases his faith and finally his entire household believe in Jesus (4:53).[628] Believing in Moses ultimately leads people to believing in Jesus (2:22; 5:46-47). Peter believed and came to the saving knowledge that Jesus is the Holy One of God (6:69).[629] Similarly, Mary of Bethany declared that Jesus is the Christ, the Son of God (11:27).[630] Through their declarations, Peter and Mary express their growth of faith in Jesus. The overflow of the Spirit in the life of a believer is delineated in 7:37-39.[631] Human beings can escape from their sins only through putting their faith in Jesus (8:24).[632] The man born blind increases his faith through various utterances about Jesus: "the man they call Jesus" (9:11, 12); "prophet" (9:17b); "Jesus is from God" (9:33); "Lord" (9:38a); and through the act of worshipping him (9:38b).[633] His final declaration in 9:38a is the end result of a series of faith reactions. Thus, the Johannine narrator demonstrates that believing in Jesus is one of the key factors for human beings to increase in life.[634]

As Jesus is the good shepherd, his sheep are expected to hear his voice and follow him. Those who listen to his voice and follow him are guaranteed the benefits of eternal life (10:26-28; 20:31).[635] When people believe in Jesus, it assures them to see the glory of God (11:40).[636] Unbelief in Jesus and in his works is understood as lack of progress in life and that in turn is considered as lack of prosperity and spiritual maturity (12:37-38).[637] As the Father and Son are one, the believers are expected to reach the maturity of oneness. The virtue of oneness among the believers inspires the world to believe in Jesus (17:21;

---

[626] *Knowing* (*ginōskein*) and *believing* (*pisteuein*) together occur in four passages (4:53; 6:69; 10:38; and 17:8). However, the cognates of *ginōskein* like *oida* and *pisteuein* also occur in 4:42; 8:31-32; 16:30; and 19:35.

[627] See Thomaskutty, *Dialogue in the Book of Signs*, 170; also see Moloney, *The Gospel of John*, 151; cf. Stibbe, *John*, 72; Bennema, *Encountering Jesus*, 96.

[628] See Witherington, *John's Wisdom*, 126-130.

[629] See Barrett, *The Gospel according to St. John*, 301; Carson, *The Gospel according to John*, 233; Thomaskutty, *Dialogue in the Book of Signs*, 238-239; Witherington, *John's Wisdom*, 161.

[630] Culpepper, *Anatomy of the Fourth Gospel*, 140-142; Thomaskutty, *Dialogue in the Book of Signs*, 380-385.

[631] See Schnackenburg, *The Gospel according to St. John*, 2:152-156.

[632] Brant, *John*, 144.

[633] Thomaskutty, *Dialogue in the Book of Signs*, 349-350.

[634] Culpepper, *Anatomy of the Fourth Gospel*, 139-140.

[635] See Moloney, *The Gospel of John*, 320.

[636] Moloney, *The Gospel of John*, 342.

[637] Schnackenburg, *The Gospel according to St. John*, 2:412-413.

cf. 19:35).[638] In John, there is a connection between seeing and believing and in that way the disciples are instructed to believe based on their witness of the events around Jesus (20:8, 27, 29).[639] But, the *makarism* in 20:29b emphasizes the aspect of prospering in faith even without seeing evidences.[640]

The above discussion gives us the following understanding regarding belief in the Fourth Gospel: first, believing in Jesus is possible through believing his words and his actions; second, there is a development expected from 'no faith' to 'developing faith' and from 'developing faith' to 'mature faith;'[641] third, those who increase in faith are expected to believe even without seeing evidences; fourth, growth in faith assures people's connectivity with Jesus/God and the resultant experience of eternal life; fifth, those who grow in faith are transformed as 'children of God'; sixth, there is a bifurcation between those who believe (i.e., those qualified to live forever) and those who do not believe (i.e., those condemned); and seventh, the aspect of increase or prosperity is understood and measured based on people's faith in Jesus.[642] As a whole, prosperity according to John functions within the Christological and soteriological framework of the Gospel and that can be achieved through appropriating faith in Jesus.

Prospering in Love

John's Gospel affirms that God's love for the world is the basis for human salvation (3:16).[643] But, people's love for darkness rather than light brought a dualistic friction in the world from below (3:19).[644] The Jews were not having the love of God in them (5:42) that made them to reject Jesus (1:10-11; 5:43).[645] While the Jews represent the unrepentant nature of the world, Jesus demonstrates the love of God through his ministry in the world. When someone accepts God as Father, s/he can do that only through loving Jesus (8:42).[646] In the family of Martha, Mary, and Lazarus of Bethany, the narrator portrays the mutual love relationship between Jesus and the members of the

---

638 See France, "Faith," 224-225.

639 Thomaskutty, *Saint Thomas the Apostle*, 64-68.

640 Culpepper, *Anatomy of the Fourth Gospel*, 123-124.

641 See Thomaskutty, *Dialogue in the Book of Signs*, 173-175.

642 See France, "Faith," 224-225.

643 See Schnackenburg, *The Gospel according to St. John*, 1:398-400.

644 See Witherington, *John's Wisdom*, 103; Schnackenburg, *The Gospel according to St. John*, 1:403-405.

645 See Leon Morris, "Love," *Dictionary of Jesus and the Gospels* (Downers Grove: InterVarsity Press, 1992), 494; cf. Schnackenburg, *The Gospel according to St. John*, 2:126-128.

646 See Witherington, *John's Wisdom*, 177-178; Schnackenburg, *The Gospel according to St. John*, 2:212.

family (11:5, 36).[647] In 13:1, it is further stated that Jesus demonstrated his love for his own. To fulfill the love of God, human beings are expected to "loving one another" (13:34). As Jesus loved the disciples even at a risk of his life, the disciples are ought to love one another (13:34). Seeing the love of the disciples among themselves, the world can perceive that they are the followers of Jesus (13:35).[648] Thus, the Johannine narrator emphasizes the need of fostering both the horizontal and the vertical love relationship over against all other material pleasures and blessings of the world.[649]

In the Fourth Gospel, loving Jesus and obeying his commandments are integrally connected. Obedience to Jesus is the outward expression of people's love for him (14:15, 21, 24).[650] People can receive the favor of the Father only through their love for Jesus. The Father and the Son come to those who love God/Son and make their home with them (14:23). In Jesus, God's demonstration of love and obedience are knitted together (14:31).[651] The aspect of love flourishes from the benevolence of the heavens: first, as the lover par excellence, the God of heavens lavishes his love on the Son; second, the Father's love reaches the people through the mediation of the Son; third, the people of the world should love Jesus to fulfill the commandments of Moses; and fourth, people's love among themselves directs the attention of the world toward God/Jesus. Human beings can prosper in their life only through stabilizing their relationship with God/Jesus and with the fellow human beings.[652]

As Jesus instructs his disciples to remain in his love, the disciples are expected to nurture their faith in the love of God and prosper in their living together (15:9-10). The epitome of Christian love is laying down life for the other (15:12-13, 17).[653] Jesus' death on the cross is the visible demonstration of God's love for the world. Jesus instructs his disciples saying that "you are my friends if you do what I command" (15:14).[654] People can achieve eternal prosperity through the means of developing friendship with Jesus. As the Father loved Jesus, Jesus loves the disciples. God expects the disciples remain in that love (15:9).[655] The love of God/Jesus for the world is the basis for

---

[647] See Thomaskutty, Dialogue in the Book of Signs, 370-374; Schnackenburg, *The Gospel according to St. John*, 2:323, 337; Esler and Piper, *Lazarus, Mary, and Martha*, 75-103.

[648] See Culpepper, *Anatomy of the Fourth Gospel*, 115-125.

[649] See J. R. Michaels, "Commandment," *Dictionary of Jesus and the Gospels* (Downers Grove: InterVarsity Press, 1992), 135-136.

[650] See Michaels, "Commandment," 135-136; Witherington, *John's Wisdom*, 103.

[651] Brant, *John*, 215-216.

[652] Michaels, "Commandment," 135-136.

[653] Witherington, *John's Wisdom*, 259.

[654] Michaels, "Commandment," 135-136.

[655] Brant, *John*, 218.

the disciples to practice love among themselves. Loving God and believing in Jesus are the requirements for Christian living (16:27). As the Father/Son loves the disciples, the disciples are ought to love (17:23).[656] As God's love is everlasting, the disciples of Jesus are expected to prosper and align themselves in the same love (17:24).[657] In his prayer in 17:26, Jesus reiterates that having God's love means having Jesus in/among the disciples.[658] In 21:15-17, Jesus initiates to bring Peter back to the love of Jesus/God to make him a leading figure.[659] Through all these means the narrator portrays divine love as the kernel point for Christian maturity and prosperity.

The above discussion invites the attention of the reader toward an integrative and interlocking relationship within John's Gospel: first, the Father's love for the world is everlasting; second, the Father loves the world through giving his begotten Son; third, the Son lavishes God's love upon the people of the world; fourth, only those who accept Jesus can accept God; fifth, people can accept the love of God only through the means of accepting each other and lavishing God's love upon the other; sixth, the unity of the Father and the Son is a paradigm for the disciples to cherish oneness among themselves; and seventh, oneness among the disciples is missional as that directs the attention of the world toward God/Jesus. The narrator of the story and the protagonist together invite the readers to prosper in the love of God/Jesus that flourishes from above. This is the standard of prosperity demonstrated within the narrative annals of John.

Prospering in Knowledge

The macro-structure of the Fourth Gospel develops through some significant ironies: "He came to that which was his own, but his own did not receive him" (1:11) and "among you stands one you do not know" (1:26).[660] In the Gospel, Jesus' "all-knowing" perspective is in sharp conflict with his interlocutors' misunderstanding and "unknowing" perspective (8:14, 19, 55).[661] His conversation with a leading Pharisee and teacher of the law in 3:10-15 reveals this contrast.[662] Jesus's statement to the Samaritan woman, "You Samaritans worship what you do not know; we [the Jews] worship what we do know, for Salvation is from the Jews," is a double-edged criticism toward both the

[656] See Culpepper, *Anatomy of the Fourth Gospel*, 115-125.

[657] See Moloney, *The Gospel of John*, 480; Beasley-Murray, *John*, 304.

[658] Brant, *John*, 227.

[659] See Witherington, *John's Wisdom*, 355-356.

[660] Brant, *John*, 48.

[661] See Moloney, *The Gospel of John*, 268-269.

[662] Thomaskutty, *Dialogue in the Book of Signs*, 118.

Samaritans and the Jews (4:22).[663] In Jesus' criticism, while the Samaritans do not know what they worship, the Jews do not perceive that salvation is from them.[664] Jesus reveals the latter fact through his conversation with Nicodemus (3:10-15) and the Jews as a whole (chaps. 7-8).[665] But, the Samaritans surpassed the Jews in their understanding of the truth by acknowledging that Jesus is truly the Savior of the world (4:42).[666] Throughout the Gospel, Jesus emphasizes that the people of the world should come to the saving knowledge.

Peter's belief that Jesus is the Holy One of God is based on certain knowledge about him. Through his utterance "we believe and know" (6:69), it is made clear that knowing and believing are integrally connected.[667] In 7:28-29, Jesus states that true knowledge is to know both the *sender* (the Father) and the *sent one* (the Son). In the Gospel, knowing the Son is tantamount with knowing the Father.[668] If they know both the sender and the sent one, then they can really become his disciples (8:31).[669] Moreover, it is stated that holding the teachings of Jesus and knowing the truth ultimately lead people to the position of enjoying the freedom (8:32).[670] The man born blind progresses in his knowledge about Jesus and that enables him to be a sheep of the flock (9:25; 10:4). The words of Jesus make it clear that knowing the voice of the shepherd and following him is true discipleship.[671] The mutual relationship between believing and knowing the shepherd is emphasized in 10:14 and 27.[672]

While "walking in the light" is identified as a figure of knowing, "walking in the darkness" is perceived as a mark of unknowing (12:35).[673] In 13:17, knowing and doing the will of God are knitted together. In that connection, "loving one another" is the fundamental discipline to make others know that the followers are indeed the disciples of Jesus (13:34-35).[674] Similarly, the virtue of unity among the disciples is a directive that brings knowledge among the people (17:23). The Johannine narrator emphasizes that those who know Jesus shall know the Holy Spirit also (14:17).[675] In the Gospel, on the one hand,

---

[663] Brant, *John*, 86.

[664] Thomaskutty, *Dialogue in the Book of Signs*, 146-147.

[665] Schnackenburg, *The Gospel according to St. John*, 1:375-379, 392-398.

[666] Thomaskutty, *Dialogue in the Book of Signs*, 161-162.

[667] Brant, *John*, 125-126.

[668] Brant, *John*, 138.

[669] See Beasley-Murray, *John*, 133.

[670] Brant, *John*, 144.

[671] Schnackenburg, *The Gospel according to St. John*, 2:282-283.

[672] Brant, *John*, 160-163.

[673] Witherington, *John's Wisdom*, 225-226.

[674] See Beasley-Murray, *John*, 247-248.

[675] See Witherington, *John's Wisdom*, 250.

the world's unknowing is repeatedly stated (15:21), on the other hand, the disciples of Jesus overcome it.[676] The Fourth Gospel describes the following things clearly: first, knowledge about Jesus leads people for their knowledge about the Father; second, knowledge functions both as a prerequisite to and after effect of believing Jesus; third, prospering in knowledge is one of the significant requirements in Christian living; fourth, knowing the Father and the Son leads people to the knowledge of the Holy Spirit; and fifth, the followers of Jesus are expected to make others know about Jesus through their oneness. Thus the Gospel of John emphasizes the aspect of knowledge about Jesus and its steady progress that ultimately leads people to a mature faith.

Having the Experience of Abundant Life

In the Fourth Gospel, Jesus appears as the source of life.[677] In John, life/eternal life is not limited to a future age but can be realized in the present by the one who believes in Jesus (3:15-18, 36).[678] The metaphor of water is mostly used in connection to the eternal life experience (4:14).[679] Similarly, the metaphor of reaping and harvest is not used in a literal sense, but rather with a spiritual sense and in relation to eschatology (4:36).[680] In the Gospel, eternal life flourishes from the Father and people can experience it through putting their faith in Jesus (5:24). The Jews understand that through diligent study of the scripture one can receive eternal life (5:39; 6:63);[681] but they do not understand that all the scriptures point to Jesus. John's Gospel affirms that eternal life is accessible to people only by believing in Jesus (20:31).[682]

In Jesus' speech, he uses "food" as a spiritual element that endures to eternal life (6:27). As he is the bread of life and provider of living water, whoever goes to him never be hungry and believes in him never be thirsty. The blessings of eternal life are assured to those who eat his flesh (6:35) and drink from his well (4:14; 7:37-39). This experience enables people to be raised up on the last day (6:40, 47).[683] The metaphorical aspects such as "eating the flesh" and "drinking the blood" are also connected to this regard (6:54-58). Some of the significant steps in experiencing eternal life include recognizing that Jesus has the words of eternal life (6:68) and believing and knowing that

---

[676] Beasley-Murray, *John*, 276.

[677] John 1:4; 5:21, 26, 40; 6:33.

[678] See D. H. Johnson, "Life," *Dictionary of Jesus and the Gospels*, 469.

[679] Culpepper, *Anatomy of the Fourth Gospel*, 136-137.

[680] Johnson, "Life," 470-471.

[681] See Moloney, *The Gospel of John*, 180-181.

[682] Johnson, "Life," 470-471.

[683] Beasley-Murray, *John*, 90-94.

he is the Holy One of God (6:69).[684] Jesus came that the sheep may have life to the full (10:10). Abundant life refers to life in its abounding fullness of joy and strength for mind, body, and soul. Reaching to such a point is considered as the joy of salvation.[685] In that sense, prosperity in John is enjoying the spiritual blessings in the present with a hope about its complete measure in the future.

Jesus lays down his life for the sheep so that the sheep can experience life in abundance (10:15, 17, 28; 15:13). In 11:28, Jesus promises eternal life and he assures that those who receive it shall never perish. In that sense, prosperity in John means eternal security of life (11:25, 26; 14:6).[686] One of the earthly standards of prosperity is the capacity to keep things for the future. On the contrary, the divine standard is that "the man who loves his life will lose it" and "the man who hates his life in this world will keep it for eternal life" (12:25, 44-46, 50; 17:2).[687] In John's terms, "Eternal life is that people may know the Father, the only true God, and Jesus Christ whom he has sent" (17:3).[688] Having abundant life is a unique privilege to exercise heavenly joy in its fullness. In sum, John explains the aspect of prosperity in terms of believing and following Jesus, exercising divine love, enjoying the indwelling of the Holy Spirit, having fellowship with the people, and thus enjoying the favors and blessings of God in abundance.

Response to Jesus: Characters and Characterization

The narrative framework of John foregrounds the characters and the characterization in a peculiar way. Rather than people search for financial stability and material well being, they increase in the divine wisdom and come to the realization of Jesus' identity as the Messiah. It is true even in the case of John the Baptist who states his unworthiness in relation to Jesus (1:26-27).[689] Though he is considered honorable among the people, he accepts the Lordship of Jesus and demonstrates his spiritual and missional maturity as a forerunner (1:7-8, 15, 29-34, 35-36; 3:22-30).[690] By introducing the Lamb of God to the world, he surrenders himself for the mission of God and fulfills the spiritual mandate entrusted on him (1:29-34). His utterance in 3:30 (that is, "He must increase, but I must decrease") provides a significant narrative clue concerning the "increase" and "decrease" pattern of the storyline.

---

[684] Beasley-Murray, *John*, 90-94.

[685] Johnson, "Life," 469.

[686] Moloney, *The Gospel of John*, 333.

[687] Moloney, *The Gospel of John*, 354; Renn, "Life, Live, Living," *Expository Dictionary of Bible Words*, 595.

[688] Moloney, *The Gospel of John*, 461.

[689] Beasley-Murray, *John*, 24.

[690] See Bennema, *Encountering Jesus*, 22-30.

In the call narratives, the characters demonstrate their search for the Messiah and all those searches come to fulfillment in Jesus. When Andrew proclaims that "we have found the Messiah" (1:41), his search for the Messiah is made obvious and that finally comes to reality in Jesus.[691] As a person who was brought to Jesus by Andrew (1:42), Peter later on declares that "Lord, to whom shall we go? You have the words of eternal life. We believe and know that you are the Holy One of God" (6:68-69).[692] Similarly, Philip utters that "we have found the one Moses wrote about in the law and about whom the prophets also wrote" (1:45).[693] Nathanael makes his profound statement as follows: "Rabbi, you are the Son of God; you are the King of Israel" (1:49).[694] In all these instances, people's search for the Messiah and the way those come to fulfillment in Jesus are made obvious. All of them were called to follow Jesus not in an occasion in which they were searching for health, wealth, or happiness in the earthly sense; but when they were searching for the Messiah. People's awareness about the Messiah, their search for him, fulfillment of their search in Jesus, and the increase of their faith and commitment are made obvious at the outset of the Gospel.

The flat nature of Nicodemus' character in 3:1-10 turns to be in developing mode as he defends Jesus in a legal court (7:50-51) and spending his finance through the means of myrrh and aloes (worth about hundred pounds) during his burial (19:39).[695] As he spends his finance to show his devotion to Jesus, the narrator focuses on the spiritual growth of the character.[696] As the Samaritan woman demonstrates her faith in Jesus, she recognizes him progressively as a "Jew" (4:9), a "teacher" (4:15, 19), a "prophet" (4:19), "Messiah" (4:25), and finally with other Samaritans "truly the Savior of the world" (4:42).[697] The progression of her spiritual maturity from the point of a beginner to the level of a full-grown believer is made obvious to the reader. The Royal man shows a kind of conditional faith at the beginning (4:48) and later on reveals his maturity in faith (4:53) as the entire family joins him in believing Jesus.[698] Though he is an influential and at the same time an affluent person, the narrator focuses on his devotion to Jesus, gradual development

---

691 Bennema, *Encountering Jesus*, 47-52.

692 Beasley-Murray, *John*, 97.

693 Thomaskutty, *Dialogue in the Book of Signs*, 63-71.

694 Bennema, *Encountering Jesus*, 64-68.

695 Culpepper, *Anatomy of the Fourth Gospel*, 134-136.

696 See Craig R. Koester, "Theological Complexity and the Characterization of Nicodemus in John's Gospel," *Characters and Characterization in the Gospel of John* (London/New York: Bloomsbury, 2013), 165-181.

697 Culpepper, *Anatomy of the Fourth Gospel*, 136-137.

698 Bennema, *Encountering Jesus*, 94-99.

of faith, and the pattern of discipleship.[699] The characters of the Gospel of John flourish not in matters of earthly blessings but in the areas of spiritual advancement. They achieve the growth in alignment with the 'from above' world and the divine principles.

The man born blind progresses as he develops his knowledge in Jesus as follows: he addresses him as the "man they call Jesus" (v. 11), a prophet (v. 17), one from God (v. 33), "Lord" (v. 38), and finally he worships him (v. 38).[700] While the Good shepherd is identified with the virtue of laying down his life for the sheep, the hired ones are identified as those who work for the earthly income.[701] In that context, the devotion of Mary and Martha is enlightening. While Judas' interest is on the finance, Mary's superabundant generosity is the emphasis in 12:1-8.[702] Mary Magdalene develops as a character under the cross alongside of other dignified women. Her witness concerning the resurrection of Jesus to her male counterparts positions her as an *apostola apostolorum*.[703] Her personal conviction that "I have seen the Lord" (20:18) later becomes a community conviction ("We have seen the Lord," 20:25).[704] Thomas appears with a determination to die with Jesus (11:16), asking about the way (14:5), declaring that Jesus is Lord and God (20:28), and being with the company of other disciples (21:2).[705] Thus, John's characters progress to the higher levels and demonstrate their spiritual prosperity.

In Cana in Galilee, Jesus is present with his mother, his brothers, and the disciples for attending a wedding feast (2:1-11). The narrator is more concerned of the scarcity of wine rather than the happiness mood of the occasion. Jesus brings happiness in an occasion where there was lack of joy.[706] The story's main thrust is not on the aspect of material prosperity and earthly happiness, but rather on the theme of divine revelation (2:11).[707] Though there is an element of happiness within the story, the overarching perspective is revelation of the truth of God for people's belief. In 2:13-22, Jesus sternly warns people who are engaged in "buying," "selling," and "making the Father's house a

---

[699] Thomaskutty, *Dialogue in the Book of Signs*, 173-175.

[700] Thomaskutty, *Dialogue in the Book of Signs*, 349-350.

[701] See Moloney, *The Gospel of John*, 303-306.

[702] See Thomaskutty, "Reading John's Gospel in the Nepali Context," 12-13.

[703] See Susan Haskins, "Apostola Apostotorum," *Mary Magdalene: Myth and Metaphor* (New York: Penguin, 1993), 55-94; Thomaskutty, "Reading John's Gospel in the Bangladeshi Context," 61-62.

[704] Beasley-Murray, *John*, 384-385.

[705] Thomaskutty, *Saint Thomas the Apostle*, 84-85.

[706] Brant, *John*, 55-59.

[707] Beasley-Murray, *John*, 34-36.

marketplace."[708] His activity of "pouring out the coins of the money changers and overturning their tables" re-establishes proper worship in the temple (2:14). In a context in which cattle, sheep, and doves were determining factors for people's wealth, Jesus' zeal for the Father's house is made obvious.[709] Similarly, while there was scarcity of finance and resources in a needy situation, the disciples inform Jesus about the impossibility of feeding a multitude of people (6:1-15).[710] But, five loaves and two fishes were sufficient in the hands of Jesus.[711] The leftover of twelve baskets full of meal symbolizes God's grace upon the people who need divine favor and require timely help.[712] In sum, the Gospel of John attunes the attention of the readers toward the matters "from above" and invites them to be enriched with the spiritual blessings. Though there are several connotations of finance and indications of earthly resources within the Gospel, the theme of Christ-centered prosperity takes the center-place of the discussion.

Conclusion

In recapitulation, the narrative annals of the Fourth Gospel demonstrate their distinctive emphases on the matters of health, wealth and happiness. The dualistic framework of the Gospel invites the attention of the reader toward the 'from above' aspects over against the matters of this world. The narratorial framework with its kernels and events attunes the reader toward the individualistic, communitarian, and universal maxims. The protagonist and the narrator together build the narrative kernels with a focus to develop a transformed community. A network of themes such as faith, love, knowledge, and abundant life are idealized with an intention of directing people's attention to Christ. John's framework employs the earthly things in order to denote their spiritual meanings. The narrative framework reflects the ethics and the values of the Johannine community and their devotion to the things from above. The themes such as abundant life and everlasting joy are not introduced merely in terms of the future, but as realities that enrich our present life. The narrator portrays the story in a Christ-centered manner over against the antagonistic trends of the Jews. In a context in which prosperity is perceived mostly in earthly terms, the Johannine narrator introduces a unique paradigm that takes the reader's attention to the individual, corporate, and universal realms. As Clement of Alexandria was addressing that the Fourth Gospel a "Spiritual

[708] Moloney, *The Gospel of John*, 80-82.

[709] Brant, *John*, 70-71.

[710] Thomaskutty, *Dialogue in the Book of Signs*, 208-216.

[711] Witherington, *John's Wisdom*, 151-153.

[712] Thomaskutty, *Dialogue in the Book of Signs*, 208-209.

Gospel,"[713] a modern reader can understand the true meaning of its spiritual aspects when s/he explores the gospel in terms of wealth, health, and happiness. The story of the Gospel is built with a universal intent that emphasizes the advancement of faith, increase of love, acquisition of knowledge, and the experience of abundant life. In that sense, the Fourth Gospel is a paradigm for interpreting the aspect of prosperity with a spiritual and gnomic intent.

[713] See Hypotyposes, cited in Eusebius, *HE*, 6.14.7; Cf. Guthrie, *NT Introduction*, 285.

Chapter 8

Characterization of Thomas in the Fourth Gospel

Introduction

Thomas appears four times within the narrative framework of the Fourth Gospel (see 11:16; 14:5; 20:24-28; 21:2). His presence in the Gospel introduces some of the strategic transitions to the macro-narrative structure.[714] The following are some of the crucial moments introduced through the entry of Thomas: first, Thomas' character is brought to the foreground toward the close of Jesus' public ministry, where a transition is in view from Lazarus' death and raising to Jesus' death and resurrection (11:16);[715] second, he appears as a significant interlocutor engaged in a dialogue so that Jesus' identity as "the way, the truth, and the life" may be revealed to the disciples during his private ministry (14:5-6); third, Thomas' character appears toward the climax of the Book of Glory (13:1-20:31) as he is instrumental in revealing the identity of Jesus as "Lord" and "God" (20:24-29); and fourth, he appears as one of the seven disciples during the post-resurrection context in Galilee (21:2). Although Thomas' character is absent at the beginning of the gospel, his presence is significantly noticeable in the above stated transitions.

---

[714] Christopher W. Skinner, *John and Thomas—Gospels in Conflict? Johannine Characterization and the Thomas Question*, PTMS (Eugene: Pickwick Publications, 2009), 43.

[715] Skinner states further: "Here, Thomas serves as a foil, being used by the narrator to create a situation where narrative tension, irony, and misunderstanding point forward to the illumination given by the 'light of the world.'" See Skinner, *John and Thomas*, 55.

The narrator orchestrates the extended story of the gospel with a view of Thomas at the transitions. The unique placement of Thomas communicates something significant about the character and his development within the narrative. As Thomas' character appears in the significant transitions of the Gospel, the reader gets the impression that he is present to reveal a universal truth. His character represents a universal ideology within the annals of the Fourth Gospel. A careful analysis of the four appearances of Thomas, that is, within the episodes they appear, as well as within the extended narrative framework of John, calls the attention of the reader toward some of the vital areas in the story. In the following sections, we will look into those aspects through an exegetical analysis.

From Lazarus' Death to Jesus' Death (11:1-12:11)

The narrator introduces Thomas in chap. 11 and the reader gets an impression that he was there with Jesus right from the beginning of his public ministry. That further means that he was following Jesus passively until now as an implicit and backgrounded character.[716] In 11:16, the passive, implicit, and backgrounded Thomas comes out as an active, explicit, and foregrounded character. The narrator of the story uses Thomas' question in v. 16 as a significant statement in order to tell the story of Jesus dynamically.[717] Thomas' saying about *going* and *dying* (*agōmen . . . apothanōmen*) and Jesus' references about *dying*, *living*, and *resurrection* (vv. 24-27) are integrally connected.[718] Why is Thomas introduced at the high point of the public ministry of Jesus? Sylva states that, "Thomas appears first at the turning point of the narrative, at the point where John is making clear that the significance of Jesus' signs is that they show that he is the one who gives eternal life."[719] Thomas appears here as a foil character to bring to the fore the aspects of the 'death' of Jesus without shifting the attention of the reader away from the protagonist.[720]

The narrator attempts to reveal a truth through constellations of words and expressions within the narrative framework. The network of expressions

---

716 Skinner, *John and Thomas*, 43.

717 Byrne considered 12:1-11 as a well-connected pericope to the story of Lazarus in 11:1-57. See B. Byrne, *Lazarus: A Contemporary Reading of John 11:1-46* (Collegeville: The Liturgical Press, 1991), 67-68.

718 R. F. Collins, *These Things Have Been Written: Studies on the Fourth Gospel* (Louvain: Peeters/Grand Rapids: Eerdmans, 1990), 84-85.

719 D. Sylva, *Thomas—Love as Strong as Death: Faith and Commitment in the Fourth Gospel*, LNTS 434 (London: Bloomsbury, 2013), 11.

720 M. M. Thompson, *John: A Commentary*, NTL (Louisville: Westminster John Knox, 2015), 242; also see T. Popp, "Thomas: Question Marks and Exclamation Marks," *Character Studies in the Fourth Gospel: Narrative Approaches to Seventy Figures in John*, WUNT (Tübingen: Mohr Siebeck, 2013), 50.

such as *going*, *dying*, *faith*, *glory*, *love*, and others are significant to note within the narrative master plan.[721] According to Popp, "the Thomas texts are not conclusive but are, rather, through their polyvalence, open to diverse interpretive possibilities."[722] Though Martha comes as the key character and confessor of Jesus in the following sections (11:17-44), her role as a whole is restricted within the present episode. But Thomas advances from here until the end of the extended Johannine story.[723] Thomas is said to have prepared the rest of the disciples for Jesus' forthcoming death.[724] In the following sections we will see how a network of expressions helps us to understand the very essence of Thomas' statement in 11:16.

Let us also go . . .

The theme of *going* appears continuously within this narrative framework. It begins with the utterance of Jesus in v. 7: "*Let us go* to Judea again."[725] Jesus' statement here is filled with missional implications as he is stepping forward for accomplishing a task. Jesus' very movement was at stake as the disciples pose a question in v. 8: "Rabbi, the Jews were just now trying to stone you, and are you *going* there again?"[726] Going ahead, irrespective of growing oppositions or threat to death, is part and parcel of Jesus' mission initiatives.[727] After these preliminary remarks based on the *going* language, the narrator introduces Thomas to the foreground with his significant utterance.

The utterance of Thomas in v. 16, "Let us also go [*agōmen*]," introduces a radical step at this critical juncture.[728] On the one hand, he takes a challenge to go against the majority view, and on the other hand, he decides to align himself to the view of Jesus that was not pleasant to the rest of his companions

[721] See P. D. Duke, *Irony in the Fourth Gospel* (Atlanta: John Knox Press, 1985), 59-61; A. J. Köstenberger, *John*, ECNT (Grand Rapids: Baker, 2004), 331-332.

[722] Popp, "Thomas: Question Marks and Exclamation Marks," 504; also see Collins, *These Things Have Been Written*, 84-85.

[723] Byrne, *Lazarus*, 46-47.

[724] See J. Bowman, *The Fourth Gospel and the Jews: A Study in R. Abika, Esther and the Gospel of John* (Pittsburgh: The Pickwick Press, 1975), 246; W. Hendriksen, *Exposition of the Gospel according to John*, New Testament Commentary (Grand Rapids: Baker, 1954), 144-145.

[725] The subjunctive plural verb is a derivation of *agō* which means "to lead." See B. M. Newman and E. A. Nida, *A Handbook on the Gospel of John* (New York: United Bible Societies, 1980), 358.

[726] Indicative present active singular verb is a derivation of *hupagō* which means 'to depart.'

[727] W. Howard-Brook, *John's Gospel and the Renewal of the Church* (Maryknoll: Orbis, 1997), 77.

[728] See R. Bultmann, *The Gospel of John: A Commentary* (Philadelphia: The Westminster Press, 1971), 400; W. Carter, *John: Storyteller, Interpreter, Evangelist* (Peabody: Hendrickson Publishers, 2006), 75.

(v. 16).[729] Popp argues that, "His [Thomas'] entrance is unmediated and abrupt. He is suddenly present as an acting character and addresses his 'fellow disciples' (*summathētais*, 11:16a). This description designates Thomas as a member of the group of disciples, thus also implying his obligation to follow Jesus."[730] In that sense, Thomas' statement takes the spirit of Jesus' missional concerns at its highest esteem.[731] His utterance is in the sense that *as Jesus goes, let us also go with Him*.[732]

While Martha and Mary *went* to meet Jesus to convey their grievances concerning their brother's death (vv. 20, 29),[733] Thomas shows a superior missional model as he encourages his colleagues to go with Jesus even if there is danger ahead.[734] He stands apart and understands the real meaning of Jesus' *going*. He was able to perceive Jesus' *going* synonymous to his death. As Bonney states, "The journey *will* lead to the crucifixion of Jesus (cf. 11:45-53)."[735] Thomas acts here as the spokesman for the Twelve. He shows willingness to go with Jesus, who was leading them to death, and to share the danger ahead.

. . . that we may die with Him

As we have seen, the linguistic phenomena help us to understand the characterization. The speech and behaviour of Thomas are important narrative clues to perceive his personality.[736] Thomas' utterance, "that we may *die* with him [Jesus]," works in a dynamic rhythm with other narrative and utterance units.[737] Charlesworth states that, "He [Thomas] exhorts his fellow disciples to follow Jesus back into Judea, even if it means martyrdom: 'Thomas, called the Twin, said to his co-disciples, *Let us also go, that we may die with him*

---

[729] Sylva, *Thomas—Love as Strong as Death*, 12.

[730] Popp, "Thomas: Question Marks and Exclamation Marks," 507.

[731] Sylva, *Thomas—Love as Strong as Death*, 11.

[732] C. Bennema, *Encountering Jesus: Character Studies in the Gospel of John*, Second Edition (Minneapolis: Fortress Press, 2009), 164.

[733] Though Mary's exemplary activity is narrated in 11:2 and 12:1-8, her role, as in the case of Martha, is restricted within this episode.

[734] E. Haenchen, *A Commentary on the Gospel of John chapters 7-21*, Vol. 2 (Philadelphia: Fortress Press, 1984), 60; U. C. Von Wahlde, *The Gospel and Letters of John*, Vol. 2 (Grand Rapids: Eerdmans, 2010), 484-502.

[735] W. Bonney, *Caused to Believe: The Doubting Thomas Story at the Climax of John's Christological Narrative* (Leiden/Boston: Brill, 2002), 138.

[736] Cf. N. R. Petersen, *The Gospel of John and the Sociology of Light: Language and Characterization in the Fourth Gospel* (Valley Forge: Trinity Press International, 1993).

[737] Byrne, *Lazarus*, 47.

(11:16).'"[738] Thomas' utterance is a narrative clue that reminds the reader that the death of Lazarus is told as a 'minor story' in order to present the 'major story' of Jesus with symbolical effect.[739]

The resolution of John's story takes shape in the current episode as it merges Lazarus' death and resurrection symbolically with the death and resurrection of Jesus.[740] The analeptic statement in v. 2 (as a reference to 12:7) attunes the reader's attention toward the death and burial of Jesus. In Jesus' statement in v. 4 it is made clear that Lazarus' death and resurrection are for God's glory, so also of the glory of the Son of Man. Here, the death and glorification of the Son of Man are in view. Thomas' utterance in 11:16 is a great pointer toward that extended story of the Gospel.[741] Jesus' determination to go to his own death and his glorification is strongly supported by the remarkable voice of Thomas.[742] Lincoln says, "Thomas' comment is truer than he suspects. In the case of Jesus what he does not yet know but what the narrator will recount is that it is precisely Jesus' act of raising Lazarus that will trigger off the events that finally lead to his death."[743] The revelatory utterance of Jesus, "I am the resurrection and the life" (v. 25), has to be interpreted also as a reaction to the utterance of Thomas in 11:16.[744] The narrator uses Martha and Mary as key figures in developing the story of Lazarus. On the other hand, he uses Thomas as the key figure to attune the story to the extended level.[745]

Within the extended framework of John's story, the utterance of Thomas creates a prolepsis with the passion and death of Jesus. Thomas' entry from the background to the foreground spearheads one of the dramatic initiatives of the narrator to develop the story with suspense and surprise. The narrative setting provides special punch for the involvement of Jesus as the life-giving saviour in the family of Lazarus. But Thomas shifts the attention of the reader away from Lazarus and his death and resurrection to the upcoming event of Jesus'

---

[738] J. H. Charlesworth, *The Beloved Disciple: Whose Witness Validates the Gospel of John* (Valley Forge: Trinity Press International, 1995), 238.

[739] Bonney, *Caused to Believe*, 137-1388.

[740] See M. W. G. Stibbe, *John's Gospel* (London and New York, 1994), 24-25.

[741] M. W. G. Stibbe, John, Readings: A New Biblical Commentary (Sheffield: Sheffield Academic, 1993), 125; Bonney, *Caused to Believe*, 138.

[742] F. J. Moloney, *Signs and Shadows: Reading John 5-12* (Minneapolis: Fortress Press, 1996), 159.

[743] A. T. Lincoln, *The Gospel according to Saint John*, BNTC (London: Continuum, 2005), 322).

[744] H. C. Waetjen, *The Gospel of the Beloved Disciple: A Work in Two Editions* (London: T & T Clark, 2005), 275; D. Rensberger, *Johannine Faith and Liberating Community* (Philadelphia: Westminster Press, 1988), 120.

[745] C. I. K. Story, *The Fourth Gospel: Its Purpose, Pattern, and Power* (Shippenburg: Ragged Edge Publication, 1997), 243.

death. The willingness of Thomas to go with Jesus irrespective of the risk of life is heroic. As Charlesworth says, "The leadership role of Thomas was made clear in chap. 11, when he exhorted his fellow disciples to follow Jesus even if it meant death (11:16)."[746] The death of Jesus and the climax of John's story are prefigured through the utterance of Thomas. Thomas stands against all odds and confirms his reaction positively to Jesus and his plans. The glorification aspect accelerates toward its climax as Thomas shifts the focus from Lazarus to Jesus. Although Thomas does not add any Christological title in his speech, his utterance marks a crucial Christological turn within and beyond the episode.

Knowing the Way (13:1-17:26)

After introducing Thomas to the reader in 11:16, the Johannine narrator foregrounds him another time in 14:5.[747] The utterance of Thomas within the Farewell Discourse resonates with other themes, character utterances, and narrative comments. While Thomas' first utterance was a significant one toward the end of Jesus' public ministry in the Book of Signs, his second utterance in the private ministry section provides additional punch to the previous utterance.[748] In the following sections, we will analyze how the utterance of Thomas resonates within the Farewell Discourse of John's Gospel.

Lord, we do not know where you are going . . .

The second utterance of Thomas (14:5) is yet another enigmatic statement that has to be explored alongside several other factors. While Thomas does not use any Christological titles to address Jesus (but only *autou*) in his previous utterance (11:16), in 14:5 he uses one of the extensively used titles, *kurios*.[749] It explicitly states that there is a development from the former appearance and utterance to the latter. The Farewell Discourse uses the title *kurios* either as an address of the disciples to Jesus (13:6, 9, 25; 14:5, 8, 22) or as a self-revelatory description by Jesus himself (13:13, 14, 16; 15:15, 20). Thomas uses a title that was familiar: first, it was used by Jesus as a self-revelatory description, and second, it was used by his colleagues to address their master.[750]

The unknowing nature of Thomas contributes semantic domains within the *statement-misunderstanding-clarification* narrative framework.[751] Sylva

[746] Charlesworth, *The Beloved Disciple*, 125.

[747] See F. F. Bruce, *The Gospel of John: Introduction, Exposition and Notes* (Grand Rapids: Eerdmans, 1983), 298-299.

[748] Sylva, *Thomas—Love as Strong as Death*, 64.

[749] J. A. Fitzmyer, "Kurios," *EDNT*, Vol. 2 (Grand Rapids: Eerdmans, 1981/1991), 329.

[750] See F. D. Bruner, *The Gospel of John: A Commentary* (Grand Rapids: Eedrmans, 2012), 811-812.

[751] J. H. Neyrey, *The Gospel of John*, NCBC (Cambridge: University Press, 2007), 243; also see Bennema, *Encountering Jesus*, 164-70.

states, "Thomas' understanding is found deficient because, loyal as he is, he has not come to know the essence of Jesus' being and the Father that this essence reveals."[752] What Sylva states here is true as Thomas reflects his character in his own idiom. John depicts the aspect of knowing at three levels: first, the all-knowing nature of Jesus; second, the ignorant nature of the world from below; and third, Thomas and his colleagues are progressive as they begin to know. Thomas' expression *we do not know* reveals this fact explicitly to the reader.[753] As a person lives in the world from below and understands the mysteries of the things from above, Thomas' character shows dullness and progress at the same time.[754]

Thomas represents a leading person among the disciples, but at the same time he expresses his views in his own terms.[755] Even after their continuous acquaintance with Jesus, the disciples are unable to understand him (14:9) and his deeds (13:7). In that sense, Thomas' perplexities in 14:5 can be understood in the following ways: first, as a human, he *was* thinking and knowing things from the point of view of this world; second, as a follower of Jesus, he *is* aware of the things from above (because Jesus makes things known to him, 17:26); and third, as a person who has dual identity, he is perplexed (but Jesus *will* make things known to him, 17:26).[756] These past, present, and future aspects reveal some of the significant aspects of the characterization of Thomas.[757] Thomas as a person under training was not able to perceive mysterious things, but Jesus promises that he will make all things known to him later (17:26).[758]

The vocabulary of going is another significant aspect in the Farewell Discourse to reckon with. Thomas' statement, "we do not know where you are going," should be looked at from the constellation of that linguistic phenomenon. In this way, as far as the character analysis is concerned, Jesus and Thomas (explicitly in 14:5 and implicitly in 14:31) are brought into contact with one another."[759] From Thomas' utterance three things are significant to note: first, in 11:16 Thomas recognizes that Jesus' going is for his death; second, Thomas is not able to see beyond Jesus' death and perceive

[752] Sylva, *Thomas—Love as Strong as Death*, 80-81; also see R. Schnackenburg, *The Gospel according to St. John*, Vol. 3 (New York: Herder and Herder, 1982), 64.

[753] Popp, "Thomas: Question Marks and Exclamation Marks," 512-513.

[754] See C. K. Barrett, *The Gospel according to St. John: An Introduction with Commentary and Notes on the Greek Text* (London: SPCK, 1962), 382; C. L. Blomberg, *The Historical Reliability of John's Gospel* (England: IVP, 2001), 198.

[755] See Popp, "Thomas: Question Marks and Exclamation Marks," 512; W. Brouwer, *The Literary Development of John 13:17: A Chiastic Reading*, SBLDS 182 (Atlanta: SBL, 2000), 90.

[756] Popp, "Thomas: Question Marks and Exclamation Marks," 512.

[757] Sylva, *Thomas—Love as Strong as Death*, 81.

[758] Popp, "Thomas: Question Marks and Exclamation Marks," 512.

[759] See Blomberg, *The Historical Reliability of John's Gospel*, 198.

the connection between his death and going to the Father; and third, while Thomas recognizes that Jesus is going to die in 11:16, he fails to understand Jesus' death as a marking point for him to go to the Father.

How can we know the way?

Thomas' utterance in 14:5 ends with a significant question: "How can we know the way?"[760] Carson maintains that "His [Thomas'] question sounds as if he interpreted Jesus' words in the most crassly natural way: he wants an unambiguous destination, for without such a destination how can one meaningfully speak of the route there?"[761] Thomas' identity, which is caught between the world from below and the world from above, makes him ask this question.[762] In John, the hour of Jesus is connected to the way to the cross (13:1; 17:1). At the same time, it marks his departure from this world (13:1; 16:5). DeConick states as follows:

> The author, by deliberately characterizing Thomas as a fool in this passage, condemns the hero of the Thomasine Christians. Moreover, his articulation of the discourse points to a particular feature of the dispute: the journey or ascent to heaven. John tells us that such ascent is not necessary, that Jesus himself is the only 'way' into heaven. This is stated in contradiction to the Thomasine belief which, from Thomas' answer in 14:5, appears to have encouraged proleptic heavenly ascents.[763]

From Jesus' utterance in 14:7, "None comes to the Father except through me," one perceives that Jesus is the way that God opened to the world.[764] Similarly, Jesus is the one who prepares a way backward to the Father. Jesus' mission of preparing a home for the faithful is in the process of its realization (14:3).[765] Peter' question in 13:36 ("Lord, where are you going?") and Thomas' question in 14:5 ("How can we know the way?") are to be perceived from this ideological constellation.[766] The conversation between Philip and Jesus

---

[760] See J. A. Brant, *Dialogue and Drama: Elements of Greek Tragedy in the Fourth Gospel* (Peabody: Hendrickson Publishers, 2004), 105.

[761] D. A. Carson, *The Gospel according to John* (Leicester: IVP/Grand Rapids: Eerdmans, 1991), 490; cf. Bultmann, *The Gospel of John*, 603-604.

[762] Bonney, *Caused to Believe*, 139.

[763] A. D. DeConick, *Voices of the Mystics: Early Christian Discourse in the Gospels of John and Thomas and Other Ancient Christian Literature*, JSNTSS 157 (Sheffield: Sheffield Academic, 2001), 73.

[764] Barrett, *The Gospel according to St. John*, 382.

[765] See Barrett, *The Gospel according to St. John*, 381-382.

[766] F. J. Moloney, *The Gospel of John*, Sacra Pagina 4 (Collegeville: The Liturgical Press, 1998), 393.

in 14:8-14 strengthens this subject matter further. Jesus speaks figuratively in saying that "In my Father's house there are many dwelling places" (14:2), "Where I am, you also may be" (14:3), and "You know the way to the place where I am going" (14:4). The narrator highlights the utterance of Jesus, "I am the way, the truth, and the life" (14:6), as the epitome of the extended discourse.[767] The coming of the Holy Spirit (14:16-17, 26; 15:26-27; 16:7-8, 13-15) further assures that Jesus had opened the way from/to heaven.

John also shows an antagonistic movement against the way: betrayal as the way of Satan (13:2, 18, 21, 26-30; 17:12), the coming of the ruler of the world (14:30; 16:11), the hate of the world towards the children of God (15:18-25; 17:15), and the hour of the enemy (16:2-4).[768] Jesus as the way to God introduces a new ethical paradigm over against the ways of Satan. Through the mediation of Jesus, the *world from above* ushers in the *world from below*. In this context, Thomas' question functions in the following ways: first, it helps as a pointer for the reader to understand the sharp contrast between the from-below and from-above ideologies; second, it is used as a rhetorical device to draw the attention of the reader toward Jesus the protagonist and his revelation as the way, truth, and life;[769] and third, it helps the reader to identify her/himself with Thomas in order to develop from *going to die* aspect (11:16) to *going to the Father* aspect (14:5).[770]

The utterance of Thomas in John 14:5 provides further understanding about his person and his ideological framework. The shift of emphasis from the previous utterance (11:16, going to Jerusalem and to death) to the latter (14:5, to the Father) has to be noticed in the process of reading the text. The narrator places the utterances of Thomas in 14:5 in order to develop the plot structure with suspense and surprise. Thomas' question adds rhetorical punch for the Farewell Discourse and it has both analeptic and proleptic functions within the narrative master plan. Thomas' role as a character that represents the rest of the disciples initiates some of the significant revelatory aspects in the Gospel. As we had already noted, the speech unit of Thomas has the following emphases: first, the title *Lord* has a specific emphasis when it is compared with the rest of the usages; second, the narrator explores the narratorial technique of *knowing-and-unknowing* contrast in its maximum; third, the aspect of *going* is introduced with a different emphasis when it is compared with 11:16; and fourth, the question "How can we know the Way?" ushers some of the revelatory and mysterious truths related to the heavenly realities and the existential struggles of the believers.

---

[767] Moloney, *The Gospel of John*, 394-395.

[768] See Brant, *Dialogue and Drama*, 220-224.

[769] Schnackenburg, *The Gospel according to St. John*, 3:64.

[770] See DeConick, *Voices of the Mystics*, 72-73.

Thomas is unique in his approach to belief as he is a seeker of truth through evidence, as he believes on the basis of seeing, and as he shows inclination toward an action-oriented and progressive movement. His character shows love and concern toward Jesus and his utterances, exemplifies frankness in speech, willingness to die for Jesus and to represent his colleagues in crucial junctures, and requires time to accept the truth of Jesus. Thomas stands tall as a character who takes the initiative to communicate the glorification aspect convincingly to the rest of the disciples/readers. Thus, Thomas emerges as a stable character and one who adds rhetorical force to the plot-structure of the story.

Recognizing Jesus as 'Lord' and 'God' (20:1-31)

John 20:1-31 is the last episode of the Book of Glory in which Thomas appears for the third time.[771] In the episode, the character of Thomas can be fully understood only in comparison to the rest of the characters and their utterances. The utterances of Mary Magdalene and the other disciples are to be compared with that of Thomas to understand the unique presence of Thomas. The extreme statements of Thomas, one to the rest of the disciples (v. 25b) and one to Jesus (v. 28), make his appearance convincing within the episode. While on the one hand he says to the disciples that "Unless I see . . . put my finger . . . I will not believe" and on the other he utters to Jesus "My Lord and my God!"[772]

Seeing and putting finger in the mark of the Nails

The vocabulary of *seeing* is rich in John 20 and that has to be analyzed seriously to understand the utterances of Thomas in vv. 24-29. Thomas' determination to see tangible evidence is made clear through his conditional statement in v. 25b.[773] His conviction about his faith in Jesus compels the reader to evaluate him in relation to the rest of the characters. While the leading characters of John 20, Mary Magdalene and the disciples (including Peter and the other disciple), declare both in the individual and corporate life that they have seen the Lord, Thomas stands out at a different level.[774] Thomas did not see Jesus as in the case of Mary and the other disciples. He declares that unless he *sees* and touches tangible evidence that Jesus is alive he will not believe (v. 25).[775]

---

[771] See more details in Thompson, *John: A Commentary*, 423; Bonney, *Caused to Believe*, 145-167.

[772] For a detailed explanation see Johnson Thomaskutty, *Saint Thomas the Apostle: New Testament, Apocrypha, and Historical Traditions*, Jewish and Christian Texts Series 25 (London/New York: Bloomsbury T & T Clark, 2018), 54-74.

[773] Bruce, *The Gospel of John*, 393; cf. Sylva, *Thomas—Love as Strong as Death*, 84-87.

[774] Sylva, *Thomas—Love as Strong as Death*, 82-83; see Haenchen, *John*, 2:211.

[775] See the expression *ean mē* in Thomas' utterance.

Jesus takes the challenge, comes to him in the presence of others, and says to him: "put your finger here and *see* my hands" (v. 27). Jesus' question in v. 29a ("Have you believed because you have *seen* [*heōrakas*] me?") cannot be considered as an exclusive response to Thomas, but has to be looked at as one to Thomas, Mary Magdalene, Peter, the other disciple, and the rest of the disciples.[776] Similarly, his makarism in v. 29b cannot be reckoned as an exclusive criticism to Thomas, but has to be understood as one to the disciples and Mary Magdalene.[777] Thomas comes out here as a figure who can better conclude the story of Jesus in the gospel. By placing Thomas, one of the leading figures of early Christianity, at center-stage the narrator deciphers the early Christian trend of *seeing and believing*.[778]

Thomas' demand for touching the mark of the nails in Jesus' hands requires special attention.[779] Though Thomas demands to touch the body of Jesus, there is no mention that he literally touched the body.[780] But, a reader can infer that Jesus' command to put his finger in his hands would have been wholeheartedly accepted by Thomas (v. 27; cf. v. 25b).[781] Theodore of Mopsuestia comments: "And when [Thomas] ever so carefully touched him and accurately ascertained the truth, he confessed his fault saying, *My Lord and My God!*"[782] Thomas' statement makes it clear that Jesus' hands were nailed and he himself was a witness of the incident. Both the Synoptic Gospels and John do not give details concerning nailing the hands (and also legs) of Jesus. Thomas is the first and only person who talks about the mark of the nails in Jesus' hands (*ton tupon tōn helōn*, v. 25).[783] In his response to Thomas, Jesus also makes a mention: "Put your finger here and see my hands" (v. 27a).[784]

Thomas' utterance concerning seeing and putting his finger in the mark of the nails is the only explicit reference about marks in the hands of Jesus.[785] His statement leads us to the following observations: first, there is every possibility that Thomas was an eye-witness of the crucifixion and that he

---

[776] In order to foreground the aspect of *seeing* the narrator uses a wide variety of vocabularies.

[777] Bennema, *Encountering Jesus*, 167.

[778] Thompson, *John: A Commentary*, 243-244.

[779] Schnackenburg, *The Gospel according to St. John*, 3:318.

[780] Barrett, *The Gospel according to St. John*, 476.

[781] Bultmann, *The Gospel of John*, 694.

[782] Theodore of Mopsuestia, *Commentary on the Gospel of John*, ACT (Downers Grove, IVP, 2010), 166; cf. Köstenberger, *John*, 578-580.

[783] Bultmann, *The Gospel of John*, 694.

[784] Brant, *Dialogue and Drama in the Gospel of John*, 88.

[785] Moloney comments, "The use of the verb *ballein* ("place") is much stronger than a simple "placing" of the finger or the hand. It conveys the idea of an energetic thrust." See Moloney, *The Gospel of John*, 539.

saw Jesus' hands were literally nailed by the soldiers; second, while the other disciples took the matter of Jesus' crucifixion in a regular sense, Thomas took that in a more serious sense; third, the wounded psyche of Thomas led him to keep himself away from the other disciples and to take an altogether different stand in his faith and discipleship; fourth, as one who was willing to go and die with Jesus and who wanted to know the 'way,' he was perplexed in his faith-journey to have tangible evidences; fifth, the narrator presents Thomas on par with Mary Magdalene as both of them saw, touched, and declared their faith-reactions, while others could only see and declare in unison; sixth, he represents all those who are determined for a good reason to believe and proves himself and his faith through seeing, touching, and proclaiming; and seventh, the narrator wanted to present him even above Mary Magdalene as Thomas' character was brought remarkably at the climax of the story. These factors prove the fact that Thomas was placed above all (even above Peter, the Beloved Disciple, and Mary Magdalene) and brings a convincing climax to the story of Jesus in John.[786]

. . . and putting hands in the side, I will not believe

As a matter of belief, Thomas also wanted to put his hands in the side of Jesus.[787] In that sense, Thomas' utterance in 20:25 forms an analepsis with 19:31-37. The narrator describes the events of the passion in an ironical fashion: first, the Jews got permission from Pilate to break the legs of the crucified ones (v. 31b), the soldiers came to break the legs of them all, they broke the legs of the ones on either side of Jesus (v. 32), and because Jesus was already dead they did not break his legs (v. 33);[788] and second, they did not pierce the sides of those on either side (vv. 31-34), but one of the soldiers pieced the side of Jesus with a spear, and at once blood and water came out (v. 34).[789] Talbert suggests that the soldier "doubtless aimed at the heart to be sure of his death."[790] John connects these two incidents with Old Testament prophesies (cf. Exo 12:46; Num 9:12; Psa 34:20; Zech 12:10).[791] From the scriptural as well as the situational evidence a reader can infer that Jesus indeed

---

[786] As Bruner comments, "Thomas is every generation's 'modern man,' sincere inquirer, and honest seeker. The Gospel is giving all such people, in Thomas' person and through his present insistence, some space, time, and respect." See Bruner, *The Gospel of John*, 1185.

[787] See Mopsuestia, *Commentary on the Gospel of John*, 165-166.

[788] W. M. Swartley, *John*, BCBC (Harrisonburg and Waterloo: Herald Press, 2013), 443.

[789] Morris, *The Gospel according to John*, NICNT, Revised Edition (Grand Rapids: Eerdmans, 1995), 723.

[790] C. H. Talbert, *Reading John: A Literary and Theological Commentary on the Fourth Gospel and the Johannine Epistles*, Revised Edition (Macon: Smyth and Helwys, 1992/2005), 245; cf. Swartley, *John*, 443.

[791] Köstenberger, *John*, 553-554.

died in a unique manner.[792] Thomas' demand in 20:25 is purely Johannine as the narrator records the event of piercing the side of Jesus.[793] The Johannine Jesus accepts the demand of Thomas by stating "reach out your hand and put it in my side."[794]

Thomas demands three things for his belief in Jesus' resurrection: first, seeing the mark of the nails in Jesus' hands; second, putting the finger in the mark of the nails; and third, putting the hand in his side.[795] Jesus' response to it cannot be taken as an unpleasant answer of a teacher, but as an acceptance of the demand of Thomas before others (v. 27).[796] A reader cannot demarcate between Thomas and the rest of the interlocutors in their faith responses. All of them believed either after seeing or after seeing and touching the evidence.[797] At the same time there is a distinction between Thomas and the rest of the characters as he puts forward detailed evidence as strong cause for his faith.[798] Thomas demands to see and touch the body of Jesus, especially two marks that are specified only in the Fourth Gospel. While recording the event of piercing the side in the passion narrative, the narrator would have foreseen Thomas at the climax of his story.[799]

My Lord and my God!

Thomas' utterance in v. 28 brings a clear dénouement to the story. The U-shaped plot structure of the story develops in the following fashion based on the utterance of Thomas: *first*, at the beginning: the story as a whole begins with a reference that the *Word was God* (1:1); *second*, at the middle: *the Word becomes flesh and dwelt among us*, i.e., Jesus' mission and ministry in the world; and *third*, at the closing: the resurrected Jesus reveals that he is *Lord and God* through the utterance of Thomas (20:28).[800] Larsson comments, "Thomas, by his confession in 20:28, shows that the faith expressed by the Evangelist in 1:1 was in the end 'gained in the actual intercourse of the disciple with Christ.'

---

[792] Mopsuestia, *Commentary on the Gospel of John*, 157.

[793] See Swartley, *John*, 463.

[794] See Bruner, *The Gospel of John*, 1190-1191.

[795] J. H. Bernard, *A Critical and Exegetical Commentary on the Gospel according to St. John*, ICC, Vol. 2 (Edinburgh: T & T Clark, 1929), 682.

[796] Köstenberger, *John*, 578.

[797] Thompson, *John: A Commentary*, 425.

[798] The narratorial comment in 19:35 states: "he who saw this has testified so that you also may believe."

[799] Skinner, *John and Thomas*, 76.

[800] B. Witherington, *John's Wisdom: A Commentary on the Fourth Gospel* (Louisville: Westminster John Knox Press, 1995), 344.

The incarnate Son is on the same level as the Father in his deeds."[801] Thomas' utterance in the gospel is the strongest and profoundest of all the utterances.[802] It brings to the fore the Christological apex of the entire gospel narrative.[803]

The above discussion helps us to gain a comprehensive view of the role and character of Thomas within the narrative framework of John 20:1-31. In 20:1-31, there is a steady progression of his character from the earlier appearances (11:16 and 14:5). A comparison between the utterances of Thomas and the rest of the disciples (and Mary Magdalene) reveal that he moved away from one extreme understanding (v. 25b) to the other extreme (v. 28). His earlier conviction was to believe in Jesus' resurrection and glorification only on the basis of seeing him and putting his finger in the mark of the nails. By bringing Thomas toward the climax of the story with his revelatory utterance ("My Lord and my God"), the narrator places him above all other characters. Thomas' demand to see the mark of the nails, putting his hands into the mark of the nails, and putting his hands into the side (v. 25b) attune the attention of the reader toward his Christological utterance (v. 28). The reader of the story cannot demarcate Thomas on the basis of his demand because all other characters along with him saw, touched and believed. His determination that *I will not believe* (v. 25b) has to be placed over against his phenomenal proclamation (v. 28). Thomas transforms radically from his earlier conviction that *I will not believe* to his current belief that Jesus is *My Lord and my God.* While Jesus' coming a week later with an exclusive focus on Thomas reveals his special love for Thomas, Thomas' confession reveals his love and devotion to Jesus. Thomas saw the glorified Jesus and that persuades him to utter his perception about the divine.

Jesus Shows Himself (21:1-25)

In the epilogue of the Gospel of John (21:1-25), Thomas' name appears in a fourth context. Whereas Thomas' role is active in the first three occasions (11:16; 14:5; 20:24-28), he appears as a passive character in 21:2. In this case he is counted as one among the seven disciples. At the same time, a reader can understand the characterization of chap. 21 as a whole only in relation to Thomas' immediately preceding appearance (20:24-28). Thomas is the

---

[801] T. Larsson, *God in the Fourth Gospel: A Hermeneutical Study of the History of Interpretation*, Coniectanea Biblica: New Testament Series 35 (Stockholm, Sweden: Almqvist and Wiksell International, 2001), 120; also see G. Mlakuzhyil, *The Christocentric Literary Structure of the Fourth Gospel* (Roma: Editrice Pontificio Instituto Biblico, 1987), 336-337. Keener further states, "Thomas' very skepticism makes him the ideal proponent of a high Christology by indicating the greatness of the revelation by which he was convinced." See Keener, *The Gospel of John: A Commentary*, 2:1211.

[802] Thompson, *John: A Commentary*, 423.

[803] Carson, *The Gospel according to John*, 659.

connecting link between the ending of the Book of Glory (20:24-28) and the beginning of the epilogue (21:2).[804] The transition and linkage through the appearance of Thomas contribute toward the narrative development of the overall story of John.

Jesus shows himself (21:1)

In chaps. 20-21, the narrator reports conversations of the resurrected Jesus with the key figures in the following sequence: Mary Magdalene (20:1-18); Thomas (20:24-29); Peter (21:15-19); and John (21:20-25).[805] In chap. 21, Peter, John, Thomas, and Nathanael appear at the outset of the narrative.[806] After concluding the main body of the Gospel which narrates Thomas' conversation with Jesus (20:24-29), the narrator invites the reader to compare Peter and John with Thomas.[807] A symbolical gesture is employed as Thomas keeps silence after the pivotal utterance in chap. 20 and Peter and John continue the discourse.[808]

In 21:1, the narrator reports that Jesus showed himself again to the disciples by the Sea of Tiberias.[809] While the disciples already *saw* (and also *touched*) and *believed* in chap. 20, here it is told that Jesus shows himself to the disciples once again.[810] The repetitive expressions such as "Jesus showed himself again" and "and he showed in this way" (v. 1) catch the attention of the reader.[811] Expressions such as, "he said to *them*" (v. 5), and "*they* cast it" and "[*they*] were not able to haul" (v. 6b), show the collective response of the disciples of whom Thomas is a key figure.[812] In vv. 7-8, Peter and John are brought to the foreground and the rest of the disciples are backgrounded. The other disciples were dragging in the net full of fish with an implicit understanding that it would have been done under the leadership of Thomas.

Thomas as one among those Gathered

The narrator introduces the disciples with the following formula, "gathered there together were."[813] Then he provides a list of the disciples in the following

---

[804] M. W. G. Stibbe, *John*, Readings: A New Biblical Commentary (Sheffield: Sheffield Academic, 1993), 206.

[805] Schnackenburg, *The Gospel of John*, 3:352.

[806] Sylva, *Thomas—Love as Strong as Death*, 93.

[807] See Thompson, *John: A Commentary*, 436.

[808] Blomberg, *Historical Reliability of the Fourth Gospel*, 272.

[809] See J. A. Brant, *John*, PCNT (Grand Rapids: Baker, 2011), 279.

[810] See Witherington, *John's Wisdom*, 328-351.

[811] Schnackenburg, *The Gospel of John*, 3:351.

[812] See Sylva, *Thomas—Love as Strong as Death*, 93-99.

[813] H. Ridderbos, *The Gospel of John: A Theological Commentary* (Grand Rapids: Eerdmans, 1987), 658-965.

sequence: Simon Peter, Thomas called the Twin, Nathanael of Cana in Galilee, the sons of Zebedee, and two others of his disciples.[814] Schnackenburg argues that, "the number 7 (the number of fullness in Semitic thought), can have a symbolic value: this group of disciples represents the future community, the Church (cf. also the seven churches in Rev 2-3)."[815] The first and third person plural pronouns in the narrative structure (v. 3) direct the attention of the reader toward the disciples among whom Thomas is a key figure: Simon Peter said to *them*, *they* said to him, *we* will go with you, *they* went out and got into the boat, and but that night *they* caught nothing.[816] It is made clear that Thomas did not detach from the group of disciples even after Jesus' death and resurrection.[817]

On the basis of the above delineation, the presence of Thomas in 21:2 can be understood as follows: first, in the "gathered there together" group Thomas is counted second only to Peter; second, Thomas' connection with Peter and other figures of early Christianity is brought to the fore; third, Thomas is one among the three disciples whose names are specified (i.e., Simon Peter, Thomas called the Twin, and Nathanael of Cana in Galilee); fourth, he was one among those who witnessed the post-resurrection revelation of Jesus in the Galilean context; and fifth, Thomas' silence in the chapter is meant in the context of his encounter with Jesus in 20:24-28. While the Gospel as a whole begins with the strongest utterance of Nathanael, it ends with the strongest of all the utterances from Thomas in 20:28.

Peter appears more often beginning from 1:40-42 until chap. 21. But, Peter's character develops through various ups and downs. The unsettled nature of his character is brought to the forefront more convincingly in chap. 21. While the references to Nathanael create an inclusion with his appearance at the beginning and end of the story, Thomas creates another inclusion by linking the two resurrection stories (i.e., the resurrection of Lazarus with the resurrection of Jesus, 11:16; 20:24-28). The narrator reaches the goal of his thesis statement ("the Word was God," 1:1) through the very utterance of Thomas in 20:28 ("My Lord and my God," 20:28).[818] The section 21:1-25 can be considered as a narrative expansion to stabilize the role and function of Thomas even more convincingly through the lagging natures of Peter and John. Thus, we note the grand inclusion that connects chap. 20 with chap. 1.[819]

---

[814] Bonney, *Caused to Believe*, 172.

[815] Schnackenburg, *The Gospel of John*, 3:352; Sylva, *Thomas—Love as Strong as Death*, 93-94.

[816] Haenchen, *John*, 2:222.

[817] As Barrett righty says, John has more to say about Thomas than any other evangelist. See Barrett, *The Gospel according to St. John*, 481.

[818] See Bonney, *Caused to Believe*, 172-173.

[819] See Thompson, *John: A Commentary*, 431.

Conclusion

The above analysis of the four passages (11:1-12:11; 13:1-17:26; 20:1-31; 21:1-25) provides us an extended understanding of the character of Thomas within the framework of John's gospel. A reader of the gospel gathers a view concerning Thomas' character with the help of a constellation of phraseologies and expressions embedded within the narrative master plan. While the character of Thomas is backgrounded in the first half of the gospel, he emerges as a developing character from chap. 11 on. The narrator advances his story to actualize the thesis statement in 1:1 through persuasive utterances and performative acts of Thomas in the second half. The presentation of Thomas alongside of his metaphorical utterances foregrounds his role and status in a unique fashion. Thomas' appearances in the transition episodes make him a figure with symbolical significance. That further helps the reader to view the role and status of Thomas in gnomic and universalistic terms.

The development of Thomas alongside of his persuasive speeches unlocks some of the key aspects of the extended story in the following fashion: first, Thomas' utterance in 11:16 directs the attention of the reader from the minor story of Lazarus to the major story of Jesus, i.e., a transition of the story from the death of Lazarus to the death of Jesus; second, his second utterance in 14:5 enables the reader to attune her/himself to *the way* that connects the world from below with the world from above, that is, with an exclusive claim that Jesus himself is the way to the Father; third, his utterances in 20:24-28 further directs the reader to understand the identity of Jesus not only as *Lord* but also as *God* in a Thomasine idiom; and fourth, his appearance as one among the seven disciples in 21:2 and the other disciples' deficient nature make the reader aware of Thomas' unique role within the narrative framework. As the narrator actualized the thesis statement of the gospel (1:1) through the character of Thomas in 20:28, Thomas' placement in the gospel has to be reckoned with rhetorical significance. As the narrator projects Thomas' character as a loyal, inquisitive, and developing model, his character advances toward a new level of faith commitment. The symbolic portrayal of the character of Thomas makes him to appear as gnomic and universalistic in his role and status.

PART III

Dynamic Localization: Johannine Texts and the Contexts

Chapter 9

Biblical Interpretation in the Global-Indian Context: Reading John 4:1-42 as a Paradigm

Introduction

In the globalized context of the early twenty-first century, a world characterized by integration and convergence, new modes of biblical interpretation are needed.[820] Interpreting Christian Scripture in the Indian and the South Asian contexts is a very different task when compared with the Euro-American ways of interpretation. In a context such as Indian in which various linguistic, religious, cultural, ideological, and symbolical diversities exist, a locally oriented interpretation that is attuned to global perspectives has the potential to strengthen the narrative voice of the text. The current essay attempts to foreground ways in which biblical worldviews and pluralistic Indian worldviews interact in the process of interpretation. Yet this interaction raises a number of challenging questions. Are existent methodologies of interpretation sufficient to address global readers? How would a 'local' to 'global' development help interpreters draw the attention of a global audience? How would the gnomic interpretative processes (in

[820] My attempt here is not to deal with aspects of globalization that indicate growing interdependence of countries and provinces through communication, finances, and governance. Rather, I intend to explore the possibilities of a renewed framework for New Testament interpretation. For more details, see Johnson Thomaskutty, "A Dialogue between 'the Eastern' and 'the Western' in New Testament Scholarship: A Proposal," *Bangalore Theological Forum,* LI/1 (June 2019); 1-27.

relation to descriptive processes) help the interpreter achieve her/his goal?[821] And, is a dialogue between biblical and Indian worldviews even possible?

In the following sections, I attempt to discuss an interpretative framework suited to the globalized India. A biblical model of interpretation that takes into account people of other faith traditions, religious scriptures, and socio-religious contexts will also be considered in the process. With that in mind, I discuss the following aspects: the necessity of crossing traditional boundaries, the importance of creating ideological constellations, the value of building dialogical relationships, and the goal of rhetorizing the discourse toward a 'third space.' The story of the Samaritan woman in John 4:1-42 will be considered as a paradigm for developing an interpretative framework.

Crossing the Traditional Boundaries

In the contemporary global context of India, crossing the traditional boundaries is one of the foremost necessities in biblical interpretation. An interpreter should begin her/his tasks with an attempt to understand differences based on prevalent casteistic, religious, linguistic, and ethnic identities. If an interpreter attends exclusively to her/his own contextual realities, a wider impact is impossible in today's global-Indian context. Yet part of attending to contextual realities in India involves understanding the "otherness" of different readers and the interpretative sensibilities.

In the story of the Samaritan woman as narrated in John 4, Jesus crosses traditional boundaries based on gender, race and culture in order to engage in a conversation with the woman. The dialogue develops in a threefold fashion, that is, the metaphor of water is discussed both in the material and spiritual sense in the beginning (4:7-15), the identity and the morality of the woman are foregrounded in the middle (4:16-18), and the theme of worship is brought to the fore toward the end (4:19-26). Though Jesus engages with the woman in a local context where she comes to carry water from Jacob's well, the dialogue as a whole develops, first, with the help of a universal metaphor (that is, water), and second, with a spiritual connotation attributed to it for gnomic significance. Here, Jesus uses a strategy of *dynamic localization* rather than a *pure localization*.[822] This can be viewed as a rhetorical strategy that directs readers from particulars to universals.

---

[821] Although in the English language "gnomic" often refers to a general maxim or a proverbial saying, with reference to a grammatical concept for *Koinē* Greek, Daniel B. Wallace states that "the gnomic present refers to a general, timeless fact" (*Greek Grammar beyond the Basics Greek Grammar Beyond the Basics*, 523). In speaking of a "gnomic present interpretation of the text," I am referring to the timeless dimensions of Scripture. But, such gnomic interpretation must also always be done in relation to a descriptive presentation of the text.

[822] In *pure localization/pure contextualization,* the interpreter attempts to emphasize the *local/contextual* aspects over against the *global/universal*. But, in *dynamic localization/dynamic*

In today's global-Indian context, an interpretative strategy of dynamic localization, wherein both the centrifugal and centripetal aspects of a text are foregrounded, is to be preferred over a purely local approach. That is, the text has to be interpreted as a source that develops from local to universal realities, and vice versa. In this way, the text can find its meaning in a wider global context. In the technologically advanced and postmodern context of India, an interpreter can adopt innovative methodologies to advance the scope of her/his initiative, aiming at a global audience. A majority of the hermeneutical questions raised in India today are inadequate to catch the attention of a wider, non-Indian audience. Pure localization methods and hermeneutical strategies employed may not make adequate sense for a wider audience. Those who interpret the text from Dalit, Tribal, and Adivasi perspectives mostly adopt pure localization methods and thus limit the scope of their hermeneutical engagement. As interpreters consider methods that focus primarily upon a reader's/community's particular context, they mostly serve the interests of a limited group of people.[823]

It is the biblical text, not the reader or the reader's context, that is a universal reality. Therefore, the text can be the starting point to familiarize semantic domains for global readers. An interpreter who advances from universals to contextuals can persuade the reader for wider efficacy. Similarly, an interpreter who foregrounds the contextual aspects in closer relationship with the textual horizons can develop the situational aspects through the framework of the text. Thus, both the centrifugal and centripetal movements would facilitate a dynamic localization rather than a pure localization. Contextual methodologies, with their parochial perspectives, perhaps overlook the global aspects of the text. In the process of contextualization, it would be more appropriate to begin with the universal metaphors of the text and connect them with the local aspects. Just as the Johannine Jesus and the narrator adopt this methodology in narrating the story of the Samaritan woman, an Indian interpreter can facilitate an inclusive and universal strategy where the universals are emphasized in relation to the particulars, and vice versa. In that sense, contextual interpretations in India should take a different stance by

contextualization the interpreter emphasizes the local in relation to the universal metaphors and other aspects.

[823] P.S. Jacob stated: "New Testament is the word of God and it cannot be confined to doctrinal interpretations alone. Word of God has 'infinite' possibilities of understanding and those possibilities should be explored as much as the interpreters can. Scholarship comes from understanding a wide range of possibilities while one holds on to one's belief and above all unfailing faith in Jesus." P.S. Jacob, "'Fifty Years as an Educator, Leader, and Theologian': A Friendly Conversation with Dr. P.S. Jacob," published in https://ntscholarship.wordpress.com/2012/01/10/fifty-years-as-an-educator-leader-and-theologian-a-friendly-conversation-with-dr-p-s-jacob/, dated January 10, 2012.

deemphasizing methodologies of pure localization. Crossing the traditional boundaries is one of the basic requirements of an interpreter/ation to address the global readers.

Creating Contextual and Ideological Constellations

Creating contextual and ideological constellations between the biblical worldview and the contemporary Indian worldviews should be prioritized in the process of interpreting the text. In John 4, Jesus interweaves the realities of the Samaritan context with that of the Jewish religious aspirations, and then he leads his interlocutor toward a new perspective on eternal life. In the story, the contextual reality of drawing material water is smoothly aligned with the spiritual levels of every human. That further means, Jesus transfers the contextual aspects to the universal realities with a gnomic intent. Since Jacob appears as a common figure both in the Samaritan and the Jewish scriptures (4:12), Jesus links Samaritan religiosity with that of Jewish religiosity.[824] Furthermore, the Messianic hope of Judaism has striking parallels with the figure of *Taheb* in the Samaritan religion.[825] These major connecting links are supported with the help of other themes in the narrative framework.[826] In this conversation, Jesus develops an ideological constellation to lead the woman toward the levels where he wanted her to be settled. This approach can be quite significant in the multi-religious and pluralistic context of India.

An adequate study of the Bible, as Paul Ricoeur has argued, must be thoroughly hermeneutical.[827] This principle has to be placed at the forefront of all interpretative ventures. Meaning of a text cannot be reduced to a single and literal sense, but the polyvalence of words and the semantic richness of larger linguistic units generate new meanings.[828] This polyvalence is a reality in all interpretations, but especially in relation to the Indian context. Interpretations should emerge out of a premise that biblical texts are paradigms with local implications and universal significance.

---

[824] Kevin Quast states that "Jacob's well was a symbolic stage setting for talk of more than living water. Being at the foot of Mount Gerizim, it also invited dialogue about worship." Kevin Quast, *Reading the Gospel of John: An Introduction* (New York/New Jersey: Paulist, 1991/1996), 35. Also see Thomaskutty, *Dialogue in the Book of Signs,* 141, 147-148.

[825] Craig Blomberg comments, "The Samaritans actually looked for a 'teacher,' 'restorer' and 'converter' figure called the *Taheb*, but John has provided the dynamic equivalent translations in both Hebrew (transliterated) and Greek" (*The Historical Reliability of John's Gospel* [Leicester: Inter Varsity, 2001], 101).

[826] Other major themes in the story are eternal life, hour, salvation, spirit and truth, belief, worship, spiritual food, and 'God is Spirit.'

[827] Paul Ricoeur, *Interpretation Theory: Discourse and the Surplus of Meaning* (Fort Worth: Christian University Press, 1976), 25-54.

[828] See Thomaskutty, *Dialogue in the Book of Signs*, 26.

Indian interpreters should strive to create an atmosphere of peace and harmony in the multi-religious context rather than creating discord and intolerance. An interpreter who perceives the realities of the world in general and the Indian realities in particular can foreground the textual message in a dynamic way. Biblical texts should be interpreted with the help of other religious expressions and cultural phenomena. Rather than imposing Christian ideologies upon others, interpreters should endeavor to create ideological constellations that can help to transfer the biblical message to people of other faith traditions. In that process, some of the challenging contextual realities of the country, such as caste-consciousness, multi-religious identities, and multi-cultural dimensions, require necessary attention. Every interpretative task should be actualized through connecting the universals with the contextuals, and vice versa.

In the process of interpretation, the text should be linked to Indian realities, but at the same time, Indian realities should be connected to a universal worldview. The Hindu names and concepts such as *Brahman*, *Isvara*, *Moksha*, *Atman*, and others should find meaning in the interpretative tasks and their implications should be explored in relation to universal readers. Similarly, the experiences of the Dalits, Tribals, Adivasis and other marginalized groups should be dynamically placed and interpreted with a gnomic intent. Just as Jesus used a constellation of words and ideas from the Samaritan context to lead his interlocutor toward certain understandings, interpreters of the Bible in India can adopt methodologies of such sort in today's context.

Building Dialogical Relationships

In the process of interpreting the Scripture in a pluralistic context, an interpreter should consider building dialogical relationships with people of other religious and cultural backgrounds. The dialogue of Jesus with the Samaritan woman reveals a universalistic, inter-religious and cross-cultural mission initiative as he breaks down the gender, ethnic and religious boundaries to be engaged in the *Missio Dei* with a gnomic intent. The inter-religious nature of the dialogue sharpens the woman's existent views and directs her to the Savior of the world. John's narrative techniques develop an unusual method of interpretation in order to accommodate the feelings and aspirations of the woman. Here, Jesus as the protagonist communicates the message of eternal life in relation to the contextual realities of his interlocutor.

The message of the Bible should be communicated distinctively from people to people and culture to culture. The Johannine narrator uses his literary skill at its best in the story of the Samaritan woman. When an ancient text is introduced to the global-Indian reader, it has to be interpreted with the help of athe narrator and the modern reader who interact with one another. While the dialogue within the text (between Jesus and the Samaritan woman) functions at the micro-level, the dialogue between the narrator and the modern reader functions at the macro-level. When the text is introduced to the modern reader through the perspective of an ever-continuing narrator, the text can accommodate existent realities and the reader can gain a new identity in relation to the textual horizon. In this way, the text can deal with the existential realities, such as gender discrimination, economic problems, caste hierarchy, and others, with a universalistic intent. A dialogue of the narrator with the global-Indian reader through the mediation of the Samaritan woman and her experiences would facilitate a dialogue that leads to liberation and transformation.

Rhetorizing the Discourse Toward a 'third space'

An interpreter is expected to lead readers toward the global-Indian context. Neither an interpreter who engages only in a descriptive analysis of the text nor one who emphasizes only the pure localized aspects of the Indian society can direct the attention of the reader toward a gnomic 'third space.' In John's discourse, the personal and moral aspects of the Samaritan woman are sandwiched between the divine aspects as follows: first, the dialogue begins with a discussion about the difference between "the gift of Jacob" and "the gift of God" (that is, between the "water of this world" and the "living water") in relation to eternal life (vv. 7-15); second, the woman's moral and personal aspects are dialogued subsequently (vv. 16-18); and third, emphasis on the need to adhere with the existent Jerusalem-centric worship in order to continue with the 'already . . . but . . . not yet' worship in spirit and truth (vv. 19-26). The dialogue reveals one of the central aspects toward the end of the conversation, that is, the revelation of the identity of Jesus as the Messiah. This development of the dialogue rhetorically persuades the reader to aspire for eternal life experience. Ultimately, Jesus leads the woman toward "eternal life" perspectives. Thus, a 'third space' (that is, eternal life experience) emerges in relation to but distinct from the first and second spaces (that is, the Jerusalem-centric spirituality and the Samaritan-centric spirituality).[829]

A distinguishing mark of Indian ethos is its profound spiritual outlook. But at the same time, there exists polarities of religious ideologies, economic disparities, and political conflicts. An interpreter of the text in the Indian context is expected to emphasize the ideological convergence between the biblical thought-world as well as the Indian socio-religious thought-world. Here, an interpreter should search for a "third space" created out of the biblical ideology which was intended for the original readers and the Indian religious insights in the local level in order to transcend boundaries. Such a

[829] Cf. Edward W. Soja, *Third Space: Journeys to Los Angeles and Other Real-and-Imagined Places* (Malden, Mass.: Wiley, 1996).

paradigm has the potential to enhance the possibility of mutual respect for different religions and to undo religious hatred. As Jesus directs the acumen of the Samaritan woman to eternal life perspectives and moves away from temple-centric religiosity, interpreters may also lead the communities toward a third space. This hermeneutical interplay would take into consideration a "life-sustaining pluralistic perspective" that distances all the existing categorizations and discriminations.[830]

In the global-Indian context, an interpreter must dwell on flesh and blood existence. The Bible has such a rich store of images it employs to enrich our understanding of God. A life-sustaining interpretation should be emphasized where people's existential needs would get attention, but that should not be done apart from the spiritual and universal aspirations of the text. Any religious tradition, including Hinduism, Islam, Buddhism, Jainism, Sikhism, and others, can be studied from a life-sustaining pluralistic perspective. Those elements from other scriptures should be used for enhancing the biblical message more convincing to the Indian audience.

Conclusion

In conclusion, prevailing biblical interpretations in India, with their pure localization strategies, do not have the potential to make a wider impact in the global context. Interpreters should employ dynamic localization strategies in order to make the scriptural texts relevant in both local and global contexts. A gnomic interpretative strategy in relation to descriptive aspects should be adopted in the global-Indian context for wider efficacy. In that process, the text should be considered as a paradigm to include the feelings and aspirations of diverse people, irrespective of their racial and national identities.

In order to achieve this goal, an interpreter, first of all, should cross traditional hermeneutical strategies, moving from pure localization to dynamic localization. Creating constellations of ideas between the biblical worldview and the Indian worldview might help interpretation in particular contexts, but such a strategy should not ignore a global audience. In a pluralistic context like India, building dialogical engagements with other religious and cultural aspects is both necessary and has the potential to enhance the scope of the interpretative task. Furthermore, through the ways of crossing the traditional boundaries, creating ideological constellations, and building dialogical relationships, the interpreter should aim to direct the global-Indians toward a "third space." Through these ways an interpreter can rhetorize his interpretative discourse in contexts both "here and now" and "everywhere and ever."

---

830 See S. Robertson, *Approaching Religion in a Pluralistic Context* (Bangalore: BTESSC/SATHRI, 2009), 128-134.

Chapter 10

"Religious Freedom and Conversion in India Today": Reading John's Gospel as a Jewish-Christian Conflict Narrative

Introduction

This chapter attempts to investigate how the narrator of the Fourth Gospel captures the socio-religious realities of the First Century CE through his narrative lens. The rhetoric of John is reflection of reality. In that sense it is a *mimesis*.[831] In a context in which emerging Christian communities were denied religious freedom and were widely persecuted, the Johannine community members realized that their very existence was at risk. The community was undergoing persecution from the hands of both the Jewish religio-political authorities as well as from the Empire of Rome.[832] Johannine community's antilanguage and its antisocial outlook placed it well over against the Jewish and Roman power structures.[833] While the narrator employs dualism as a major narrative means to decipher the realities, the *from above* ideology of Jesus is

[831] It is the Greek word for imitation, a central term in aesthetic and literary theory since Aristotle. See C. Baldick. *The Concise Oxford Dictionary of Literary Terms* (Oxford/New York: Oxford University Press, 1990), 137.

[832] In this essay, we will look at the conflict between the Jews and the Christians and the related aspects.

[833] Malina and Rohrbaugh state that, "Antilanguage derives from an antisociety that is set up within another society as a conscious alternative to it." See B. J. Malina and R. L. Rohrbaugh, *Social-Science Commentary on the Gospel of John* (Minneapolis: Fortress Press, 1998), 46.

in constant conflict with the *from below* ideology of the Jews. In this way, two ideologies are brought into a sharp conflict.[834] Through the usage of conflict and characterization as a major narrative device, the narrator adds vigor and flavor to the narrative dynamics of the story and its discourse in order to turn it out as a dramatic masterpiece.[835]

This situation persuades the reader to pose the following questions: How does the narrator of John's Gospel exemplify religious freedom and persecution both in explicit and implicit terms? How does the narrator convert the message from the *Sitz im Leben Jesu* to the *Sitz im Leben Kirche*?[836] How does the narrator employ the narrative techniques of *mimesis* and *diegesis*?[837] How can the Johannine community realities be used as a paradigm in the contemporary Indian context where religious freedom and conversion remain as prima factors?[838] The task of the paper is threefold: *first*, to identify the Johannine tenets of narration to decipher the socio-religious realities; *second*, to investigate how religious freedom and persecution are used as elements that propel the narrator to foreground the contextual realities; and *third*, to understand the relevance of the topic in the present day Indian context where anti-conversion activities are widely practiced. While the Johannine story remains as a gnomic rhetoric, the Indian situation reverberates the Johannine situation. In that way, the global and the local dynamisms come into play when we read John as a paradigm to the Indian realities.

Social Milieu of the Johannine Community

In a patron-client social context in which one's honor/shame was determined on the basis of several factors, people had to strive hard to usurp the superiority

---

[834] See N. R. Petersen, *The Gospel of John and the Sociology of Light: Language and Characterization in the Fourth Gospel* (Eugene, Oregon: Wipf & Stock, 1993).

[835] For more details about conflict and characterization, see J. H. Neyrey, *The Gospel of John in Cultural and Rhetorical Perspective* (Grand Rapids, Michigan: William B. Eerdmans Publishing Company, 2009), xi-xii; Baldick, *The Concise Oxford Dictionary of Literary Terms*, 61-2; S. Chatman, *Story and Discourse: Narrative Structure in Fiction and Film* (Ithaca: Cornell University, 1978).

[836] These expressions mean: *the life situation of Jesus* and *the life situation/s of the early Christian community/ies*. See W. Marxen, *Der Evangelist Markus* (Eng. Tr. Mark the Evangelist, 1959/1969).

[837] Baldick says *diegesis* as "an analytic term used in modern narratology to designate the narrated events or story (French, *histoire*) as a 'level' distinct from that of the narration." See Baldick, *The Concise Oxford Dictionary of Literary Terms*, 57; also see A. J. Greimas and J. Courtés, *Semiotics and Language: An Analytical Dictionary* (Bloomington: Indiana University Press, 1979), 79.

[838] R. V. Peace, *Conversion in the New Testament: Paul and the Twelve* (Grand Rapids: Eerdmans, 1999).

status over against the prevailing inferiorities.[839] It was in such a context the Christian communities, especially the Johannine community as an emerging group, had to undergo constant existential struggles.[840] As a newly emerged community, i.e., without having canonized scriptures and a highly organized ecclesiastical set up, it had to suffer persecution both from the conservative religious Jews and from the imperial authorities. The attitudinal trends of the religious Jews described in the Gospel of John provide ample details pertinent to questions such as: How does the Judaism of the day tolerate minority faith/religious communities? How were the minority communities affected due to religious intolerance? How were the Johannine sectarians persecuted extensively?[841] The very existence of the Johannine community was in danger as it was a minority community without power and influence.[842] The bossy attitude of the Jewish religious authorities toward the emerging Christian community/ies led the situation to violent and traumatizing ends.

John the narrator captures *the story of Jesus* the protagonist in order to re-tell and re-interpret that with greater efficacy. In *the story of Jesus*, his mission initiatives were extended from Jerusalem to Cana (2:1-11; 4:46-51), Capernaum (4:46-51; 6:22-59), Sychar (4:1-42), Bethany (11:1-42), and other Israelite provinces.[843] In that sense, Jesus' mission flourished from the southern provinces to the northern parts of the country. The engagement of Jesus as an agent of God resulted into the establishment of several faith communities across the Israelite context. A good number of communities emerged during the time of Jesus later on accepted John the Beloved Disciple as their leader. In that sense, the Johannine church was not merely a Jerusalem-centric congregation at its beginning stages but rather a confederation of several churches.[844] The community/ies had to bear with and overcome the growing opposition from

---

[839] See D. A. deSilva, "Patronage," *Dictionary of NT Background*, eds. C. A. Evans and S. E. Porter (Downers Grove: InterVarsity Press, 2000), 766-771.

[840] See C. S. Keener, *The IVP Bible Background Commentary: New Testament* (Downers Grove: InterVarsity Press, 1993), 827; cf. deSilva, "Patronage," *DNTB*, 766-771. For Keener, a 'client' is "a person socially dependent on a patron in Roman society." See Keener, *IVP Bible Background Commentary*, 824.

[841] Köstenberger says that, "John acknowledges that 'salvation comes from the Jews' (4:22), yet he portrays Israel as part of the unbelieving world that rejects Jesus. Jesus' 'own' (the 'Jews') did not receive him (1:11). In their place, the Twelve, who are now 'his own,' become the recipients of his love (13:1; cf. chap. 17). The Jewish leaders, on the other hand, are said not even to belong to Jesus' flock (10:26)." See A. J. Köstenberger, *John*, BECNT (Grand Rapids: Baker Academic Press, 2004), 15.

[842] The members of the community would have been people like fisherfolk, Samaritans, Galilean peasants, and the healed ones (i.e., invalids, blind, and poor). Also see Köstenberger, *John*, 15-16.

[843] And also to some Greeks (cf. 12:20-25).

[844] The North and South riddles of the Gospel clearly bring this aspect to the fore.

the part of the Jerusalem-and temple-centric religious authorities. While Jesus' ministry was mostly concentrated in the Jerusalemite context in John, later on the community of the Beloved Disciple flourished from its Jerusalem-rootedness to the Ephesus-centric Gentile context.[845] The narrator adds further ingredients to *the story of Jesus* (i.e., *Sitz im Leben Jesu*) in order to re-create and re-tell it according to the new demands of his situation (i.e., *Sitz im Leben Kirche*; see Figure 2).[846]

Figure 2: *Sitz im leben Jesu* to *Sitz im leben Kirche*

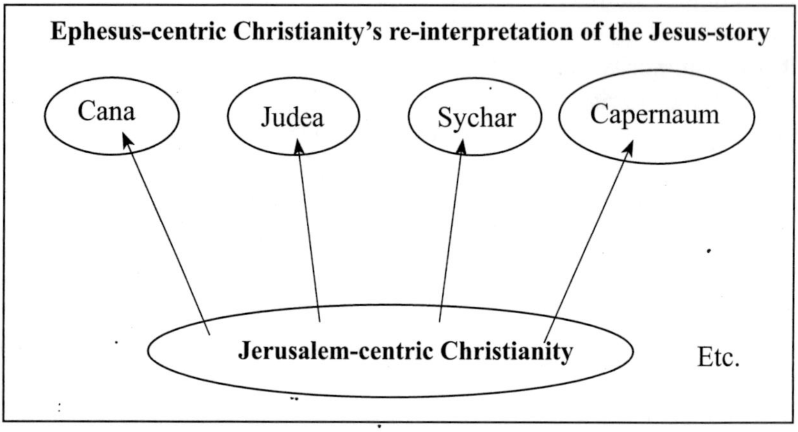

Toward the end of the First Century CE, John's community started to flourish circumscribed around a leading person called the Beloved Disciple. As Martyn explains, the story of Jesus was used as a paradigm to reinterpret and implicate to the Johannine situation where the community had to undergo persecution from the hands of 'the Jews' and the Empire of Rome.[847] The Ephesus-centric Johannine community focused on the person and work of Jesus, his life situation, and his *ethos-pathos-logos* as kernels to develop their ideological and epistemological framework. The community's theology emerged out of their ideological conflicts and contextual beckoning in its developmental stages. Keener is of the view that, "The Johannine Christians had been made

[845] In that sense, the Johannine community had several stages of development [cf. J. L. Martyn, *History and Theology in the Fourth Gospel* (Nashville: Abington, 1968); R. E. Brown, *The Community of the Beloved Disciple* (New York: Paulist, 1979)]. The community would have changed its headquarters from Jerusalem to Ephesus due to constant persecutions from the side of the Jews. Cf. A. J. Köstenberger, *The Mission of Jesus and the Disciples: According to the Fourth Gospel* (Grand Rapids: Eerdmans, 1998).

[846] One has to understand that Johannine church had roots in both the Israelite and the Gentile contexts. Cf. Marxsen, *Der Evangelist Markus*.

[847] See Martyn, *History and Theology in the Fourth Gospel*.

unwelcome by local synagogue authorities, treated as if their very Jewishness was held in question because they believed in Jesus as the Messiah. The Roman authorities were also suspicious of people who did not worship the emperor but were not Jewish."[848] As the Johannine narrator merges the *Sitz im Leben Jesu* with the *Sitz im Leben Kirche*, the conflicting situation of Jesus in the thirties was familiarized in relation to the Johannine community struggles in the latter half of the century (see Figure 2).[849]

The Jews are presented in the Gospel as hostile to Jesus and all those who confess that he is the Christ (cf. 9:22; 12:42; 16:2). Their antagonistic trends are widespread in the narrative framework of the Fourth Gospel (cf. 11:45-53; 18:28-19:16; 19:17-22; 20:19).[850] Moloney says that, "The conflicts between Jesus and 'the Jews' are more the reflection of a christological debate at the end of the first century than a record of encounters between Jesus and his fellow Israelites in the thirties of that century."[851] Thus John's typical vantage point enables him to realign *the story of Jesus* within the narrative framework of *the story of the Johannine community*.[852]

The geographical/topographical details and the eye-witness statements of the Fourth Gospel provide ample evidences concerning the attachment of the Beloved Disciple in the mission initiatives of Jesus.[853] The narrator portrays Jesus as the incarnated Word, the agent of God, the Savior of the world, and the glorious Son of Man.[854] This portrait of Jesus introduces a conflicting situation

---

[848] See Keener, *IVP Bible Background Commentary*, 261. Köstenberger states that, "If Thomas' confession of Jesus as 'my Lord and my God' is intended to evoke associations of emperor worship under Domitian (81-96 CE), a date after 81 CE would appear most likely." See Köstenberger, John, 8; cf. R. E. Brown, *The Gospel according to John (i-xii)*, The Anchor Bible, Vol. 1 (Garden City: Doubleday, 1966), lxx-lxxv; J. H. Neyrey, *The Gospel of John*, The New Cambridge Bible Commentary (Cambridge: Cambridge University Press, 2007), 30-31.

[849] See F. J. Moloney, *The Gospel of John*, Sacra Pagina Series, ed. D. J. Harrington (Collegeville: The Liturgical Press, 1989/1998), 9; cf. C. L. Blomberg, *The Historical Reliability of John's Gospel: Issues and Commentary* (Leicester: Apollos, 2001); Marxsen, *Der Evangelist Markus*.

[850] See Moloney, *The Gospel of John*, 9-11; C. Bennema, "A Comparative Approach to Understanding Character in the Gospel of John," *Character and Characterization in the Gospel of John*, ed. C. W. Skinner (London/New York: Bloomsbury, 2012/2013), 44.

[851] See Moloney, *The Gospel of John*, 10; see G. R. Beasley-Murray, *John*, Word Biblical Commentary, Vol. 36 (Waco, Texas: Word Books Publisher, 1987), xliv; also see Brown, *The Gospel according to John*, 1:lxx-lxxv.

[852] See D. Tovey, *Jesus, Story of God: John's Story of Jesus* (Adelaide: ATF Press, 2007).

[853] Cf. J. C. S. Redman, "Eyewitness Testimony and the Characters in the Fourth Gospel," *Character and Characterization in the Gospel of John*, ed. C. W. Skinner (London/New York: Bloomsbury, 2012/2013), 59-78.

[854] See M. W. G. Stibbe, *John*, Readings: A New Biblical Commentary (Sheffield: Sheffield Academic, 1993), 16-17.

between the traditional Judaism and the newly emerged Christian community.[855] John's two-level drama brings to the foreground a conflicting situation of the Johannine church in rhetorical and performative means to the reader. While the Qumran community adopted a *rhetoric of distance,* the Johannine community maintained a *rhetoric of difference.*[856] Johannine community was a resistance movement that emphasized an ideological conflict between *from above* and *from below* rather than a conflict between *this aeon* and *coming aeon.*[857] Thus, Johannine eschatology is more convincingly realized and existential.

The Christology of John coupled with his eschatology derives its roots out of the existential struggles of the people. Brown says that, "John emphatically insists that Jesus is the Messiah, the very claim that the Jews rejected. John uses the Greek form of this title (*christos*) more frequently than does any other Gospel and is the only Gospel to use the transliterated form *messias* (1:41; 4:25)."[858] The emphasis on Jesus' messiahship enabled the community to develop their own idiom in performative linguistic pattern.[859] Borchert says that, "The Johannine community, which probably developed within the context of a Jewish cradle, was . . . unable to continue within the protected status of Judaism as a *religio licita* (a licensed religion) in the Roman world."[860] Thus, the narrative master plan of John draws the attention of the reader toward the social realities of the First Century CE. This was actualized with the help of merging the story of Jesus with the story of the Johannine community, and with the help of both the techniques of *showing* and *telling*.

---

[855] A. J. Kelly and F.J. Moloney, *Experiencing God in the Gospel of John* (New York: Paulist Press, 2003), 44-48.

[856] Though we outline a lot of similarities between Qumran and Johannine communities, this difference is one of the striking areas to be seriously considered in the process of interpretation.

[857] The *vertical eschatology* of John develops steadily within the framework of the 'from above' and 'from below' conflict. But, in the Synoptics a *horizontal eschatology* is at focus as 'this aeon' is in conflict with 'coming aeon.' Cf. J. Thomaskutty, "Glo[b/c]alization and Mission[s]: Reading John's Gospel," *New Life Theological Journal*, Vol. 5/1 (Jan.-June 2015/4), 57.

[858] Cf. B. Milne, *The Message of John*. The Bible Speaks Today (Downers Grove: InterVarsity Press, 1993), 25-27; Stibbe, *John*, 19; Namita, *A New Paradigm for Evangelization in the Third Millennium* (Bangalore: St. Peter's Pontifical Institute Publications, 2000), 21-22.

[859] See M. Huie-Jolly, "Maori 'Jews' and a Resistant Reading of John 5:10-47," *John and Postcolonialism: Travel, Space and Power*, eds. M. W. Dube and J. L. Staley (London/New York: Sheffield Academic Press, 2002), 94; K. Quast, *Reading the Gospel of John: An Introduction* (New York/Mahwah: Paulist Press, 1991/1996), 5.

[860] See G. L. Borchert, *John 1-11*, The New American Commentary (Nashville: B&H Publishing Group, 1996), 72-73; L. Morris, *The Gospel according to John*, Revised Edition (Grand Rapids: Eerdmans, 1995), 35-42; Blomberg, *The Historical Reliability of John's Gospel*, 62; Quast, *Reading the Gospel of John*, 4-5.

Synagogue-and-Church Conflict within the Story of John

The narrator of the story uses the *ipsissima vox* of Jesus (very *voice* of Jesus) rather than *ipsissima verba Jesu* (very own *words* of Jesus) in order to narrate it in his own idiom.[861] This narratorial trend enabled him to delineate the synagogue-and-church conflict in a dynamic way with the help of dialogue at the *intradiegetic* (i.e., among the characters within the story) and *metadiegetic* (i.e., between the narrator and the reader) levels.[862] The narrator of the story convinces the reader the underlying disputation through the narratorial phenomenon called conflict and characterization. The agent of God schema where Jesus comes to the world as *one from above* over against the prevailing schema of *the world from below* brings out a conflict of its own.[863]

In the story of the blind man turned healed (in chap. 9:1-41), the synagogue-and-church conflict comes out in convincing terms. One of the conspicuous factors is the progress of the man in his apprehension about the person of Christ: *first*, "the man called Jesus" (v. 11); *second*, "He is a prophet" (v. 17); *third*, he talks about fearing God and being obedient to his will (vv. 30-33); *fourth*, he calls him 'Lord' and tells him 'I believe' (v. 38); and *fifth*, he 'worshipped him' (v. 38).[864] As a member of the local synagogue, he makes all these assertions and comprehensions; but the religious authorities categorically reject them all.[865] This situation introduces a conflicting situation within the synagogue.[866] In order to convince the reader the narrator adds more material to the story of Jesus from within the existential struggles of the community.[867] Petersen says, "John's community is an *anti-society* because it understands itself as other to the dominant society that has made it other. The very identity of his people is dependent upon their being other, and this is evident in their

---

[861] *Ipsissima Vox* is a Latin expression meaning "the very voice," and describes the view that the NT Gospel-accounts capture the concepts that Jesus expressed, but not exact words. *Ipsissima Vox* is contrasted with *Ipsissima Verba*, meaning "the very words."

[862] Culpepper quoted in Thomaskutty, *Dialogue in the Book of Signs*, x. These terms were introduced by G. Genette, *Narrative Discourse: An Essay in Method* (Ithaca: Cornell University, 1980), 228-234.

[863] Cf. Martyn, *History and Theology in the Fourth Gospel*, 24-36; J.G. Van der Watt, *An Introduction to the Johannine Gospel and Letters*, T&T Clark Approaches to Biblical Studies (New York: T&T Clark, 2007), 112-114.

[864] See Thomaskutty, *Dialogue in the Book of Signs*, 349-350; Köstenberger, *John*, 277-296; R. A. Culpepper, *Anatomy of the Fourth Gospel: A Study in Literary Design* (Philadelphia: Fortress Press, 1983), 140.

[865] See Martyn, *History and Theology in the Fourth Gospel*, 24-36.

[866] See Moloney, *The Gospel of John*, 10; also see Brown, *The Gospel according to John*, Vol. 1, lxxiii-lxxv; Martyn, *History and Theology in the Fourth Gospel*, 37-62.

[867] Cf. Brown, *The Community of the Beloved Disciple*, 1979.

special use of the everyday language of the society that has rejected them."[868] Thus, the Johannine polyvalence is exemplified through its layered treatment of contexts and issues.

Just as *the story of Jesus* developed in the Israelite context, initially *the story of the Johannine community* developed in the surroundings of the temple at Jerusalem. Later on the community flourished in the North Israelite (i.e., Galilee and Samaria) and in the Gentile (most possibly to Ephesus) contexts. The shift of the community's setting from Jerusalem to Ephesus can be inferred from the geographical/topographical details and narrative asides that include the transliteration of Hebrew terms in the text.[869] While the Northern and Southern Israelite contexts introduce a riddling situation at the local level, the Israelite and Gentile contexts introduce a wider riddling situation within the narratorial framework of the Gospel. Moloney says that, "The community began as a small group of Jerusalem Christians and its members developed an increasingly unique understanding of Jesus as they responded to a variety of experiences, both religious and social."[870] In the Gospel, Jesus is introduced as an agent of transformation over against the existing socio-political and religio-cultural phenomena. He invites people toward a new experience under the power of God. Believing in Jesus is suggested as the foundational step in order to experience life in its abundance.[871]

People without repentance and an experience of *metanoia* cannot enter into such a situation. This messianic axiom divides *the world from below* into two groups, those who follow the light-logos-life (*licht-liebe-leben*; i.e., converted) and those who follow the way of the world and hence under darkness (i.e., non-converted).[872] This religious scenario introduces a conflictive situation within the socio-political and religious context. From all these details it is evident for the reader that the Johannine community underwent opposition and persecution from the hand of Jewish religious authorities both within the Palestinian and Gentile contexts.

The motif of 'newness' in the deeds and discourses of Jesus and its further propagation by the Johannine community usher a conflicting situation between the 'old' hierarchical system of Judaism and the newly advancing

---

[868] See Petersen, *The Gospel of John and the Sociology of Light*, 89, 108.

[869] The narratorial techniques used in the Gospel are with an aim to describe the story of Jesus with a larger intent. Hence, the narrator describes the geographical/topographical details, Hebrew/Aramaic terms, concepts and chronological aspects.

[870] See Moloney, *The Gospel of John*, 12; also see R. Kysar, "The Whence and Whither of the Johannine Community," *Life in Abundance: Studies of John's Gospel in Tribute to Raymond E. Brown*, ed. J. R. Donahue (Collegeville: Liturgical Press, 2005), 65-81.

[871] See Stibbe, *John*, 9-19.

[872] See G. Voigt, *Licht-Lieve-Leben: Das Evangelicum nach Johannes* (Gottingen: Vandenhoeck & Ruprecht, 1991).

group of John.[873] The introduction of the *new Genesis* (1:1-18), *new wine* (2:1-11), *new temple* (2:19-22), *new birth* (3:3), *new water* (4:13-14; 7:37-38), *new life* (4:46-54; 11:1-54), *new exodus* (6:16-21), *new manna* (6:22-59), *new Moses* (6:22-59),[874] *new bread* (6:22-59), *new light* (8:12; 9:5), and the like were severe attacks on the existence and sustenance of the age old Jewish hierarchical system.[875] Köstenberger says that, "Like his portrait of Jesus, John's presentation of the new messianic community follows a salvation-historical pattern. In keeping with OT typology, believers are described as a 'flock' (chap. 10) and as 'branches' of the vine (chap. 15). John, however, does not teach that the church replaces Israel. Rather, he identifies *Jesus* as Israel's replacement: *he* is God's 'vine' taking the place of God's OT 'vineyard,' Israel (Isa 5)."[876] Thus, the incarnation of *logos* as the fulfiller of the Messianic hopes and as the harbinger of a new covenantal relationship was against the axioms of the Jewish religious authorities.

The presentation of Jesus as the 'first utterance' and the 'wisdom of God' facilitated the idea that Jesus supersedes everything before.[877] John as a genre mosaic vibrantly enthuses the reader to get involved in the story-world. The focalization of the story develops as the voices of the protagonist (i.e., Jesus) and the narrator merge together and persuasively influence the implied/historical/contemporary reader(s) of the text. This facilitates the *gnomic* (rather than the *descriptive*) significance of the Johannine story.[878]

In Jesus' arguments with the Jews, as Brown states, "There is an attack . . . against the religious position of Judaism—Jesus is the Messiah, and in his presence and face to face with that he has done, Judaism has lost its pre-eminence."[879] Moreover, as Martyn elaborates, there were debates within the synagogue and the introduction of the curse of the heretics or deviants

[873] See J. Thomaskutty, "Reading John's Gospel to the Nepali Context," *Nepali Theological Journal* (South Korea: ACTS College, 2015/3), 63-82.

[874] See Petersen, *The Gospel of John and the Sociology of Light*, 104-109.

[875] See C. S. Keener, *The Gospel of John: A Commentary*, Vol. 1 (Peabody: Hendrickson, 2003), 68.

[876] See Köstenberger, *John*, 15; also see W. F. Howard, *The Gospel according to St. John*, The Interpreter's Bible, Vol. 8 (New York/Nashville: Abingdon Cokesbury Press, 1952), 449-450; Morris, *The Gospel according to John*, 55.

[877] See Kelly and Moloney, *Experiencing God in the Gospel of John*, 43-48.

[878] See J. Thomaskutty, "Biblical Interpretation in the Global-Indian Context," *Fuller Magazine: Reading Scripture Globally* 8 (2017), 64-68.

[879] See Brown, *The Gospel according to John*, Vol. 1, lxx-lxxv; see Bennema, "A Comparative Approach," 14; cf. Thomaskutty, "Glo[b/c]alization and Mission[s]," 64; C. H. Dodd, *The Interpretation of the Fourth Gospel* (Cambridge: The University Press, 1960), 289-443.

in Judaism (*Birkat ha-Minim*).[880] Martyn's thesis certainly has attracted a great deal of attention that involves exclusion from the synagogue and the relationship of this exclusion to the conflict texts in John.[881] Manns says that, "The 'benediction' of the *Minim* no longer allowed members of the two communities to pray together. Discussions on the person of Jesus were at the origin of the 'benediction' of the *Minim*. John attaches great importance to these discussions (7:26-28; 7:40-43; 12:34)."[882] The emerging opposition in Jerusalem (chap. 5), in Galilee (chap. 6), the domination of the Pharisees (chaps. 7-10), the domination of the chief priests (chap. 11), and Jesus' trial and death (chaps. 18-19) are the local manifestations of the plot of this world against Jesus.[883]

The "sending out of the synagogue" (*aposunagogē*) and the struggle of the newly emerged Johannine community are vividly portrayed by the narrator with the help of both explicit and implicit terms.[884] Painter says that, "In the *diaspora* the Johannine Christians were excommunicated from the synagogue. The threat of excommunication was a fearful weapon as is evidenced by John 9:22; 12:42. At some stage it was the purpose of the Johannine tradition to encourage secret believers to confess their faith and to face excommunication."[885] The dualistic contrast and the performative linguistic phenomenon of the Johannine text dramatically foreground the community conflict in the First Century context. The contrast between the 'believing' and 'unbelieving,' 'sons of light' and 'sons of darkness,' and 'world from above' and 'world from below' rhetorically introduces the Jewish-Christian conflict with the help of figurative language and with the help of socio-political and

---

[880] See Martyn, *History and Theology in the Fourth Gospel*, 92, 131; see Borchert, *John 1-11*, 46; F. Manns, *John and Jamnia: How the Break Occurred between Jews and Christians* (Jerusalem: Franciscan Printing Press, 1988).

[881] Bennema says that, "'The Jews' consist of those Jews who are hostile and opposed to Jesus, especially from among the religious leaders in Jerusalem (e.g., 1:19; 5:16-18; 6:41, 52; 7:1; 8:31-59; 9:13-34; 10:31-39)." See Bennema, "A Comparative Approach," 13; cf. Borchert, *John 1-11*, 47.

[882] See Manns, *John and Jamnia*, 32; also see C. Bennema, *Excavating John's Gospel: A Commentary for Today* (Delhi: ISPCK, 2005), 13-14; Quast, *Reading the Gospel of John*, 5.

[883] Van der Watt sees a contrast between 'the family of God' and 'the children of devil' within John's narrative framework. See Van der Watt, *An Introduction to the Johannine Gospel and the Letters*, 30-77; also see Thomaskutty, "Glo[b/c]alization and Mission[s]," 64; Neyrey, *The Gospel of John*, 5-9.

[884] See Martyn, *History and Theology in the Fourth Gospel*, 37-62; Brown, *The Community of the Beloved Disciple*; Tovey, *Jesus, Story of God*, 148-152.

[885] See J. P. Painter, *The Quest for the Messiah: The History, Literature and Theology of the Johannine Community* (Nashville: Abingdon, 1993), 128; also see Quast, *Reading the Gospel of John*, 59-77.

religio-cultural phenomena.[886] Thompson says that, "The plot of the Gospel cannot be determined unless the readers comprehend the dialectical structure. In John's Gospel, God incarnate in Jesus has a controversy with the world, the Jewish leaders who epitomize the world in its opposition to the Gospel (John 5:16, 18; 6:41; 7:1; 10:31; 11:8)."[887] This reality is at the heart of John's Gospel. A paradigmatic reader of John's Gospel can understand the larger picture only by means of grasping the narratorial dynamism which elucidates the Synagogue-and-Church conflict and the subsequent minority assaults in the First Century context/s.

Dialogue at the Center of the Johannine Narrative

The narrator of the Johannine story develops his rhetoric by placing a Jewish-Christian dialogue at the centre. The narrator aligns the characterization of *the story of Jesus* within *the story of the Johannine community* context, i.e., as one between the protagonists (the followers of Jesus/the community of John) and the antagonists (the religious Jews in the socio-religious context). This narrative tendency helps the reader to understand the *macro*-structure of the gospel through the medium of the *micro*-and *meso*-structures. Keener is of the view that, "Most of Jesus' discourses in John 3-12 are conflicts with the Jewish authorities and thus bear some resemblances to the briefer rabbinic accounts of arguments with opponents."[888] John's Gospel is structured as a multi-layered drama at the *exchange*, *episode* and *narrative* levels.[889] The Jewish-Christian conflict is narrated in a concentrated form in chaps. 7-8, 9, and 11-12. The narrator uses dialogic trends at the *intradiegetic* and *metadiegetic* levels.[890] The aspects of dialogue and drama within the story of John make it a persuasive artistry. The narrator as a riddler captures the attention of the reader toward the underlying conflict and the resultant characterization through the means of the two-level story.[891]

Some of the prominent dialogues between Jesus and the Jewish leaders are narrated as follows: Jesus and the religious leaders in Jerusalem in 5:16-47 and 7:14-8:59; with the crowd and the Jewish leaders in 6:25-59; with the Greeks and the Jerusalem crowd in 12:20-36; with the high priest and the

---

[886] See Moloney, *Gospel of John*, 11; Borchert, *John 1-11*, 47-49; Howard, *The Gospel according to St. John*, 449-450.

[887] See Thompson, 1992, 373; also see J. Thomaskutty, "Dialogical Nature of John's Prologue," *Union Biblical Seminary Journal*, Vol. 8.2-9.1 (Sep. 2013-Mar. 2015), 13.

[888] See Keener, *The IVP Bible Background Commentary*, 262.

[889] See Thomaskutty, *Dialogue in the Book of Signs*.

[890] *Intradiegetic* means "dialogue among the characters within the story," and *metadiegetic* means "dialogue between the author/narrator and the reader of the story."

[891] See Martyn, *History and Theology in the Fourth Gospel*; P. N. Anderson, *The Riddles of the Fourth Gospel: An Introduction to John* (Minneapolis: Fortress Press, 2011).

guard in 18:19-24; and with Pilate (18:28-19:16).[892] These dialogues develop in antonymous terms as the religious ideologies of the Jews are in sharp conflict with the ideologies of Jesus. In chap. 5, a dramatic protagonist-and-antagonist conflict begins to develop and the protagonist takes full control by turning the dialogue into a monologue.[893] Johannine dialogues are reproductions of constant interactions, encounters, conflicts, and 'accommodation and disruption' tendencies developed within the Johannine community context.

The Johannine community was a marginal group expelled from the synagogue (16:2) and had to deal with the issues of: *first*, their relationship to Judaism; *second*, questions of self-identity; *third*, minority status; and *fourth*, oppression.[894] The narratives play a vital role at the intervals of utterance-units, as in chap. 6, as they add dramatic setting to the story. The *murmuring* scene in v. 41, *argument* scene in v. 52, and *grumbling* scene in vv. 60-61 are implicitly introduced as 'community dialogues.'[895] The Johannine community concerns over against the other majority cultures are reflected through the dialogic interactions of the characters.[896] In order to sharpen the conflicts, plot features such as *reversal*, *recognition* and *suffering* are integrally embedded within the dramatic narrative.[897]

In chaps. 7-8, the responses and actions of the Jews over against Jesus are mostly without evidence, shallow in description, emotional in attitude, verbally abusive, unknowing and misunderstanding in sense, and violence-ridden.[898] In chap. 9, "The Jews are viewed as 'unbelieving' and antagonistic characters, who misunderstood the words of Jesus, and revile and drive out the 'believing.'"[899] In John's dialogue, Jesus, the protagonist, is in constant dialogue with his interlocutors in order to reveal his messiahship and to lead them toward eternal life perspectives. On several occasions, the narrator employs the *question-and-answer*, *request-rebuke-response*, and *challenge-*

---

[892] Cf. Anderson, *The Riddles of the Fourth Gospel*, 13-14.

[893] While vv. 1-18 develops in the form of dialogues, vv. 19-47 develops mostly as a single monologue. Cf. Quast, *Reading the Gospel of John*, 59-77.

[894] For more details, refer to J. Thomaskutty, *Proefschrift: The Nature and Function of Dialogue in the Book of Signs* (Nijmegen: Radboud Universiteit Nijmegen, 2014).

[895] Cf. Culpepper, *Anatomy of the Fourth Gospel*, 127.

[896] See Thomaskutty, *Proefschrift*, 289.

[897] See Thomaskutty, *Proefschrift*, 289; Dodd, *The Interpretation of the Fourth Gospel*, 297-389.

[898] See Thomaskutty, *Dialogue in the Book of Signs*, 308; Dodd, *The Interpretation of the Fourth Gospel*, 297-389; Quast, *Reading the Gospel of John*, 59-77.

[899] See Thomaskutty, *Dialogue in the Book of Signs*, 349; Quast, *Reading the Gospel of John*, 59-77.

and-riposte methods to maintain the dialectical nature of the dialogues.[900] Thus, the majority religion of Judaism is portrayed as antagonistic and as a great threat for the faith and practices of the newly emerged Johannine community.

The dialogues at the *micro*-level are flavored and supplemented with several literary devices. Dialogue forms such as *double meaning-misunderstanding-clarification* (see 8:12-20, 21-30; 9:39-41; 11:7-16, 17-27; 12:12-36a),[901] *question-and-counter question* (6:60-66), *community type* (7:37-44; 9:8-12), *religious-theological* (7:14-36; 8:31-59), *controversial* (5:1-13; 6:22-59; 7:14-36; 8:31-59; 9:1-41; 11:7-16, 17-27; 12:12-36a), *forensic* (7:45-52; 8:31-59; 9:8-12, 13-17, 18-23, 24-34, 39-41; 10:22-39) and others appear at the exchange level.[902] At the *meso*-level, the conflicting ideologies of the protagonist and his interlocutors are delineated in detail.[903] At the *macro*-level, especially in the Book of Signs, all the dialogues are dynamically interlocked within the narrative framework (cf. 1:19-12:50).[904]

The animosity-centered and dualistic pattern of the Book of Signs provide insights concerning the 'hate' language of the Jews over against Jesus the protagonist, his speeches, and his mission initiatives. Their hate language is explicit through their activity of naming him a 'deceiver' (7:12), 'demonic' (7:20; 8:48, 52; 10:20-21), 'Samaritan' (8:48), and 'Son of Joseph' (6:42).[905] Other aspects of 'hate' language such as *diminution* and *reduction* are also obvious in the language of the Jews (6:42, 52).[906] The narrator's memory of the actual speeches and events concerning Jesus is reproduced in the light of the ongoing struggles of the community.[907]

The violent actions of Jesus' interlocutors are beyond the pattern of the dialogue.[908] The antagonistic and exclusivistic attitudes of the Jews toward those who do not hold on to their religious ideologies are obvious through

---

[900] See Thomaskutty, *Dialogue in the Book of Signs*, 446; Baldick, *Concise Oxford Dictionary of Literary Terms*, 56.

[901] Cf. Neyrey, *The Gospel of John*, 12-13, 78, 90-91, 195-196.

[902] See J. D. Hernando, "Episodes of Personal Encounter: Inquiry into John's Christology," *But These are Written . . . Essays on Johannine Literature in Honor of Professor Benny C. Aker*, eds. C. S. Keener, J. S. Crenshaw, and J. Daniel May (Eugene: Pickwick Publications, 2014), 80-90.

[903] See Dodd, *The Interpretation of the Fourth Gospel*, 297-389.

[904] See Quast, *Reading the Gospel of John*, 59-77.

[905] Roy explains four language structures: naming, diminutives, reduction, and metaphors. See J. M. Roy, *Love to Hate: America's Obsession with Hatred and Violence* (New York: Colombia University Press, 2002), 25-42.

[906] Cf. Roy, *Love to Hate*, 32.

[907] See Thomaskutty, *Dialogue in the Book of Signs*, 466-7; Dodd, *Interpretation of the Fourth Gospel*, 297-389; Martyn, *History and Theology in the Fourth Gospel*, 24-151.

[908] See Martyn, *History and Theology in the Fourth Gospel*, 24-151.

the ongoing vocal exchanges within John's narrative.[909] This is portrayed vividly through their actions: i.e., "attempting to kill Jesus" on several occasions (5:18; 7:19-20, 25; 11:45-53), "driving" the healed man out of the synagogue (9:34b), and "plotting to kill Lazarus" (12:9-11).[910] John's dialogue has polyvalent connections within the narratorial framework as it works well with the *sign language* and the "I AM" sayings. The signs and dialogue are integrally connected in John and together they help the protagonist to reveal himself.[911]

Moreover, Jesus' revelatory aspects are potentially reflected through his "I AM" sayings (see 6:35, 48; 8:12; 9:5; 10:7, 9, 11; 11:25; 14:6; 15:1, 5).[912] Through all these the narrator foregrounds the undercurrent struggles and conflicts of the Johannine community. Furthermore, dialogue development is significant in chaps. 18-19. The Passion Discourse includes the verbal interactions during Jesus' betrayal and arrest (18:1-11), Jesus' conversation with Pilate and the Jews (18:28-19:15), post-crucifixion events (19:16-24), and Jesus' words from the cross (19:25-30) in dialogue-centric and dramatic fashion.[913] Thus, the conflict stories are fashioned with the help of dialogues, the controversies are discussed from the point of view of eternal life, and the characterization is portrayed with the help of dualistic terms and themes.

To show the undercurrents and the conflicts between the Jewish and Johannine communities, the narrator uses socially intertwined linguistic phenomena. Brant sees *episodic structure* and *transitions* as key elements in the organization of the Johannine plot. She identifies *peripeteia*,[914] *anagnōrisis*, and *pathos* as the significant plot elements.[915] Within the dramatic plot structure

---

[909] See Thomaskutty, *Dialogue in the Book of Signs*, 468; Quast, *Reading the Gospel of John*, 59-77.

[910] Cf. Neyrey, *The Gospel of John*, 210-211.

[911] See Thomaskutty, *Dialogue in the Book of Signs*, 447.

[912] Refer to Thomaskutty, *Dialogue in the Book of Signs*, 450; Dodd, *Interpretation of the Fourth Gospel*, 297-389.

[913] D. A. Carson, *The Gospel according to John* (Leicester: IVP/Michigan: Eerdmans, 1991); Quast, *Reading the Gospel of John*, 59-77.

[914] Brant says that, "The idea of peripeteia as a single event or as a simple reversal of fortune belies the complexity of how reversals are handled in Greek tragedies." J. A. Brant, *Dialogue and Drama: Elements of Greek Tragedy in the Fourth Gospel* (Peabody: Hendrickson Publishers, 2004), 26-32, 42-63.

[915] Brant describes: "When Aristotle asks what sort of action is appropriate to drama, he identifies three means of moving the soul to pity and fear (the emotions that drama ought to arouse): reversal (*peripeteia*), recognition (*anagnōrisis*), and suffering (*pathos*)." See Brant, *Dialogue and Drama*, 42-43; also see Stibbe, *John*, 13-14; cf. *Poet.* 1450a 34-35; 1452b 8.

the narrator adds significant elements that propel the story.[916] The narrator of the story uses several other literary and linguistic aspects in order to interlock the reader with the text. Brant says that, "The exchanges of insults that occur in the Fourth Gospel may not simply be pieces of reciprocal verbal abuse. Such interactions in Greek tragedy belong to a literary type of scene and category of dramatic dialogue known as 'flyting.'"[917] The usage of 'flyting' helps the narrator to show the conflicting nature of the story.[918] The Sabbath conflicts in chaps. 5 and 9 brings out the conflicting nature at their maximum.[919] The author includes several group encounters (other than the individual encounters) in 6:41-59; 7:11-24; 8:13-47; 9:40-10:18; 10:22-39; 11:3-16; and 12:27-36.[920]

The above discussion gives us ample evidences to prove the fact that the dialogue that developed between Jesus and the Jews was not synonymous but antithetical in every sense. Through these dialogues the narrator points out the following things: *first*, the Johannine community didn't enjoy religious freedom as the Jewish authorities never allowed them to do so; *second*, as a community that was comprised of Jewish converts (and also others), the Jews always considered them as anti-religious and anti-social; and *third*, the narratorial framework, antithetical dialogue, dualistic language, and the literary dynamism of the Gospel facilitate a protagonist-and-antagonist duel both at the ideological and contextual levels.

Religious Freedom and Conversion in Today's Context

How the Johannine phenomenon of Religious Freedom and Conversion be understood in relation to the existent struggles of the Christian communities in India? While Indian constitution provides freedom to express and propagate one's religion, the Hindu fundamentalist groups go against the very rights of the minority religions. In that sense, the struggles of the Christian communities in India are in several ways equivalent to the struggles of the Johannine community. In the multi-religious Indian context, politicization of religion and communal tendencies are rampant and the minority rights are not at all protected. These contextual realities invite the attention of the reader to look at

---

[916] Cf. T. L. Brodie, *The Gospel according to John: A Literary and Theological Commentary* (New York/Oxford: Oxford University Press, 1993); G. L. Parsenios, *Rhetoric and Drama in the Johannine Lawsuit Motif*, WUNT 258 (Tübingen, Germany: Mohr Siebeck, 2010).

[917] See Brant, *Dialogue and Drama*, 123-124.

[918] Also refer J. A. Brant, *John*, Paideia Commentaries on the New Testament (Grand Rapids, Michigan: Baker Academic, 2011); Stibbe, *John*, 13-14.

[919] See D. M. Smith, *John*, Abingdon New Testament Commentary (Nashville: Abingdon Press, 1999), 35; also see Asiedu-Peprah, *Johannine Sabbath Conflicts as Juridical Controversy* (Tübingen: Mohr Siebeck, 2001), 12.

[920] See Painter, *The Quest for the Messiah*, 125; Quast, *Reading the Gospel of John*, 7; Hernando, "Episodes of Personal Encounter," 81, 88-90.

the things from a *gnomic* perspective rather than *descriptive* perspectives. In the contemporary context, John's Gospel can be better understood by way of aligning the *Sitz im Leben Jesu* and the *Sitz im Leben Kirche* within the *Sitz-im-leben India*.[921] While Martyn perceives the Gospel of John as a *two-level drama*, an Indian reader who looks at the Gospel from her/his existential struggles can better understand it as a *tri-level drama* (see Figure 3).[922]

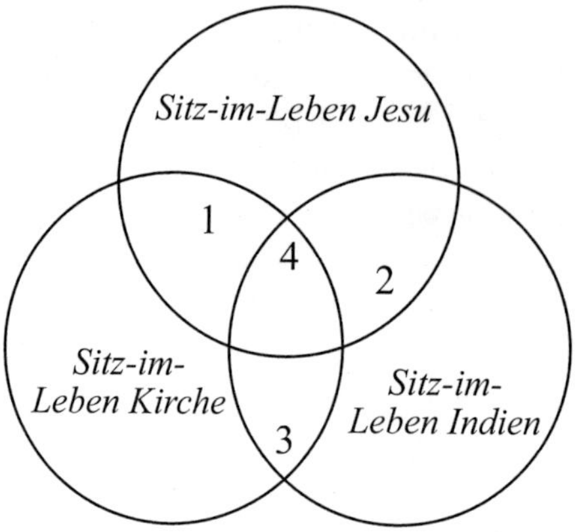

Figure 3: *Sitz-im-Leben Jesu*, *Sitz-im-Leben Kirche*, *Siz-im-Leben Indien* interaction: space #1 is the *Sitz-im-Leben Jesu* and *Sitz-im-Leben Kirche* meeting point; space #2 is the *Sitz-im-Leben Jesu* and *Sitz-im-Leben Indien* meeting point; space #3 is the *Sitz-im-Leben Kirche* and *Sitz-im-Leben Indien* meeting point; and space #4 is the common meeting point of all

In today's context, the BJP-led Indian Government does not protect the minority rights. The Christian communities are persecuted throughout the country by way of aggressive *Ghar Wapsi* campaign and other anti-conversion means.[923] These issues and others at the local and national levels called into question the very nature of religious freedom and conversion. This situation invites the reader of the Gospel of John to merge *the story of the Indian context* with that of *the story of the Johannine community*. In that sense, John has the accommodative power to encompass the feelings and existential struggles

[921] Marxsen distinguished between three *Sitz-im-Leben*: "The first is the *Sitz-im-leben* in the life of Jesus himself and has to do with the relationship between written records and actual events. The second has to do with the *Sitz-im-Leben* of the early church and its illuminated by form-critical attempts to differentiate community theology from the words and acts of Jesus. The third has to do with the authors and strives to delineate the theology of the evangelists as distinguished from the community theology." See Marxsen, *Der Evangelist Markus*, quoted in Guthrie, *New Testament Introduction*, 237-238.

[922] See Martyn, *History and Theology in the Fourth Gospel*.

[923] See S. M. Michael, *Challenges to Christian Mission: Problems and Prospects* (Pune: Ishvani Kendra, 2014), 30.

of the Indian masses. In this way the Gospel functions as a persuasive and performative artistry.

John provides us with ample evidences to cross-pollinate our contextual struggles with that of the story world of the Fourth Gospel. In the Gospel of John, 'freedom' (*eleutheria*, 8:31-47) is understood as freedom from the bondage of sin. In that sense, freedom is emphasized to be the inner spiritual aspect of a believer. Inner spiritual aspect of freedom is not just an end in itself, but the cause to further freedom in the personal and collective experience of eternal life in the world. This holistic aspect must be emphasized if the freedom is to be understood and experienced in its complete sense.[924] In that sense, in John, experiencing the freedom is not only individualistic but also relational. One who experiences the freedom is obligated to invite others to have the same experience. There comes the role of evangelism and missions. That further leads to religious conversion. This aspect of the Johannine ideology is distinct in its orchestration from that of the Jewish and Hindu ideologies. Hence, there are conflicts within the *Sitz-im-Leben Kirche* and in the *Sitz-im-Leben Indien*. Wingate says that, "The Christian encounter with India produces particular issues, because it has been, in the religious area, primarily an encounter with Hinduism."[925] An extreme view expressed by the Rashtriya Swayam Sevak (RSS) can be stated below:

> The non-Hindu people in Hindustan must adopt Hindu culture and language, must learn to respect and hold in reverence to Hindu religion, must entertain no idea but those of the glorification of the Hindu race and culture . . . They must cease to be foreigners or may stay in the country completely subordinate to the Hindu nation, claiming, deserving no privileges or any preferential treatment, not even citizens' rights.[926]

The above statement is by all means anti-nationalistic in its essence. In spite of the freedom of religion being guaranteed as a fundamental right, several attempts have been made in state and central assemblies or in committees to overthrow the essence of Article 25 of the Indian Constitution.[927] This is

---

[924] Cf. Martyn, *History and Theology in the Fourth Gospel*; Brown, *Community of the Beloved Disciple*.

[925] See A. Wingate, *The Church and Conversion: A Study of Recent Conversions to and from Christianity in the Tamil Area of South India* (Delhi: ISPCK, 1997/1999), 232.

[926] Quoted in Wingate, *The Church and Conversion*, 234; R. Robinson and S. Clarke, eds., *Religious Conversion in India: Modes, Motivations, and Meanings* (New Delhi: Oxford University Press, 2003).

[927] Thavare says that, "Conversion from one religion to another has always been an issue of friction in a pluralistic situation, where the process of change affects one's religion, society, and culture. Conversion has become a controversial issue in India and has led to serious communal

the situation in which the Johannine community feelings and struggles are to be reinterpreted. Moreover, the rhetorical and dramatic configuration of Johannine story enables the Indian readers to understand its efficacy in their existential struggles *here* and *now*. The *gnomic* rather than *descriptive* linguistic phenomenon of the Gospel makes it a paradigm for the Christian communities in India to reinterpret their contextual struggles.[928]

Conclusion

In recapitulation, the genre components such as *content*, *form*, and *function* of the Fourth Gospel incorporate the existent struggles of the Johannine community. The *church-and-synagogue conflict* lies at the heart of the narrative which in turn provides both explicit and implicit clues pertinent to the Johannine social dynamics. The narrator's attempt to merge the *story of Jesus* with the *story of the community* persuades the reader to consider the Gospel as a paradigm in the contemporary Indian context. The *story of the Indian church*, which delineates the existent struggles of the Christian community within the extended socio-religious milieu, has to be merged with the Johannine story in order to recreate the Indian realities with efficacy. As in the case of the Johannine community, the Indian church suffers from the minority-and-majority issues. In the Johannine narrative framework, Jesus' dialogue with his interlocutors foregrounds the antonymous trends, verbal duel, and the violent attitudes of the religious leaders. The same is obvious in the contemporary Indian context as the bossy and dehumanizing tendencies of the Hindu fundamentalists are categorically manifested.

In a context in which freedom of expression and freedom of belief are at risk, the Johannine narrator persuades the reading community to develop a *rhetoric of difference* rather than a *rhetoric of distance*. The Johannine narrator develops his discourse through the means of a protagonist-and-antagonist dialogue, and that further impacts the reader/s to take side with Jesus. In today's context, the church should take advantage of the ongoing antagonism of the Hindu fundamentalists by placing Jesus at the center of the Christian discourse. The Johannine narrator does not background the person and work of Jesus even in the face of growing opposition. But he foregrounds the messiahship of Jesus in dramatic and rhetorical terms in order to stabilize the kernel of his story. The Indian church should adopt the same (i.e., a Christ-

---

conflicts and tensions, and has resulted in law and order problems in some places." See B. Tavare, "Trends in Theology of Conversion in India," in K. C. Marak and P. S. Jacob, ed., *Conversion in a Pluralistic Context: Perspectives and Perceptions* (Pune/Delhi: CMS/ISPCK, 2000), 47.

[928] While *descriptive linguistic phenomena* guide the reader to the *there and then* aspects, *gnomic linguistic phenomena* guide the reader to the *everywhere and ever* perspective. See Thomaskutty, "Biblical Interpretation in the Global-Indian Context," 64-68.

centered missiology and ecclesiology) irrespective of the growing antagonism against its missions and ministry. Thus, the Gospel of John can be considered as a *tri-level drama* in order to accommodate the struggles and aspirations of the Christian communities in the Indian context. As John is both localizing and globalizing in its scope, an Indian reader of the Gospel can derive meaning in her/his own terms and situational demands. This peculiarity of the Gospel affirms its gnomic and universalistic nature.

Chapter 11

Johannine Women as Paradigms in the Indian Context

Introduction

The current essay is an attempt to see how the female characters appear within the narrative framework of the Gospel of John. We intend to foreground the role and status of the women characters of John in relation to Jesus and other characters of the Gospel. In order to achieve that goal, we employ certain principles of characterization and narrative analysis. In the final section of the paper, we will see the relevance of the study in the contemporary Indian context. In the process of finding the implications in the Indian context, we will see the necessity to develop an Indian Christian feminist methodology and also demonstrating the aspect of 'woman-power' as a hermeneutical key to explore the text.

The following questions will play significant role in the process of interpretation: How the women play their role and status within the narrative framework of John's Gospel? What are the ways and means through which we can demonstrate 'women-power' in the Gospel of John? How can John be presented as a paradigm in the contemporary Indian context? What message the Indian women can derive from the characterization of women in the Fourth Gospel? We will analyze the following texts and characters in that process: first, the Mother of Jesus (2:1-5; 19:25-27); second, the Samaritan woman (4:1-26, 39-42); third, Martha and Mary of Bethany (11:1-45; 12:1-8); and fourth, Mary Magdalene (19:25; 20:1-2, 11-18). The presenter, first of all, as a Johannine researcher, develops a Johannine paradigm of women characters; second, as an interpreter with a gnomic intent, attempts to bridge the gap between the first century and twenty-first century CE contexts; and third, as an Indian, researches about the impact and influence of the Johannine text in the contemporary Indian scenario. The localizing and globalizing aspects of the Fourth Gospel shall be foregrounded through the dynamic localization method adopted here for interpretation.

The Mother of Jesus (2:1-5, 12; 19:25-27)

Mary appears on two different occasions within the narrative framework of John, one at the beginning (2:1-12) and another at the climax (19:25-27) of Jesus' public ministry.[929] The narrator describes her as 'mother (*mētēr*) of Jesus' (2:1, 3) and 'his mother' (2:5, 12; 19:25, 26a, 26b).[930] In both the passages, Jesus addresses her as 'woman' (Gk. *gunai*; 2:4; 19:26).[931] While the narrator mentions her as *mētēr* to make her identity known to the reader, Jesus addresses her *gunai*. Johannine Jesus addresses her as 'woman' in order to de-emphasize his earthly origin.[932] As the incarnation of Jesus is made obvious in the human sphere, he emphasizes his divine identity and prepares to fulfill the 'hour' of the Father.[933] In the process of emphasizing the heavenly origin, his earthly origin receives lesser attention.

Jesus' address to Mary as *gunai* should be understood within this ideological framework of John. The narrator makes it plain that the mother of Jesus was there in the wedding place at Cana in Galilee (2:1). Mary's presence with the family during this auspicious occasion is noticeable. She

---

[929] The Synoptic evangelists mention her name in Matt 1-2; 13:55; Mark 6:3; Luke 1-2; and also in Acts 1:14. See Scholer, "Women," *DJG*, 884-885; also see Gaventa, *Mary: Glimpses of the Mother of Jesus*, 81-95.

[930] Jesus' mother is mentioned in the discussions of the Jews in 6:42. Blomberg comments that, "That John calls Mary simply 'Jesus' mother' fits ancient practice in referring to well-known figures and presupposes some knowledge of her within the Johannine community." See Blomberg, *Historical Reliability of John's Gospel*, 86.

[931] Bruce comments that, "Our Lord addressed his mother by this same term (Gk. *gynai*, vocative of *gynē*) when he hung on the cross (19:26); and indeed the term was consonant with the utmost courtesy, being translatable as 'madam' or 'my lady.'" See Bruce, *Gospel of John*, 69; also see Stibbe, *John*, 44; Brown, *Gospel according to John 1-12*, 98; Borchert, *John 1-11*, 154-155; Milne, *Message of John*, 64.

[932] Scholer states that, "Jesus' conversation with her [Mary] in John 2 does not indicate disrespect, but rather shows John's emphasis on Jesus' own authority and responsibility for his mission and implies Mary's discipleship. Mary is understood as a disciple (see John 19:25-27; Acts 1:14)." See Scholer, "Women," *DJG*, 885; also see Morris, *Gospel according to John*, 158; Köstenberger, *John*, 94; Coloe, *Mother of Jesus*, 210; Stagg, *Woman in the World of Jesus*, 236.

[933] See Moloney, *Gospel of John*, 67; also see Stibbe, *John*, 44; Beasley-Murray, *John*, 34-35.

is introduced as the initiator of a dialogue with Jesus to solve an important problem. The dialogue begins as she brings an important concern to him, i.e., the lack of wine at the wedding banquet.[934] The presence of Mary as the first reported character (2:1), Jesus and his disciples as invited guests (2:2), and the brothers of Jesus as walk-on characters (2:12) strengthen the argument that the wedding was of one of the closer relatives, or at least one of the friends, of the family.[935] Although, Jesus' attempt is to emphasize his heavenly origin, his earthly mother receives attention at some of the crucial junctures of his public ministry.

Mary's presence and her speech in 2:1-5 are to be understood as the first female presence and voice within the narrative framework of John.[936] As she appears at the outset of Jesus' public ministry, she expresses her voice in order to invite Jesus' attention.[937] When she utters that "they have no wine" (2:3b), she reflects her attachment with the family and her knowledge about the top secrets of the banquet room.[938] As the woman approaches Jesus with her request, expresses her expectation (2:3b), and instructs the servants (2:5), she lavishes her trust in Jesus.[939] Mary's implied thoughts are made explicit through her performative speech in v. 3b and the subsequent instruction to the servants in v. 5. Coloe states that, "The Mother's apparently neutral comment, 'they have no wine,' can be understood as a linguistic strategy of indirectness where without making an explicit request, she presumes, because of her relationship with her son, that he will hear the implied request."[940] When Jesus states to Mary (v. 4) and also to his brothers (7:6) that his hour has not yet come, a reader can infer a conflict within his family set up about the concept of hour.[941] While the hour of his earthly family members is scheduled according to the

---

[934] See Thomaskutty, *Dialogue in the Book of Signs*, 79; cf. Köstenberger, *John*, 93-96; Culpepper, *Anatomy of the Fourth Gospel*, 133-134.

[935] See Kanagaraj, *Gospel of John*, 98-99; also see Chatman, *Story and Discourse*, 173-195.

[936] See Bruce, *Gospel of John*, 69.

[937] As Moloney states, "She [the mother of Jesus] was the first character introduced and she initiates action with her statement." See Moloney, *Gospel of John*, 67; also see Morris, *Gospel according to John*, 158.

[938] In 2:1-11, Mary, the mother of Jesus, makes her son aware of the wedding party's need. See Thomaskutty, "Reading John's Gospel in the Nepali Context," 12; cf. Thomaskutty, "Reading John's Gospel in the Bangladeshi Context," 59-60; also see Milne, *Message of John*, 63; Bennema, *Excavating John's Gospel*, 38.

[939] See Bruce, *Gospel of John*, 70; also see Köstenberger, *John*, 92, 96.

[940] See Coloe, *Mother of Jesus*, 205.

[941] Neyrey comments that "When Jesus declares that 'my hour has not yet come,' this speaks of God's providential orchestration of Jesus' high status as he returns to God and glory." See Neyrey, *Gospel of John*, 63. For more syntactical aspects of v. 4, see Wallace, *Greek Grammar Beyond the Basics*, 150-151.

worldly standards (7:6b), Jesus works according to the hour of his Father in heaven. The story also has to be viewed from the cultural dynamics of 'honor and shame.'[942] While the so-called honorable are seated at the table as guests, a woman, in the role of a host, is concerned of extending hospitality to them and sustaining the dignity of the family. As wine was metaphorically equated to joy in Jewish culture, she is instrumental in bringing the lost joy of the family back in place.[943] Jesus' going down to Capernaum with his mother, brothers, and disciples and their stay together for a few days are further indicated in v. 12.[944] While Mary's trust and devotion to Jesus are conspicuous in 2:1-5 and 19:25-27, his brothers' unbelief is made obvious in 7:1-9.

A second time Mary appears near the cross of Jesus (19:25-27). As the narrator positions her presence explicit right at the beginning and at the end of Jesus' public ministry, a reader can conjecture her association with Jesus throughout the Johannine story.[945] The suspense that is emerged in 2:1-11 concerning Jesus' relationship with his 'worldly mother' is resolved when the 'hour' of Jesus comes into a full circle in 19:25-27.[946] While she appears in the Galilean context for the first time (2:1-11), in 19:25-27 she appears in the Judean setting. As Jesus was at the point of a shameful death, standing near the cross also was considered shameful.[947] The brothers of Jesus are settled in Galilee (7:1-9) and there is no mention about their presence near the cross.[948] In such a context, Mary's association with the crucified Jesus is intriguing. Jesus utters to his lonely mother, "woman, here is your son" (19:26), and thus

---

[942] See Neyrey, *Gospel of John*, 16-21.

[943] See Borchert, *John 1-11*, 155. Milne comments that, "Mary's sharing her dilemma with Jesus was possibly a habit bred of long years of family dependence, in the apparent absence of Joseph (Mark 6:3)." See Milne, *Message of John*, 63; cf. Brown, *Gospel according to John 1-12*, 97-99; McReynolds, "Mary, the Mother of Jesus," 446.

[944] Brashler states that, "John 2:12 mentions that the brothers of Jesus accompanied him to Capernaum and they later tauntingly suggest that Jesus should publicly demonstrate his great deeds at the Feast of Tabernacles (7:3, 5, 10)." See Brashler, "Jesus, Brothers and Sisters of," 3:820.

[945] See Milne, *Message of John*, 278; cf. Calvin, *Gospel of John 1-11*, 53.

[946] Coloe states that, "The importance of her relationship as mother of Jesus, in this Gospel, will only be revealed in 'the Hour.' The Cana miracle happens, but Jesus' apparent reprimand creates a puzzle that will not be resolved until the Passion." See Coloe, *Mother of Jesus*, 207.

[947] Stibbe states that, "Jesus' reference to his 'hour' here (the hour of his return to the Father, embracing his death), links the Cana episode to the crucifixion where the mother of Jesus is also present." See Stibbe, *John*, 44.

[948] The Synoptics also associate the brothers and sisters of Jesus in the Galilean context. Cf. Mark 6:3 = Matthew 13:56; Mark 3:31-32 = Matthew 12:42 and Luke 8:19-20. See Brashler, "Jesus, Brothers and Sisters of," 3:819.

he extends his care and protection to her.[949] Moreover, it is surprising that there was no second view from his brothers when Jesus entrusted their mother under the care of the Beloved Disciple. Stagg states that, "His brothers in the flesh were not there; but for Jesus a 'soul brother' was there who could be a 'son' to Mary and Mary a 'mother' to him."[950] The Johannine narrator does not give the role and status of James, the so-called brother of Jesus,[951] and Joseph, the Father (cf. 1:45 and 6:42), at this point.[952] On the other hand, the Beloved Disciple receives the responsibility to take care of his Lord's mother (v. 27).[953] As Morris states, "It is perhaps a little strange that Jesus commends Mary to the beloved disciple rather than to his brothers. But, they did not believe in him (7:5) and Mary did."[954] Jesus' mother was welcomed to the company of the believing rather than being under the care of her unbelieving children.[955] Mary's character demonstrates her leadership role at the wedding place and her deep devotion to Jesus near the cross.

The Samaritan Woman (4:1-26, 39-42)

Jesus crosses the existing social, racial, and moral barriers when he engages in a dialogue with the Samaritan woman (4:1-26).[956] In his analysis of the scripture, Stibbe observes both *realistic* and *representative* aspects in the portrayal of the woman.[957] In the episode, she is presented in a more favorable light than her male counterparts.[958] The woman's coming to the well during the

---

[949] It is stated that her sister, Mary the wife of Clopas, was with her. See Beasley-Murray, *John*, 349.

[950] See Stagg, *Woman in the World of Jesus*, 236.

[951] See Gillman, "James, Brother of Jesus," 620.

[952] Porter says that, "Apart from John (1:45; 6:42), where Jesus is twice referred to as the 'son of Joseph,' Joseph is only mentioned in the birth and childhood stories of Jesus." See Porter, "Joseph, Husband of Mary," 3:974.

[953] See Moloney, *Gospel of John*, 503.

[954] See Morris, *Gospel according to John*, 718; also see Borchert, *John 12-21*, 269. Brashler states that, "Acts 1:14 . . . includes the brothers of Jesus as part of a group praying together after the crucifixion with the 11 disciples and some women, including Jesus' mother Mary." See Brashler, "Jesus, Brothers and Sisters of," 3:820.

[955] Culpepper considers Mary that she symbolically represents Judaism, Jewish Christianity, the new Eve, and the Church. See Culpepper, *Anatomy of the Fourth Gospel*, 133; also see Kanagaraj, *Gospel of John*, 98.

[956] For more details about "Samaria" and "Samaritans," refer to Purvis, "Samaria (City)," 5:914-921; Anderson, "Samaritans," 5:940-947. Also see Thomaskutty, "Reading John's Gospel in the Nepali Context," 12.

[957] The woman appears as a realistic person without any mask and representative as the narrator presents her even without mentioning her name. See Stibbe, *John*, 66-67.

[958] See Stibbe, *John*, 62. The dialogue between Jesus and the woman educates about the universalistic, inter-religious and cross-cultural mission initiatives as the protagonist breaks the

midday and her presence in the scorching sunlight are reflective of her social status as a person who was rejected in the society due to her shameful past (vv. 16-18).[959] After crossing all the human made boundaries, Jesus asks her for a drink (v. 7). The woman's surprising answer to Jesus enables the reader to understand how the Jews treated the Samaritans for centuries (v. 9).[960] As a representative figure, her response to Jesus cannot be considered in a minimal sense; rather it has to be construed as her voice for justice and equality with a gnomic and universal intent.[961] Jesus' response concerning the living water and her misunderstanding response reveal the conceptual conflict between Jesus' eternal perspective and her temporal point of view (vv. 10-12).

Jesus' speech in v. 10 makes it obvious that his interlocutor was unaware of God's gift and its provider.[962] But, her inquisitive nature enables Jesus to make his identity known to her in a progressive manner. The conversation brings to the foreground the underlying contrast between Jacob's well and Jesus' provision of the water that gushes up to eternal life (vv. 12-14). In v. 15, the woman's perplexity is once again made explicit as she expresses her views from a parochial perspective.[963] The *all-knowing* perspective of Jesus and the *unknowing* perspective of the woman are in sharp contrast within the story. In vv. 7-15, the metaphor of water is used to distinguish between the 'from above' and 'from below' perspectives. Even when she was continually misunderstanding, she was demonstrating brevity to develop and thus was at a progressive mode in her encounter with Jesus.[964] In vv. 16-19, the woman's personal identity is brought to the focus. When Jesus enquires about her husband, she responds to him that she does not have one (vv. 16-17). Jesus

---

ethnic, cultural, religious, and sexual boundaries in order to speak and engage in the Missio Dei. See Kok, "As the Father Has Sent Me, I Send You," 168; cf. Thomaskutty, *Dialogue in the Book of Signs*, 167-168.

[959] See Kanagaraj, *Gospel of John*, 142.

[960] Williamson comments that, "The parenthetical comment in verse 9 about Jewish-Samaritan relations following the woman's expression of surprise that Jesus should ask her for a drink is probably not a general statement, but reflects a halakhic ruling (mid-first century?) that 'the daughters of the Samaritans are menstruants from their cradle' (*b. Nid.* 31b) and hence that the vessels which they handle are unclean." See Williamson, "Samaritans," 728; also see Neyrey, "What's Wrong with This Picture?" 110.

[961] 'Gnomic,' here means, 'timeless' facts, which works efficaciously with an 'everywhere' and 'ever' sense. See Thomaskutty, "Biblical Interpretation in the Global-Indian Context," 66; Brown, *Gospel according to John 1-12*, 168-172; Köstenberger, *John*, 149.

[962] See Köstenberger, *John*, 149-150.

[963] See Bennema, *Encountering Jesus*, 88.

[964] Bennema, *Encountering Jesus*, 88.

brings the realities behind her personal life (v. 18) and she acknowledges him as a prophet (v. 19).[965]

The dialogue develops further as the theme shifts from 'water' (vv. 7-15) and 'woman' (and her personal identity, vv. 16-19) to the theme of 'worship' (vv. 20-26).[966] The woman reflects her wider knowledge in matters of worship as she distinguishes between her ancestors' worship on 'this mountain' and the worship of the Jews in Jerusalem (v. 20).[967] In Jesus' response, he directs her attention away from the 'first space' (i.e., Mount Gerizim) and the 'second space' (i.e., Jerusalem) to a 'third space' (i.e., 'worship in spirit and in truth,' v. 23).[968] Jesus' intention of the worship in spirit and in truth is to direct her attention toward the eternal life experience. This equips her to express her expectation and knowledge about the coming Messiah (v. 25).[969] Borchert states that, "The woman's expectation of the coming messianic figure was of one who would reveal 'all things,' consistent with the Samaritan expectation of a Mosaic-like Prophet or *Taheb*."[970] The woman's statement about her expectation persuades Jesus to reveal his messianic identity (v. 26).[971] Thus, the dialogue as a whole develops in a triadic fashion: the 'water' that Jesus provides is introduced (vv. 7-15); the 'woman' and her personal identity are brought to the limelight (vv. 16-19); and the 'worship' in spirit and in truth is prophesied (vv. 20-26).[972]

The water jar that the woman leaves is a *prop*.[973] It symbolically speaks of her leaving the worldly water in order to proclaim about the living water (v. 28). The woman proclaims about Jesus to her own people in a persuasive

---

[965] Moloney states that, "Much is made of the five husbands, a number beyond the possibilities allowed by Jewish practice, as a possible symbolic use of the number five to refer to the five gods of Samaria (cf. *Ant.* 9.288), or the five books of the Samaritan Pentateuch, or the five foreign cities that brought their gods with them (cf. 2 Kings 17:27-31." See Moloney, *Gospel of John*, 131-132; also see Brown, *Gospel according to John 1-12*, 171; Carson, *Gospel according to John*, 221.

[966] See Thomaskutty, *Dialogue in the Book of Signs*, 145-147.

[967] See Morris, *Gospel according to John*, 237.

[968] See Thomaskutty, *Dialogue in the Book of Signs*, 147-149; Brown, *Gospel according to John 1-12*, 180-181.

[969] Morris comments that, "The Samaritans acknowledged no prophet after Moses other than the one spoken of in Deuteronomy 18:18, and him they regarded as the Messiah. For her to speak of Jesus as a prophet was thus to move into the area of messianic speculation." See Morris, *Gospel according to John*, 236.

[970] See Borchert, *John 1-11*, 209; cf. Keener, *Gospel of John*, 619-620.

[971] See Borchert, *John 1-11*, 209-210.

[972] See Thomaskutty, *Dialogue in the Book of Signs*, 145-147.

[973] The woman's leaving of the 'water jar' is a *prop* used to reveal the symbolical activity of leaving 'Jacob's water' and proclaiming the 'living water.' See Thomaskutty, *Dialogue in the Book of Signs*, 152.

manner (v. 29) and drives them from the city to the savior (v. 30).[974] Culpepper comments that, "The woman becomes a missionary to her people. She evokes, therefore, the mission to the Samaritans."[975] The narrator states that many Samaritans from the city believed in Jesus because of her word about him (v. 39).[976] After their personal encounter with Jesus, the Samaritans are no more believing because of the woman's words but because of their own personal witness about him (vv. 40-42).[977]

The woman, who had been confined to her own house, realized a sense of freedom after her encounter with Jesus to face her own people and introduce the savior to them.[978] Their final utterance that Jesus is 'truly the Savior of the World' is the paramount utterance of the story (v. 42b).[979] Though the woman is considered as an outsider, unclean, and shameful person, she is a representative character who turns to be a proclaimer.[980]

Martha and Mary of Bethany (11:1-45; 12:1-8)

The sisters in 11:1-45 and 12:1-8 reflect their devotion to Jesus and also demonstrate their unique model of discipleship. Not only was Bethany known in their names but also Lazarus is introduced as their brother.[981] While the disturbed sisters sent a message to Jesus indicating Lazarus' illness (v. 3), they show their trust in him and on the other hand Jesus' love for the family. The message of the sisters persuades Jesus to declare one of his glorification motifs

---

[974] See Scholer, "Women," 883, 886; Köstenberger, *John*, 152-154; Keener, *Gospel of John*, 622.

[975] See Culpepper, *Anatomy of the Fourth Gospel*, 137.

[976] Bauckham states that, "Though the Samaritan woman in John 4 is not a model of respectable women's behavior, there is probably nothing improper about the way she spreads her news throughout her village (John 4:28-30, 39)." See Bauckham, *Gospel Women*, 292.

[977] See Anderson, "Samaritans," 5: 940-947; also see Köstenberger, *John*, 163-164. Stagg comments that, "With dramatic skill, the storyteller moves the Samaritan woman from a very shady character to one of great stature. Next to Jesus, she dominates the story." See Stagg, *Woman in the World of Jesus*, 237.

[978] See Kanagaraj, "The Profiles of Women in John," 63-64; also see Chakkuvarackal, "'Woman-Power' in the Canonical Gospels," 71.

[979] The inter-religious nature of the dialogue sharpens the woman's existent views and directs her to the Savior of the world. See Koester, "'The Savior of the World' (John 4:42)," 665-680; Thomaskutty, "Biblical Interpretation in the Global-Indian Context," 66.

[980] Neyrey states, "The cultural world of the Gospel highly valued female sexual exclusivity, the core of a female's virtue and worth. Thus a female with five husbands and a current companion not her spouse mocks this criterion; hardly virtuous, she is instead a *sinner*, an *adulterous*, a *shameless person*." See Neyrey, *Gospel of John*, 95.

[981] Köstenberger states that, "Martha was the older of the two, since she acts as the hostess in the Lukan passage." See Köstenberger, John, 326; cf. Stagg, *Woman in the World of Jesus*, 238; also see Luke 10:38-42:

in v. 4.[982] While Martha went out to meet Jesus, Mary stays at home in deep distress (v. 20).[983] In both Luke and John, Martha is represented primarily as a rather determined worker (Luke 10:41; John 12:2) and Mary as the worshipful one (Luke 10:39, 42; cf. John 11:2; 12:3).[984] In vv. 20-27, Martha appears to the foreground as she engages in a dialogue with Jesus.[985] She begins the conversation with Jesus stating that, "Lord, if you had been here, my brother would not have died" (v. 21).[986] She is assured of the fact that God can give whatever Jesus asks (v. 22). While Jesus assures that her brother will rise again in the present life, she states her assurance about its happening on the last day (vv. 23-24).[987]

The utterances of Martha reflect her complete trust in Jesus, but she is oriented toward the 'future' rather than the 'present.' Jesus reveals his identity by stating that "I am the resurrection and the life" (v. 25).[988] Once when Jesus states to her about the necessity to believe (vv. 25b-26), she affirms her faith in a profoundest fashion that addresses him as "Lord," "Messiah," "Son of God," and "the one coming into the world" (v. 27).[989] Köstenberger states that, "Martha's almost creedlike confession of Jesus as 'the Christ, the Son of God—the one who is coming into the world' strikingly anticipates the purpose statement at the end of the Gospel (20:30-31)."[990] The return of Martha back to home and her call of Mary are reflective of her witnessing attitude (v. 28).[991] In performing this, she moves from a confessor to a witness.[992]

Mary is introduced as one who anointed the Lord with perfume and wiped his feet with her hair (11:2; cf. 12:1-8).[993] She kneels down before Jesus and

---

982 See Borchert, *John 1-11*, 350.

983 See Brown, *Gospel according to John*, 423.

984 Stibbe states that, "She [Martha] goes out alone to meet Jesus and, like the Samaritan woman, is portrayed as one who grows in faith and understanding." See Stibbe, *John*, 125; also see Borchert, *John 1-11*, 349.

985 See Neyrey, *Gospel of John*, 197.

986 See Bruce, *Gospel of John*, 243.

987 See Köstenberger, John, 334-335.

988 See Borchert, *John 1-11*, 356; cf. Dodd, *Interpretation of the Fourth Gospel*, 366.

989 Neyrey states that, "In a Gospel where confessions are rare and reserved for elite people, Martha declares that she 'knows' that Jesus is Messiah, Son of God, and the one coming into the world." See Neyrey, *Gospel of John*, 196.

990 See Köstenberger, *John*, 336. Neyrey states, "the narrative attributes to Martha very high status by virtue of Jesus' revelations, but not a formal role." See Neyrey, *Gospel of John*, 197.

991 Mary and the people consoling her go to the place where Jesus was. The people consoled and following her thought that she was going to weep at the tomb (v. 31).

992 See Brant, *John*, 175-176; Stibbe, *John*, 125.

993 Esler and Piper attempt to understand Lazarus, Mary and Martha as prototypes of identity for Christ-followers. See Esler and Piper, *Lazarus, Mary and Martha*, 17-22; also see

speaks the same utterance that Martha declared in v. 21 (v. 32). That shows that the declaration "Lord, if you had been here, my brother would not have been died" (vv. 21, 32) was their family confession. Jesus was deeply moved and greatly disturbed in spirit when he saw that Mary and the people followed were weeping (v. 33).[994] Borchert says that, "Mary expressed her loss differently from Martha. Mary's tears have in fact taken the place of most of Martha's words."[995] Jesus' inner movements and outer expressions enable the Jews to ponder the depth of his love for Martha, Mary, and Lazarus (vv. 35-37).[996] After introducing Mary's entry to the stage, Martha once again appears as a dialogue partner with Jesus. Upon Jesus' request of moving the stone from the entrance, Martha responds by saying about the period of time Lazarus' body was laid inside the tomb and the aspect of stent (v. 39).[997] At that point Jesus once again stabilizes Martha's belief and prepares her to see the glory of God (v. 40).[998]

While Martha expresses her faith based on her 'future' eschatological hope, Jesus shapes her faith based on the 'present' realities. The sisters' message to Jesus (v. 3), their family confession (vv. 21, 32), constant conversation and expression of emotion, and growth in faith in Jesus made him to glorify the name of the Father (v. 40; cf. v. 4).[999] Stagg states that, "John gives great prominence to Mary and Martha throughout the story. Jesus dominates the story, but otherwise the sisters command the center of the stage."[1000] The women characters such as Martha and Mary are genuine disciples in their own ways and they demonstrate their faith in Jesus in their own ways.[1001] In 12:1-8, the sisters along with their brother who was raised from death appear once again on stage.[1002] The three members of the family are involved in different

---

Thomaskutty, "Reading John's Gospel in the Bangladeshi Context," 61.

[994] See Brown, *Gospel according to John*, 424-425; Köstenberger, *John*, 339; Neyrey, *Gospel of John*, 198-199.

[995] Cf. Culpepper, *Anatomy of the Fourth Gospel*, 140-142; Borchert, *John 1-11*, 359; Stibbe, *John*, 126.

[996] See Brown, *Gospel according to John*, 424-425.

[997] See Bruce, *Gospel of John*, 247-248.

[998] As the episode begins with a glory proposal (v. 4) and ends with a glory fulfillment, it can be considered as a *glory-focused revelatory dialogue*. See Thomaskutty, *Dialogue in the Book of Signs*, 368-404; Brant, *John*, 176; Culpepper, *Anatomy of the Fourth Gospel*, 140-142; Witherington, *John's Wisdom*, 204.

[999] Cf. Culpepper, *Anatomy of the Fourth Gospel*, 140-142; Thomaskutty, *Dialogue in the Book of Signs*, 403.

[1000] See Brant, *John*, 175-176; Stagg, *Woman in the World of Jesus*, 238.

[1001] See Thomaskutty, *Dialogue in the Book of Signs*, 400-404.

[1002] Cf. Witherington, *John's Wisdom*, 203-205; Stagg, *Woman in the World of Jesus*, 238-239.

ways in the story: Martha is serving (v. 2a);[1003] Mary anoints the feet of Jesus (v. 3); and Lazarus is reclining at the table with the guests (v. 2b).[1004] Here the narrator foregrounds the character of Mary over against Judas Iscariot.

There are five contrasts brought out between Judas Iscariot (a male disciple) and Mary of Bethany (a follower of Jesus): first, while Judas *speaks* like a concerned person (vv. 4-5), Mary *acts* in a gentle way (v. 3); second, while Judas betrays Jesus for *thirty* pieces of silver (Matthew 26:15), Mary spends *three hundred* denarii and shows her superabundant generosity (v. 5);[1005] third, while Judas *fills his heart* with evil thoughts (vv. 5-6), the woman *fills the home* with the fragrance of the perfume (v. 3b); fourth, while Judas accuses the woman although he is a *guest*, Mary lavishly spends as an honorable *host*; and fifth, while Judas betrays Jesus and that led to his *arrest* (18:2), Mary prepared herself for the day of her master's *burial* (v. 7).[1006] Schnackenburg comments that, "Mary has recognized the dignity and greatness of Jesus and, in an exemplary action, has shown the others who they have in their midst."[1007] While Martha receives special attention in chapter 11, Mary receives more attention in 12:1-8. The role and status of Martha and Mary establish above several of the male characters in the Fourth Gospel.[1008] Both of them are paradigms for ideal discipleship and hence for effective leadership because they exhibited the qualities of devotion, sacrificial attitude, service, belief in Jesus and apostolic witness.[1009] They were closely bound with Christ and to his mission of accomplishing God's redemptive plan.[1010]

Mary Magdalene (19:25; 20:1-2, 11-18)

In John, Mary Magdalene appears for the first time in the company of a group of women under the cross. She is present with the mother of Jesus, her sister, and wife of Clopas. Mary's presence reveals her association with some of the significant women of the early Jesus movement (19:25). Her appearance is

---

[1003] Schnackenburg states that, "The remark about Martha's waiting at the table resembles Luke 10:40, but the evangelist may also have been familiar with this tradition in some way." See Schnackenburg, *The Gospel according to Saint John*, 2:366.

[1004] See Dodd, *Interpretation of the Fourth Gospel*, 368-370.

[1005] See Schnackenburg, *Gospel according to Saint John*, 3:368.

[1006] See Blomberg, *Historical Reliability of John's Gospel*, 175-178; Bruce, *Gospel of John*, 255-257.

[1007] See Schnackenburg, *Gospel according to Saint John*, 2:370.

[1008] See Brant, *John*, 179-180.

[1009] Witherington states that, "Mary also seems to be assuming the role of a servant, for it was the servant's task to anoint the master's feet when he came off the dusty highways of Judea." See Witherington, *John's Wisdom*, 207.

[1010] See Kanagaraj, "The Profiles of Women in John," 70; cf. Chakkuvarackal, "'Woman—Power' in the Canonical Gospels," 71.

brought to the foreground in 20:1-2 and 20:11-18 during the post-resurrection period. At the tomb of Jesus, Mary witnesses that the stone had already been removed from its entrance (v. 1).[1011] She reports Peter and the Beloved Disciple that Jesus' body has been taken away from the tomb. Brant comments that, "A woman who comes alone in darkness to such a place abandons propriety and safety in order to commemorate Jesus with her grief. John represents her anxiety by focalizing the setting through her eyes: she sees the stone has been removed from the tomb (20:1)."[1012] Her misapprehension is mentioned through her statement that "we do not know where they have laid him" (v. 2). After testifying about the empty tomb to the disciples, the woman stands outside of it and weeps (v. 11).[1013] This incident reveals her lamenting attitude when it was not expected from her.[1014] As Jesus was weeping outside the tomb of Lazarus (11:35), Mary Magdalene weeps outside of her Lord's tomb.[1015] As Stibbe states, "This echo effect suggests a Christ-like quality to Mary's characterization."[1016] The conversation between the woman and the angels makes it once again explicit that she was deeply disturbed within (vv. 12-13). Her devotion to Jesus is made clear as she attempts to regain the corpse of her Lord.[1017] Her turning around to see and unrecognition of the identity of Jesus reveal some of the realistic aspects of Johannine story-telling.[1018]

The character of Mary captures attention of the reader as she progresses in her faith in Jesus. Her unrecognition of Jesus in v. 14 would have been based on several reasons: first, as Mary was settled in her mundane and 'from below' perception that Jesus was indeed dead, she was unable to understand the supernatural and 'from above' aspects; second, she already witnessed the death of Jesus, noticed that the stone was rolled away, perceived that the body was taken from there, and saw that the disciples themselves confirmed it; and third, the tears from her eyes would have blurred her eyes from recognizing Jesus (v. 14).[1019] While Jesus asks her the reason behind her weeping and also about the identity of the person whom she searches, she further responds in a natural way (v. 15). Mary's response to the disciples (v. 2b), to the angels

---

[1011] See Schnackenburg, *Gospel according to Saint John*, 3:307-308.

[1012] See Brant, *John*, 266.

[1013] See Witherington, *John's Wisdom*, 330; also see Kanagaraj, *Gospel of John*, 643-649.

[1014] See Moloney, *Gospel of John*, 527.

[1015] See Schnackenburg, *Gospel according to Saint John*, 3:315.

[1016] See Stibbe, *John*, 205.

[1017] See Culpepper, *Anatomy of the Fourth Gospel*, 144; also see Stagg, *Woman in the World of Jesus*, 239.

[1018] See Schnackenburg, *Gospel according to Saint John*, 314-320. Stibbe states that, "She [Mary] is portrayed in a stylized fashion." See Stibbe, *John*, 205.

[1019] See Bauckham, *Gospel Women*, 262-276.

(v. 13b), and to Jesus (v. 15b) reflect her settled view that Jesus' body was removed by somebody from the site.[1020] Mary's words and actions together perform the narrative with a lot of reality effects.[1021]

In v. 16, John narrates that Jesus calls the woman by name (that is, "Mary") and she recognizes him in return (that is, "Rabbouni," v. 16).[1022] Jesus' address and her response reflect the acceptance and recognition aspects of the story.[1023] As Jesus' ascension to the Father is imminent, he requests the woman not to cling on to him (v. 17a). The resurrected Jesus appoints Mary as the first person to proclaim the good news to others and she announces that to the disciples (v. 18a).[1024] The woman's personal conviction and proclamation (that is, "I have seen the Lord") to the disciples later on becomes the early Christian community's conviction and proclamation (that is, "We have seen the Lord," v. 25a).[1025] Jesus appoints Mary as a witness to announce the good news of his resurrection and his imminent ascension to the Father.[1026] Mary's proclamation to the male disciples saying, "I have seen the Lord" (v. 18), has apostolic significance.[1027] This would have persuaded many to hail her as 'apostle to the apostles.'[1028]

Johannine Women in the Indian Context

As we have analyzed and identified, Johannine women show devotion toward Jesus and affirm their faith with profundity than some of their male counterparts.[1029] As part of the community of John, they seemingly enjoyed considerable freedom in matters of exercising their spirituality, expressing views openly at the public places, and developing faith in Jesus as a powerful means to come out of their parochial worldviews.[1030] Jesus' position as the protagonist of the story and Johannine community's reinterpretation of the events from the *Sitz im Leben Jesu* to address the existential struggles of the

---

[1020] See Bruce, *Gospel of John*, 387.

[1021] See Jones, *Women in the Gospel of John*, 58-59; also see Bennema, *Excavating John's Gospel*, 213-215.

[1022] See Neyrey, *Gospel of John*, 321-325.

[1023] See Brant, *John*, 270; also see Moloney, *Gospel of John*, 528.

[1024] See Culpepper, *Anatomy of the Fourth Gospel*, 144; also see Jones, *Women in the Gospel of John*, 58-59.

[1025] See Stibbe, *John*, 204-206.

[1026] See Bennema, *Excavating John's Gospel*, 214; also see Beasley-Murray, *John*, 376.

[1027] See Kanagaraj, "The Profiles of Women in John," 37; also see Chakkuvarackal, "'Women-Power' in the Canonical Gospels," 72.

[1028] See Thomaskutty, *Reading John's Gospel in the Bangladeshi Context*, 61; also see Haskins, "Apostola Apostolorum," 55-94.

[1029] See Beirne, *Women and Men in the Fourth Gospel*, 1-41.

[1030] See Witherington, *Women in the Earliest Churches*, 175-182.

Sitz im Leben Kirche enable the narrator to sustain some of the values and virtues of the Jesus movement.[1031]

John sustains women's representation from varied levels of life situations: Jesus' mother appears both in the context of a celebrative mood (2:1-5) as well as a lamenting situation (19:25-27); the unnamed woman appears at a public well in the Samaritan context (4:1-42); Martha and Mary appear both in a bereaving situation (11:1-44) as well as in a context in which they show superabundant generosity (12:1-8); and Mary Magdalene is in a lamenting attitude at the tomb of Jesus and she proclaims the resurrected Jesus (20:1-2 and vv. 11-18).[1032] The above indications reveal that Johannine women exercised their faith both at the public and private sectors of life. Their representation from varied walks within the life situation of Jesus and the reinterpretation of those kernels into the life situation of the Johannine community reveals their openness even in the case of women's status and role.[1033] In the process of interpreting John into the Indian context, we need to adopt a third life situation (that is, *Sitz im Leben Indien*) in order to further interpret the story of the Fourth Gospel.[1034]

In the Indian context, atrocities against women are on the rise and the rights of the women are not protected. Women are considered inferior to men and are treated with low esteem. These contextual realities persuade the attention of the reader of John to look at the text from a *gnomic* rather than *descriptive* perspective.[1035] While Louis Martyn perceives the Fourth Gospel as a *two-level* drama, an Indian reader who interprets the text from her/his existential realities can better understand it as a *tri-level* drama.[1036] John frequently describes Jesus as empowering women and setting their belief against the unfaithfulness of men.[1037] In the Indian context, women's empowerment is one of the significant concerns, as they are often illiterate, without political power or voice in religion, and ostracized by leading elements of the society.

[1031] These expressions mean: The life situation of Jesus and the life situation/s of the early Christian community/ies. See Marxen, *Der Evangelist Markus*.

[1032] See Witherington, *Women in the Earliest Churches*, 175-182.

[1033] John the narrator captures the story of Jesus as the protagonist in order to re-tell and re-interpret that with greater efficacy. See Thomaskutty, "Reading John's Gospel as a Jewish-Christian Conflict Narrative," 141.

[1034] See Thomaskutty, "Reading John's Gospel as a Jewish-Christian Conflict Narrative," 158; also see Martyn, *History and Theology in the Fourth Gospel*, 24-151.

[1035] While *descriptive linguistic phenomena* guide the reader to the *there and then* aspects, *gnomic linguistic phenomena* guide the reader to the *everywhere and ever* perspective. See Thomaskutty, "Biblical Interpretation in the Global-Indian Context," 64-68.

[1036] See Thomaskutty, "Reading John's Gospel as a Jewish-Christian Conflict Narrative," 158.

[1037] See Kanagaraj, "The Profiles of Women in John," 60-61.

Like the Johannine women, the women of modern India can be effective agents of liberation and transformation.[1038] The following roles of Johannine women are influential in the Indian context: as Mary the mother of Jesus was playing significant roles during the wedding banquet and near the cross, Indian women should take initiative to lead the country in order to fulfill the divine tasks; as the woman at the well was instrumental in bringing the gospel to her own people, the village women of India can play transformative roles in their respective areas of life; as Martha and Mary were believing and ministering to Jesus in Bethany, our women should take challenges in fostering the missionary tasks and ministerial duties entrusted unto them; and as Mary Magdalene was sharing the good news of Jesus' resurrection with her male counterparts, women of India should take active steps in gospel propagation.[1039] Women figures like Pandita Ramabhai (1858-1922), Mother Teresa, and others were devoting themselves for the tasks of Christ and using their intrinsic power in the areas of leadership and missional engagements.[1040] They followed the path of Johannine women and introduced radical transformation in their respective areas of life.[1041]

Discriminatory thinking and practices against women persist in the Indian society although the Indian Constitution guarantees equality of sexes. India is also a signatory to the UN Charter affirming equal rights of the sexes.[1042] Against such contextual realities, the Johannine women and the Johannine community experiences suggest alternative views. The Samaritan woman had an encounter with Jesus and that resulted into her experience of acquiring greater knowledge. This unique experience enabled her to lead her people toward the "truly Savior of the world." The Samaritan woman's involvements can be introduced as a paradigm for the Indian women so that they may develop themselves from misunderstanding situations to greater understanding, awareness about the 'past' to a transformative living in the 'present,' and emphasizing the older traditions to life affirming newer experiences. Martha and Mary of Bethany can be followed as models to shift away from future-oriented eschatological hopes to present-affirming and living experiences. The sisters' positive qualities such as hospitality, generosity, and devotion to Christ are to be exercised for transformative living in the contemporary Indian context.

Mary Magdalene outsmarts her male counterparts as she was exemplifying her devotion to Jesus both through proclamations and actions. As she was

---

[1038] See Thomaskutty, "Reading John's Gospel in the Nepali Context," 13.

[1039] Thomaskutty, "Reading John's Gospel in the Nepali Context," 62.

[1040] See Chakkuvarackal, "Glimpses of the 'Feminine' in the Indian Religion and Society," 88.

[1041] Chakkuvarackal, "Glimpses of the 'Feminine' in the Indian Religion and Society."

[1042] See Das, *Christian Ethics and Indian Ethos*, 160.

demonstrating her profoundest proclamation, keeping up fellowship with the community of God, and involving dynamically around and beyond the tomb of Jesus, her character can be hailed as a model for women in the oppressive socio-religious structures. Just as these Johannine women exemplified their leadership roles, devotion to Jesus, progress in understanding Jesus, and witnessing Christ to diverse walks of life, Indian women at varied life situations can demonstrate their intrinsic qualities to transform themselves and the society. As Rekha M. Chennattu proposes, Indian interpreters of the text should emphasize "an ethics of giving life in abundance as a hermeneutical key" for interpreting John. She further states that, "such a premise presupposes a principle of combined radical equality and inclusiveness and a process of dialogue at all levels."[1043] What Chennattu suggests here is significant in the Indian context as the people as a whole expect a paradigm to liberate the ostracized communities of the nation.

Conclusion

The above analysis enables us to see how the women of John's Gospel appear in relation to Jesus and other characters of the macro-story. Though they were considered as powerless in their own socio-religious and politico-cultural contexts, they assume power both within the *Sitz im Leben Jesu* and within the *Sitz im Leben Kirche*. We observed that as part of the Johannine community, women of John enjoyed considerable freedom. Mary the mother of Jesus demonstrates her leadership quality at the wedding in Cana and her deep devotion to Jesus near the cross. Though the woman at the well was misunderstanding in nature and parochial in perception, her progress in realizing the prophet-Messiah and guiding Samaritans toward the "truly Savior of the world" is persuasive. Martha and Mary of Bethany show their family confession that if Jesus was with them Lazarus would not have died. They develop in their faith and devotion in Jesus. While Martha develops from her future-oriented eschatological hope to the present-oriented realization of the Messianic age, Mary demonstrates her identity through her superabundant generosity.

Mary Magdalene's speeches and actions reveal the fact that she was a paradigmatic personality for the early Christian communities including the male characters of the story. Her personal proclamation (i.e., "I have seen the Lord") later on became the community proclamation (i.e., "We have seen the Lord"). In their encounter with Jesus, all these women showed their love and devotion to their Lord. All of them used their intrinsic "woman-power" to come out of their narrow confines of life. These women of the Gospel of John can be presented as paradigms in the Indian context as the women of India

[1043] See Chennattu, "Life in Abundance," 200.

eagerly waiting for a message of liberation and transformation. By developing a hermeneutics of suspicion and an Indian feminist methodology, Indian feminists of our times should foster gnomic interpretative strategies over against the prevailing descriptive strategies. As Jesus liberated women from the confines of social, religious, geographical, moral, and sexual barriers and the women of John are living examples of such a movement, our attempt in the contemporary Indian context should be developing new hermeneutical keys to unlock the grand-narratives of the text. In that process, the riddle of globalizing and localizing within the Fourth Gospel has to be adequately explored.

Chapter 12

The Event of Foot Washing in John 13:1-20 as a Paradigm for Witnessing Christ in the Indian Context

Introduction

The event of foot washing in John 13:1-20 functions as one of the significant narrative masterpieces with a lot of theological insights. The pericope as a whole requires narrative and theological appreciation as it invites the reader toward a unique activity of Jesus. In the current essay, we will look at John 13:1-20 both within the framework of the Farewell Discourse as well as from the overall structure of the Fourth Gospel. It is primarily an attempt to see the *being* and *becoming* natures of Jesus and his instructions for disciples' *doing*. This symbolic act of Jesus is performed with a universalistic intent in mind.

The study attempts to see how the narrative exists as a paradigm in the contemporary missional and ministerial context of India. John's Gospel can be considered as a flexible, accommodative, and gnomic literary work that absorbs the situational aspects of people 'everywhere and ever.' Keeping all these in mind, this essay endeavors to answer the following questions in brief: What is the message the event of foot washing communicates to the global context? How does the event function as a paradigm for the contemporary India for Christian witnessing? How does the event function within the Farewell Discourse in particular and in relation to the events such as the incarnation and the death of Jesus in general? How does the event function within the narrative framework of John as a paradigm for Jesus' servanthood? The task of the study is threefold: first, as a Johannine student, exploring the literary and theological aspects of John 13:1-20; second, as a gnomic interpreter, investigating the universal and accommodative tendencies of the Fourth Gospel; and third, as an Indian contextual reader of the text, fusing the textual and contextual horizons for application.

John 13:1-20 within John's Narrative Framework

John's style of demonstrating the discourses and narratives is characteristic. While the Synoptic evangelists narrate the instructions of Jesus to his disciples throughout his ministry, John amasses the whole set of instructions and presents them together in the context of the Last Supper.[1044] The Farewell Discourse of John in chaps. 13-17 follows the literary style of *farewell discourses* or *testaments* of famous men.[1045] John shares some of the literary features parallel to *The Testaments of the Twelve Patriarchs* that contains the last words of each of the patriarchs to their people.[1046] Moreover, John's tradition also shows striking similarities with some of the Greco-Roman symposium traditions.[1047] John's style of presenting the Farewell Discourse in conformity with other literary styles demonstrates his gnomic interest.

Within the larger framework of the Gospel, there is a shift of emphasis that happens from the public ministry of Jesus (chaps. 2-12) to his private ministry

---

[1044] See Mark 4:10-20; 6:7-13, expanded by Matthew in 10:1-42; Mark 8:14-21, 27-33; 9:1-13, 33-41; 10:23-45. The instructions in Mark 13 are expanded in Matthew 24-25. Also see Mark 14:3-42; Beasley-Murray, *John*, 222; Köstenberger, *John*, 396-397; J. C. Stube, *Greco-Roman Rhetorical Reading of the Farewell Discourse*, LNTS 309 (London/New York: T & T Clark International, 2006), 1-2; Cornelis Bennema, *Excavating John's Gospel: A Commentary for Today* (Delhi: ISPCK, 2007), 140.

[1045] Collins says, "It is now commonly asserted that John 13:31-16:33 is written according to the literary genre of the farewell discourse. Approximately fifty speeches ascribed to famous men in anticipation of their deaths have been preserved for us in biblical and extra-biblical sources." See R. F. Collins, *These Things Have been Written: Studies on the Fourth Gospel* (Louvain: Peeters Press, 1990), 221; also see F. F. Bruce, *Gospel of John: Introduction, Exposition and Notes* (Grand Rapids: Eerdmans, 1983), 278.

[1046] See the OT parallels in Gen 49; Josh 22-24; and 1 Chron 28-29. Beasley-Murray comments that, "The most important example of this kind of writing, however, is the Book of Deuteronomy, which could well have been in the Evangelist's mind when composing the discourses of the Upper Room. This work in its entirety consists of the farewell discourses of Moses to Israel." See Beasley-Murray, *John*, 222-223; G. L. Borchert, *John 12-21*, The New American Commentary, Vol. 25B (Nashville: B & H Publishers, 2002), 72-90; T. Engberg-Pedersen, "A Question of Genre: John 13-17 as *Paraklēsis*," *The Gospel of John as Genre Mosaic* (Gōttingen: Vandenhoeck & Ruprecht, 2015), 283-302.

[1047] Just like the symposium traditions, we see in John 13-17 a formal banquet, a symposium, i.e., a conference or discussion on a particular subject, took place (see Plato's *Symposium*). See Bennema, *Excavating John's Gospel*, 140.

(chaps. 13-17).[1048] While John places 1:1-18 at the outset of the *Book of Signs* with a punch line that *the Word became flesh and dwelt among humanity* (1:14), later on he places 13:1-20 as an introductory narrative for the *Book of Glory* with an emphasis on *the Teacher-Lord became a servant among his disciples* (13:14).[1049] On the one hand, in John, the Passover was celebrated on the eve of the festival (13:1; 18:28); on the other hand, the Synoptic Gospels indicate that Jesus celebrated it with his disciples (see Mark 14:12; Luke 22:15).[1050] In John's portrayal, he attempts to foreground Jesus as the Passover lamb.

John 13:1-30 falls into two major sections: vv. 1-20, describing the foot washing of the disciples by Jesus; and vv. 21-30, the announcement of Jesus of his impending betrayal by a disciple.[1051] The event of foot washing in vv. 4-11 and the succeeding interpretation of it are persuasive within John's narrative framework. Keener considers "the foot washing as the narrative introduction to the Farewell Discourse that prefigures the passion."[1052] This nature of the story underscores its feature as a *hypodeigma* (i.e., an 'example,' v. 15).[1053] Interspersing the event of foot washing (vv. 1-20) with the betrayal (vv. 21-30) demonstrates the imminent death of Jesus.[1054] Jesus' servant-model in 13:1-20

[1048] See Leon Morris, *The Gospel according to John* (Grand Rapids: Eerdmans, 1971), 610. Moloney says that, "No doubt the constituent parts of 13:1-17:26 had their own history in the storytelling of the Johannine community, but the process of telling and retelling produced a Gospel that is thoroughly Johannine in all its parts." See F. J. Moloney, *Gospel of John*, Sacra Pagina 4 (Collegeville: The Liturgical Press, 1989/1998), 370.

[1049] Keener says that, "The foot washing in John is the narrative introduction for the final discourse, part of the lengthy prolegomena to the Passion Narrative. Jesus' impending death dominates with foreshadowing of his betrayal (13:2, 10-11, 18-30), then opens directly into discussion about Jesus' departure by way of the cross (13:36-38; 14:3-6). This scene therefore paves the way for the Farewell Discourse (13:31-17:26)." See C. S. Keener, *Gospel of John: A Commentary*, Vol. 2 (Peabody: Hendrickson Publishers, 2003), 899.

[1050] Beasley-Murray states that, "Not frequently it is maintained that the Fourth Evangelist knowingly altered the date of the trial and death of Jesus in the interests of his theology, namely to show that Jesus died as God's Passover Lamb (1:29; 19:31-37)." See Beasley-Murray, *John*, 224. The division of the Gospel of John as Book of Signs and Book of Glory can be found in Brown's two-volume commentary. See Brown, *Gospel according to John*, 2:555.

[1051] Beasley-Murray says that, "In vv. 21-30 a brief dialogue of dramatic intensity takes place, wherein Jesus both makes known that one of the disciples at the table will betray him and actually precipitates the act of betrayal by his words in v. 27b." See Beasley-Murray, *John*, 230.

[1052] Keener says that, "Just as Mark 13 interprets the imminent passion of Mark 14-15 for the disciples in terms of their future tribulation, so Jesus' final discourse in John's Gospel interprets the meaning of Jesus' passion for his disciples: they will share both his sufferings and his resurrection life." See Keener, *Gospel of John*, 2:891.

[1053] See Beasley-Murray, *John*, 230; also see R. A. Culpepper, "The Johannine *hypodeigma*: A Reading of John 13:1-38," *Semeia* 53 (1991), 135.

[1054] See D. A. Carson, *Farewell Discourse and Final Prayer of Jesus*, An Evangelical Exposition of John 13-17 (Grand Rapids: Baker Academic Press, 1980), 11-18.

introduced at the outset of the *Book of Glory* becomes an indication for the glorification motif ahead.

The narrative elements of John 13:1-20 initiates the resolution of John's macro-story. Jesus' 'servant-model' has to be looked at from an 'honor and shame' context.[1055] Johannine irony comes into its culmination here in 13:1-20, where servanthood is portrayed as masterhood.[1056] Thus prefigures to the motif of Jesus' passion in John, in which death is portrayed as glorification.[1057] In v. 1, the narrator indicates that Jesus knew his hour had come (cf. 12:23). In the Gospel, the 'hour' of Jesus is an indication to the death/glorification of the Son of Man.[1058] It is over against the trend of the first twelve chapters where Jesus mostly states that his hour has not yet come.[1059]

In the context of foot washing, the presence of Judas is once again brought to the foreground (v. 2; cf. v. 18). That shows the connection between the foot washing event and the anticipated death of Jesus within John's narrative framework. The entire event of foot washing is narrated within an inclusion with a reference to Judas in vv. 1 and 18. In v. 3, the incarnation of Jesus and the 'U-shaped' plot-structure of John are inscribed: Father had given all things into his [Jesus'] hands (as the pre-existent son); that he had come from God (his incarnation to the world); and was going to God (Jesus' returning back to the Father).[1060] Paschal sees two levels of interpretations based on varied viewpoints of scholars like Brown and Boismard: first, a soteriological/christological interpretation in 13:6-10; and second, a moral interpretation

---

[1055] See J. H. Neyrey, *Gospel of John in Cultural and Ideological Perspective* (Grand Rapids: Eerdmans, 2009), 305-307.

[1056] See Borchert, *John 12-21*, 75.

[1057] See K. Quast, *Reading the Gospel of John: An Introduction* (New York/Mahwah: Paulist Press, 1991/1996), 112-114.

[1058] In the first half of the Gospel, the hour of Jesus is a highly anticipated moment in the ministry of Jesus (2:4; 4:21; 5:25; 7:30; 8:20). In the second half of the book, readers discover that Jesus comes upon his hour (12:23, 27; 13:1; 17:1). See D. Senior, *Passion of Jesus in the Gospel of John* (Collegeville: The Liturgical Press, 1991), 36-38.

[1059] See Morris, *Gospel of John*, 613-615. Keener states that, "At this point, however, John underlines a different aspect of the chronology: Jesus loved his own 'to the end' (13:1). This is Johannine double entendre: it can imply 'to the utmost,' 'fully,' as well as 'to the point of his death.'" See Keener, *Gospel of John*, 2:899.

[1060] See J. L. Resseguie, *The Strange Gospel: Narrative Design and Point of View in John*, Biblical Interpretation Series 56 (Leiden/Boston: Brill, 2001), 171.

in 13:12-17.[1061] In Bultmann's interpretation, he suggests that the evangelist wove the two together.[1062]

Based on the coherent pattern of the narrator and the speech-and-action integration of the protagonist, readers can perceive John 13:1-20 as a gently plotted and sequentially interweaved story. The Farewell Discourse follows its own literary format (13:1-30 [a narrative]; 13:31-16:33 [discourse/s]; and 17:1-26 [a prayer]) in which the foot washing event sustains a distinct literary style from the rest of the materials.[1063] A comparison between Jesus' speeches in the Farewell Discourse and Moses's Deuteronomistic instructions suggest the covenantal language in both of the masterpieces and demonstrates the way Jesus is cast as the new Moses who institutes a new covenant with the new Israel.[1064] The event of foot washing plays a significant role that leads the readers toward the covenantal discourses as well as the death of Jesus. While the Deuteronomistic instructions focus on the temporal Iasrael, the Farewell Discourses focus on the new Israel as a liberated community from all places and from all times. This aspect of the Fourth Gospel reveals its universalistic nature. In the following sections, we will expound some of the key factors within the narrative framework of John 13:1-20.

Jesus's Nature of 'Being': Indications about His Divine Attributes

Jesus' nature of 'being' is understood in terms of his universality (4:42), supernatural power (6:1-15) and existence as one 'from above' (8:23).[1065] God's eternal existence and essential unity with the Son became a "historical

---

[1061] See R. W. Paschal, "Service," Dictionary of Jesus and the Gospels (Downers Grove: InterVarsity Press, 1992), 749. Also see R. E. Brown, *The Gospel according to John XIII-XXI*, The Anchor Bible, Vol. 29A (Garden City: Doubleday, 1990), 2:559-572; M. E. Boismard, "Le Lavement des Pieds (John 13:1-17)," *RB* 71 (1964), 5-24.

[1062] Morris says that, "Before the sustained instruction begins there are two significant actions performed by our Lord. The first, that of washing the disciples' feet, is pregnant with meaning, the meaning of the cross which now loomed before Jesus. The second, that of giving the sop to Judas, taken with Jesus' words to the traitor, set in motion the events leading to the passion." See Morris, *Gospel of John*, 611; also see Brown, *Gospel according to John*, 558-559; Bultmann, *The Gospel of John*, 348-351.

[1063] See Moloney, *Gospel of John*, 370; also see F. F. Segovia, *The Farewell of the Word; The Johannine Call to Abide* (Minneapolis: Fortress Press, 1991), 1-58; Brown, *Gospel according to John*, 559-562.

[1064] See Köstenberger, *John*, 398.

[1065] For more details about Jesus' divine nature, refer to M. F. Bird, C. A. Evans, and S. J. Gathercole, eds., *How God Became Jesus: The Real Origins of Belief in Jesus' Divine Nature* (Grand Rapids: Zondervan, 2014), 1-30; S. H. Webb, *Jesus Christ, Eternal God: Heavenly Flesh and the Metaphysics of Matter* (Oxford/New York: Oxford University Press, 2012), 75-94.

and dynamic reality in Jesus as the Christ."[1066] The Son's existence in relation to the eternals rather than the temporal aspects demonstrates his being beyond time and space.[1067] This nature of Jesus is foregrounded within the macro-narrative framework of the Fourth Gospel.

Within John's macro-structure, Jesus is introduced from the eternal point of view and his presence is delineated in the following ways: he was with God right from the beginning (1:1b), he was God himself (1:1c), all things came into being through him (1:2), the 'Word' became flesh and dwelt among humanity (1:14a), and he shared the glory, grace, and truth of the Father (1:14b). Jesus' identity and authority as the begotten Son of God (1:14b, 18; 3:16) enabled him to appear as a distinct figure within John's narrative framework.[1068] The interlocutors of Jesus recognize him as 'Teacher' or 'Rabbi'/'Rabbouni' in several narrative intervals (1:49; 3:2; 4:31; 11:8; 20:16).[1069] His conversations with Nicodemus (3:1-10), the Samaritan woman (4:7-26), the Jews in the Synagogue at Capernaum (6:24-59) and during the Feast of Tabernacles (7:10-21) affirm his role and status as a teacher.[1070] Moreover, his position as 'Lord' is proclaimed alongside of the title 'Teacher.'[1071] These titles in John do not function in parochial senses, but rather they demonstrate Jesus' divine attributes as he is the teller of heavenly truths and as one who executes authority from above.

While the signs in John reveal his lordship over the created things (2:1-12; 4:43-54; 5:1-18; 6:1-15, 16-21; 9:1-41; 11:1-54),[1072] his 'I AM' sayings demonstrate his role as an authentic teacher of heavenly realities (6:35, 48; 8:12; 9:5; 10:7, 9, 11; 11:25; 14:6; 15:1).[1073] It is further supported by the utterances of the Johannine characters: "Lord, to whom can we go?" (Simon Peter, 6:68); "Lord, I believe" (the healed man [9:38]; and Martha [11:27]); "I have seen the Lord" (Mary Magdalene, 20:18); "We have seen the Lord"

[1066] See M. J. Harris, *Jesus as God: The New Testament Use of Theos in Reference to Jesus* (Eugene/Origen: Wipf & Stock, 1992), 291.

[1067] For a more detailed explanation of 'being,' refer to *The Oxford English Dictionary*, Vol. 1, 777.

[1068] See Beasley-Murray, *John*, 6-17.

[1069] See Beasley-Murray, *John*, 27, 47, 63, 188, 374-376.

[1070] See Moloney, *Gospel of John*, 89-103, 115-145, 239-246.

[1071] See Moloney, *Gospel of John*, 375.

[1072] Thompson says that, "A sign is . . . properly understood when it is seen as pointing to God's work through the person of Jesus to effect salvation." See M. M. Thompson, "John, Gospel of," *Dictionary of Jesus and the Gospels* (Downers Grove: InterVarsity Press, 1992), 379; Thomaskutty, *Dialogue in the Book of Signs*, 447-450.

[1073] See G. M. Burge, "'I AM' Sayings," *Dictionary of Jesus and the Gospels* (Downers Grove: InterVarsity Press, 1992), 354-356; Thomaskutty, *Dialogue in the Book of Signs*, 450-452.

(the disciples, 20:25); and "It is the Lord" (Beloved Disciple, 21:7).[1074] But Thomas's utterance, "My Lord and my God," takes the attention of the reader one step further to the oneness motif and to the divine realities (20:28).[1075]

Jesus' vertical christological attributes are emphasized within the micro-narrative structure of 13:1-20. Within the macro-structure of John, there is a higher regard for Jesus' 'being' as the Son of God and as the Lord-Teacher from above (cf. 3:2).[1076] The very act of Jesus rising up from the table (13:4) is symbolical that indicates his departure from the elevated 'position' and 'honor' to the status of service.[1077] Through his utterances and actions, Jesus proved that he is a teacher par-excellence and the Lord of all times. As the ancient rhetoric rightly suggests, Jesus' speech here is supplemented by his actions.

In 13:1, the narrator states about Jesus' departure from the world of 'becoming' to the world of 'being.' The 'hour,' 'glorification,' and 'lifting up' of the Son of Man are revealed through Jesus' death on the cross (cf. v. 1b).[1078] While the event of 'word becoming flesh' brings about a transition in Jesus' mission from the 'world from above' to the 'world from below' (1:3c-4, 14),[1079] the hour/glorification/lifting up on the cross reveals the reversal of the event.[1080] While, at the beginning, Jesus appears from the 'world of being' to the 'world of becoming,' at the end, a transition occurs when Jesus moves from the 'world of becoming' to the 'world of being' (v. 1).[1081]

The references about his knowing in vv. 1 and 3 are clear marks of his 'being' nature over against his interlocutors' unknowing character. Borchert comments that, "Building upon the statements concerning Jesus' knowledge of his hour in v. 1, the evangelist expands the idea here to remind the reader that

---

[1074] See Ben Witherington, "Lord," *Dictionary of Jesus and the Gospels* (Downers Grove: InterVarsity Press, 1992), 490-491.

[1075] See Thomaskutty, *Saint Thomas the Apostle*, 64-68; M. J. Wilkins, "Disciples," *Dictionary of Jesus and the Gospels* (Downers Grove: InterVarsity Press, 1992), 180.

[1076] See Morris, *Gospel of John*, 611-623; cf. Bruce, *Gospel of John*, 82.

[1077] Borchert states that, "In a society that was very conscious of status symbols of shame and honor, such as the touching and washing of feet, was an extremely important matter." See Borchert, *John 12-21*, 79; also see Köstenberger, *John*, 400-409; Brown, *Gospel according to John*, 2:563-572.

[1078] Moloney says, "The hour is to be a moment when Jesus will depart from the sphere of everyday events. The one who has been sent by the Father will return to the Father, but during his ministry he has gathered disciples, a group called 'his own' (v. 1b: *hoi idioi*. Cf. 1:11-12; 10:3, 4, 12), and his passage through the hour will be a supreme demonstration of his love for them." See Moloney, *Gospel of John*, 373.

[1079] See Moloney, *Gospel of John*, 38.

[1080] See Moloney, *Gospel of John*, 373.

[1081] See Borchert, *John 12-21*, 77.

Jesus was clearly knowledgeable about his origin and his goal or destiny."[1082] Thus Jesus' omniscient nature is made obvious within the narrative master plan of the Gospel.[1083] While the Father committing "all things" (*panta*) into Son's hands as an active partner in creation (1:3), Jesus appears as an authoritative and powerful figure in human history.[1084] Jesus' knowledge, love, and action in contrast to the unrecognizing, hateful, and misunderstanding natures of the Jews [and the disciples] reveal his divine attributes (vv. 1-5).[1085]

Jesus knows that the Father had given all things into his hands, his coming from God, and his going back to God (v. 1). Jesus' statement in v. 13 is significant to note here: "You call me Teacher and Lord—and you are right, for that is what I am." While Peter in his personal conversation calls Jesus "Lord" (vv. 6, 9), the disciples as a whole address him as "Teacher" and "Lord" (vv. 13-14).[1086] Jesus acknowledges their utterances and affirms his status as "I am." While Nicodemus refers him as a heavenly teacher, the title has overtones of divinity (3:2).[1087] Jesus' nature as a sent one of God is highlighted in v. 20. As Jesus is 'from above' (*ek tōn anō*, 8:23), seeing him is seeing God. As an agent of God, he has life in himself and has authority to execute judgment (5:26-27). These divine attributes of Jesus enable him to be the authoritative one of God.[1088]

Jesus's Nature of 'Becoming': His Servant Model

The Gospel of John as a whole describes how God himself became a human being. Jesus' descend from the heavens, total identification with the humans (1:14), and his service in the world (13:1-20) are emphasized by the Fourth Evangelist. John 13:1-20 also demonstrates the horizontal and humanitarian aspects in the ministry of Jesus.

In the first century CE context, foot washing was considered as a menial work and was usually practiced by slaves and Gentiles.[1089] In the episode, Jesus' posture of getting up from the table, taking off his outer robe, tying a

---

[1082] See Borchert, *John 12-21*, 78.

[1083] Borchert says, "'Coming from' (*exerchesthai* plus *apo*) and 'going to' (*hypagein* plus *pros*) was the way John here described the broad dimensions of Jesus' earthly existence and his relationship to the eternal God." See Borchert, *John 12-21*, 79.

[1084] See Borchert, *John 12-21*, 79.

[1085] See Moloney, *Gospel of John*, 373-374.

[1086] See Morris, *Gospel of John*, 617-618.

[1087] See Morris, *Gospel of John*, 620.

[1088] See Borchert, *Gospel of John*, 79.

[1089] Keener states that, "Thus people often washed their feet when returning home; washing one's feet was common enough that 'unwashed feet' became proverbial in some places for 'without preparation.' The face, hands, and feet seem to have been the most critical parts of the body to wash." See Keener, *Gospel of John*, 2:903.

towel around, pouring water into a basin, washing the feet of the disciples, and wiping them with a towel that was tied around him demonstrates his serving attitude (v. 4).[1090] Michaels says that, "When his work is done, he will reverse those actions: 'So, when he had washed their feet, he took his garments and reclined again' (v. 12)."[1091] While reclining at the table is symbolical of his honorable position, washing the feet of the disciples demonstrates his gesture of humility.[1092] The narrative makes it clear that though Jesus was honorable he came to serve humanity.[1093] The event of washing the feet exemplifies Jesus' pattern of sacrificial and costly service. It is in this manner the disciples are expected to show their *agapē* to one another as they are engaged in witnessing Christ in the world (13:34-35).[1094] This understanding of John's Christology goes in alignment with the suffering servant motifs in the Book of Isaiah and the Gospel of Mark (see Isa 52:13-53:12).[1095]

While Mark delineates a 'theology of power' at the outset of the Gospel (chaps. 1-8), later on he shifts the emphasis to a 'theology of suffering' (Mark 10:45).[1096] Such a paradigmatic presentation of Christ's work is obvious within the narrative framework of John 13:1-20. On the one hand, Jesus' *being* nature is presented at a vertical level, and on the other hand, his *becoming* nature is shown at a horizontal level. These extreme positions cannot be considered as contrasting elements within Johannine Christology. Rather, they should be perceived as Christological elements that progress from one level to the other.

[1090] Bruce states that, "So he dresses himself like a household servant and performs a servant's task." See Bruce, *Gospel of John*, 280; also see J. H. Bernard, *Gospel according to St. John*, International Critical Commentary (New York: Charles Scribner's Sons, 1929), 458-459.

[1091] Michaels says that, ". . . the writer is content to let the death of Jesus remain implicit here, just as it remained implicit in the account of Mary anointing Jesus' feet at the earlier 'supper' in Bethany (see 12:3-8)." See J. R. Michaels, *The Gospel of John*, NICNT (Grand Rapids: Eerdmans, 2010), 724-725; also see Bernard, *Gospel according to St. John*, 465.

[1092] See Bennema, *Excavating John's Gospel*, 142-143; also see Bernard, *Gospel according to St. John*, 454-476.

[1093] Keener (2003: 2: 904) states that, "Washing feet was a menial task, and one who sought to wash another's feet normally took the posture of a servant or dependent." See Keener, *Gospel of John*, 2:904.

[1094] See Paschal, "Service," 750; also see Bernard, *Gospel according to St. John*, 476-477.

[1095] See J. Blenkinsopp, *Isaiah 40-55: A New Translation with Introduction and Commentary* (New Haven/London: The Anchor Yale Bible, 2002), 338-356.

[1096] Guthrie comments that, "It is supposed that Mark sees the disciples as spokesmen for a theology of glory linked to the Hellenistic divine man idea. According to this view, Mark 1-8 presents a triumphalistic wonder-worker, where the rest of the gospel sees Jesus in terms of the Suffering Servant." See Donald Guthrie, *New Testament Introduction* (Downers Grove: InterVarsity Press, 1961/1990), 68; also see R. H. Stein, *Mark*, BECNT (Grand Rapids: Baker Academic Press, 2008), 486-490, 632-634.

Jesus' love for his disciples extends until the end (v. 2). It demonstrates how love as the essential truth of God extends from heaven to earth. In v. 3, the narrator places the clause on Jesus' coming from God at the center with a purpose. While the construction "Father had given all things into his [Jesus'] hands" (the pre-incarnate stage) is placed at the beginning and the expression "he [Jesus] was going to the Father" (the ascension to heaven) at the end, the expression "he [Jesus] had come from God" (his descent from heaven) emphasizes a significant aspect within the passage. As Jesus is the word that became flesh, he reveals his characteristic role of servant leadership. Jesus' statement to the disciples, "your Lord and Teacher . . . washed your feet" (v. 14), emphasizes the aspect of humility and servant leadership.[1097] He further states that "servants are not greater than their master nor are messengers greater than the one who sent them" (v. 16).[1098] This speech has to be understood in the light of his statement in v. 20: "whoever receives one whom I send receives me; and whoever receives me receives him who sent me."

Jesus' statement here indicates that no one can respect a master or a sender without respecting his/her servant and messenger. Thus, His servanthood in relation to the Father and the disciples' servanthood in relation to Jesus are interknitted together. Peter was hesitant to see "the Holy One of God" humbling himself and perform such a menial service for one so unworthy (vv. 6-11).[1099] In a context in which 'clean' and 'unclean' are interpreted on the basis of the laws of purification and 'honor' and 'shame' on the basis of role and status, Jesus shares his views from an eternal and heavenly perspective.[1100]

Peter's appointment as a disciple (1:42) and his presence with Jesus in the Synagogue at Capernaum (6:66-71) would have made him clean.[1101] What Jesus spoke to the disciples was spirit and life (6:63). Peter in his conversation acknowledges that Jesus possesses words of eternal life (6:68). As he is internally cleansed, he and those who follow Jesus need only the washing of the feet (6:60-71).[1102] Jesus washes their feet as a symbolical gesture and

---

[1097] See Beasley-Murray, *John*, 232-237; also see Bruce, *Gospel of John*, 284-285. Morris says that, "Jesus gently discourages excess. The imagery is that of a man going to a feast. He will bathe at home. Then when he arrives he needs only to wash his feet to sit at table wholly clean." See Morris, *Gospel according to John*, 618.

[1098] See Bruce, *Gospel of John*, 286.

[1099] Cf. Michaels, *Gospel of John*, 726.

[1100] Bruce states that, "the foot washing symbolizes Jesus' humbling himself to endure the death of the cross and the cleansing efficacy of his death for the believer." See Bruce, *Gospel of John*, 281-283; also see Morris, *Gospel according to John*, 618; also see Borchert, *John 12-21*, 82.

[1101] See Bruce, *Gospel of John*, 281-282; also see Köstenberger, *John*, 401-409..

[1102] See Michaels, *Gospel of John*, 732.

as a model of service in order to communicate with them certain lessons.[1103] Jesus, as the Paschal Lamb (1:29, 36; 19:36), demonstrates an image of sacrifice through washing the feet of the disciples.[1104] His act in this passage prefigures his imminent passion and death on the cross.[1105] The event as a whole foreshadows Jesus' service to the world as a paschal lamb.[1106] Thus the text bridges between the "local" and the "global" with a gnomic intent in mind.

Jesus' Instruction on 'Doing': A New Lesson for the Disciples

In vv. 14-15, Jesus instructs his disciples that they should wash one another's feet. In v. 15, He tells his disciples that "you should do (*poiēte*) as I have done (*epoiēsa*) to you" (v. 15b). While *poiēte* remains as the present active subjunctive form and *epoiēsa* as the aorist active indicative form of *poiēo*, the pointed activity of Jesus and the subsequent instructions for the disciples to practice are indicated.[1107] In this context, Jesus illustrates the event as an example (*hypodeigma*) for the disciples to practice in the future. He insists that the disciples should do as he has done to them (vv. 14-15).[1108] Through Jesus' activity and the subsequent instruction, the disciples are prepared to carry out the virtue of humility through the act of service.[1109]

The narrator of the story points out that the disciples are expected to demonstrate the aspect of *Imitatio Christi*.[1110] Michaels says that, "The noun 'example' and the repetition of 'you too' make it clear that Jesus is calling

---

[1103] See Blomberg, *Historical Reliability of the Fourth Gospel*, 188-192; also see Bennema, *Excavating John's Gospel*, 142-143; also see Köstenberger, *John*, 401-409.

[1104] Merkle states that, "Biblical leadership is humble, servant leadership. Jesus gave the perfect example of humility when he washed the feet of his disciples (John 13:1-20)." See B. L. Merkle, *Why Elders? A Biblical and Practical Guide for Church Members* (Grand Rapids: Kregel Publications, 2009), 45.

[1105] Paschal says that, "The foot washing is a drama of Jesus' act of sacrifice on the cross." See Paschal, "Servant," 750; also see Köstenberger, *John*, 401-409.

[1106] Paschal states that, "The servant sayings of Jesus in John 13:12-17 have christological implications that we should not miss: the Lord of the disciples is also the obedient son and servant of the Father (cf. John 14:10-12; 17:1-5)." See Paschal, "Servant," 750; also see Blomberg, *Historical Reliability of John's Gospel*, 189-192.

[1107] See J. W. Wenham, *Elements of New Testament Greek* (Cambridge: Cambridge University Press, 1965), 96, 159-160. Michaels says, "the present subjunctive, 'might do,' in contrast to the aorist, 'just as I did,' implies that he is urging them to continue to do repeatedly what he has done for them once and for all." See Michaels, *Gospel of John*, 735.

[1108] See Blomberg, *Historical Reliability of John's Gospel*, 190-191.

[1109] Paschal suggests that, "The humility that Jesus is pressing on Peter is both to accept the gracious gift of service from the Master and to accept a common human need for the same gift." See Paschal, "Service," 750.

[1110] See Jôel B. Green, *Death of Jesus: Tradition and Interpretation in the Passion Narrative* (Eugene/Oregon: Wipf & Stock, 1988), 112.

on his disciples to do for each other exactly what he has done for them. The repetition of the verb 'to do'—'just as I did' and 'that you might do'—confirms that he is urging them to imitate not just his humble attitude, but the literal action of washing feet."[1111] While Jesus initiates the service as an honorable task, the society considers that as an act of the weak.[1112] As Jesus does the will of God and serving the humanity at the same time, the disciples are instructed to do the same. Through the very activity of Jesus, the Johannine community is instructed in a special way to follow a pattern of sacrificial and costly service to humanity.[1113]

The *agapē*-centric ethics of the Fourth Gospel is foreshadowed in its apex level within the Farewell Discourse. The Johannine ethics that are recapitulated within a punch line phrase like "love one another" (13:34). This phraseology of John can be considered as a call for caring the poor and outcaste within varied life situations.[1114] As the Johannine community was an expelled messianic group from the synagogue, their mutual relationship and service among themselves in utter humility are emphasized. As Jesus was selflessly serving them and sacrificing himself for the humanity even to the point of the cross, the disciples are asked to follow his steps to witness Christ through the gesture of service.[1115]

The narrator foregrounds the relationship among the Father, the Son, and the believers (vv. 16-18). When God the Master sends his Son as a Servant, the Son exemplifies a servant model of leadership. Though he possesses a superior status on a par with the Father and belongs to the world of *being*, Jesus turns to be a servant and he exemplifies selfless model of leadership on earth. Jesus' humility and servanthood provide the disciples practical lessons to remain as faithful servants of God.[1116] Furthermore, while God the Father functions as the sender, Jesus the Son appears as the messenger of God. As Jesus proceeds from the world of the 'sender,' he exists in the world below as the messenger of God. As Jesus the messenger turns to be the 'sender' of God, he sends the disciples as messengers of God. Here Jesus prepares his disciples to do what he has already done for them.[1117]

[1111] See Michaels, *Gospel of John*, 735.

Bennema comments that, "Jesus regards the acts of service to others as honorable, whereas the society of that time considered them as sign of weakness." See Bennema, *Excavating John's Gospel*, 143.

[1113] See Bennema, *Excavating John's Gospel*, 140-144.

[1114] See Paschal, "Service," 750.

[1115] See Paschal, "Service," 750.

[1116] See Bruce, *Gospel of John*, 282-288.

[1117] See Bruce, *Gospel of John*, 286-287.

Jesus, being master and sender, comes in the form of a servant/messenger and instructs the disciples to witness God even at the point of death.[1118] If the disciples continue to know the things that Jesus actualized in this world and imitate his activities, they will be considered as blessed (v. 17).[1119] While Peter is foregrounded as an insider whom Jesus instructs the truth, Judas is identified as a representative of the outsiders.[1120] Paschal comments that, "As Peter represents the community of faith, Judas represents those who reject Jesus' sacrificial gift and its concomitant demand for service to others."[1121] In that sense, the *hypodeigma* is also demonstrated through the faith responses of Simon Peter and Judas Iscariot. Jesus instructs here that people can do the will of God through their faith response to Jesus, attitude of loving relationship with one another, and the virtue of servant model of discipleship. In short, Jesus, the 'sent one,' functions as 'the sender.'[1122] When the disciples receive Jesus and accept his authority to send, they shall be turned to be messengers of the eternal truth of God.[1123]

Relevance of the Study in the Indian Context

John 13:1-20 recapitulates the theological master plan of the Fourth Gospel. Jesus' being nature and divine status, his becoming nature as servant of God, and his glorification on the cross are demonstrated in a nutshell in the episode.[1124] The narrator of the story attempts to merge the theme of servanthood with the glorification aspect. Jesus' movement as a messenger of God flourishes from his divine nature (the pre-incarnate stage) to the human form (the incarnate Word) and further to the divine nature (through revealing the hour/glorification/lifting up of the Son of Man).[1125]

[1118] Beasley-Murray comments that, "The comparison of v. 13 is deepened by a saying drawn from the tradition of Jesus's sayings (cf. Matthew 10:24); here 'student' and 'teacher' are replaced by 'slave' and 'master,' and 'one sent' along with the 'superior who sends' him." See Beasley-Murray, *John*, 236.

[1119] Moloney comments that, "The blessedness of the Johannine believer flows from the living out, the 'doing' of all that is implied by entering into discipleship through baptism." See Moloney, *Gospel of John*, 379.

[1120] See Blomberg, *Historical Reliability of John's Gospel*, 189.

[1121] Paschal further says that, "Not to accept Jesus' death for us is to betray him, to leave the community of faith and embrace the darkness (13:30)." See Paschal, "Service," 750.

[1122] See Blomberg, *Historical Reliability of John's Gospel*, 190-191; Moloney, *Gospel of John*, 378-379.

[1123] See other New Testament parallels in Mark 10:35-45; Matthew 20:20-28; and Luke 22:24-28. Also see Blomberg, *Historical Reliability of John's Gospel*, 189-190.

[1124] See Moloney, *Gospel of John*, 370-372.

[1125] See William Loader, *Jesus in John's Gospel: Structure and Issues in Johannine Christology* (Grand Rapids: Eerdmans, 2017), 225.

The movement of Jesus 'from heavenly to earthly' and again 'from earthly to heavenly' forms the 'U shaped plot structure' of the Fourth Gospel. In the event of foot washing, Jesus' posture of sitting at the table (v. 4a), his washing of the feet of the disciples (v. 4b-11), and his reclining back to the table (v. 12) symbolically demonstrates the 'U shaped plot structure' of the story.[1126] As Jesus' identity is delineated in relation to a prop like a table at the beginning and at the end (vv. 4a, 12) and his attitude of service at the middle (vv. 4b-11), the narrator demonstrates a 'U shaped plot structure' at the micro-level with symbolical underpinnings.[1127]

While sitting at the table is symbolical of the status of 'honor,' washing the feet is identical to Jesus' becoming nature. Jesus' attitude of life-giving is resulted into his death and the death is identified as the glorification of the Son of Man.[1128] The event of foot washing and the successive Farewell Discourse intimate the reader a clue concerning the imminent death of Jesus. The event as a whole prepares way for the narrator to identify the betrayer in 13:21-30.[1129] The Farewell Discourse ultimately leads the protagonist to his death and that further demonstrates his glory. In that way, the event in its semantic domains can be considered as a foundational activity with a lot of symbolical aspects. The suffering servant motif is obviously reflected through the event (cf. Mark 10:45).[1130]

John's Gospel is a contextually adaptable and theologically enriched masterpiece that can absorb concepts from 'everywhere and ever' in order to provide a 'gnomic' and 'universal' appeal.[1131] A thorough analysis of the Gospel will enable us to understand the flexible nature of John—its adaptability to new situations and the reverberation of its impact through space and time.[1132] A gnomic reading of the Fourth Gospel, one that explores its message for all times and all places, will help us to understand its significance for the people of India today.[1133]

[1126] See Resseguie, *The Strange Gospel*, 171.

[1127] The expressions like *egeiretai ek tou deipnou* (v. 4a) and *anepesen palin* (v. 12) make us to think of a table at view.

[1128] See Loader, *Jesus in John's Gospel*, 225.

[1129] See Bennema, *Excavating John's Gospel*, 140-146.

[1130] See Beasley-Murray, *John*, 222-240.

[1131] See Johnson Thomaskutty, "Biblical Interpretation in the Global-Indian Context," *Fuller Magazine* (Pasadena: Fuller Theological Seminary, 2017), 64-68.

[1132] See Johnson Thomaskutty, "Reading John's Gospel in the Nepali Context," *Journal of Asian Evangelical Theology* (March 2016), 6.

[1133] See Johnson Thomaskutty, "Glo(b/c)alization and Mission(s)," *New Life Theological Journal* (January 2015), 56-77; also Thomaskutty, "Reading John's Gospel in the Nepali Context," 5-6.

John's narrative master plan enables the readers aware of the superiority of Jesus as 'one who was in the beginning' (1:1), 'all things came into being through him' (1:2), and 'in him was life and the life was light of all people' (1:4).[1134] In 13:1-20, Jesus reveals his 'honorable' position in contextual and social terms as a 'teacher' and 'Lord.'[1135] But his posture of washing the feet of the disciples is, in social terms, a 'shameful' activity. The church in India should 'do what it speaks' as Jesus 'did what he talked.'[1136] As Jesus accommodated the human world and its cultures through his very nature of becoming (see 'Word became flesh,' 1:14), the Indian church should take active steps in witnessing Christ to the suffering humanity of the country. The mission model of identifying with people has long lasting effects in witnessing Christ in the pluralistic context of the country.[1137]

As the servant-model of leadership demonstrated both at the *micro* (13:1-20) and *macro* levels of the Gospel, the church in India should prioritize this model both in its ministerial and missional engagements.[1138] Missional and ministerial aspects of the church should not be limited to people's *coming* to the church but it should also prioritize church's *going out* to the people groups. In that sense, Christian mission in India can be actualized mainly through servanthood model and praxis-oriented strategies.[1139] As M. M. Thomas and P. D. Devanandan suggests, the church in India should get involved in the very act of nation building and she should serve the country through humanization.[1140]

As Johannine Jesus, who turns to be a servant of God, uplifted the marginalized sections of the society, the Indian church, as an agent of mission, should uplift the Dalit, Tribal, and other marginal groups of the society.[1141] In that sense, as Jesus manifested his glory through service until his death, the church should also exemplify its service to the community and reveal Christ's honor in the public. As Jesus appears to be a 'sent one of God' to send people for witnessing, the Church as the 'sent one' in the world is expected to send people for witnessing Christ at varied levels of community life.

[1134] See Moloney, *Gospel of John*, 34-39.

[1135] See Bruce, *Gospel of John*, 281-283; Morris, *Gospel according to John*, 618; also see Borchert, *John 12-21*, 82.

[1136] See Thomaskutty, *Dialogue in the Book of Signs*, 450-452.

[1137] See Paschal, "Service," 749-750.

[1138] Paschal, "Service," 749-750.

[1139] See C. Perry, *A Bibliographical History of the Church in Nepal* (Kathmandu: Nepal Church History Project, 2000), 17-19, 30-31; S. Pandey, *Christianity in Nepal: Unity in Diversity* (Kathmandu: National Churches Fellowship of Nepal, 2003), 1-50.

[1140] See M. M. Thomas and P. D. Devanandan, *Christian Participation in Nation Building* (Bangalore: NCCI and CISRS, 1960), 2-3, 48-50, 154-155, 209-210, 227-242, 266-289, 290-305.

[1141] See Thomaskutty, "Reading John's Gospel in the Nepali Context," 20.

The Indian church should transcend all sorts of human made boundaries for witnessing Christ and also she should prioritize loving kindness as the greatest virtue of God (13:34-35; 14:18-24; 17:23).[1142] In the Indian context, the church should function as an agent of charity, reconciliation, and liberation. As Jesus exemplifies a 'U shaped' witnessing model within John's micro-and macro-narrative frameworks, Christian communities in India can adopt a 'U shaped' mission model to attune people to the experience of eternal life.[1143] On the one hand, the church can sustain its values and spiritual norms as 'honorable' human beings, and on the other hand, she can extend her services to the betterment of the society. The church's service to the suffering humanity can enable her to regain the honorable status. The praxis oriented standards of Jesus' witnessing, which interlocks both kerygmatic and praxis-oriented mission strategies, can be a paradigm for the Indian church for her mission in the pluralistic context of the country.[1144]

In Jesus' ministry, the event of foot washing was foreshadowing his imminent passion, crucifixion, and death on the cross as a servant of God.[1145]. In that sense, the Indian church should endeavor for witnessing Christ irrespective of the increasing oppositions, persecutions, and martyrdoms. The church's struggles in witnessing Christ can be transformed as honorable and glorious occasions. Even when the church remains as a minority community, she should attempt to balance between the kerygmatic and practically oriented aspects of mission in the Indian context.[1146] As a two-level drama, the Fourth Evangelist emphasizes the event of foot washing with a purpose of educating his community the lessons of mutual love and service in corporate living.[1147] John's community considers Jesus as a model of servant leadership and his performances as *hypodeigmata* for social living.[1148] All the above factors reveal John's gnomic significance in the Indian context.

[1142] See F. J. Moloney, *Love in the Gospel of John* (Grand Rapids: Baker Academic, 2013), 26-99; J. Varghese, *Imagery of Love in the Gospel of John* (Roma: Gregorian & Biblical Press, 2009), 11-24.

[1143] See Resseguie, *The Strange Gospel*, 171.

[1144] See Thomaskutty, "Reading John's Gospel in the Nepali Context," 14.

[1145] See D. Sylva, *Thomas—Love as Strong as Death* (London/New York: Bloomsbury T & T Clark, 2013), 54.

[1146] See Perry, *A Bibliographical History of the Church in Nepal*, 17-19; also see Pandey, *Christianity in Nepal*, 1-50.

[1147] See J. L. Martyn, *History and Theology of the Fourth Gospel* (Nashville: Abingdon, 1968), 24-36.

[1148] In John, Jesus is the 'Word became flesh and dwelt among humanity' and one who 'washed the feet of the disciples.' See M. L. Coloe, "Sources in the Shadows," *New Currents Through John* (Atlanta: Society of Biblical Literature, 1976), 69-82.

Conclusion

The above discussion enables us to understand that John 13:1-20 is a unique literary masterpiece that functions paradigmatically both within the narrative framework of the Farewell Discourse and within the macro-structure of the Gospel. The event recapitulates the 'U shaped' plot structure of the entire Gospel with an emphasis on the *being* and *becoming* natures of Jesus and his instruction for *doing*. That reveals the *hypodeigmatic* function within and beyond the text. In a context in which people's social positions such as 'honor' and 'shame' were perceived in a hierarchical way, Jesus' action of washing the feet of the disciples overturns the prevailing norms of the society. While the divine attributes of Jesus plotted dynamically within the textual horizon of John, his *being* nature is brought to the foreground. The narrator designs the story with an ever-continuing and universalistic effect.

The symbolical act of washing the feet of the disciples demonstrates his servant model of leadership and thus the *becoming* nature. Jesus' instruction to the disciples for *doing* it in their future witnessing exposes the event to the level of an example story. The usage of the expressions like "got up from the meal" (v. 4) and "returned to his place" (v. 12) and the ordering of the event of washing the feet at the center (vv. 4b-11) amply show the plot dynamics of the event to communicate the message in a unique fashion. Moreover, the connection of the event with the *agapē*-centric utterances of Jesus in the Gospel and his demonstration of love on the cross provide in-depth meaning to the event.

The message of the event can be adopted as a paradigm in the Indian context for Christian witness, mission, and evangelism. As the Johannine community re-interpreted the event in relation to the incarnation, servant model, and death of Jesus and in congruence with their own *Sitz im Leben*, the Indian Christian community should demonstrate its ethos through serving others even at the point of death. Service to humanity should be prioritized in order to inculcate a praxis-oriented witnessing. Church's servanthood model reveals her identity as a worthy community in the present and thus achieving a glorious future. John's gnomic and universal tendencies can be adopted as means of hermeneutical key in order to make John's semantic domains conducive and reverberating in the pluralistic context of India. As a classical masterpiece and a universal maxim, the Fourth Gospel is inclusive in its nature and it can dynamically absorb the local situations into its narrative framework for a renewed understanding.

Chapter 13

Faith and Theology in the Johannine Community and in the Reformation: A Paradigm in the Indian Context

Introduction

The following essay deals with the relationship between the faith of the believing community and theology within the academic set-up. The Reformation movement with its emphasis on *sola scriptura, sola fide*; and *solus Christus* attempted to build a bridge between faith and theology. While the Reformers derived their core concepts and theological ideas mostly from the Pauline corpus, in the current investigation, I seek to explore the connection between the Johannine understanding of faith and theology and its significance in the Reformation context. The following questions are given prominence here: how did the Johannine community deal with the issues of the relationship between faith and theology in their personal and corporate living? How did the Reformers follow the ideology of the Johannine community in their interpretative endeavours in relating faith in the ecclesiastical set-up and the theology in the academic circles of their times? How did the Reformation movement influence Indian Christianity and its reinterpretation of faith and theology? How did the characteristic features of the Johannine community serve as a model to the Reformers and also to the post-Reformation Indian believers/scholars in developing their ideological and theological framework?

An attempt is made to analyze the way in which Christ-centred interpretations work in the Johannine, in the Reformation, and in the Indian

Christian contexts. At the integrative level, we will also explore the analeptic (to the Johannine community) and the proleptic (to the Indian Christian context) connection of the Reformation Movement. The unique feature of the Reformation, as it relates to both the biblical past and the global future, gives us a significant outlook concerning the movement and its growth. As a Johannine scholar, I will, first, analyse faith and theology within the narrative framework of the Gospel of John; second, as a person influenced by Protestant theology, I will describe the connection of these two areas in the Reformation traditions; and third, as an Indian, I will study the impact and influence of the Johannine and the Reformation principles both in the historical and in the contemporary Indian scenario.

Faith and Theology in the Johannine Community Context

As a gnomic interpreter, the Johannine narrator recreates the story of Jesus with innovative techniques, immediate effects, and universal significance.[1149] Louis Martyn conceives the Gospel of John as a two-level drama.[1150] For him, the Fourth Gospel "seems far more detached from its ancient setting." Martyn says, "The very mention of this Gospel causes most of us to think of those marvellous discourses of Jesus, in the reading of which one feels immediately warmed by such 'spiritual' and timeless affirmations as, 'I am the way, and the truth, and the life.'"[1151] Raymond E. Brown explains the tension between Church and Synagogue and the polemic between Jews and the Johannine sectarians,[1152] arguing that the Johannine Christians, as a sectarian group expelled from the Synagogue, constructed a theology according to their existential demands and based on their faith affirmations.[1153] In the Johannine community context, the aspect of faith was dealt with using an entirely different emphasis and perspective. In the words of Kysar, "Community experience was

---

[1149] While *descriptive linguistic phenomena* guide the reader to the *there and then* aspects, *gnomic linguistic phenomena* guide the reader to the *everywhere and ever* perspective. Here the expression *gnomic* is used to indicate the sense of language that explores the general and universal maxims. See See Johnson Thomaskutty, "Reading John's Gospel as a Jewish-Christian Conflict Narrative: A Paradigm for Contemporary India," *Religious Freedom and Conversion: Papers from the 4th SAIACS Academic Consultation* (Bengaluru: SAIACS Press, 2017), 160.

[1150] See J. Louis Martyn, *History and Theology in the Fourth Gospel*, Revised and Enlarged (Nashville: Abingdon, 1968/1979), 129; Robert Kysar, "The Whence and Whither of the Johannine Community," *Life in Abundance: Studies of John's Gospel in Tribute to Raymond E. Brown*, ed. John R. Donahue (Collegeville: Liturgical Press, 2005), 68.

[1151] Martyn, *History and Theology in the Fourth Gospel*, 15.

[1152] See Brown, *The Gospel according to St. John*, lxx-lxxiv.

[1153] Wayne A. Meeks, using the methods of a sociology of knowledge, "examines the descent/ascent motif in John and proposes that it comprises a myth by which the Johannine Christians understood and strengthened their status as a sectarian counter-culture group." See Wayne A. Meeks, "The Man from Heaven in Johannine Sectarianism," *JBL* 91 (1972), 44-72.

understood to be the key that unlocked the puzzles of the gospel—both its theological themes and the language it uses to tell its story of Jesus."[1154] The communitarian tendencies of the Fourth Gospel enable the reader to relate the characters and the events from an 'everywhere and ever' point of view rather than from a 'there and then' perspective.[1155]

In the words of Clement of Alexandria, John positions his Gospel over against the 'external facts' of the Synoptic Gospels, as the Fourth Gospel is a narrative filled with 'internal facts' that qualifies this Gospel to be called 'a spiritual Gospel.'[1156] This general framework persuades a reader to perceive the contemporaneous outlook of the Gospel. The questions to be answered in this paper are: 'How did the situation of the Johannine community inform the reformulation of their faith along soteriological and eschatological lines?' 'How can the community's theological engagements be a paradigm in the contemporary Indian context?' 'What insights can an overview of the experiences of the Johannine community in relation to the Indian Christian situation offer into the connection between faith and theology in the contemporary world?'

In the Fourth Gospel, while the noun *pistis* does not occur, the verb *pisteuō* occurs nearly one hundred times.[1157] R. T. France states, "At any rate, the verb expresses a vital component in John's understanding of salvation. It summarizes what God requires of his people (6:28-29)."[1158] John's usage of the verb can be briefly outlined as follows: first, the intellectual content of the verb is expressed twelve times by *pisteuō* with *hoti* (literally, "believe that"). All these uses (except 9:18) refer to a Christological conviction, i.e., the belief that Jesus the Messiah, the Son of God, has come from God (6:69; 8:24; 11:27, 42; 13:19; 17:8, 21; 14:10-11; 16:27, 30; 20:31);[1159] second, in no less than thirty-six cases it is expressed with *pisteuō eis* (literally, "believe into"), and

---

[1154] Kysar, "The Whence and Whither of the Johannine Community," 70.

[1155] Warren Carter says, "Reading John's narrative [...] is an ongoing interpretive task that engages the narrative and its good news in ever-changing and new circumstances." Warren Carter, *John: Storyteller, Interpreter, Evangelist* (Peabody: Hendrickson Publishers, 2006), 218.

[1156] Quoted in Eusebius, *Ecclesiastical History* 6.14.7.

[1157] In Johannine theology *pisteuō* (98 occurrences in the Gospel, 9 in 1 John; *pistis* only in 1 John 5:4) occupies a position of central importance. See G. Barth, "Pistis," *Exegetical Dictionary of the New Testament*, Vol. 3, eds. Horst Balz and Gerhard Schneider (Grand Rapids: Eerdmans, 1994), 95-96; Schnelle, *Theology of the New Testament*, 717. Apart from 1 John 5:4, where *hē pistis hēmōn* is called the power which overcomes the *kosmos*, the noun *pistis* does not occur in the Gospel or Epistles of John. See Bultmann, "The *pistis* Group in the New Testament," *TDNT* 6, ed. Gerhard Friedrich (Grand Rapids: Eerdmans, 1968), 222.

[1158] R. T. France, "Faith," *Dictionary of Jesus and the Gospels*, eds. Joel B. Green, Scot McKnight, and I. Howard Marshall (Downers Grove: InterVarsity Press, 1992), 224-225.

[1159] Dodd, *Interpretation of the Fourth Gospel*, 179.

once *pisteuō en* ("believe in"; see 2:11; 3:15, 16, 18a, 36; 4:39; 6:29, 35, 40; 7:31, 48; 8:30; 9:36; 10:42; 11:45, 48; 12:11, 42; 14:1a; 17:20).[1160] All these usages except two refer to a belief "into Jesus," or "into the name of Jesus" (1:12; 2:23; 3:18);[1161] third, in thirty cases *pisteuō* is used absolutely, with no explicit indication of the object of belief. Often these uses follow closely on references to believing "into Jesus" (see 3:18; 4:39, 41; 6:40, 47; 9:35-38).[1162] In the words of Udo Schnelle, "In the majority of cases, *pisteuō* is combined with *eis* (in or on), which indicates a fundamental characteristic of the Johannine understanding of faith."[1163] It demonstrates a complete commitment and personal union between the believer and Christ.

Believing in Jesus means to receive him (1:12; 5:43; 13:20), to receive his testimony (3:11), and to receive his words (12:48; 17:8).[1164] In that sense, faith is used as a shorthand expression for a Christian commitment that is mostly or even fully directed to Jesus.[1165] Here we see John's distinctive linguistic usage of faith that is remarkably single-minded. While a few of John's uses of *pisteuō* appear with the dative and refer to God or Scripture (or Moses) or a word spoken, in the vast majority of cases the object of faith is the person of Jesus himself.[1166] This understanding of the verb in John informs the reader about the following things: first, believing is significantly connected to the person and work of Jesus; second, it is a soteriologically loaded term that functions both at the *intradiegetic* (within the story of John) and *metadiegetic* (in relation to the readers) levels;[1167] and third, it is an existential demand or requirement to establish the identity of the community.

The first time the word "faith" in verbal form (pisteusōsin) appears in 1:7. John the Baptist came as a witness to testify to the light, so that all might believe through him. In 1:12, it is said that believing (*pisteuousin*) in Jesus' name will give people "power to become children of God."[1168] These initial and other

---

[1160] See France, "Faith," 225.

[1161] The two exceptions are references to belief in God (12:44; 14:1), but in each case this is combined directly with belief in Jesus.

[1162] John speaks of saving faith as both *pisteuō hoti* and *pisteuō eis/en*. To 'believe that' Jesus is the Christ, the Son of God (20:31), is soteriologically equivalent to 'believing in' him for eternal life (3:15-16). See Thomas L. Stegall, *The Gospel of Christ: A Biblical Response to the Crossless Gospel Regarding the Contents of Saving Faith* (Milwaukee: Grace Gospel Press, 2009), 170.

[1163] Schnelle, *Theology of the New Testament*, 717.

[1164] See George Eldon Ladd, *A Theology of the New Testament* (Grand Rapids: Eerdmans, 1974), 308.

[1165] France, "Faith," 225.

[1166] See France, "Faith," 225.

[1167] Schnelle, *Theology of the New Testament*, 717; also see Barth, "Pistis," 96.

[1168] Schnelle, *Theology of the New Testament*, 717; cf. Ladd, *A Theology of the NT*, 308.

references to "believing" are well-aligned with the purpose statement of the Gospel leading up to the climax of the story. In 20:31, the narrator concludes: "But these are written so that you may come to *believe* (*pisteuēte*) that Jesus is the Messiah, the Son of God, and that through *believing* (*pisteuontes*) you may have life in his name." Commenting on John 20:31, L. W. Hurtado states that, "The acclamation of Jesus as 'the Christ' forms a central part of the author's own summary of Christian faith."[1169] In 20:30, the narrator gives an impression that the content of the Gospel is understood to be signs performed by Jesus (cf. 2:11, 23; 4:54; 12:37). In 2:11 disciples believed in Jesus as a result of a sign and revelation of his glory. Believing in Jesus as a result of seeing signs is repeated in 2:23 and 4:53-54. In 14:12 Jesus says that the one who believes in him will do the works that he does and, in fact, will do greater works than him.[1170] In all these cases the fourth evangelist emphasizes the following aspects: first, those who take the decision to follow Jesus should affirm their faith in him; second, Jesus is the focal point of Christian faith;[1171] third, signs are used as powerful means to invite faith in Jesus; fourth, those who believe in him are expected to invite others to faith through greater works; and fifth, through believing in Jesus, people can attain eternal life. These aspects make the reader aware that the Johannine faith is primarily based on people's response to Jesus and that the terminology is marked by contextual and theological underpinnings.[1172]

In the Fourth Gospel, the substance of faith is comprised of the following: Jesus is the Holy One of God (6:69); he is the Christ, the Son of God (11:27); God has sent him (11:42; 17:8, 21); he is one with the Father (14:10-11); he has come from the Father (16:27, 30); and he is the 'I am' (8:24; 13:19).[1173] Such faith in Jesus' person is the way to eternal life and is the reason why the Gospel was written (20:31).[1174] Hans Conzelmann places faith and obedience in relational terms. He says, "Faith and obedience are not [...] twofold, in the sense that faith first arises as the right religion and then obedience follows

---

[1169] See L. W. Hurtado, "Christ," *DJG* (Downers Grove: InterVarsity Press, 1992), 114-15.

[1170] But, on some occasions, although Jesus performed many signs, his interlocutors did not believe in him (12:37).

[1171] See Dunn, *Unity and Diversity in the New Testament*, 27.

[1172] James D. G. Dunn says, "Believing that Jesus is the Christ, the Son of God, leads to *life*. Here is another important and characteristic theme in John: verb and noun ('live,' 'life') together 97 times in the Johannine Gospel and letters." See Dunn, *Unity and Diversity in the New Testament*, 28.

[1173] Ladd, *A Theology of the New Testament*, 271.

[1174] According to G. Barth, "Faith is oriented toward the assertions that Jesus is sent by the Father (5:24, 38; 6:29; 12:44; 17:8, 21), went out from the Father (16:27, 30; 17:8), is in the Father and the Father in him (14:10-12; 17:21), is the Christ, the Son of God (3:18; 11:27; 1 John 3:24; 5:1, 5), and is he who came into the world (John 11:27; 12:46)." See Barth, "Pistis," 96; also Ladd, *A Theology of the New Testament*, 271.

as the right morality. Faith is the obedience that God wills. And vice versa: obedience is simply believing God."[1175]

People are called upon to believe the witness of the Scriptures (2:22), Moses (5:46) and his writings (5:47), and beyond this to believe the words (2:22; 4:50; 5:47-49) and works (10:38) of Jesus, which in turn means believing Jesus himself (5:38, 46b; 6:30; 8:31, 45, 46; 10:37, 38a). To believe Jesus and his word means to believe God (5:24) and to be obedient to his will.[1176] This understanding of faith in John is at the same time theological and Christological.[1177] Schnelle summarizes the theological program of the Gospel in the following words, "theology as Christology, without thereby minimizing the fundamental importance of theology in the proper sense."[1178] In that sense, faith in John is a divine-human means of interaction that enforces a believer to act obediently and to progress in union with Christ. Faith persuades a believer to remain as an active companion of Jesus and as a dynamic member of the community of God. Thus faith in John is one of the overarching concepts that interweaves soteriology with Christology and theology.

In John, faith results from the signs of Jesus, not vice versa.[1179] John has apparently taken up a tradition in which *pisteuein* is bound to Jesus' miracles: Jesus' *sēmeia* lead to faith in him (2:11, 23; 4:53; 7:31; 11:15, 42, 45; 12:37; 20:31; according to 10:25, 37-39; 14:11, Jesus' *erga* should do this).[1180] The signs/works reveal Jesus'/God's glory and thus lead people to belief in Jesus.[1181] Another significant aspect of the theme of faith is its polyvalent connection with other themes. In the Gospel, "believing" is closely related to "knowing."[1182] According to G. Barth,

---

[1175] Conzelmann, *An Outline of the Theology of the New Testament*, 172.

[1176] Ladd, *A Theology of the New Testament*, 271.

[1177] In John, faith plays a role in salvation that is mostly absent in the Synoptics. See Ladd, *A Theology of the New Testament*, 271.

[1178] Udo Schnelle, *Theology of the New Testament* (Grand Rapids: Baker Academic, 2007), 660. The term *theos* (God) occurs eighty-two times in the Fourth Gospel, mostly in genitive constructions determined by Christology. The Synoptic counterpart is that faith is used as a prerequisite to receive a miracle.

[1179] The Synoptic counterpart is that faith is used as a prerequisite to receive a miracle.

[1180] France says, "And even this connection is of limited value—a faith based *solely* on miracles is superficial and inadequate (2:23-25; 4:48; 6:26-29)." Also see 14:10-11; 20:29; cf. France, "Faith," 225; Barth, "Pistis," 96; Ladd, *A Theology of the New Testament*, 272-75.

[1181] Schnelle, *Theology of the New Testament*, 717.

[1182] See the usage of *ginōskein* and its cognate *oidamen*; cf. 4:42; 6:69; 8:31-32; 10:38; 16:30; 17:8; 19:35; also see 1 John 4:16. France says, "If to believe is the key to eternal life (3:16 etc.), so also is 'to know' (17:3). 'Believing' and 'knowing' appear as virtual synonyms in 6:69. There is no trace in John of the modern dichotomy between faith and knowledge." France, "Faith," 225. In the view of James D. G. Dunn, "Believing . . . means both accepting the veracity of the claim that 'Jesus is the Christ, the Son of God' (belief *that*—e.g. 6:69; 8:24; 11:27; 16:27; 20:31;

> Since God's eschatological revelation has come in Jesus, the believer already participates in eschatological salvation (John 3:18, 36; 5:24; 6:40, 47; 11:25-27; 17:3). Yet it is necessary to "abide" in Jesus (15:4, 7; 1 John 2:6, 28; 3:6), which means nothing other than to abide in his word (8:31) and thus in his love (15:9) and to keep his commandments (15:10; 14:15, 21; 1 John 2:3-5; 3:24). Since the knowledge bequeathed to faith is knowledge of God's love, faith must necessarily lead to love (John 17:26; 1 John 3:23; 4:16), a love directed above all toward one's brother.[1183]

Another central feature of the Johannine understanding of faith is its connection with "seeing" (*horaō, blepō, theōreō*).[1184] Schnelle says, "For the evangelist John the miracle effects faith; seeing the *sēmeion* (sign, miracle) is followed by *pisteuein eis Iēsoun Christon* (believing in Jesus Christ). This utterly non-dualistic link between seeing and believing is made explicit in John 2:11, 23; 4:53; 6:14; 7:31; 9:35-38; 10:40-42; 11:15, 40, 45; 12:11; 20:8, 25, 27, 29a, so that it plays a central role in the way the Fourth Evangelist understands faith."[1185] Thus in John believing, seeing, knowing, obeying, and the work of God/Jesus are connected terms in relation to soteriology and eschatology.

As stated above, faith and knowledge are integrally connected in John. Knowledge sometimes precedes faith (16:30; 18:8), which makes it impossible to differentiate knowledge and faith as the initial and the final stages of Christian experience. As Ladd perceives, knowledge can be considered as a constitutive element in genuine faith.[1186] When faith in Jesus guarantees someone's salvation, it entails a certain level of knowledge. As Dieter Lührmann elaborates, "Salvation is accomplished in the sending of Jesus; faith, the acceptance of this salvation, means salvation, so that the believer already possesses eternal life (3:15-17, 36; 5:24; 6:40, 47; 11:25-27)

---

1 John 5:1, 5), and commitment to this Jesus (belief *into*—the predominant and characteristic Johannine usage—e.g. John 1:2; 3:16; 6:29; 11:25-27; 17:20; 1 John 5:10). Distinctive also of Johannine usage is the extent to which the verb 'know' (56 times) has become a near equivalent to 'believe.'" See James D. G. Dunn, *Unity and Diversity in the New Testament: An Inquiry into the Character of Earliest Christianity*, Second Edition (London: SCM Press, 1977/1990), 26-27; C. H. Dodd, *The Interpretation of the Fourth Gospel* (Cambridge: Cambridge University Press, 1953/1960), 179.

[1183] Barth, "Pistis," 96. Also see Bultmann, "The *pistis* Group in the New Testament," 227. Hanz Conzelmann equates faith with knowledge. See Hanz Conzelmann, *An Outline of the Theology of the New Testament*, New Testament Library (London: SCM Press, 1969), 172; also see Schnelle, *Theology of the New Testament*, 719.

[1184] See Schnelle, *Theology of the New Testament*, 719-720.

[1185] See Schnelle, *Theology of the New Testament*, 718.

[1186] Ladd, *A Theology of the New Testament*, 277.

and no longer comes into judgment (3:16, 18)."[1187]In that sense, believing plays a central role in the whole system of John's theology of salvation. It is a response to revelation, and it enhances knowledge about the truth and results, further, in eternal life.[1188] As Dodd comments, "Faith, then, is a form of vision. When Christ was on earth, to have faith was to 'see His glory'—to apprehend and acknowledge the deity through the veil of humanity. Now that he is no longer visible to the bodily eye, faith remains the capacity for seeing His glory. This understanding is vital to the evangelist's whole conception of the incarnation."[1189] That further means that people's knowledge about the revelation and their positive response to it in faith lead them to the experience of eternal life.

The Johannine community as a newly emerged Christian group developed its theology out of existential struggles.[1190] Their expulsion from the Synagogue and the resultant minority status in society forced them to develop an "insider" versus "outsider" dialectic. The existential demands persuaded them to redefine their soteriology in relation to eschatology and theology.[1191] In the process of contextualization, the community described its ideas with a situational rhetoric and that enabled them to develop a semiotics of resistance. As a result, the theme of faith was conceptualized in the community with significant theological emphases. The above discussion helps us to understand the role of faith in the theological discourses of the Johannine community: first, the community members emphasized a Christocentric theology where faith in Jesus was placed as a significant requirement; second, the community demanded the faith reactions of its members with an aim to promote a soteriology that takes into account seeing, knowing, and obeying Jesus as important requirements; third, the community considered faith as an existential demand or requirement for establishing people's community identity; fourth, in the community, because the signs Jesus performed were powerful means for inviting faith in Jesus, those who believed in Jesus were expected to attract other followers through their similar, even greater works; fifth, people's knowledge about the superior revelation of Jesus and their positive response to

---

[1187] Dieter Lührmann further comments that, "In taking up the linguistic usage and the intention of his 'gospel of signs,' John therefore specifies the content of faith with the faith that is connected to salvation." See Dieter Lührmann, "Faith," *The Anchor Bible Dictionary*, Vol. 2 (New York/London: Doubleday, 1992), 755.

[1188] France, "Faith," 225.

[1189] Dodd, *Interpretation of the Fourth Gospel*, 186.

[1190] See Johnson Thomaskutty, "Reading John's Gospel as a Jewish-Christian Conflict Narrative: A Paradigm for Contemporary India," *Religious Freedom and Conversion in India: Papers from the Fourth SAIACS Academic Consultation* (Bengaluru: SAIACS Press, 2017), 140-41.

[1191] See Thomaskutty, "Religious Freedom and Conversion in India Today," 57-61.

it through faith led them to experience eternal life; sixth, faith was the means through which the members of the community facilitated union with Christ and exercised the charismatic gifts; and seventh, faith was one of the overarching concepts that interweave soteriology with Christology and theology. The insider dynamism was developed first to establish its community identity and then to expand its faith-centred and interactive theology to outsiders. Thus, it is obvious that fostering faith in Jesus during existential struggle enabled the community to develop an intra-ecclesial theology with special emphasis on "life/eternal life."

Faith and Theology in the Reformation Context

The emphasis laid on the experiential/living faith in the Johannine community enabled them to connect the eschatological, soteriological, and Christological aspects with their existential struggles.[1192] In John's community, faith was not considered as an abstract concept, but as people's response to Jesus and as a significant requirement for community identity. As a result, faith as an active response was actualized through an emphasis on seeing, knowing, obeying, and involving.[1193] Faith as an existential demand enabled them to possess their theology not as a remote entity but as a lived-out experience.[1194] It was conceived through the appropriation of faith and hence was a theology of the people, by the people, and for the people. This model of the community can be considered as a paradigm in the contemporary context.

The following principles are important to consider at this juncture: first, the Johannine community's Christocentric lifestyle, lived-out faith, and emphasis on salvation through faith identify them as a unique group of people; second, the community's existential struggles and the subsequent demands enable them to link the higher theology and the lower theology;[1195] and third, the community's emphasis on the aspect of life/eternal life attune the attention of the readers to their situation in life.[1196] In this context, the concept of the

---

[1192] Allison says, "In the Johannine thought eternal life (6:47), living water (4:14), bread from heaven (6:25-34), divine sonship (1:12) and even the resurrection (5:25)—all things traditionally associated with the eschaton—may be experienced now." See D. C. Allison, "Eschatology," *DJG*, ed. Joel B. Green (Downers Grove: IVP, 1992), 209. Also see Schnelle, *Theology of the New Testament*, 741-46.

[1193] See France, "Faith," 224-25.

[1194] France, "Faith," 224-225.

[1195] Here, higher theology is more of the conceptualized, theoretical, and elevated levels of theology. In that sense, lower theology emerges out of the existential strugglers.

[1196] See D. H. Johnson, "Life," *DJG*, ed. Joel B. Green (Downers Grove: IVP, 1992), 469-71. For more details about the community aspects in John, see Johnson Thomaskutty, "Reading John's Gospel as a Jewish-Christian Conflict Narrative: A Paradigm for Contemporary India," *Religious Freedom and Conversion in India* (Bengaluru: SAIACS Press, 2017), 138-51.

Faith and Theology Conference held in Wittenberg during the 500th anniversary of Reformation plays a key role. It elaborates as follows, "The Reformation, with its principle of *sola fide* on the one hand and its institutionalization of the Scripture-based academic theology on the other hand, drew particular attention to the tension between faith and theology and suggested new answers to that problem."[1197] The above statement makes us aware that the Reformers, following the model of the Johannine community, also attempted to bring faith and theology together as closer realities.

Martin Luther's emphasis on believing in Christ as he was part of the ecclēsia and his approach to the Scripture as a professor enabled him to bring faith and theology closer to one another.[1198] He affirmed the need to believe in Christ and attempted to facilitate faith both in personal and corporate settings. For him, faith was not something to be exercised solely within the limits of someone's personal, spiritual, and ecclesiastical affairs. It was thanks to this careful calibration of faith and science—as a professor full of faith, and believer committed to intellectual rigor—that Luther was able to challenge the church and the society to renewed and transformed living. This resembles the believing aspect of the Johannine community with its profound attachment to the aspects of knowing, seeing, and obeying.

The Reformation principles of interpretation emphasized the following things: the interpreter needed to seek the illumination of the Spirit of God; the Bible was the supreme and final authority in all matters and is above the authority of the Church; and the aim of all interpretation was to find Christ.[1199] These emphases of the Reformation align well with the Johannine community situation, where a profound pneumatology is developed with a focus on the Holy Spirit as an illuminator and instructor which reminds the followers of the teachings of Jesus (John 14:15-17, 26; 15:26; 16:7-8).[1200] As the Johannine Christians considered the proclamation of Jesus in the *Sitz im Leben Jesu* as supreme, the Reformers emphasized the original setting of the Bible and the words of Jesus as supreme authority (*sola scriptura*).[1201]

1197 See 'Faith and Theology: Basic Insights of the Reformation in Ecumenical Debate,' *Conference on the Reformation Anniversary in Wittenberg* (2017), 1.

1198 This paragraph was written after my visit to the historical places in Lutherstadt Wittenberg, Germany, and after having discussions with colleagues in the church and academy.

1199 See Isaak A. Dorner, *History of Protestant Theology*, Vol. 1 (Eugene: Wipf & Stock, 1970), 81-86.

1200 See M. M. B. Turner, "Holy Spirit," *DJG*, ed. Joel B. Green (Downers Grove: IVP, 1992), 347-51.

1201 See Thomaskutty, "Reading John's Gospel as a Jewish-Christian Conflict Narrative," 157-160.

As in the Johannine community, the Reformers attempted to find Jesus through their interpretative endeavours (*solus Christus*).[1202] That means that a faith-based and theologically grounded reinterpretation of the Jesus movement and Christ himself was emphasized by the Reformers in the *Sitz im Leben Kirche*.[1203] According to Thomas Schreiner in his introductory chapter, *sola fide* declares that "salvation does not come from looking at our own works of righteousness, but from looking outside ourselves to another, to the person and work of Jesus Christ."[1204] This aspect of faith in the Christian community was actualized through people's integral relationship with Christ. Keith Clements says, "*sola fide* does not denigrate the true place of good works in the Christian life. Rather, he [she] who rests in faith upon Christ and his righteousness is made one with Christ, the loving actions flow naturally from this union with the living Christ."[1205] Thus the Reformers interpreted faith and theology in a Johannine way.

A faith that is intelligible and liberative is at the root of the Reformation. The Reformers placed this aspect at the centre of their hermeneutical and theological engagements. Spivey states, "The shift to a faith-oriented hermeneutic began with Luther's *sola fide*: faith alone justifies. This soteriological principle undergirded an epistemological emphasis on faith."[1206] Luther and Calvin understood biblical truth as inaccessible to human reason unless the interpreter's mind was first informed by faith and illumined by the Spirit of God.[1207] A faith that is informative and Spirit-illumined lies at the heart of Reformation theology. Such a faith has two sources: first, it is rooted in an intuitive knowledge of Christ, God's Word revealed personally to the believer by the Spirit of God; and second, it derives from a confidence that the Bible is the self-authenticating Word of God: the message itself and the influence of the Spirit of God convince the believer of this fact.[1208] Here, the

---

[1202] The Reformers emphasized: "Only through God's gracious self-revelation in Jesus do we come to a saving and transforming knowledge of God." See http://www.christianity.com/church/church-history/the-five-solas-of-the-protestant-reformation.html, on 1 Oct., 2017.

[1203] See Thomaskutty, "Reading John's Gospel as a Jewish-Christian Conflict Narrative," 157-160.

[1204] Thomas Schreiner, *Faith Alone, the Doctrine of Justification* (Grand Rapids: Zondervan, 2015).

[1205] Keith Clements, "Sola Fide," *A New Dictionary of Christian Theology*, eds. Alan Richardson and John Bowden (London: SCM Press, 1983), 545.

[1206] See James T. Spivey, "The Hermeneutics of the Medieval and Reformation Era," *Biblical Hermeneutics: A Comprehensive Introduction to Interpreting Scripture*, Eds. Bruce Corley, Steve W. Lemke, and Grant I. Lovejoy, Second Edition (Nashville: B & H Publishing Group, 2002), 112-113.

[1207] See Spivey, "The Hermeneutics of the Medieval and Reformation Era," 112-113.

[1208] Spivey, "The Hermeneutics of the Medieval and Reformation Era," 112-113.

believer as the subject is guided by the Scripture and the illumination of the Spirit of God to direct her/his faith solely to Jesus.[1209] In that sense, faith is the means by which a believer can have access to Jesus. That further shows that faith is a response to the saving act of Jesus and that through faith one can have access and union to/with Jesus. The union with Christ through faith is the eschatological, soteriological, and Christological basis of Christian theology.

Moreover, pneumatological insights strengthen the above-stated aspects of theology and their formulation. In that sense, the Reformation theology pays more attention in bridging two spheres, i.e., the living faith of the believer in day-to-day affairs and her/his engagement as a seeing, knowing, and obeying figure in the organizational and theological discourses.[1210] The connection of seeing, knowing, and obeying with believing in both personal and corporate settings informs the people about their identity as "insiders" over against the unbelieving "outsiders" (i.e., those who do not hold the view of *sola fide*). Thus the Reformers, as in the case of the Johannine sectarians, emphasized a faith-centered and a theologically-engaged Christian way of life.

As in the case of John, Luther was an *existential* theologian. Timothy George says, "When we call Luther an *existential* theologian, we mean that for him concern with God was a life-and-death matter, involving not merely one's intellect but one's whole existence. For Luther, theology was always intensely personal, experiential, and relational."[1211] In that sense, for Luther theology was not merely something practiced in the academic setting, but was integrally connected to the people and their life as a whole. Similarly, Christian faith is individualistic and at the same time rooted in the community of believers. Tyron Inbody states, "Christian faith is not merely generic faith (our common human spirituality), but is a way of life that entails a dialectic between, on the one hand, specific stories, symbols, practices, and beliefs that you learn (*the Christian* faith) and, on the other, your experience of the living Christ within your life as a believer (Christian *faith*)."[1212] The individual and

---

[1209] See Schnelle, *Theology of the New Testament*, 704-712.

[1210] See Timothy George, *Theology of the Reformers* (Nashville: B & H Publishing Group, 2013), 59.

[1211] See George, *Theology of the Reformers*, 59. Martin Junge says, "Undoubtedly, the Reformation's insight of justification by faith alone is a deeply theological issue. The power of that insight, however, and the wave of transformation it unleashed, can only be explained against the background of the immense, complex, and demanding changes in the sixteenth-century western European societies." See Martin Junge, "Global Perspective on the Reformation," *Global Perspectives on the Reformation: Interactions between Theology, Politics and Economics*, The Lutheran World Federation 61, eds. Anne Burghardt and Simone Sinn (Leipzig: Evangelische Verlagsanstalt, 2016), 10.

[1212] Tyron Inbody, *The Faith of the Christian Church: An Introduction to Theology* (Grand Rapids/Cambridge: Eerdmans, 2005), 1-2.

corporate aspects of Christian faith co-exist in a believer as a unique spiritual experience and thus make Christian living a characteristic engagement in the world.[1213] This level of faith rests in our direct experience of God and the intensity of our relationship with Christ.[1214] In short, the faith and theology of the Reformation align well with the Johannine communitarian context. The individual, corporate, and organizational aspects of faith and theology were emphasized among the Johannine Christians both in their vertical and horizontal relationships. This demonstrates that faith and theology were integrally connected in the Johannine context and that was further emphasized by the Reformers.

Faith and Theology: Indian Explorations

As in the case of the Johannine sectarians, the Reformers attempted to bridge confessional faith and academic theology. The current section discusses the balance between a faith-centered and theologically relevant Christian way of life in the Indian context. In the course of so doing, insights from the Johannine community and from the Reformation contexts are brought to the fore. Mission in India is, first of all, attributed to Didymus Judas Thomas, one of the profoundest Johannine characters, who conceived Jesus as "My Lord and my God" (20:28). The apocryphal documents such as *The Gospel of Thomas*, *The Book of Thomas the Contender*, *The Acts of Thomas*, and *The Infancy Gospel of Thomas* supplement the portrayal of Thomas in John as a character who expressed his faith and conviction, as he demonstrated that believing is as result of seeing and knowing.[1215] Being integrally connected to the Indian situation, the Thomas Christians follow Jesus as believing Christians and as committed members within an organizational set-up. They attempt to bridge their faith on the confessional levels and theological institutions. This heritage of the Thomas Christians is both Johannine and Thomasine and had a closer relationship with the Protestant mission at a much later stage.

The Protestant Mission came to India through Lutheran missionaries from Halle, Germany, Bartholomäus Ziegenbalg and Heinrich Plütschau,

[1213] Brennan R. Hill, Paul Knitter, and William Madges argue, "Christian faith is both individual and communal. It is a commitment to a way of life, a spirituality." Brennan R. Hill, Paul Knitter, and William Madges, *Faith, Religion, and Theology: A Contemporary Introduction* (Mystic: Twenty-Third Publications, 2004), 64.

[1214] Tyron Inbody, "Disciplined thinking within the life of faith is necessary for clarity, new insights, and direction. World construction (a linguistic framework) is necessary to understand the Bible and the faith of the church. It contributes to a vital and open faith by enabling us to make new connections." See Inbody, *Faith of the Christian Church*, 8-9.

[1215] See more details in Johnson Thomaskutty, *Saint Thomas the Apostle: New Testament, Apocrypha, and Historical Traditions*, Jewish and Christian Texts Series 25 (London/New York: Bloomsbury T&T Clark, 2018).

in Tranquebar on 9th July 1706.[1216] Robin Boyd states that, "Ziegenbalg was a scholarly man and a firm believer in the basic principle of Protestant missions."[1217] The expressions "scholarly man" and "firm believer" attributed to him exemplify the nature of the people involved in the first Protestant Mission in the Indian context.[1218] Ziegenbalg and his colleagues initiated a mission theology that prioritized a life-affirming, people-oriented, and faith-centered interpretation of the Scripture.[1219]

In India, a new era of Protestant missionary work was inaugurated in 1793 by William Carey of Serampore, who, like Ziegenbalg, soon found himself grappling with the relationship between the simple belief of the people and rigorous theological inquiry.[1220] The Serampore mission attempted to get involved in the mission of Bible translation at the grass-root levels to facilitate faith among the people and to establish a theological institution like Serampore College in West Bengal.[1221] These are grand models of bridging faith and theology in the Indian context. As faith and theology were integrally connected in the Johannine community context and as that was later on carried over by the Reformers, one can witness how these two movements lie at the root of the Indian scenario.[1222] The pluralistic context of India is rich with various faith traditions, religious identities, and theological positions.

[1216] See Robin Boyd, *An Introduction to Indian Christian Theology* (Delhi: ISPCK, 1969/2000), 15. Also see E. Arno Lehmann, *It Began at Tranquebar* (Madras: CLS, 1956). For more details about the mission, read: Daniel Jeyaraj, *Bartholomäus Ziegenbalg, the Father of Modern Protestant Mission: An Indian Assessment* (Delhi: ISPCK; Chennai: Gurukul, 2006).

[1217] Boyd, *An Introduction to Indian Christian Theology*, 15. Also see V. V. Thomas, "The Impact of Reformation on Indian Church and Mission: A Historical Perspective," *SATHRI Journal*, Vol. 11/1 (April 2017), 101-103.

[1218] See Daniel Jeyaraj, "Indian Participation in Enabling, Sustaining, and Promoting Christian Mission in India," *India and the Indianness of Christianity*, ed. Richard Fox Young (Grand Rapids: Eerdmans, 2009), 26-40.

[1219] See David Bosch, *Transforming Mission: Paradigm Shifts in Theology of Mission*, Twentieth Anniversary Edition (Maryknoll: Orbis Books, 1970/2011), 259-261. Also see Heike Liebau, *Cultural Encounters in India: The Local Co-workers of Tranquebar Mission, 18th to 19th Centuries* (London/New York: Routledge, 2018), 131.

[1220] Boyd, *An Introduction to Indian Christian Theology*, 15-16. Also see A. Christopher Smith, "Carey, William," *Bibliographical Dictionary of Christian Missions*, ed. Gerald H. Anderson (Grand Rapids: Eerdmans, 1999), 115.

[1221] A similar pattern we see in Luther as he was a translator of the Scriptures and at the same time a professional theologian at the academic levels. Ziegenbalg also was involved in the translation of the Scriptures and at the same time he was a learned person.

[1222] V. V. Thomas says, "Although late, its [Reformation Movement] arrival in India created several ripples that is still being experienced in various aspects of not only the church in India but even in the social, political, economic aspects of the Indian society." See V. V. Thomas, "The Impact of Reformation on Indian Church and Mission," 119.

In India, when it comes to faith and theology, three different trends may be observed: first, a new trend of Christianity that distances itself from higher theological education; second, a strand of theologians who do not closely associate themselves with the faith and confessional levels of the church; and third, theologians who themselves are part and parcel of the church and thus form a closer relationship between the believing level of their lives and the systematization of their faith. While the first group mostly emerges without a closer relationship with the academy, the second group distances itself from a relationship with the *ekklēsia*. Above all, the third group seems to be more influential in bridging the gap between the faith levels of the communities and the systematization of the beliefs and practices.[1223] In the ecclesial context, while these distinctions are noticeable, those who associate themselves with both levels make greater impact. They attempted to relate the two realms in a positive manner. The effect of the Johannine community traditions coupled with the Reformation insights is especially obvious among the third group.

Theologians like Sadhu Sundar Singh (1889-1929) and others attempted to reflect on the church from a systematic theological perspective.[1224] Sundar Singh's description of his work as "the water of life in an Indian cup" is to approach theology in a Johannine way.[1225] While Ayadurai Jesudason Appasamy (1891-1975) emphasized "Christianity as *Bhakti Marga*,"[1226] Chenchiah laid an emphasis on "the theology of the new creation."[1227] Chakkarai, on similar lines, created an awareness of a "Christology of the Spirit."[1228] The rethinking group of Christianly remained within the church and elaborated profound theological ideas like "*Logos* as *antaryāmin* [indweller]," "God and the world," "Jesus as the *avatāra* [incarnation]," "sin and *karma* [work]," "the *yoga* of the Spirit and ecclesiology," "Christ and the Spirit," "the *bhakti* of the cross," and "Hindu terminology and Christian theology" in the contextual levels of the faith communities.[1229] They also attempted to discuss faith and theology in the ecclesial, political, and socio-economic with regard to the spheres of the people.

[1223] Robin Boyd provides ample evidences from the post-Reformation context and the theological developments in India. See Robin Boyd, *An Introduction to Indian Christian Theology*.

[1224] See Boyd, *An Introduction to Indian Christian Theology*, 86-109.

[1225] See Boyd, *An Introduction to Indian Christian Theology,* 86-109.

[1226] See Boyd, A*n Introduction to Indian Christian Theology*, 110-143.

[1227] See Boyd, A*n Introduction to Indian Christian Theology*, 144-164.

[1228] See Boyd, A*n Introduction to Indian Christian Theology*, 165-185.

[1229] *Bhakti* here means devotional worship directed to one supreme deity. See Boyd, *An Introduction to Indian Christian Theology*, 86-185.

The initiatives of the Reformers in elaborating a theology of the "body of Christ" as a distinct identity within society and also as a relational community in the public arena are some of the emphases of their theological positions.[1230] In the words of John D. Roth, "Theology is always embedded in larger political and economic contexts."[1231] Roth's statement makes sense in the context of Reformation theology, as the Reformers emphasized the individual, religio-cultural, and socio-political transformation. But, as an exception, among the newly emerging congregations, there are intentional attempts to distance themselves from the theological insights that emerged from the Reformers. Although they emphasize dicta such as *sola scriptura*, *sola fide*, and *sola gratia*, they do not advance to the higher levels of theology. Those who are theologically equipped and have a zeal for systematizing the faith and academy can take a leading role in the process. Bernd Oberdorfer says, "The specific theological insights, based on the liberating concept of justification by grace through faith, gave theology a new relevance which, in many ways, permanently shaped society."[1232] This is the truth of the matter when we discuss the Indian church during the post-Reformation era. The insights from the Reformation play a significant role in equipping the faith communities to engage in the societal realities as agents of transformation.

The Lutheran World Federation International Conference in Namibia (2015) identified four core features of transformative theology that inform and are informed by political and economic realities: contextual, critical, creative, and concrete. In India, the post-Reformation period witnessed a considerable theological advancement that emphasized a contextualization of the Gospel message, a critical engagement with the biblical worldview, a creative elaboration of the biblical and contextual ideas, and a concrete affirmation of the faith. There were theologians from the West who attempted to inculcate the biblical message in India with profound influence from the Reformation. In his *The Christ of the Indian Road*, E. Stanley Jones attempted to outline some of the significant aspects in theology such as "growing moral and spiritual supremacy of Jesus," "Jesus through experience," "Christ and the other faiths," "concrete Christ," "Indian interpretation of Jesus," and "Christ

---

[1230] Petri Merenlahti, "You Cannot Serve God and Wealth," *Global Perspectives on the Reformation* (Leipzig: Evangelische Verlagsanstalt, 2016), 98.

[1231] See John D. Roth, "Just Peacemaking: Christian Pacifism as a Form of Political Responsibility," *Global Perspectives on the Reformation: Interactions between Theology, Politics and Economics*, The Lutheran World Federation 61, Eds. Anne Burghardt and Simone Sinn (Leipzig: Evangelische Verlagsanstalt, 2016), 43.

[1232] See Bernd Oberdorfer, "Law and Gospel and Two Realms: Lutheran Distinctions Revisited," *Global Perspectives on the Reformation: Interactions between Theology, Politics and Economics*, The Lutheran World Federation 61, Eds. Anne Burghardt and Simone Sinn (Leipzig: Evangelische Verlagsanstalt, 2016), 31.

of the Indian road" with an intention of *Indianizing* the Gospel.[1233] In his other titles, such as *The Word Became Flesh* and *Abundant Living*, Jones related some of the Johannine ideas to the Indian context.[1234] In his interpretative endeavours Jones approached contextual issues in a Christ-centered way as it was in the case of the Reformation traditions. Jones dealt with that which made the Christian religion unique and enduring among other religions. He emphasized the authority of the Scripture and proclaimed the universality of salvation.[1235] In the Reformation traditions these aspects of Christianity were strongly emphasized.

In his book *The Gospel in a Pluralist Society* Lesslie Newbigin strongly emphasized the following aspects: the "gospel in the pluralist society" and "Christian faith in the Indian context."[1236] Newbigin demonstrated his ideas with insights from both the biblical worldview and the Reformation traditions, and he attempted to relate the Church and society in a unique way. Following the footprints of Stanley Jones and Lesslie Newbigin, Indian Christian theologians also attempted to relate the Gospel to the social and cultural heritage of India. While M. M. Thomas emphasized the acknowledged Christ of the Indian Renaissance,[1237] P. D. Devanandan, Stanley Samartha, and others elaborated the necessity for engaging in inter-religious dialogue.[1238] Moreover, P. D. Devanandan and M. M. Thomas elaborated their ideas with a keen interest on Christian participation in nation building.[1239] Thus, a unique mode of contextualization, critical engagement, creative elaboration, and concrete emphasis on the Gospel and the faith of the community were highlighted for theological advancement and engaged mission.

In today's post-Reformation Indian context, we observe the obvious differences between the teachings of the Scripture at the church level and the exegetical and hermeneutical readings of it at the academic level. In the ecclesiastical context, there is a general tendency of enhancing faith-based and faith-generating teaching methods. On the higher educational levels, learning takes place in a systematic and rational way. The academicians systematize the contents of their scriptural understanding and theology with the help

---

1233 See E. Stanley Jones, *The Christ of the Indian Road* (Kessinger Publishing, 2005).

1234 See E. Stanley Jones, *The Word Became Flesh* (Abingdon Press, 2006).

1235 See E. Stanley Jones, *Abundant Living* (Hodder & Stoughton, 1946).

1236 See Lesslie Newbigin, *The Gospel in a Pluralist Society* (Grand Rapids: Eerdmans, 1989).

1237 Paul M. Collins, *Christian Inculturation in India* (New York: Routledge, 2016), chap. 3.

1238 See Boyd, *An Introduction to Indian Christian Theology*, 186-205.

1239 See Veli-Matti Kärkkäinen, *An Introduction to the Theology of Religions: Biblical, Historical and Contemporary Perspectives* (Downers Grove: IVP Academic, 2003), chap. 28; P. D. Devanandan and M. M. Thomas, eds., *Problems of Indian Democracy* (Bangalore: CISRS, 1962); P. D. Devanandan and M. M. Thomas, *Christian Participation in Nation Building* (Bangalore: The National Christian Council of India and the CISRS, 1960).

of various hypotheses and pedagogies and attempt to attune the learners to certain expectations and accomplishments. Often Christian theologians combine critical approaches of academy with the basic or "simple" teachings of faith. Although these two levels are mutually compatible to a certain extent, it is not true in all cases. As part of the plan of educating theologians, the institutions may have to go extra miles in their pedagogical programs. Among many methods, analytical, empirical, literary, historical-critical, grammatical, theological, sociological, and other approaches are employed in the higher academic settings.

The post-Reformation period witnessed the social impact of Christian mission and the period focused on the lower strata of Indian society. V. V. Thomas says, "The social impact of the Christian mission in India is an important aspect of the Protestant churches. Faced with the age-old discrimination in the caste system and other related issues, people from the lower strata of Indian society were waiting for a way out. The coming of the Protestant mission to India became a great boost for such people."[1240] In that sense, theology in the academy is more of a kind of systematization of a socio-religious life-style, comparative aspects, scientific approaches, rational thinking, and innovative methods. As John combines the faith aspects of the community in relation to their eternal life perspectives, Indian Christian theologians attempt to interpret the Scriptures at an academic level with insights from the life situations of the people. This is especially evident in the initiatives of the contributors of Indian Christian theology during the post-Reformation era.

In India, Christian theology was mostly discussed in symposiums, conferences, and other forums of Christianity. The Senate of Serampore College (SSC) and Asia Theological Association (ATA) offer exclusive theological degree programs. A recent development is that some of the secular universities like the University of Madras, the University of Mysore, and others have started to offer theological degree programmes through their Christian Studies Departments, and as a result there are wider interactions between theology and other disciplines. With the emergence of Christian Studies Departments in the secular universities, a new way forward is initiated in systematizing theological discourses. It further opens up new opportunities of awareness in the public arena. That means that in today's context Christian theology functions as part of a wider academic discourse. As the academic community represent both the Catholic and Protestant strands of thought and also from inter-religious and inter-disciplinary strands, the views expressed in the discourses are mostly dialogical, interdenominational, interreligious, and ecumenical.

[1240] See V. V. Thomas, "The Impact of Reformation on Indian Church and Society," 111.

In the public arena the arts, iconographies, newspapers, television channels, and the social media play significant roles in bridging the gap between faith and theology. The Protestants use the media for various noble endeavours. In that sense, the effect of the Reformation in India was/is significant as its Scripture-centered and theologically-motivated discourses challenge the faith and the academic levels. The Reformation continues to influence the individuals, the churches, the academy/sciences, and the general public. As Antje Jackelén says, "Today's challenges are no longer defined by local or national borders. They are glocal, both global and local. Borders are no longer what they used to be. That should not scare us. Because at the centre of Christianity, there is a God crossing the most dramatic border of all: the one between divine and human."[1241] As we live in a world that is borderless and glocal where information and knowledge are accessible through media, drawing a strict borderline between faith and theology is a difficult task.

The Johannine sectarians as a faith-oriented community with an emphasis on the *Sitz im Leben Jesu*,[1242] reinterpretation of the *Verba Jesu* within the *Sitz im Leben Kirche*, Messianic interpretation of the Old Testament, and the theological and philosophical elaboration within the community context laid emphasis on the relationship between faith and theology. John's narrative framework oscillates between the "simple" and the "profound" and between the "spiritual" and the "rational" aspects of Christianity. This trend of the Johannine hermeneutic is as multifaceted as it is faith-oriented, scripturally based, and theologically insightful in nature. The Reformers, in their reflections and articulations, followed a Johannine trend in dealing with the tension between faith and theology. The Reformation, with its principle of *sola fide* on the one hand and its institutionalization of a Scripture-based academic theology on the other hand, drew particular attention to this tension.

During the post-Reformation Indian context, Protestant theologians strove hard to keep up this principle derived from both the Johannine thought and the Reformation principles in their academic and theological discourses.[1243] Thus the paradigm developed here is biblically-based (John's Gospel), historically accepted (Reformation), and contextually applicable and transformative (India). As the Gospel of John is considered a Gospel with an Indian mind, a large number of the Indian interpreters identify its ideological and contextual relevance in the country. A Johannine and at the same time Reformational

---

[1241] See Antje Jackelén, "Justification and Justice: The Relevance of Lutheran Distinctions in Church and Society," *Global Perspectives on the Reformation: Interactions between Theology, Politics and Economics*, The Lutheran World Federation 61, Eds. Anne Burghardt and Simone Sinn (Leipzig: Evangelische Verlagsanstalt, 2016), 21.

[1242] See Johnson Thomaskutty, "Religious Freedom and Conversion in India Today," 50-72.

[1243] See the previous paragraphs for more details.

exegesis and hermeneutics in India have introduced a radical transformation in bridging the ecclesiastical aspects with the profound theological discourses. It further enables interpreters to be theologically sensitive and ecclesiastically inclined within the wider pluralistic context as informed and responsible citizens of the country.[1244]

Conclusion

The above discussion demonstrates how the Johannine community, the Reformation Movement, and Protestant Christianity in India relate theological reflection with 'living' devotion. In John's community, the aspect of faith was considered confessional, not in a simplistic sense, but rather as an important requirement integrating seeing, working, knowing, and obeying. This characteristic aspect in the community, alongside the structural, contextual, and organizational relevance of theology, enabled the community to balance between faith and theology. In the Reformation, a similar trend was sustained through the fusion of the principle of *sola fide* and the institutionalization of a Scripture-based academic theology. There was an emphasis on the individualistic, ecclesiastical, critical and academic, and wider communal aspects to deal with the tension between faith and theology. It shows the mutual compatibility of faith and theology.

During the post-Reformation period, the Protestant missionary movements and theologians in the Indian context incorporated Johannine and Reformational aspects in their homiletical, missional, exegetical, and hermeneutical engagements. Academic theology began to include wider perspectives and other disciplines like inter-religious dialogue, science and religion, interdisciplinary approaches, historical-critical methods, the treatment of the sacred in relation to the secular, by and large the integration of church, academy, and the wider public. Moreover, there emerged a growing tendency of doing biblical hermeneutics with the help of critical approaches over against the prevailing uncritical practices. The innovative contents, standards, and methods of Protestant theology introduced a transformative movement that impacted not only the ecclesiastical thought-world but also the wider arenas of public life. As a wider contextual movement, the Reformation functioned as charismatic in its scope, evangelical in its sharing, ecumenical in its spirit, and liberative in its engagements; as a critical movement it endeavoured for a reasonable and inclusive faith; and as a creative movement it aimed at holistic transformation aspects. These various characteristics show the gnomic significance of the Reformation Movement, just as in the case of the Johannine community, both in the local and in the global arenas.

[1244] See Antje Jackelén, "Justification and Justice: The Relevance of Lutheran Distinctions in Church and Society," 21-29.

Chapter 14

Reading John's Gospel in the Nepali Context

Introduction

The Gospel of John is quite flexible in its relationship to time and space. Although, it was written twenty centuries ago in a context entirely different from that of the present-day Nepal, its message does not seem strange to a contemporary Nepali reader. Richard Burridge describes the Gospels as documents "about people, by people, for people."[1245] A gnomic reading of the Fourth Gospel, one that explores its message for all times and places, will help us to understand its significance for the people of Nepal today.[1246]

This essay will consider the following questions: How does the gnomic language of John's Gospel help the reader to understand its message in her/his own terms? How does John's Gospel address the contemporary realities of the Nepali people? How does John's Gospel present a paradigm for mission and evangelism in today's Nepali scenario? How does John's Gospel help us join our actions to our words as two sides of the same coin in that context? In addressing those questions from a paradigmatic point of view, not as first-time readers but constrained and guided by our prior faith commitment,[1247] we

---

[1245] Richard A. Burridge, "About People, by People, for People: Gospel Genre and Audiences," *The Gospels for All Christians: Rethinking the Gospel Audiences*, ed. Richard Bauckham (Grand Rapids: Eerdmans, 1998), 113-145.

[1246] See also Johnson Thomaskutty, "Glo(b/c)alization and Mission(s): Reading John's Gospel," *New Life Theological Journal*, Vol. 5, No. 1 (Jan.-June 2015), 56-77.

[1247] On this distinction, see Mark W. G. Stibbe, *John*, Readings: A New Biblical Commentary (Sheffield: JSOT Press, 1993), 16-17.

will attempt to bridge the gap between the Johannine community of the first century and the Nepali communities of the twenty-first century, relating the gospel dynamically and conveying its message with efficacy. The purpose of this essay is to develop an interpretive framework for the gospel that will be effective in today's globalized Nepali context.[1248]

John's Gospel and Its Relation to the Nepali Context(s)

A study of some of John's themes and their dynamic function within his narrative framework will help us to understand the flexibility of the Fourth Gospel—its adaptability to new situations and the reverberation of its impact through space and time. A proper grasp of the following aspects is fundamental to contextualizing the gospel message for Nepal.

The Setting

John's story develops in a unique context. The narrator presents Jesus in Jewish, Galilean, and Samaritan settings in order to show the all-inclusive nature of his ministry. The larger setting is the land of Israel, which borders the Dead Sea, the lowest point on earth. When we interpret the stories of John's Gospel for the Nepali context, we are reinterpreting these stories for different people and a very different place, for the inhabitants of a land that is commonly referred to as "the top of the world."[1249] But in both Israel and Nepal, mountains play a significant role. Just as the Samaritan woman says, "Our ancestors worshiped on this mountain" (John 4:20), many Nepalese can claim, "Our ancestors worshiped on these great mountains, the Himalayas." As with the Samaritan woman, Jesus' response to the Nepalis would surely be, "The hour is coming when you will worship the Father neither on these mountains nor in Jerusalem….A time is coming and has now come when the true worshipers will worship the Father in spirit and truth."[1250]

Discipleship

Discipleship is one of the significant themes of John's Gospel. At its outset the evangelist presents five models: the discipleship of John the Baptist, who was *sent* from God (*apestalmenos para theou*, 1:6); the discipleship of Andrew, who *heard* about Jesus and followed (*ēkousan/akolouthēsan*, 1:37);

[1248] It is estimated that about two million Nepalis are scattered around the world today. Tan Tai Yong and Md Mizanur Rahman, "Introduction: Diaspora Engagement and Development in South Asia," *Diaspora Engagement and Development in South Asia*, eds. Tan Tai Yong and Md Mizanur Rahman (New York: Palgrave Macmillan, 2013), 3.

[1249] See Jeannette P. Windham, *At the Top of the World: Let's Travel to Nepal Together*, Windows on the World Series, No. 3 (Tampa: Global Age Publishing, 1995).

[1250] Compare John 4:21, 23. C. K. Barrett, *The Gospel According to St. John: An Introduction with Commentary and Notes on the Greek Text* (London: ISPCK, 1955), 197-199.

the discipleship of Peter, who was *led* to Jesus by another disciple (ēgagen, 1:42); the discipleship of Philip, whom Jesus himself *found* and commanded to follow (*heuriskei*, 1:43); and the discipleship of Nathanael, whom another disciple *found* and who was accepted by Jesus into their company (*heuriskei*, 1:45).[1251] Nicodemus and the Samaritan woman offer two more discipleship models, one a member of the Jewish religious elite (3:1-21), the other a woman living in a Samaritan village (4:1-26).[1252]

The invalid who is healed in 5:1-18 and the blind man whose sight is restored in 9:1-41 embody two very different responses to the experience of healing. While the invalid fades from the scene without showing any desire to become a disciple, the formerly blind man grows remarkably in his faith and understanding of Jesus.[1253] In 4:46-54, the official whose son is healed advances from partial, conditional faith (4:48) through developing faith and finally to mature faith in Jesus, bringing his entire family with him (4:53).[1254] Thus the point that discipleship involves development is obvious from the beginning of this Gospel.

The contrast between genuine and counterfeit discipleship is a theme that runs through much of John's narrative. For example, the conflict within Jesus' own family is revealed through the presentation of his brothers' unbelief in 7:1-9. The Jews, as antagonists, reveal their unbelief in Jesus the protagonist through their duel with him in the Tabernacles Discourse of chapters 7 and 8. The narrator, urging his readers to find their place in Jesus' sheepfold (10:1-18), draws a sharp contrast between Jesus the Good Shepherd and irresponsible hirelings. In chapters 11 and 12, members of Lazarus's family are introduced as committed followers of Jesus. In 12:1-8, the narrator juxtaposes genuine with counterfeit discipleship by setting the behavior of Mary of Bethany alongside the response of Judas Iscariot.[1255]

In 13:1-20, Jesus teaches the disciples the value of a servant model of discipleship. Three things are highlighted: his superiority as their Teacher and Lord (v. 13); his voluntary inferiority as their servant (v. 14); and his mandate for them to follow his example as servants to one another (vv. 15-17).[1256] His act of washing their feet, followed by his instruction, "You should do as I

[1251] Barrett, *Gospel According to St. John*, 125-156.

[1252] Leon Morris, *The Gospel According to John*, rev. ed., New International Commentary on the New Testament (Grand Rapids: Eerdmans, 1995), 184-252.

[1253] Kanagaraj, *The Gospel of John*, 167-174, 301-320.

[1254] Moloney, *The Gospel of John*, 150-163; Johnson Thomaskutty, "The Nature and Function of Dialogue in the Book of Signs (John 1:19-12:50)" (Ph.D. diss., Radboud University Nijmegen, 2014), 197-210; R. V. G. Tasker, *John*, Tyndale New Testament Commentaries (Leicester, England: InterVarsity Press, 1960), 80-83.

[1255] Tasker, *John*, 137-146.

[1256] Tasker, *John*, 153-158.

have done for you" (v. 15), rhetorically interlocks the reader with the text. It is not only Jesus, the first *parakletos*, but also the Spirit of Truth, the second *parakletos*, who will guide and counsel the disciples (14:16, 26; 15:26; 16:7). Remaining (*menein*) in Jesus is emphasized (15:1-11) in a model of discipleship resting on the foundation of believers' love and unity (17:1-26).[1257]

In the Nepali context, the church should function as an agent of love, peace, reconciliation, and liberation. Christian communities should follow a servant model in order to attune people to the experience of eternal life. Just as the Johannine Jesus stands out as an agent of God who transcends all boundaries, the Nepali church should rise above all socio-religious and politico-cultural barriers with a discipleship model rooted in love. Jesus emphasizes love as the greatest commandment (14:18-24; 17:23). Such an approach would greatly benefit the Nepali church.[1258]

Persecution

The Gospel of John reflects the experience of persecution at several levels. First of all, Jesus himself was verbally attacked by his enemies, with their opposition finally leading to his execution (11:45-53).[1259] At another level, members of the Johannine community, like other early believers, were harassed and treated unfairly. The practice of putting followers of Jesus out of the synagogue (9:22, 34; 16:2) would eventually lead the Christian community to an identity crisis.[1260] Yet even in such a context, the community did not follow a "rhetoric of distance," as in the case of the Qumran community, but a "rhetoric of distinction."[1261]

The Christian community of Nepal necessarily functions within the socio-religious and politico-cultural context of that country. Nepali believers struggle when other Nepalis struggle, and they are at ease when other Nepalis are at ease. Although, persecution of Christians is less common today than before the end of the monarchy in 2008, churches are still striving to gain the freedom that other religious communities already enjoy. In this regard, there are several striking similarities between the Johannine community and the Nepali Christian community. The Johannine community developed in a context in which Jewish religious fundamentalism was at its peak, leading to

---

[1257] Beasley-Murray, *John*, 269-275.

[1258] Cindy Perry, *A Biographical History of the Church in Nepal*, 3rd ed. (Kathmandu, Nepal: Nepal Church History Project, 2000), 10-11, 17-19, 32-43.

[1259] Thomaskutty, "The Nature and Function of Dialogue in the Book of Signs," 554.

[1260] Morris, *John*, 433-435; Blomberg, *The Historical Reliability of John's Gospel*, 150-157.

[1261] On this terminology, see Warren Carter, *John and Empire: Initial Explorations* (T & T Clark, 2008), 14, 15, 20.

constant conflict between the two groups. In reinterpreting the story of Jesus for that context, the narrator presents him as a model for the community who has endured trials and persecution much as they have. Similarly, the Nepali church constantly struggles with the nation's mainstream religious establishment. In Nepal, as in the Johannine narrative, non-Christians are on one side, and the church as an emerging movement is on the other side. This bifurcation between believing insiders and unbelieving outsiders has to be taken seriously in the development of effective missional practices for Nepal.

Mission and Eschatology

God sent his Son to fulfill his mission in this world.[1262] The mission of God is preparing a family for God. Those who believe and become followers of Jesus are reckoned as members of that family.[1263] In Roman Palestine, Jesus worked among the masses, especially those who were poor, marginalized, and ostracized. He became bread for those who were hungry (6:22-59),[1264] light for those who were in darkness (9:1-41), the door for those who would be put out of the synagogues (10:1-7), the good shepherd for those who had been led astray (10:11), the resurrection and the life for those who were in the clutches of death (11:25),[1265] the way, the truth, and the life to lead people away from misdirection, falsehood, and death (14:6), and the true vine to bring joy into this world.[1266] The Gospel's theme of life, especially eternal life, spoke to a context in which people were dying in sin.[1267] Jesus was a hero of the poor and marginalized. As the agent of God, he was a witness to God's truth before people who were in crisis. John's emphasis on a vertical eschatology ('from above' versus 'from below') over against the synoptic prevalent *horizontal eschatological phenomenon* ('this *aeon*' [this age] and 'the coming *aeon*' [the coming age]) is noticeable in this regard. The vertical eschatology of John helps the readers come in *imminent* and *realizing* relationship with Jesus.

[1262] David Bosch, *Transforming Mission: Paradigm Shifts in Theology of Mission* (Maryknoll: Orbis, 1990), 390.

[1263] Jan van der Watt interprets the entire gospel of John from a family of God metaphor. See Van der Watt, *Family of the King*.

[1264] Jan van der Watt, "I Am the Bread of Life: Imagery in John 6:32-51," *Acta Theologica* 27, No. 2 (December 2007), 186-204; Thomaskutty, "Nature and Function of Dialogue in the Book of Signs," 241-295.

[1265] Thomaskutty, "Nature and Function of Dialogue in the Book of Signs," 441-484.

[1266] In his monograph, Ball describes I AM sayings of Jesus in detail. See D. M. Ball, *"I Am" in John's Gospel: Literary Function, Background, and Theological Implications,* Journal for the Study of the New Testament Supplement Series 124 (Sheffield, England: Sheffield Academic Press, 1996).

[1267] D. H. Johnson, "Life," *Dictionary of Jesus and the Gospels*, ed. Joel B. Green (Leicester: InterVarsity Press, 1992), 469-471.

The mission of God through Jesus is introducing *soē*[1268] as a divine gift available to all 'here' and 'now' (*realized eschatology*) and can be a force that leads people of God toward the coming *aeon* (*futuristic eschatology*).[1269] This present and future aspect of eschatology enables the insiders to be responsible citizens in the present time. In that sense, the narrator affirms that *our present guarantees our future*. This dynamic way of interlocking the present and the future aspects of eschatology provide wider meaning for the narrative annals of John. In Nepali Christian context, this method of emphasizing the life aspects and the mission orientation among the poor communities help the emerging and flourishing community of God to attract the masses toward the message of the gospel. The church should emphasize both the aspects of charity and gospel sharing.[1270] These two aspects must go hand in hand in order to have efficacy in the role and function of the church in the multi-religious and multi-cultural context of the country. Poor and needy people like the people of the wedding house in Cana (2:1-11), Samaritan woman (4:1-42), the royal man (4:46-54), the invalid person (5:1-18), the hungry masses (6:1-15), the blind man (9:1-41), and the sisters of Lazarus (11:1-44; 12:1-8) must be placed in the Nepali context in order to see their relevance as symbolic figures.

Women and Mission

John uses the role of women as a significant phenomenon within his narrative framework. In 2:1-11, Mary the mother of Jesus functions as a significant character who connects Jesus with the needy situation of the family.[1271] In 4:1-42 the role of the Samaritan woman is significant as Jesus crosses the religious, racial, and sexual barriers in order to transform her from Samaritan religiosity to eternal life centered religiosity.[1272] A woman who was alien to the Jewish religiosity witnessed the truth and started to develop in her understanding of the Messiah. Her witness about Jesus to her own people challenges them to realize the presence of the "Savior of the world."[1273] In chap. 11 the sisters of Lazarus, i.e., Mary and Martha, function significantly as

[1268] The Greek word means "life." Refer to Johnson, "Life," *Dictionary of Jesus and the Gospels*, 469-471.

[1269] Jan van der Watt, "Eschatology in John: A Continuous Process of Realizing Events," 109-140.

[1270] Simon Pandey emphasizes these aspects in his overall framework of the book. Refer to Simon Pandey, *Christianity in Nepal: Unity in Diversity* (Kathmandu: National Churches Fellowship of Nepal, 2003).

[1271] Morris, *John*, 153-64; Thomaskutty, *Nature and Function of Dialogue in the Book of Signs*, 80-88.

[1272] See Thomaskutty, *Nature and Function of Dialogue in the Book of Signs*, 153-196.

[1273] Thomaskutty, *Nature and Function of Dialogue in the Book of Signs*, 153-196.

effective characters who appeal for their brother.[1274] In 12:1-8, the two women characters work significantly as one serves at Jesus and the other spends expensive perfume to anoint the feet of Jesus. The narratorial technique of conflict and characterization (through the medium of contrast) is conspicuous as the narrator places Mary of Bethany over against Judas Iscariot.[1275] While Mary of Bethany rhetorizes her presence by her silence and her superabundant generosity shown to Jesus, Judas' presence is portrayed by the help of his hypocritical and long concerned speech. While Jesus praises the action of the lady, he condemns the speech of Judas.[1276]

In chap. 20, Mary's boldness to come to the tomb at the early morning is clearly mentioned. She becomes instrumental in proclaiming the good news concerning the resurrection of Jesus. Thus the evangelist presents her as an "apostle to the apostles."[1277] In John, Jesus empowers the woman characters and presents them over against misunderstanding, unbelieving, and unfaithful men characters.[1278] In today's Nepali context women empowerment is significant as they are educationally illiterate, politically powerless, religiously voiceless, and culturally ostracized sections of the society. The role of women in the family, church, and society is significant as they are enabled by Jesus to work dynamically as harbingers of the gospel.[1279] As Mary was instrumental in a family set up, Samaritan women was instrumental in bringing the gospel to the village of Sychar, Martha and Mary were loyal to Jesus in the context of Bethany, Mary was superabundantly generous, and Mary Magdalene was instrumental to share the good news even to their male counterparts, the Nepali women can function as powerful members in the family, church, and social contexts as agents of mission and ministry.[1280]

"I AM" Sayings

Now let's see how the "I AM Sayings" of Jesus in John are significant in the Nepali context.[1281] In John, Jesus' action and speech go synonymously. One who is able to feed the five thousand people with physical bread (6:1-15) is

---

[1274] Jey J. Kanagaraj, "The Profiles of Women in John: House-Bound or Christ-Bound?" *Bangalore Theological Forum*, Vol. XXXIII, No. 2 (December 2001), 60-79.

[1275] D. M. Scholer, "Women," *Dictionary of Jesus and the Gospels* (Leicester: InterVarsity Press, 1992), 880-887.

[1276] Thomaskutty, *Nature and Function of Dialogue in the Book of Signs*, 491-95.

[1277] *John 11-21 and 1 John*, Calvin's New Testament Commentaries (Grand Rapids: Eerdmans, 1959), 191-214.

[1278] Kanagaraj, "The Profiles of Women in John: House-Bound or Christ-Bound?" 60-79.

[1279] Cf. Kanagaraj, "The Profiles of Women in John: House-Bound or Christ-Bound?" 60-79.

[1280] See Perry, *A Biographical History of the Church in Nepal*, 17-19, 30-31.

[1281] See G. M. Burge, "I AM Sayings," *Dictionary of Jesus and the Gospels* (Leicester: InterVarsity Press, 1992), 354-356.

declared as the bread from heaven (6:22-59).[1282] The festival of Tabernacles is actualized by the very presence of Jesus as the light of the world (8:12). Moreover, one who is able to give physical sight to the blind is introduced as the "light of the world" (9:5). Jesus is standing right out there as the "door of the sheep" (10:7) when the sheep are sent out of the synagogue (9:34).[1283] While the leaders of the synagogue function as hirelings (9:1-41), Jesus functions as the "good shepherd" as he solves the lifelong struggles and issues of the blind man (10:11).[1284] One who is able to give back life is the "resurrection and life" (11:25). One who is "the way, truth, and life" prepares a way and a house in heaven (14:6). And he also sends the "Spirit of Truth" among the people so that the people of God may live their life under his guidance (14:15-31; 15:26; 16:12).[1285] One who is able to provide physical wine (2:1-11) is the "true vine" (15:1-11). Thus, the utterances of Jesus are proved through his very actions. The signs are rhetorical and are external proofs in order to prove the very utterances of Jesus. In the contemporary Nepal, the propagators of the gospel must attempt for action oriented gospel. The efficacy of the gospel should be foregrounded through actions of love. As Jesus emphasizes the significance of the commandment of love, the unity of the believers among themselves and the expression of their love toward the outside world are to be brought to the fore.

Jesus can be presented as the model of mission in the pluralistic context of Nepal. The philosophy of witnessing by example has to be exemplified in this context. Jesus' method was not simply witnessing the truth through the means of revelatory utterances but also through signs and actions. Jesus was teaching the message of the Father through action-oriented messages. The interlocking of utterances and actions in the mission and ministry of Jesus can be considered as a better paradigm in the Nepali context. In a context in which religious and philosophical ideologies are enormous and they remain mostly in vocal format, Jesus' action-oriented format is significant to reckon with. Jesus says, "whoever does not love me does not keep my words; and the word that you hear is not mine, but is from the Father who sent me" (14:24).[1286] Those who do the 'action of love' are considered as those who hear the words of Jesus. The ethical and moral actions centered on love are considered as ultimate concerns and characteristics of Jesus' mission. The Nepali church must emphasize love centered and action-oriented ethical and moral standards of mission in order

---

[1282] Tasker, *John*, 92-100; Van der Watt, "I AM the Bread of Life," *Acta Theologica*, 186-204.

[1283] Thomaskutty, *Nature and Function of Dialogue in the Book of Signs*, 532-534.

[1284] Tasker, *John*, 122-31.

[1285] *John 11-21*, Calvin's NT Commentaries, 82.

[1286] Moloney, *Gospel of John*, 405; Leon Morris, "Love," *Dictionary of Jesus and the Gospels* (Leicester: InterVarsity Press, 1992), 492-495.

to develop the mission boundaries. A church that is dogmatically oriented cannot attract the poor, marginalized, and dehumanized sections of the society. In Nepali context, the majority community is underprivileged. So the church must pay special attention in emphasizing the love-centered ethics of Jesus.[1287] This is rooted in the narrative frame work of John's Gospel.

The Rhetoric of Signs

The signs of the gospel function in a dynamic way as they contribute semantically to the narrative framework of the Gospel. Jesus turns water into wine in a wedding set up in order to solve the situational issues of a house (2:1-11).[1288] The protagonist heals the royal man's son and he develops from step to step in his journey of faith (4:46-51).[1289] The sign of healing the invalid symbolizes Jesus' generous attitude even toward strangers (5:1-18). In both 4:46-54 and 5:1-18, the time of dialogue is identified as the time of sign. The feeding of the five thousand reveals Jesus' attitude toward the hungry and the extended world of his time (6:1-15). Jesus as the one who walks on the water reveals his power and authority over the nature (6:16-21).[1290] The healing of the blind man helps the readers to understand the way a sign results into the faith development in a person (9:1-41).[1291]

Jesus' sign of bringing Lazarus back to life helps the readers to understand the way Jesus shows concern toward the community of God (11:1-44). The signs of the Book of Signs proleptically propel the attention of the readers toward the grand sign of the gospel, i.e., the resurrection of Jesus. While Jesus was engaged in the mission of God he uses signs as tools in order to reveal his identity.[1292] The poor and physically challenged people of Nepal may find hope in the mission initiatives of Jesus. The poor and oppressed people of the country must find hope in the community of God. Church must function as an agent of holistic transformation in order to root out poverty and inability from the socio-religious and politico-cultural context.[1293] The Father of the Johannine Jesus and Jesus himself should be introduced as holistic healers. As the agents of the Father/Son the church must perform its duties with an emphasis on

---

[1287] Jan van der Watt, "Ethics through the Power of Language: Some Explorations in the Gospel According to John," *Moral Language in the New Testament* (Tübingen: Mohr Siebeck, 2010), 139-167.

[1288] See Beasley-Murray, *John*, 32-37.

[1289] Barrett, *John*, 205-8.

[1290] Beasley-Murray, *John*, 85-96; Van der Watt, "I AM the Bread of Life," 186-204.

[1291] Barrett, *John*, 292-304.

[1292] Kobus Kok, "As the Father has sent me, I send you: Towards a missional-incarnational Ethos in John 4," *Moral Language in the New Testament* (Tübingen: Mohr Siebeck, 2010), 168-196.

[1293] Perry, *Biographical History*, 1-48. Refer to Bruce J. Malina and Richard L. Rohrbaugh, *Social-Science Commentary on the Gospel of John* (Minneapolis: Fortress Press, 1998), 1-22.

holistic healing. Church should remain as an agent of transformation and change in order to impact societal arenas. Here the Johannine Father/Jesus remains as a model for our mission and ministry.

Parakletos as an Agent of Mission

The Farewell Discourse of Jesus in chaps. 13-17 is intended to comfort the disciples who are in a perplexed and distressed situation.[1294] The hour/lifting up/glorification of Jesus is impending and the disciples are prepared to face the situation in the absence of Jesus. The coming up of "another paracletos" and his ministry of teaching/comforting/counseling/advocating is introduced in a more extended way in chaps. 14-16.[1295] The need of the disciples to remain (*menein*) in Jesus (15:1-11; 17:1-26) and their movements in the world under the guidance of the paracletos are instructed in detail in this section (14:15-31; 15:26; 16:12).[1296] Another significant feature of the discourse is addressing the Holy Spirit as "Spirit of Truth."[1297] The mission of the paracletos or Spirit of Truth is teaching, guiding, counseling, and comforting the disciples. The Spirit of God is still working in the day to day affairs of the church and that helps the church to be active witness of the truth of God in the world.[1298] In the Nepali context, the church should accept and acknowledge the affairs of the Holy Spirit and should go ahead in its mission activities. The mission of God can be actualized in a Johannine way by accepting the guidance of the Holy Spirit and by evangelizing/witnessing the truth to the outsiders. This can be done both through words and actions. The *kerygmatic*, *didactic*, *koinonic*, and *diakonic*[1299] mission models that the Johannine Jesus affirms can be considered as a paradigm in the Nepali context.

Dialogue as a Means of Mission

John's Gospel emphasizes the aspect of dialogue as a significant tool in order to reveal the identity of Jesus. The protagonist Jesus and the narrator John together construct the story from an eternal point of view. The dialogue of

---

[1294] *John 11-21*, Calvin's NT Commentaries, 55-152.

[1295] J. Joubert, "Johannine Metaphors/Symbols Linked to the Paraclete-Spirit and their Theological Implications," *Acta Theologica*, Vol. 27/1 (June 2007), 83-103.

[1296] Tasker, *John*, 163-88.

[1297] Joubert, "Johannine Metaphors/Symbols Linked to the Paraclete-Spirit and their Theological Implications," *Acta Theologica*, 83-103.

[1298] Köstenberger's understanding of the gospel from a missional point of view throw light on this. See Andreas Köstenberger, *The Missions of Jesus and the Disciples According to the Fourth Gospel: With Implications for the Fourth Gospel's Purpose and the Mission of the Contemporary Church* (Grand Rapids: Eerdmans, 1998).

[1299] *Kerygmatic* means "proclamatory," *didactic* means "instructional," *koinonic* means "fellowship-oriented," and *diakonic* means "service-centered."

Jesus with Nicodemus reveals the necessity of being "born from above" and "born of water and spirit." In the story, Jesus the Rabbi is placed over against a Jewish Rabbi called Nicodemus. Thus the dialogue is introduced as a pedagogical dialogue or a dialogue between two teachers.[1300] Jesus affirms the Kingdom perspective and invites his interlocutor to accept the call.[1301] In chap. 4, the dialogue is taking place in a Samaritan context. As the extended story of John progresses Jesus is introduced over against the invalid, the crowd, the Jews, the blind man, the sisters of Lazarus, and the like.[1302] The verbal duel of Jesus with various walks of people enables him to express his views at multifarious levels. Jesus' ultimate intention was to fulfill the will of the Father and to extend the Family of God in this world.[1303] The contrast between the world from above and the world from below is expressed in a dynamic way through dialogues in order to develop the narrative. In the Gospel, God the Father, Jesus the Agent of God, and Holy Spirit the Paracletos are introduced in terms of both explicit and implicit dialogues and their active interactions.[1304] In a multi-religious and multi-cultural context like Nepal dialogue has a significant role to play.[1305] The church must be dialogic rather than monologic in its missional and ministerial endeavors.

Characterization

John's Gospel has a well developed characterization within its narratorial framework. The characters and their utterances and gestures are rhetorically presented with the help of literary devices and narratorial techniques.[1306] The protagonist uses double meaning, the characters misunderstand, and the protagonist clarifies the things he had already addressed persuasively. This trend with the help of the characterization helps the narrator to communicate his

---

[1300] See Thomaskutty, *Nature and Function of Dialogue in the Book of Signs*, 113-136.

[1301] See C. C. Caragounis, "Kingdom of God/Heaven," *Dictionary of Jesus and the Gospels* (Leicester: InterVarsity Press, 1992), 417-430.

[1302] Refer to Thomaskutty, *Nature and Function of Dialogue in the Book of Signs*, 47-574.

[1303] Again Van der Watt's understanding of the gospel from the perspective of family metaphor is significant to reckon with. See Van der Watt, *Family of the King: The Dynamics of Metaphor in the Gospel of John*.

[1304] Joubert, "Johannine Metaphors/Symbols Linked to the Paraclete-Spirit and their Theological Implications," *Acta Theologica*, 83-103.

[1305] Malina and Rohrbaugh take up the social, religious, and cultural context of the First Century CE seriously in relation to the Johannine community aspects. Refer to Malina and Rohrbaugh, *Social-Science Commentary on the Gospel of John*, 1-22.

[1306] See Jan van der Watt, "Double Entendre in the Gospel According to John," *Theology and Christology in the Fourth Gospel* (Leuven: University Press, 2005), 463-481.

story performatively to the ever present reading community.[1307] A paradigmatic reader of the Johannine story may identify the characters of the story as living examples within his/her context in the process of reading the text.[1308] A Nepali reader can identify several higher caste Hindu and Buddhist personnel who seek to understand Jesus. When such personnel seek the wisdom of God we may remember the personality of Nicodemus.[1309] Samaritan woman is remembered when we enter into village set ups and when we address the lower caste women of that region.[1310]

The royal man is remembered when the higher authorities seek the wisdom of the believers and the church community in their troubles. The invalid is right in front of us when we go for evangelization to various walks of people. The crowd in chap. 6 is reminiscent to the gatherings in our own contexts. The blind man, the family of Lazarus, Mary Magdalene, Thomas, Nathanael, Peter, Philip, and all other characters are seemingly similar to the people whom we come across on a regular basis.[1311] Among them the secret Christian communities, i.e., those who have belief in Jesus but unable to take a step to be part of the Christian community, are found identical to Nicodemus and Joseph of Arimathea. The characters whom we find in John are seemingly living among and around us. This is the peculiar narrative dynamic and performative nature of John's story-telling.[1312] In our reading we find Johannine characters as Nepalese. The Johannine characters represent several ideologies and philosophies and at the same time they represent people from our own context.

In John, the characters are introduced with local colors. They represent specific socio-religious locations. But, they are presented not by way of descriptive present tenses but through gnomic present tenses.[1313] Though they are introduced within their specific contexts, they are transformed as universal figures.[1314] This inter-relation between local and universal is running all through the Gospel of John. In the contemporary Nepali context this phenomenon has to be signified. A local mission with universal significance

---

[1307] Cf. Van der Watt, "Ethics through the Power of Language," *Moral Language in the New Testament*, 139-167.

[1308] Stibbe, *John*. Readings: A New Biblical Commentary, 16-17.

[1309] See Blomberg, *The Historical Reliability of John's Gospel*, 91-95.

[1310] Moloney, *The Gospel of John*, 113-150.

[1311] Refer to Stibbe, *John*. Readings: A New Biblical Commentary, 1-30.

[1312] See Mark W. G. Stibbe, *John as Storyteller: Narrative Criticism and the Fourth Gospel*. SNTS Monograph Series 73 (Cambridge: Cambridge University Press, 1992).

[1313] Refer to Wallace, *Greek Grammar beyond the Basics*.

[1314] Thomaskutty, "Glo[b/c]alization and Mission[s]: Reading John's Gospel," 1-16.

should be emphasized in a content in which globalization is at the fore.[1315] That further means a mission model that is glocal in nature and function.[1316]

Ministry: Individual, Public and Private

In John the narrator explains three significant aspects of Jesus' ministry: individual, Public and private. The individual aspects of Jesus' ministry are spread all through the Gospel. Jesus' dealings with individuals and their concerns are rhetorically brought to the notice of the reader through his treatment of the individuals and their concerns. For example, Philip, Peter, Andrew, Nathanael, Nicodemus, Samaritan woman, royal man, invalid, and the blind man are confronted by Jesus through one-on-one interactions.[1317] At the same time, the individuals are introduced as representatives of the general public. In chaps. 1-12 the narrator attempts to introduce the public ministry of Jesus. The signs are performative and the utterances are persuasive in a context in which Jesus' ministry was initiated over against the Jewish religio-political and politico-cultural scenario.[1318] In these chapters the 'from above' concerns of Jesus the protagonist and the 'from below' concerns of Jews the antagonists are efficaciously brought out through dialogues and actions. The setting is mostly in and around the temple of Jerusalem and places adjacent to that. But in chaps. 13-17 the narrator introduces a private setting in which only Jesus and the disciples are present. The private ministry of Jesus is initiated soon after the introduction of the impending hour of Jesus (12;20-36).[1319] As the glorification of Jesus is very near the protagonist takes initiative to comfort his disciples and deliver the farewell discourse.[1320] In the context of Nepal the church must initiate these three models of ministries. The individuals of the society must be singled out and the gospel should be shared according to their existent concerns. The mission and ministry programs of the church should be community focused and publicly inclined. Similarly the ministry of Jesus should be emphasized within the church context. The church has a greater role

[1315] Malcolm Walters (1995; quoted in Araujo, 2003: 230; cf. Steger, 2013: 1-145) defines "Globalization as a concept refers to both the compression of the world and the intensification of consciousness of the world as a whole . . . both concrete global interdependence and consciousness of the global whole." In this context, Marshall McLuhan's (1960: 97) idea of "the global village" is significant to consider with. See Thomaskutty, "Glo[b/c]alization and Mission[s]: Reading John's Gospel," 56-77.

[1316] Thomaskutty, "Glo[b/c]alization and Mission[s]: Reading John's Gospel," 56-77.

[1317] See Thomaskutty, "Glo[b/c]alization and Mission[s]: Reading John's Gospel," 56-77.

[1318] Refer to Malina and Rohrbaugh, *Social-Science Commentary on the Gospel of John*, 1-22.

[1319] Cf. Blomberg, *The Historical Reliability of John's Gospel*, 180-184.

[1320] G. M. Burge, "Glory," *Dictionary of Jesus and the Gospels* (Leicester: InterVarsity Press, 1992), 268-270.

in forming evangelists, teachers, and apostles in order to shape the future of the Christian community.

The "Newness" Motif

The motif of "newness" in John is significant to reckon with. The theme of "new vine" symbolizes the aspect of "new joy." Jesus admonishes his disciples to abide in him (i.e., the Vine) and to love one another so that their joy may be complete. In 2:13-21, the narrator introduces the theme of "new temple" over against the established nature of the temple at Jerusalem. The theme of "new birth"[1321] in the conversation with Nicodemus is introduced as a requirement to see the kingdom of God (3:3-5).[1322] The theme of "new life" is introduced in the context of the healing of the royal man's son in 4:46-54. This story as well works within the narrative framework of John. The theme of "new law" in chap. 5 is followed by the theme of "new bread" (6:22-59). The theme of "new light" in the tabernacles discourse (chaps. 7-8) is followed by the theme of "new sight" in chap. 9. Through these the narrator dynamically and symbolically introduces the "newness" motif over against the "old" things. Jesus and his eternal life perspectives should be presented as a "new paradigm" over against the traditional and "old" beliefs and practices of the Nepali context. In that sense, John's Gospel can be used as a paradigm for the Nepali context in order to transform individuals, establishments and communities.

Dalits and John

The Dalit communities of Nepal suffer due to economic deprivation, social vulnerability, and religious dehumanization. During the kingly rule their concerns were not at all taken into consideration. The church of Nepal is mostly a church of the Dalit communities. The growth of the church in Nepal is possible only through concentration among these ostracized communities. In our missiological and theological endeavors our attempt must be giving voice to the voiceless. The Dalit communities of Nepal, as in the case of the Indian context, should be given their due respect and identity so that they may be transformed from their current status of "no people" to the status of a "new people." The Gospel of John provides us insights concerning Jesus' attitude toward the poor, oppressed, and marginalized.[1323] Jesus' activity of transforming the Samaritan woman from her life-long marginalization to a new identity has to be considered as a mission

---

[1321] W. L. Kynes, "New Birth," *Dictionary of Jesus and the Gospels* (Leicester: InterVarsity Press, 1992), 574-576.

[1322] Refer to Caragounis, "Kingdom of God/Heaven," *Dictionary of Jesus and the Gospels*, 417-430.

[1323] See P. H. Davids, "Rich and Poor," *Dictionary of Jesus and the Gospels* (Leicester: InterVarsity Press, 1992), 701-710; *Expository Dictionary of Bible Words* (A Modern

model to be exemplified in the Nepali context.[1324] The invalid and the blind man were people without proper recognition and identity in the socio-religious set up. Through Jesus they found a new identity and holistic transformation. In John, Jesus' mission model expects people's faith in the Father and in him. Through trusting in him or putting faith in him a person enters into the eternal life experience. A believer's existence as a redeemed person begins right there. The Nepali church of the contemporary context must take up the mission model of Jesus considerably in its day-to-day affairs.

Conclusion

The above mentioned Johannine aspects in connection to the socio-religious and politico-cultural background provide us enough insights concerning our mission and ministry in the contemporary Nepali context. A mission that is taking into consideration the Trinitarian mission model of the Gospel of John may bring significant impact in the present day context of ours. Our mission must focus on *anthropo*-centric and *cosmo*-centric aspects with ultimate concern and must follow the footprints of Jesus in that regard. As the Father, Son, and the Holy Spirit are actively involved in the mission and ministry both within and outside the church, the Nepali church of our time must come out as an agent of mission, ministry, and transformation. A radical contextualization by neglecting the biblical worldview is not our concern. Rather we initiate for a dynamic contextualization in which we attempt to interlock the biblical worldview of the first century with our own worldview. The church of Nepal can consider the mission model of the Gospel of John as a paradigm in its initiatives in the contemporary context. The aspects of "sending" (by the Father), "being sent" (by the Son), and "comforting or teaching or counseling or advocating" (by the Paracletos) can be brought at the center of the mission and ministry of the church. Our attempts by following the Johannine mission model would ultimately orient us toward a *dynamic Nepalization* in the present day context.

Replacement for the Classic Vine's Expository Dictionary (Peabody, Massachusetts: Hendrikson Publishers, 2005), 742-743.

[1324] Beasley-Murray, *John*, 56-66; Moloney, *The Gospel of John*, 113-149.

Chapter 15

Reading John's Gospel in the Bangladeshi Context

Introduction

The rhetoric of John's Gospel can encompass the feelings and aspirations of people 'there and then' and 'here and now.' This unique characteristic of the Gospel manifests its gnomic significance in a context in which various issues and interpretative necessities arise. John's narrative masterpiece takes into consideration both the individual and the corporate aspects of humanity. The *gnomic* rather than *descriptive* nature of the text calls our attention toward its global hermeneutical significance.[1325] In the contemporary context, Bangladesh is no more the 'old Bangladesh,' now it has to be considered as the 'global Bangladesh.' Despite its poor-country status, increasing numbers of tourists visit the country.[1326] This situation requires our attention and we should consider that as an occasion to inculcate missional and theological interpretation of the scriptures. The Gospel of John has the potential to persuade the contemporary Bangladeshi context in a positive manner. The following two questions lie at the center of our discussion: How can we create contextual and ideological constellations between the first century Johannine community context and the twenty-first century Bangladeshi context? How a 'third space' can be created

---

[1325] See Thomaskutty, "Biblical Interpretation in the Global-Indian Context," 64-68.

[1326] Tourism in the early 1980s amounted to some 49,000 visitors per year, but by 1986 more than 129,000 tourists—mostly from India, the United States of America, Britain, and Japan—visited Bangladesh. See http://www.assignmentpoint.com/arts/sociology/report-on-social-problems-in-bangladesh.html, on 22 Feb 2017.

out of the dialogue between the Johannine world-view and the Bangladeshi world-view?[1327] The sections below will address some of the significant issues of the Bangladeshi context in relation to the realities of the Johannine community.

Some of the Contextual and Hermeneutical Aspects

This essay is basically an endeavor to understand the relatedness of John's message to the contemporary socio-religious and politico-cultural realities of the nation of Bangladesh and the Bangladeshis.[1328] An attempt to study some of John's themes and other aspects and their dynamic function within the narrative framework of the Gospel helps us to understand its flexibility to adopt new situations and its reverberating effects beyond space and time. A proper understanding of the following aspects might enable us to contextualize the gospel message adequately to the nation of Bangladesh.

Power Misuse and Corruption

Power misuse and corruption are some of the important concerns to be taken up seriously when we discuss the political scenario of Bangladesh. The hunger for power among the elites and the influential in the country has to be addressed in the process of contextualizing the gospel message. The wealth and resources of the nation are controlled by the rich and powerful and thus the poor citizens of the country remain at the periphery. The disparity between the rich and the poor is on an increase in the nation as the business and educational sectors are in the hands of the elite class.

Jesus' model in the Gospel of John, as one who comes from the world 'from above' to the world 'from below,' can be considered as a paradigm in this context. His incarnational model of transferring from a powerful position (that is, sitting at the right hand of God in heaven) to 'Word becoming flesh' (that is, total identification with humanity, 1:14) is worth investigating and re-interpreting.[1329] In the words of John the Baptist, Jesus is the 'Messiah' and the 'Lamb of God' (1:19-34);[1330] in the words of Andrew, he found Jesus as the

---

[1327] See Edward W. Soja, *Third Space: Journeys to Los Angeles and Other Real-and-Imagined Places* (Malden: Wiley, 1996).

[1328] See the social function of John's narrative in Mark W.G. Stibbe, *John as Storyteller: Narrative Criticism and the Fourth Gospel*, SNTSMS 73 (Cambridge: Cambridge University Press, 1992), 50-66.

[1329] See Beasley-Murray, *John*, 13-14; Adele Reinhartz, *The Word in the World: The Cosmological Tale in the Fourth Gospel*, SBLMS 45 (Atlanta: Scholars Press, 1992), 20-23; Thomaskutty, "Dialogical Nature of John's Gospel," 1-17.

[1330] See Beasley-Murray, *John*, 1999, 24-26.

'Messiah' (1:41);[1331] in the words of Philip, Jesus is 'one Moses wrote about in the Law, and about whom the prophets also wrote' (1:45);[1332] and in the words of Nathanael, he is 'Rabbi,' 'the Son of God,' and 'the King of Israel' (1:49).[1333] Toward the end of the Gospel, Jesus' Lordship and God-ship are brought to the foreground through the utterance of Thomas (20:28).[1334] Jesus follows a model that invites people toward the family of God.[1335]

Thus Jesus' incarnation model is one of accommodation in which he becomes 'one among humanity.'[1336] This model can be considered as a supreme model in a context in which people strive hard to usurp positions, show hunger for hegemony, and misuse their power. The incarnational model of Jesus beckons the elites both in the church and society to adopt and enhance an accommodative strategy for the common good of the country.

Children at Risk

According to the information from UNICEF, the following things are important to make note with regard to the children of Bangladesh: first, twenty-six million children live below the national poverty line, typically deprived of four out of seven of the following basic services: water, sanitation, nutrition, education, health, information, and shelter; second, Bangladesh has one of the highest rates of child marriage in the world. Sixty-six per cent of women (aged 20 to 24) were married before they turned 18; third, thirteen per cent of children are involved in child labor. Child laborers are frequently denied an education and are vulnerable to violence and abuse; fourth, Bangladesh has one of the lowest rates of birth registration in the world. This makes it difficult to protect children from trafficking, child labor and child marriage.[1337] In this context, Johannine portrayal of Jesus' incarnation as a child of God requires our attention.

What Marianne Meye Thompson proposes in her article looks like a good model as far as my knowledge is concerned.[1338] By placing the theme

---

[1331] See Herman Ridderbos, *The Gospel of John: A Theological Commentary* (Grand Rapids: Eerdmans, 1987/1997), 84-85.

[1332] See Ridderbos, *Gospel of John*, 87-88.

[1333] See Marianne Thompson, *John: A Commentary*, 53-58.

[1334] Thompson, *John: A Commentary*, 425-427.

[1335] Jan G. van der Watt relates the metaphor 'family (of God)' with almost every aspects of the Johannine narrative. See Van der Watt, *Family of the King*.

[1336] See Greg McKinzie, "The Hermeneutics of Incarnational Evangelism: Reading the Gospel with Peruvians," *Fuller Magazine: Reading Scripture Globally*, Issue. 8 (May 2017), 56-59.

[1337] See https://www.unicef.org/bangladesh/overview_4841.html, on 22 Feb 2017.

[1338] Marianne Meye Thompson, "Children in the Gospel of John," *The Child in the Bible* (Grand Rapids: Eerdmans, 2008), 195-214.

of life at the center of the Fourth Gospel, Thompson beautifully foregrounds the relationship between God the Father and his children. She emphasizes the following expressions with greater theological significance in the process of interpreting the Fourth Gospel: first, children in John are "any and all persons as children of God"; second, they are "reborn as children of God"; third, their identity as "being in the eternal life experience"; fourth, as a "new nascent messianic community"; and fifth, they are ultimately a "new community."[1339] When Louis Martyn suggested the Gospel of John as a two-level drama, he was in reality unlocking something intriguing.[1340] At the first level of the drama, the story revolves around Jesus, the child par excellence, as a paradigm for humanity in relation to God the Father. At the second level of the drama, the same is expected from the children of God as they are a model community following the grand model of Jesus the eternal child of God.

Johannine community as the children of God differs in several ways from other communities including the Qumran community. While the Qumran community adopted a rhetoric of distance, John's community accepted a rhetoric of difference. It further suggests that Johannine community, as Marianne Meye Thompson suggests, as "a lived out identity in the world in reference to messianic community with social consequences."[1341] I may re-emphasize the following things for clarity: first, Johannine narrator presents Jesus himself as a paradigm of God's child; second, the community of John was expected to adopt the Father/God-and-Son/Jesus relationship as their paradigm model in this world; third, the world can follow the model of the children of God/Johannine community that was shaped by the ideologies of Jesus the child of God; and fourth, while those who accept this model are considered as "children of light," those who do not accept are considered as "children of darkness."[1342] Thus John suggests a model that can be appropriated through people's acceptance or rejection.

The theme of 'God becoming Child' to make all people 'children of light' can be considered as a paradigm in the Bangladeshi context on the following grounds: first, the underprivileged children are ostracized in the contemporary Bangladeshi society, hence the church has a greater role to redeem them from clutches and also to give them dignity and hope as 'children of God'; second, the Bangladeshi church exists as a minority religious group and at

---

[1339] See more details here: https://ntscholarship.wordpress.com/2016/02/01/children-in-the-gospel-of-john-joy-clement-daniels-questions-and-johnson-thomaskuttys-responses/, on 30 June 2017.

[1340] See Martyn, *History and Theology in the Fourth Gospel.*

[1341] See Thompson, "Children in the Gospel of John," 195-214.

[1342] See more details here: https://ntscholarship.wordpress.com/2016/02/01/children-in-the-gospel-of-john-joy-clement-daniels-questions-and-johnson-thomaskuttys-responses/, on 30 June 2017.

the same time a voiceless community, hence the Christian children are double marginalized. As the Johannine community encouraged a Father [God]—Son [Jesus]—Children [believers] relationship, the church in Bangladesh should facilitate all measures to liberate children from both physical and spiritual bondages; and third, the message of the Gospel of John can be presented in the Bangladeshi context as a model message to transform the social order irrespective of age, religion, class, and caste structures.

Next Generation Nationals

Bangladesh is rich in its adolescents and young people. The country has an adolescent and youth population of approximately 52 million, amounting to one/third of the country's total population.[1343] But, the lack of access to higher quality education, absence of decent work opportunities, unavailability of comprehensive health including sexual and reproductive health (SRH) services, exclusion and marginalization from civil participation and policies and laws which act against the best interest of young people are but a few challenges which they have to contend with on a regular basis.[1344] This is the context in which we need to present the mission model of Jesus based on the Johannine narrative framework. In the Fourth Gospel, Jesus is portrayed as an agent of both personal and corporate transformation. The narrator combines the story of Jesus with the story of the Johannine community. All the individual characters of the extended story are later on function as agents of transformation. They adopt a Jesus model.

In his call narratives, young people like Andrew, Simon Peter, Philip, and Nathanael are transformed.[1345] After receiving spiritual insights from Jesus, they function at the communitarian level as agents of liberation. The same can be viewed in the lives of the Samaritan woman and the Samaritan villagers (4:1-43), the royal man and his son (4:46-54), the invalid at the pool (5:1-18), the crowd on a mountainside and in the synagogue (6:1-71), many during the Feast of Tabernacles (chaps. 7-8), the blind man turned healed (9:1-43), the family of Lazarus (chap. 11) and many others.[1346] They were transformed by the words and activities of Jesus. Similarly, the church in Bangladesh should

---

[1343] See http://www.thedailystar.net/adolescents-and-young-people-of-bangladesh-54257, on 22 Feb 2017.

[1344] See http://www.thedailystar.net/adolescents-and-young-people-of-bangladesh-54257, on 22 Feb 2017.

[1345] See Carson, *The Gospel according to John*, 154-165.

[1346] See Carson, *Gospel according to John*, 228-232, 238-239, 240-250, 267-304, 305-358, 359-377, 403-423; also see Beasley-Murray, *John*, 56-81; F. F. Bruce, *The Gospel of John: Introduction, Exposition, and Notes* (Grand Rapids: Eerdmans, 1983), 100-141.

take initiative to transform the next generation Bangladeshis in the country.[1347] The Johannine characters represent different philosophical and ideological points of view. The transformation of these characters as believers and their identification with the Johannine community can be a model for missional hermeneutics in the Bangladeshi context.

Women and their Concerns

Bangladesh's socio-cultural environment contains pervasive gender discrimination, so girls and women face many obstacles to their development. Girls are often considered to be financial burdens on their family, and from the time of birth, they receive less investment in their health, care and education. With the advent of puberty, differences in the ways that adolescent girls and boys are treated become much more pronounced.[1348] Adolescence is not viewed as a distinct phase of life; instead the onset of physical maturity is seen as an abrupt shift from childhood to adulthood. At puberty, girls' mobility is often restricted, which limits their access to livelihood, learning and recreational and social activities.[1349] Bangladesh's rates of child marriage and adolescent motherhood are among the highest in the world. Maternal mortality rates also remain extremely high. Poor maternal health is the result of early marriage, women's malnutrition, a lack of access to and use of medical services and a lack of knowledge and information.[1350] Most women give birth without a skilled attendant.[1351]

John delineates the role of women significantly within his narrative framework. In 2:1-11, Mary the mother of Jesus functions as an influential character and she connects Jesus with the needy situation of the family.[1352] In

---

[1347] See Muhammad Ibrahim, *Providing Education for Out-of-School Youth in Bangladesh* (London: Commonwealth Secretariat, 2002), 21; Yedla C. Simhadri, *Development of Emerging World Youth* (Delhi: Mittal Publications, 1989), 155.

[1348] See Ataur Rahman Belal, *Corporate Social Responsibility Reporting in Developing Countries: The Case of Bangladesh* (London/New York: Routledge, 2008), 55-56.

[1349] See Sangh Mittra and Bachchan Kumar, eds., *Encyclopedia of Women in South Asia*, Vol. 3 (Delhi: Kalpaz Publications, 2004), 68; also see Margaret Alston, *Women and Climate Change in Bangladesh*, ASAA Women in Asia Series (London/New York: Routledge, 2015), 62-63.

[1350] See Royeka Kabir, "Cyclones: The Days After," *DHA News* (Geneva: Department of Humanitarian Affairs, April/May 1997); also see *International Monetary Fund Staff Council Reports*, Bangladesh: Poverty Reduction Strategy Paper (2005 IMF, IMF Country Report Number 05/410: November 2005), 150.

[1351] UNICEF, *State of the World's Children: The Double Dividend of Gender Equality*, 2007. See https://www.unicef.org/bangladesh/Women_and_girls_in_Bangladesh.pdf, on 22 Feb 2017.

[1352] Leon Morris, *The Gospel according to John*, NICNT, Revised Edition (Grand Rapids: Eerdmans, 1995), 153-64; Thomaskutty, *Nature and Function of Dialogue in the Book of Signs*

4:1-42 the role of the Samaritan woman is unique as Jesus crosses the religious, racial, and sexual barriers in order to transform her from Samaritan religiosity to eternal life-centered religiosity.[1353] A woman who was alien to the Jewish religiosity witnesses the truth and starts to develop her understanding of the Messiah.[1354] Her witness about Jesus to her own people challenges them to realize the presence of the "Savior of the world."[1355] In chap. 11 the sisters of Lazarus, i.e., Mary and Martha, function significantly as effective characters who appeal for their brother.[1356] In chap. 12:1-8, the two women characters work significantly as one serves at Jesus and the other spends expensive perfume to anoint the feet of Jesus. The narratorial technique of conflict and characterization (through the medium of contrast) is conspicuous as the narrator places Mary of Bethany over against Judas Iscariot.[1357] While Mary of Bethany rhetorizes her presence with her silence and her superabundant generosity shown to Jesus, Judas' presence is portrayed with the help of his hypocritical and seemingly concerned speech.[1358] While Jesus praises the action of the lady, he condemns the speech of Judas.[1359]

In chap. 20, Mary Magdalene's boldness to come to the tomb at the early morning is clearly mentioned. She is instrumental in proclaiming the good news concerning the resurrection of Jesus. Thus, the evangelist presents her as an "apostle to the apostles."[1360] In John, Jesus empowers the woman characters and presents them over against misunderstanding, unbelieving, and unfaithful men characters.[1361]

In today's Bangladeshi context, empowerment of women is a necessity as they appear as educationally illiterate, politically powerless, religiously

---

(John 1:19-12:50), 80-88. Also see Margaret M. Beirne, *Women and Men in the Fourth Gospel: A Genuine Discipleship of Equals*, JSNTSS 242 (Sheffield: Sheffield Academic Press, 2003), 42-66; Culpepper, *Anatomy of the Fourth Gospel*, 133-134.

[1353] See Thomaskutty, *Nature and Function of Dialogue in the Book of Signs*, 153-196.

[1354] See Thomaskutty, "Biblical Interpretation in the Global-Indian Context," 64-68.

[1355] Beirne, *Women and Men in the Fourth Gospel*, 68-104. Also see Thomaskutty, *Nature and Function of Dialogue in the Book of Signs*, 153-196; Culpepper, *Anatomy of the Fourth Gospel*, 136-137.

[1356] Kanagaraj, "The Profiles of Women in John: House-Bound or Christ-Bound?" 60-79.

[1357] Scholer, "Women," 880-887

[1358] See Beirne, *Women and Men in the Fourth Gospel*, 140-169.

[1359] Thomaskutty, *Nature and Function of Dialogue in the Book of Signs*, 491-95.

[1360] *John 11-21 & 1 John*, Calvin's New Testament Commentaries (Grand Rapids: Eerdmans, 1959), 191-214.

[1361] Kanagaraj, "The Profiles of Women in John: House-Bound or Christ-Bound?," 60-79; also see Thomaskutty, "Reading John's Gospel in the Nepali Context," 12-13.

voiceless, and culturally ostracized sections.[1362] The role of women in the family, church, and society is signified by Jesus as they are enabled in His ministry to work dynamically as harbingers of the gospel.[1363] As Mary the mother of Jesus was instrumental in a family set up, Samaritan women was instrumental in bringing the gospel to the village of Sychar, Martha and Mary were loyal to Jesus in the context of Bethany, Mary was superabundantly generous, and Mary Magdalene was instrumental to share the good news even to their male counterparts, the Bangladeshi women can function as powerful members in the family, church, and social contexts as agents of mission and ministry.[1364] Toward that end, the church of Bangladesh should function as an agent of social transformation and liberation.

Religious Persecution

Christianity is a minority religion in the Bangladeshi context. Within the total population, the country accommodates less than one per-cent Christians. We can draw several similarities between the Johannine community in relation to the Jewish religious context and the Bangladeshi Christian community in relation to the Islamic context of the country. The Gospel of John reflects the aspect of persecution at several levels. First of all, in Jesus' own situation in life, the protagonist was verbally attacked by the antagonists and the conflict finally ended up in the execution of the Son of Man (11:45-53).[1365] At another level, within the Johannine community context, the attitude of the unbelieving Jews towards the believers was not fair. The practice of 'sending [the followers of Jesus] out of the synagogue' led many to identity crises (9:22, 34; 16:2).[1366] The Johannine sect was constantly undergoing struggles from the part of the synagogue authorities. Even in such a context, the community was not fleeing away from the mainstream Jewish community (as in the case of the Qumran community) but they remained within the society.[1367] The Christian

---

[1362] See R. Jahan, "Women in Bangladesh," *Women for women, Bangladesh 1975* (Dhaka: Women for Women Research and Study Group, 1975), 1-30.

[1363] Cf. Kanagaraj, "The Profiles of Women in John: House-Bound or Christ-Bound?," 60-79.

[1364] Cf. Cindy Perry, *A Biographical History of the Church in Nepal*, Third Edition (Kathmandu, Nepal: Nepal Church History Project, 2000), 17-19, 30-31.

[1365] The violent actions of the interlocutors are beyond the patterns of the dialogue. The antagonistic and exclusive attitudes of the Jews toward those who do not hold on to their religious ideologies are obvious through the ongoing vocal exchanges within the Gospel. See Thomaskutty, *Nature and Function of Dialogue in the Book of Signs*, 554.

[1366] Morris, *Gospel according to John*, 433-35. Also see Blomberg, *The Historical Reliability of John's Gospel,* 150-157.

[1367] While the Qumran community went away from the mainstream Jewish community and lived nearby the Dead Sea area, the Johannine community remained in the public domains and

communities of Bangladesh function within the socio-religious and politico-cultural context of the country. They struggle while the country struggles and enjoy when the country enjoys. Though persecution is comparatively less, the Christian communities of the country undergo struggles to get the freedom that other religious communities enjoy. The Johannine community was developing in a context in which Jewish religious fundamentalism was at its peak.[1368]

The Johannine community as a new religious movement arose in constant struggle with the fundamentalist Jews. As a sectarian group the Johannine community underwent persecutions and trials on several grounds. In the process of re-interpreting the Jesus story into the Johannine community context the narrator attempts to present Jesus as a model figure who underwent trials and persecutions.[1369] Similarly, Bangladeshi church is a movement that has constant struggles with the mainstream religious communities of the nation. Just as in the Johannine set up, in Bangladesh, the non-Christian Bangladeshis stand on the one side and the church as an emerging movement stands on the other side. The bifurcation between the believing *insiders* and the unbelieving *outsiders* has to be considered seriously in the process of missional interpretations and practices in Bangladesh.[1370] The contextual relevance of the Johannine message should be investigated in closer relationship with the Bangladeshi context and propagated as a paradigm for social and religious transformation in the country.

The Meaning of Resurrection

In the Bangladeshi context, the significance of Jesus' resurrection is multi-faceted. When I attempt to relate Jesus' resurrection in the multi-cultural and pluralistic context of Bangladesh, I need to re-interpret it for the diverse communities of the country. The salvific significance of Christ's work on the cross and his resurrection should first and foremost be taught and proclaimed as the good news of salvation for the various religious and ethnic communities. Harold W. Attridge rightly says:

> The reality of resurrected life in the present is given definition as a life of Spirit-filled love that issues in forgiveness. But that realized experience of the way in which a believer abides with Father and Son in a mysteriously glorious present is rooted in the physical reality of the resurrected Christ. The evangelist seems most interested in the ways in which resurrected life have meaning in the present,

existed as a distinct community.

[1368] See Thomaskutty, "Reading John's Gospel in the Nepali Context," 12-13.

[1369] Thomaskutty, *Dialogue in the Book of Signs,* 249-309, 466-470.

[1370] Cf. Paul Trebilco, *Self-designations and Group Identity in the New Testament* (Cambridge: University Press, 2012), 11-12.

> but he insists that they are intimately tied to the resurrected reality of Christ, and with this reality abides a hope for the continued relationship that the presence of the Spirit portends.[1371]

Further, Udo Schnelle says that:

> Johannine Christology is characterized by a comprehensive program: Preexistence and incarnation, sending and exaltation/glorification on the cross intersect in the idea of love. The Father's love for the Son before the foundation of the world and the sending of the Son coincide just as much, according to 17:24-25, as the sending of the Son and his path to the cross motivated by love for the world (3:13-14, 16; 10:17; 13:1).[1372]

As Attridge rightly points out, the significance of the resurrection of Jesus in the present (that is, in relation to the past event) should take precedence in our missional hermeneutics. As Udo Schnelle connects the resurrection event as a mark of love, our hermeneutical task in the Bangladeshi context should uphold the crucified and resurrected Jesus and his love for the universe. When we witness Christ for instance to the poor and marginalized, also called the dust of the dust, we need to use Christ's resurrection as a model for liberation out of the clutches of oppression and dehumanization.[1373] As Christ was humiliated on the cross, and was raised by the Father from the grave, so also, Christian mission should focus on the upliftment of the oppressed out of the bondages of poverty, casteism, sin and injustice. Resurrection is therefore a unique missional paradigm, comprising the historical reality of Christ's resurrection, its salvific significance, as well as its social implications.[1374]

Walking the Talk

In his ministry, Jesus of John's Gospel was establishing his speeches by putting them into actions. Let us see how the "I AM Sayings" of Jesus in

---

[1371] See Harold W. Attridge, "From Discord Rises Meaning: Resurrection Motifs in the Fourth Gospel," *The Resurrection of Jesus in the Gospel of John*, WUNT 222, eds. Craig R. Koester and Reimund Bieringer (Tübingen: Mohr Siebeck, 2008), 19.

[1372] Udo Schnelle, "Cross and Resurrection in the Gospel of John," *The Resurrection of Jesus in the Gospel of John*, WUNT 222, eds. Craig R. Koester and Reimund Bieringer (Tübingen: Mohr Siebeck, 2008), 150.

[1373] See Craig R. Koester, "Jesus' Resurrection, the Signs, and the Dynamics of Faith in the Gospel of John," *The Resurrection of Jesus in the Gospel of John*, WUNT 222, eds. Craig R. Koester and Reimund Bieringer (Tübingen: Mohr Siebeck, 2008), 47-74.

[1374] Read the original form of the interview: http://resurrectionhope.blogspot.com/2011/05/christs-resurrection-as-unique.html, on 22 Feb 2017; also see Michael Gorman's blog: http://www.michaeljgorman.net/2011/05/31/a-missional-paradigm-for-the-resurrection/, on 22 Feb 2017.

John are significant in the Bangladeshi context.[1375] Jesus' action and speech develop synonymously within Johannine narrative framework. One who is able to feed five thousand people with physical bread (6:1-15) is declared as the bread from heaven (6:22-59).[1376] The festival of Tabernacles is actualized with the very presence of Jesus as the light of the world (8:12).[1377] Moreover, one who is able to give physical sight to the blind is introduced as the "light of the world" (9:5).[1378] Jesus is standing right out there as the "door of the sheep" (10:7) when the sheep are sent out of the synagogue (9:34).[1379] While the leaders of the synagogue function as hirelings (9:1-41), Jesus functions as the "good shepherd" as he solves the lifelong struggles and issues of the blind man (10:11).[1380] One who is able to give back life is the "resurrection and life" (11:25). One who is "the way, truth, and life" prepares a way and a house in heaven (14:6).[1381] And he also sends the "Spirit of Truth" among the people so that the people of God may live their life under his guidance (14:15-31; 15:26; 16:12).[1382] One who is able to provide physical wine (2:1-11) is the "true vine" (15:1-11).[1383] Thus, the utterances of Jesus are proved through his very actions. The signs are rhetorical and are external proofs in order to demonstrate the very utterances of Jesus.[1384] In the contemporary Bangladeshi context the propagators of the gospel must attempt for action-oriented gospel. The efficacy of the gospel should be foregrounded through actions of love. As Jesus emphasizes the gnomic significance of the commandment of love, the believing community of Bangladesh should exemplify unity among themselves and extend the same virtue toward the outside world.

Jesus can be presented as the model of mission in the pluralistic context of Bangladesh. The philosophy of witnessing by example has to be shown in this context. Jesus' method was not simply witnessing the truth through the

---

[1375] Refer to G. M. Burge, "I AM Sayings," *Dictionary of Jesus and the Gospels* (Leicester: InterVarsity Press, 1992), 354-356.

[1376] R. V. G. Tasker, *John*, TNTC (Grand Rapids: Eerdmans, 1960/1995), 92-100; Van der Watt, "I AM the Bread of Life," 186-204.

[1377] Ball, *'I AM' in John's Gospel*, 155. Ball says that, "In John 8:12, Jesus explicitly applies to himself the theme of light which applied to the Word of the prologue (1:4, 5, 9, 10). It is thus made clear to the reader that Jesus is the Word of which the prologue spoke."

[1378] See Ball, *'I Am' in John's Gospel*, 80-93.

[1379] Thomaskutty, *Nature and Function of Dialogue in the Book of Signs*, 532-534.

[1380] Tasker, *John*, 122-31.

[1381] See Ball, *'I Am' in John's Gospel*, 119-128.

[1382] *John 11-21*, Calvin's NT Commentaries, 82.

[1383] See Ball, *'I Am' in John's Gospel*, 60-145.

[1384] Refer to George A. Kennedy, *New Testament Interpretation through Rhetorical Criticism* (Chapel Hill/London: The University of North Carolina Press, 1984).

means of revelatory utterances but also through signs and actions.[1385] Jesus was teaching the message of the Father through action-oriented messages. The interlocking of utterances and actions in the mission and ministry of Jesus can be considered as a better paradigm in the Bangladeshi context. In a context in which religious and philosophical ideologies are enormous and they remain mostly in vocal format, Jesus' action-oriented format is significant to reckon with. Jesus says, "whoever does not love me does not keep my words; and the word that you hear is not mine, but is from the Father who sent me" (14:24).[1386] Those who do the 'action of love' are considered as those who hear the words of Jesus. The ethical and moral actions centered on love are considered as ultimate concerns and characteristics of Jesus' mission. The Bangladeshi church must emphasize love centered and action-oriented ethical and moral standards of mission in order to expand the mission boundaries. A church that is dogmatically oriented cannot attract the poor, marginalized, and dehumanized sections of the society. In Bangladeshi context, the majority community is underprivileged. So, the church must pay special attention in emphasizing the love-centered ethics of Jesus.[1387] This is rooted in the narrative frame work of John's Gospel.[1388]

Signs are Rhetoric

The signs of the gospel function in a dynamic way as they contribute semantically to the narrative framework of the gospel. Jesus turns water into wine in a wedding set up in order to solve the situational issues of a house (2:1-11).[1389] The protagonist heals the royal man's son and he develops from step to step in his journey of faith (4:46-51).[1390] The sign of healing the invalid symbolizes Jesus' generous attitude even toward strangers (5:1-18). In both 4:46-54 and 5:1-18, the time of dialogue is identified as the time of sign. The feeding of the five thousand reveals Jesus' attitude toward the hungry and the extended humanity of his time (6:1-15). Jesus as the one who walks on the water reveals his power and authority over the nature (6:16-21).[1391] The

---

[1385] Se Ball, *'I Am' in John's Gospel*, 177-254.

[1386] Moloney, *The Gospel of John*, Sacra Pagina Series, Vol. 4 (Collegeville, Minnesota: The Liturgical Press), 405; Leon Morris, "Love," *Dictionary of Jesus and the Gospels* (Leicester: InterVarsity Press, 1992), 492-495.

[1387] Jan van der Watt, "Ethics through the Power of Language: Some Explorations in the Gospel according to John," *Moral Language in the New Testament* (Tübingen: Mohr Siebeck, 2010), 139-167.

[1388] See Thomaskutty, "Reading John's Gospel in the Nepali Context," 13-14.

[1389] See Beasley-Murray, *John*, 32-37.

[1390] C. K. Barrett, *The Gospel according to Saint John: An Introduction with Commentary and Notes on the Greek Text* (London: SPCK, 1978), 205-8.

[1391] Beasley-Murray, *John*, 85-96; Van der Watt, "I AM the Bread of Life," 186-204.

healing of the blind man helps the readers to understand the way a sign results into a person's faith development (9:1-41).[1392]

Jesus' sign of bringing Lazarus back to life helps the readers to understand the way Jesus shows concern toward the community of God (11:1-44). The signs of the Book of Signs proleptically propel the attention of the readers toward the grand sign of the gospel, i.e., the resurrection of Jesus. While Jesus was engaged in the mission of God he uses signs as tools in order to reveal his identity.[1393] The poor and physically challenged people of Bangladesh might find hope in the mission initiatives of Jesus. The poor and oppressed people of the country must find hope in the community of God. Church must function as an agent of holistic transformation in order to root out poverty and inability from the socio-religious and politico-cultural context.[1394] The Father of Johannine Jesus and Jesus himself should be introduced as holistic healers. As the agents of the Father/Son the church must perform its duties with an emphasis on holistic healing. Church should remain as an agent of transformation and change in order to impact societal arenas. Here the Johannine Father/Jesus remains as a model for our mission and ministry.

Parakletos as an Agent of Mission

John has a well-developed pneumatology in comparison to the rest of the NT writings. While in chaps. 1-12 he presents the Holy Spirit in synonymous terms to the Synoptics, in chaps. 13-17 a personified form of the Holy Spirit is brought to the fore. In the Farewell Discourse, the identity formation of the disciples is emphasized.[1395] And the aspects such as individuals in relation to the church and in relation to the world are highlighted. The Paraklete assures God's continuing presence within the community of faith and that remains as a source of the wisdom of God (cf. 14:15-17, 26; 15:26-27; 16:7-11, 12-14; 1 John 2:1).[1396]

The Farewell Discourse of Jesus in chaps. 13-17 is intended to comfort the disciples who are in a perplexed and distressed situation.[1397] The hour/lifting up/glorification of Jesus is impending and the disciples are prepared to face the situation in the absence of Jesus. The coming of "another parakletos" and his ministry of teaching/comforting/counseling/advocating is introduced

---

[1392] Barrett, *Gospel according to Saint John*, 292-304.

[1393] Kok, "As the Father has sent me, I send you." 168-196.

[1394] Perry, *Biographical History*, 1-48; cf. Malina and Rohrbaugh, *Social-Science Commentary on the Gospel of John*; also see Thomaskutty, "Reading John's Gospel in the Nepali Context," 14-15.

[1395] See Thomaskutty, "Glo[b/c]alization and Mission[s]: Reading John's Gospel," 61-62.

[1396] See Thomaskutty, "Glo[b/c]alization and Mission[s]: Reading John's Gospel," 61-62.

[1397] *John 11-21*, Calvin's NT Commentaries, 55-152.

in a more extended way in chaps. 14-16.[1398] The need of the disciples to remain (*menein*) in Jesus (15:1-11; 17:1-26) and their movements in the world under the guidance of the parakletos are instructed in detail in this section (14:15-31; 15:26; 16:12).[1399] Another significant feature of the discourse is addressing the Holy Spirit as "Spirit of Truth."[1400] The mission of the parakletos or Spirit of Truth is teaching, guiding, counseling, and comforting the disciples.

The Spirit of God is still working in the day to day affairs of the church and that helps the church to be an active witness of the truth of God in the world.[1401] In the Bangladeshi context, the church should accept and acknowledge the affairs of the Holy Spirit and should go ahead in its mission activities. The mission of God can be actualized in a Johannine way by accepting the guidance of the Holy Spirit and by evangelizing/witnessing the truth to the outsiders. This can be done both through words and actions. The *kerygmatic*, *didactic*, *koinonic*, and *diakonic*[1402] mission models that the Johannine Jesus affirms can be considered as a paradigm in the Bangladeshi context.

The "Newness" Motif

The motif of "newness" in John is significant to reckon with. The theme of "new vine" symbolizes the aspect of "new joy." Jesus admonishes his disciples to abide in him (i.e., the Vine) and to love one another so that their joy may be complete. In 2:13-21, the narrator introduces the theme of "new temple" over against the established nature of the temple at Jerusalem. The theme of "new birth"[1403] in the conversation with Nicodemus is introduced as a requirement to see the kingdom of God (3:3-5).[1404] The theme of "new life" is introduced in the context of the healing of the royal man's son (4:46-54). This story as well works well within the narrative framework of John. The theme of "new

---

[1398] J. Joubert, "Johannine Metaphors/Symbols Linked to the Paraclete-Spirit and their Theological Implications," *Acta Theologica*, Vol. 27/1 (June 2007), 83-103.

[1399] See Chrys C. Caragounis, "'Abide in Me': The New Mode of Relationship between Jesus and His Followers as a Basis for Christian Ethics (John 15)," *Rethinking the Ethics of John: 'Implicit Ethics' in the Johannine Writings*, WUNT 291, eds. Jan G. van der Watt and Ruben Zimmerman, Vol. 3 (Tubingen: Mohr Siebeck, 2012), 250-263; Tasker, *John*, 163-88.

[1400] Joubert, "Johannine Metaphors/Symbols Linked to the Paraclete-Spirit and their Theological Implications," *Acta Theologica*, 83-103.

[1401] See Andreas J. Köstenberger, *The Missions of Jesus and the Disciples: According to the Fourth Gospel* (Grand Rapids: Eerdmans, 1998); also see Thomaskutty, "Glo[b/c]alization and Mission[s]: Reading John's Gospel," 62.

[1402] *Kerygmatic* means "proclamatory," *didactic* means "instructional," *koinonic* means "fellowship-oriented," and *diakonic* means "service-centered."

[1403] W. L. Kynes, "New Birth," *Dictionary of Jesus and the Gospels* (Leicester: InterVarsity Press, 1992), 574-576.

[1404] See Caragounis, "Kingdom of God/Heaven," *Dictionary of Jesus and the Gospels*, 417-430.

law" in chap. 5 is followed by the theme of "new bread" (6:22-59). The theme of "new light" in the tabernacles discourse (chaps. 7-8) is followed by the theme of "new sight" in chap. 9. Through these the narrator dynamically and symbolically introduces the "newness" motif over against the "old" things. Jesus and his eternal life perspectives should be presented as a "new paradigm" over against the traditional and "old" beliefs and practices of the Bangladeshi context. In that sense, John's Gospel can be used as an epitome for the Bangladeshi context in order to transform individuals, establishments and communities.[1405] Jesus as an agent of newness can persuade the masses of Bangladesh to leave the old and follow the harbinger of a new world order.

Other Concerns

Various other issues of the Bangladeshi context require radical transformation. Jesus' utterances and actions in the Gospel of John can be introduced to the contextual realities of the nation for a paradigm shift. In the context of substance abuse and immoral behavior of the people, Jesus' concern to provide living water (4:9-10) and bread of life (6:35-51) are significant. Jesus' message attunes human acumen toward the spiritual water and bread and can persuade the readers to leave the transient pleasures of this world. A context in which people face scarcity, Jesus' provision to turn water into wine can be introduced as a model of transformation. According to Jewish understanding, wine is a symbol of joy. In a context in which wine (or joy) was totally absent, Jesus turns water into wine and provides new wine (or new joy; 2:1-12). That is a phenomenal incident to be celebrated. In a context in which polygamy is widely practiced, Jesus' attitude toward a woman who have had already five husbands and at the moment a sixth illegal relationship is noticeable. Jesus accepts her as she is and attunes her acumen toward the savior of the world and also to the eternal life experience. In the Bangladeshi context, it is a unique model to adopt in the mission of liberation.

Jesus' concern for those who are in darkness is exemplified through the stories of Nicodemus (3:1-21), the invalid person (5:1-18), and the blind man (9:1-41). Jesus introduces himself as the light of the world (8:12; 9:5) for those who are in darkness. In this context, the light symbolism of John's Gospel can be used as a missional model in the Bangladeshi context. The model of Jesus as a teacher both at the public (chaps. 1-12) and at the private (chaps. 13-17) levels can be used in the Bangladeshi context in order to engage people both in the public and private arenas. While in the public ministry, Jesus' concern was missional transformation, in the private ministry, his concern was mostly pastoral edification.

[1405] See Thomaskutty, "Reading John's Gospel in the Nepali Context," 19-20.

In Bangladesh, both the missional and pastoral models are to be utilized for wider efficacy. As Jesus is introduced as a dialogue partner in the annals of John's narrative framework, in the Bangladeshi context, mission should be dialogical in nature.[1406] As John emphasizes the theme of belief and the resultant salvation, the eternal life experience should find meaning in our exegetical and hermeneutical endeavors in Bangladesh. The purpose statement of the Gospel aims at the following: "that you [the readers] may believe that Jesus is the Christ, the son of God, and that by believing you may have life in his name" (20:31). The life that Jesus provides, according to John, is not only spiritual, but also physical in the existential context. In that sense, salvation in John is holistic in every sense.

Conclusion

The Gospel of John provides hermeneutical stimulus for us not simply in the 'there and then' context, but also in the 'here and now' and 'everywhere and ever' contexts. In that sense, John's Gospel is globally significant. It has a message for the pluralistic Indian contexts, the American nationals, the European communities, the hill country of Nepal, and the Bangladeshis of our time. The messages of peace, love, faith-centered life, salvation, and the mission of God play significant roles in the life and the sustenance of the Bangladeshis. It liberates and transforms human communities with a holistic and gnomic impact. A missional hermeneutics is possible in the Bangladeshi context through crossing traditional boundaries of interpretation, creating ideological constellations in exegetical analyses, and building dialogical relationships between the biblical worldview and the contemporary worldview. This process will enable the contemporary reader of the Gospel of John in Bangladesh to direct the communities toward a 'third space.'[1407] This aspect of the Gospel of John is paradigmatic for the Bangladeshi communities in today's context.

[1406] See Thomaskutty, "Reading John's Gospel to the Nepali Context," 16-17.

[1407] See Soja, *Third Space*.

Bibliography

A

Abbott, E. A., 1906. *Johannine Grammar*. London: Adam and Charles Black.

________, 1905. *Johannine Vocabulary: A Comparison of the Words of the Fourth Gospel with Those of the Three*. London: Adam and Charles Black.

Allison, D. C., 1992. "Eschatology." *DJG*. Ed. Green, J. B. Downers Grove: IVP.

Alston, M., 2015. *Women and Climate Change in Bangladesh*. ASAA Women in Asia Series. London/New York: Routledge.

Anderson, P. N., 2011. *The Riddles of the Fourth Gospel: An Introduction to John*. Minneapolis: Fortress Press.

________, 2008. "From One Dialogue to Another: Johannine Polyvalence from Origins to Receptions." *Anatomies of Narrative Criticism: The Past, Present and Future of the Fourth Gospel as Literature*. Leiden/Boston: Brill.

________, 2007. "Bakhtin's Dialogism and the Corrective Rhetoric of the Johannine Misunderstanding Dialogue: Exposing Seven Crises in the Johannine Situation." *Bakhtin and Genre Theory in Biblical Studies 63*. Ed. Roland Boer. Atlanta: SBL.

Anderson, R. T., 1992. "Samaritans." *The Anchor Bible Dictionary*. Vol. 5. New York: Doubleday.

Arangadan, C., 1993. "Carey's Legacy of Bible Translation." *Carey's Obligation and India's Renaissance*. Eds. Daniel, J. T. K., and Hedlund, R. E. Serampore: Council of Serampore College.

Ashton, J., 1992. "Paraklete." *The Anchor Bible Dictionary*. Ed. Freedman, D. N. New York: Doubleday.

Asiedu-Peprah., 2001. *Johannine Sabbath Conflicts as Juridical Controversy*. Tübingen, Germany: Mohr Siebeck.

Athithan, A., 1989. *Linguistic Structures in Tamil, A Historical Study: The Grammar of Tolkappiyam and the Language of Pathinenkilkkanakku, A Comparative Study*. Madurai: Madurai Kamaraj University.

Attridge, H. W., 2008. "From Discord Rises Meaning: Resurrection Motifs in the Fourth Gospel." *The Resurrection of Jesus in the Gospel of John*. WUNT 222. Eds. Koester, C. R., and Bieringer, R. Tübingen: Mohr Siebeck.

Aune, D. E., 2003. "Dialogue." *The Westminster Dictionary of New Testament and Early Christian Literature and Rhetoric*. Louisville/London: Westminster John Knox Press.

________, ed., 1988. "Introduction." *Greco-Roman Literature and the New Testament*. Society of Biblical Literature. Atlanta: Scholars Press.

________, 1987. *The New Testament in Its Literary Environment*. Philadelphia: The Westminster Press, 1987.

B

Bailey, J. L., and Vander Broek, L. D., 1992. *Literary Forms in the New Testament: A Handbook*. Louisville: Westminster John Knox Press.

Bakhtin, M. M., 1984. *Speech Genres and Other Late Essays*. Theory and History of Literature 8. Minneapolis: University of Minnesota Press.

________, 1984. "Toward a Reworking of the Destoevsky's Book." *Problems of Dostoevsky's Poetics*. Theory and History of Literature 8. Minneapolis: University of Minnesota Press.

Baldick, C., 1990. *The Concise Oxford Dictionary of Literary Terms*. Oxford/New York: Oxford University Press.

Ball, D. M., 1996. *"I Am" in John's Gospel: Literary Function, Background, and Theological Implications*. Journal for the Study of the New Testament Supplement Series 124. Sheffield, England: Sheffield Academic Press.

Banerjee, T., 2001. "Growth and Development of Bengali Literature from Serampore." *Carey Day Souvenir*. Serampore: Serampore College.

Barr, J., 2004. *The Semantics of Biblical Language*. Eugene, Oregon: Wipf & Stock.

Barrett, C. K., 1982. *Essays on John*. London: SPCK.

Barry, J. G., 1970. *Dramatic Structure: The Shaping of Experience*. Berkeley, Los Angeles: University of California Press.

________, 1978. *The Gospel according to St. John*. London: SPCK.

Barth, G., 1994. "Pistis." *Exegetical Dictionary of the New Testament*. Vol. 3. Eds. Horst Balz and Gerhard Schneider. Grand Rapids: Eerdmans.

Bartholomä, P. F., 2010. *The Johannine Discourses and the Teaching of Jesus in the Synoptics: A Comparative Approach to the Authenticity of Jesus' Words in the Fourth Gospel*. A PhD Dissertation. Heverlee: The Evangelical Theological Faculty.

Barus, A., 2006. "John 2:12-25: A Narrative Reading." *New Currents through John: A Global Perspective*. Leiden/Boston: Brill.

Bauckham, R., 2011. *Jesus: A Very Short Introduction*. Oxford: University Press.

________, 2002. *Gospel Women: Studies of the Named Women in the Gospels*. Grand Rapids: Eerdmans.

________, 1998. "For Whom Were the Gospels Written?" *The Gospel for All Christians: Rethinking the Gospel Audience*. Grand Rapids: Eerdmans.

Beasley-Murray, G. R., 1999. *John*. Word Biblical Commentary. Vol. 36. Second Edition. Dallas/Nashville: Thomas Nelson.

________, 1992. "Synoptics and John." *Dictionary of Jesus and the Gospels*. Eds. J. B. Green and S. McKnight. Downers Grove: InterVarsity Press.

Beets, M. G. J., 1995. *The Voice of Reason: a Philosopher's Approach to St. John's Gospel*. Amsterdam: Hilversum.

Behm, 1967. "Parakletos." *Theological Dictionary of the New Testament*. Ed. and Tran. Geoffrey W. Bromiley. Grand Rapids: Eerdmans.

Beirne, M. M., 2003. *Women and Men in the Fourth Gospel: A Genuine Discipleship of Equals*. JSNT Supplement Series 242. London: Sheffield Academic Press.

Belal, A. R., 2008. *Corporate Social Responsibility Reporting in Developing Countries: The Case of Bangladesh*. London/New York: Routledge.

Bennema, C., 2012/2013. "A Comparative Approach to Understanding Character in the Gospel of John." *Character and Characterization in the Gospel of John*. Ed. Skinner, C.W. London/New Delhi/New York/Sydney: Bloomsbury: 36-58.

________, 2009. *Encountering Jesus: Character Studies in the Gospel of John*. Bangalore: Primalogue.

________, 2005. *Excavating John's Gospel: A Commentary for Today*. Delhi: ISPCK.

Bernard, J. H., 1929. *A Critical and Exegetical Commentary on the Gospel according to St. John*. International Critical Commentary. Vol. 2. New York: Charles Scribner's Sons.

Berney, C. F., 1925. *The Poetry of Our Lord*. Eugene, Oregon: Wipf & Stock.

Bhattacharya, K., 2014. *Ravindranath Tagore: Adventure of Ideas and Innovative Practices in Education*. Springer Briefs in Education. Heidelberg/New York: Springer.

Bird, M. F., Evans, C. A., and Gathercole, S. J., eds., 2014. *How God Became Jesus: The Real Origins of Belief in Jesus' Divine Nature*. Grand Rapids: Zondervan.

Blenkinsopp, J., 2002. *Isaiah 40-55: A New Translation with Introduction and Commentary*. The Anchor Bible 19A. New Haven/London: The Anchor Yale Bible.

Blomberg, C. L., 2010. *A Handbook of New Testament Exegesis*. Grand Rapids: Baker Academic Press.

________, 2001. *The Historical Reliability of John's Gospel: Issues and Commentary*. Leicester: InterVarsity Press.

Bloomfield, L., 1935/2005. *Language*. Delhi: Motilal Banarsidass.

Blount, B. K., 1995. *Cultural Interpretation: Reorienting New Testament Criticism*. Minneapolis: Fortress Press.

Bodine, W. R., 1992. "Linguistics and Biblical Studies." *Anchor Bible Dictionary*. Vol. 4. New York: Doubleday.

Boismard, M. E., 1964. "Le Lavement des Pieds (John 13:1-17)." *RB* 71: 5-24.

________, 1957. *St. John's Prologue*. London: Blackfriars.

Bonney, W., 2002. *Caused to Believe: The Doubting Thomas Story at the Climax of John's Christological Narrative*. Leiden/Boston: Brill.

Booser, K. D., 1993. "The Literary Structure of John 1:1-18: An Examination of Its Theological Implications concerning God's Saving Plan through Jesus Christ." *Evangelical Journal* 16.

Borchert, G. L., 2002. *John 12-21*. The New American Commentary. Vol. 25B. Nashville: B & H Publishers.

________, 1996. *John 1-11*. The New American Commentary. Nashville, Tennessee: B & H Publishers.

Bosch, D. J., 1991/2006. *Transforming Mission: Paradigm Shifts in Theology of Mission*. Maryknoll: Orbis Books.

Bowman, J., 1975. *The Fourth Gospel and the Jews: A Study in R. Abika, Esther and the Gospel of John*. Pittsburgh: The Pickwick Press.

Boyd, R. M., 1969/2000. *An Introduction to Indian Christian Theology*. Delhi: ISPCK.

Brant, J. A., 2011. *John*. Paideia Commentaries on the New Testament. Grand Rapids, Michigan: Baker Academic.

________, 2004. *Dialogue and Drama: Elements of Greek Tragedy in the Fourth Gospel*. Peabody: Hendrickson.

Brashler, J. A., 1992. "Jesus, Brothers and Sisters of." *The Anchor Bible Dictionary*. Vol. 3. New York: Doubleday.

Brodie, T. L., 1993. *The Gospel according to John: A Literary and Theological Commentary*. New York/Oxford: Oxford University Press.

Brouwer, W., 2000. *The Literary Development of John 13:17: A Chiastic Reading*. SBLDS 182. Atlanta: SBL.

Brown, R. E., 2009. *An Introduction to the New Testament*. Bangalore: Theological Publications in India.

________, 1979. *The Community of the Beloved Disciple: The Life, Loves, and Hates of an Individual Church in New Testament Times*. New York: Paulist Press.

________, 1970. *The Gospel according to John XIII-XXI*. The Anchor Bible. Vol. 29A. Garden City: Doubleday.

________, 1966. *The Gospel according to John i-xii*. Vol. 1. Garden City, New York: Doubleday.

Bruce, F. F., 1983. *The Gospel of John: Introduction, Exposition and Notes*. Grand Rapids: Eerdmans.

Bruner, F. D., 2012. *The Gospel of John: A Commentary*. Grand Rapids: Eedrmans.

Bultmann, R., 1971. *The Gospel of John: A Commentary*. Ed. Beasley-Murray, G. R. Oxford: B. Blackwell/Philadelphia: Westminster.

________, 1968. "The *pistis* Group in the New Testament." *TDNT* 6. Ed. Gerhard Friedrich. Grand Rapids: Eerdmans.

________, 1963/1968. *The History of the Synoptic Tradition*. Tran. Marsh, J. Oxford.

________, 1958. *Jesus Christ and Mythology*. New York: Charles Scribner's Sons.

Burge, G. M., 1992. "Glory." *Dictionary of Jesus and the Gospels*. Leicester: InterVarsity Press.

________, 1992. "'I AM Sayings." *Dictionary of Jesus and the Gospels*. Eds. Green, J. B., and McKnight, S. Downers Grove: InterVarsity Press.

Burnett, F. W., 1993. "Characterization and Reader Construction of Characters in the Gospels." *Semeia* 63.

Burridge, R., 1992. *What are the Gospels?: a Comparison with Greco-Roman Biography*. Cambridge: Cambridge University Press.

Buss, M. J., 2007. "Dialogue in and among Genres." *Bakhtin and Genre Theory in Biblical Studies*. Ed. Boer, R. Atlanta: SBL.

Buth, R., 1992. "*Oun*, *De*, *Kai*, and Asyndeton in John's Gospel." *Linguistics and New Testament Interpretation: Essays on Discourse Analysis*. Ed. Black, D. A. Nashville: Broadman Press.

Byrne, B., 1991. *Lazarus: A Contemporary Reading of John 11:1-46*. Collegeville: The Liturgical Press.

C

Cabezón, J. I., 2017. *Sexuality in Classical South Asian Buddhism*. Studies in Indian and Tibetan Buddhism. Somerville: Wisdom Publications.

Caird, G. B., 1980. *The Language and Imagery of the Bible*. Philadelphia: The Westminster Press.

Calvin, J., 1553. *The Gospel of John 1-11*. Vol. 1. The John Calvin Bible Commentaries. North Charleston: Createspace.

Caragounis, C. C., 2012. "'Abide in Me': The New Mode of Relationship between Jesus and His Followers as a Basis for Christian Ethics (John 15)." *Rethinking the Ethics of John: 'Implicit Ethics' in the Johannine Writings*. WUNT 291. Eds. Van der Watt, J. G., and Zimmerman, R. Vol. 3. Tübingen: Mohr Siebeck.

________, 1992. "Kingdom of God/Heaven." *Dictionary of Jesus and the Gospels*. Leicester: InterVarsity Press.

Carey, S. P., 1923. *William Carey: The Father of Modern Missions*. London: Wakeman Trust.

Carson, D. A., 1996. *The Gagging of God: Christianity Confronts Pluralism*. Grand Rapids: Zondervan Academics.

________, 1991. *The Gospel according to John*. Leicester: IVP/Michigan: Eerdmans.

________, 1980. *The Farewell Discourse and Final Prayer of Jesus*. An Evangelical Exposition of John 13-17. Grand Rapids: Baker Academic Press.

Carter, W., 2008. *John and Empire: Initial Explorations*. New York/London: T & T Clark.

________, 2006. *John: Storyteller, Interpreter, Evangelist*. Peabody: Hendrickson Publishers.

________, 1990. "The Prologue and John's Gospel: Function, Symbol and the Definitive Word." *Journal for the Study of the New Testament* 39.

Chakkuvarackal, J., 2003. "Toward a Spirit-centered Biblical Theology: The 'From Below' Aspects of the Holy Spirit." *Bangalore Theological Forum*. Vol. 35/1.

________, 2003. "The Serampore Mission and the Linguistic Renaissance in India." *Bangalore Theological Forum*. Vol. XXXV/2.

________, 2002. "Important Issues in the Translation of the Bible in the Indian Context." *Bangalore Theological Forum*. Vol. XXXIV/1.

________, 2002. "Glimpses of the 'Feminine' in Indian Religion and Society: A Christian Perspective." *Indian Journal of Theology*. Vol. 44/1-2.

________, 2002. "'Woman-Power' in the Canonical Gospels: A Paradigm for the Modern Patriarchal Societies." *Bangalore Theological Forum*. Vol. 34/2.

Charlesworth, J. H., 1995. *The Beloved Disciple: Whose Witness Validates the Gospel of John*. Valley Forge: Trinity Press International.

Chatman, S., 1978. *Story and Discourse: Narrative Structure in Fiction and Film*. Ithaca: Cornell University Press.

Chatterjee, S. K., 1993. "William Carey and the Linguistic Renaissance in India." *Carey's Obligation and India's Renaissance*. Eds. Daniel, J. T. K., and Hedlund, R. E. Serampore: Council of Serampore College.

Chennattu, R. M., 2017. "Life in Abundance: Johannine Ethics from an Indian Feminist Perspective." *The Bible and Catholic Theological Ethics*. Eds. Chan, Y. S. L., Keenan, J. F., and Zacharias, R. New York: Orbis Books.

Chow, E. N., and Berheide, C. W., eds., 1996. *Women, the Family, and Policy: A Global Perspective*. Atlanta, Georgia: Scholars Press.

Claassens, L. J. M., 2003. "Biblical Theology as Dialogue: Continuing the Conversation on Mikhail Bakhtin and Biblical Theology." *JBL* 122/1.

Clements, K., 1983. "Sola Fide." *A New Dictionary of Christian Theology*. Eds. Richardson, A., and Bowden, J. London: SCM Press.

Collins, P. M., 2016. *Christian Inculturation in India*. New York: Routledge.

Collins, R. F., 1990. *These Things Have been Written: Studies on the Fourth Gospel*. Louvain Theological and Pastoral Monographs 2. Louvain: Peeters Press.

________, 1976. "Representative Figures in the Fourth Gospel, I and II." *The Downside Review* 94.

Coloe, M. L., 2013. "The Mother of Jesus: A Woman Possessed." *Character Studies in the Fourth Gospel*. Eds. Hunt, S. A., Tolmie, D. F., and Zimmermann, R. Grand Rapids: Eerdmans.

________, 1989/2007. *Dwelling in the Household of God: Johannine Ecclesiology and Spirituality*. Collegeville, Minnesota: Liturgical Press.

________, 1976. "Sources in the Shadows: John 13 and the Johannine Community." *New Currents Though John: A Global Perspective*. Eds. Lozada, F., and Thatcher, T. Atlanta: Society of Biblical Literature.

Cone, J., 1975/1997. *Speaking the Truth: Ecumenism, Liberation, and Black Theology*. Second Edition. Maryknoll: Orbis Books.

Conzelmann, H., 1969. *An Outline of the Theology of the New Testament*. New Testament Library. London: SCM Press.

Cotterell, P. and Turner, M. *Linguistics and Biblical Interpretation*. Leicester and Downers Grove: InterVarsity Press, 1989.

Culpepper, R. A., 1991. "The Johannine *hypodeigma*: A Reading of John 13:1-38." *Semeia* 53: 133-152.

________, 1998. *The Gospel and Letters of John*. Nashville: Abingdon.

________, 1983. *Anatomy of the Fourth Gospel: A Study in Literary Design*. Philadelphia: Fortress Press.

________, 1980. "The Pivot of John's Prologue." *NTS 27*.

D

Das, S., 2001. *Christian Ethics and Indian Ethos*. Delhi: ISPCK.

Davids, P. H., 1992. "Rich and Poor." *Dictionary of Jesus and the Gospels*. Leicester: InterVarsity Press.

Davies, M., 1992. *Rhetoric and Reference in the Fourth Gospel*. JSNT Supplement Series 69. Sheffield: JSOT Press.

De, S. K., 2018. *History of Bengali Literature in the Nineteenth Century, 1800-1825*. Chizine Publications.

DeConick, A. D., 2001. *Voices of the Mystics: Early Christian Discourse in the Gospels of John and Thomas and Other Ancient Christian Literature*. JSNTSS 157. Sheffield: Sheffield Academic.

De Jonge, M., and Van Duyne, H. M. J., 1978. *Taal en Teken: Ontmoetingen met Jezus in het Evangelie van Johannes*. Nijkerk: Uitgeverij G. F. Callenbach b. v.

De Klerk, J. C., and Schnell, S. W., 1987. *A New Look at Jesus: Literary and Sociological-Historical Interpretations of Mark and John*. Pretoria: J. L. van Schaik.

Delon, M., ed., 2001. "Grammar." *Encyclopedia of the Enlightenment*. Vol. 1. London/New York: Routledge.

Denning-Bolle, S., 1992. *Wisdom in Akkadian Literature: Expression, Instruction, Dialogue*. Leiden: Ex Oriente Lux.

deSilva, D.A., 2000. "Patronage." *Dictionary of NT Background*. Eds. Evans, C.A., and Porter, S.E. Downers Grove, Illinois: InterVarsity Press.

Devanandan, P. D., and M. M., Thomas, M. M., eds., 1962. *Problems of Indian Democracy*. Bangalore: CISRS.

________, 1960. *Christian Participation in Nation Building*. Bangalore: The National Christian Council of India and the CISRS.

Devasahayam, V., ed., 1996. *Dalit Theology.* Chennai: Gurukul Lutheral Theological College.

Dodd, C. H., 1963. *Historical Tradition in the Fourth Gospel*. Cambridge: University Press.

________, 1952/1953/1960. *The Interpretation of the Fourth Gospel*. Cambridge: University Press.

Domeris, W. R., 1983. "The Johannine Drama." *Journal of Theology for Southern Africa* 42.

Dorner, I. A., 1970. *History of Protestant Theology*. Vol. 1. Eugene: Wipf & Stock.

Duke, P., 1985. *Irony in the Fourth Gospel*. Atlanta: John Knox.

Dunn, J. D. G., 1977/1990. *Unity and Diversity in the New Testament: An Inquiry into the Character of Earliest Christianity*. Second Edition. London: SCM Press.

E

Eco, U., 1979. *The Role of the Reader: Explorations in the Semiotics of Texts*. Bloomington/London: Indiana University Press.

Elam, K., 1980. *The Semiotics of Theatre and Drama*. London/New York: Methuen.

Ellis, P. F., 1984. *The Genius of John: A Composition Critical Commentary on the Fourth Gospel*. Collegeville, Minnesota: Liturgical Press.

Engberg-Pedersen, T., 2015. "A Question of Genre: John 13-17 as *Paraklēsis*." *The Gospel of John as Genre Mosaic*. Ed. Larsen, K. B. Gōttingen: Vandenhoeck & Ruprecht: 283-302.

Esler, P. F., and Piper, R. A., 2006. *Lazarus, Mary and Martha: Social-Scientific Approaches to the Gospel of John*. Minneapolis: Fortress Press.

F

Fitzmyer, J. A., 1997. *The Semitic Background of the New Testament*. Grand Rapids: Eerdmans.

________, 1981/1991. "Kurios." *EDNT*. Vol. 2. Grand Rapids: Eerdmans.

Flemming, D., 2005. *Contextualization in the New Testament: Patterns for Theology and Mission*. Illinois: InterVarsity Press.

Fogle, J., 2007. *One Flesh: A Biblical Perspective on the Permanence of Marriage*. Eugene, Oregon: Wipf & Stock.

France, R. T., 1992. "Faith." *Dictionary of Jesus and the Gospels*. Eds. Green, J. B., McKnight, S., and Marshall, I. H., Downers Grove: InterVarsity Press.

Funk, R. F., 1988. *The Poetics of Biblical Narrative*. Sonoma, California: Polebridge Press.

G

Gardner-Chloros, P., 2009. *Code-Switching*. Cambridge: Cambridge University Press.

Garver, E., 1994. *Aristotle's Rhetoric: An Art of Character*. Chicago/London: The University of Chicago Press.

Gaventa, B. R., 1999. *Mary: Glimpses of the Mother of Jesus*. Minneapolis: Fortress Press.

Gench, F. T., 2007. *Encounters with Jesus: Studies in the Gospel of John*. Louisville/London: Westminster John Knox Press.

Genette, G., 1980. *Narrative Discourse: An Essay in Method*. Ithaca, NY: Cornell University Press.

George, K. M., 1992. *Modern Indian Literature and Anthology*. Vol. 1. New Delhi: Sahitya Akademi.

George, T., 2013. *Theology of the Reformers*. Nashville: B & H Publishing Group.

Gibson, A., 2001. *Biblical Semantic Logic: A Preliminary Analysis*. The Biblical Seminar 75. London/New York: Sheffield Academic Press.

Gillman, F. M., 1992. "James, Brother of Jesus." *The Anchor Bible Dictionary*. Vol. 3. New York: Doubleday.

Gine, P. C., 2001. *'Nomos' in Context: Philo, Galatians and the Bengali Bible*. Delhi: ISPCK.

Green, J. B., 1988. *The Death of Jesus: Tradition and Interpretation in the Passion Narrative*. Eugene, Oregon: Wipf & Stock.

Greimas, A. J., and Courtés, J., 1979/1982. *Semiotics and Language: An Analytical Dictionary*. Bloomington: Indiana University Press.

Grelot, P., 2006. *The Language of Symbolism: Biblical Theology, Semantics, and Exegesis*. Peabody: Hendrickson Publishers.

Gromacki, R. G., 1974. *New Testament Survey*. Grand Rapids: Baker Book House.

Gundry, R. H., 1964. "The Language Milieu of First-Century Palestine." *Journal of Biblical Literature* 83.

Gupta, R. K. D., 1993. "William Carey and Bengali Grammar." *Carey's Obligation and India's Renaissance*. Eds. Daniel, J. T. K., and Hedlund, R. E. Serampore: Council of Serampore College.

Guthrie, D., 1990. *New Testament Introduction*. Fourth Revised Edition. Downers Grove: InterVarsity Press.

Guthrie, W. K. C., 1975. *A History of Greek Philosophy*. Vol. 4. Cambridge: University Press.

Gutiérrez, G., 1988. *A Theology of Liberation: History, Politics, and Salvation*. Maryknoll: Orbis Press.

H

Haenchen, E., 1984. *A Commentary on the Gospel of John chapters 7-21*. Vol. 2. Philadelphia: Fortress Press.

Hahn, F., 1963. *Theologie Des Neuen Testaments: Band I*. Tübingen: Mohr Siebeck.

Halliday, M. A. K., 1978. *Language as Social Semiotic: The Social Interpretation of Language and Meaning*. Baltimore: University Park.

Harnack, A. V., 1982. "Ubes das Verhaltnis des Prologs des Vierten Evangeliums." *Zeitschrift fur Theologie und Kirche* 2.

Harris, E., 1994. *Prologue and Gospel: The Theology of the Fourth Evangelist*. Sheffield: Sheffield Academic Press.

Harris, M. J., 1992. *Jesus as God: The New Testament Use of Theos in Reference to Jesus*. Eugene, Oregon: Wipf & Stock.

Haskins, S., 1993. "Apostola Apostolorum." *Mary Magdalene: Myth and Metaphor*. New York: Penguin Press.

Hays, R. B., 1996. *The Moral Vision of the New Testament: Community, Cross, New Creation: A Contemporary Introduction to NT Ethics*. New York: Harper Collins.

Heever, V. D., 1992. "Theological Metaphors and the Metaphors of John's Gospel." *Neotestamentica* 26/1.

Hellholm, D., 1986. "The Problem of Apocalyptic Genre and the Apocalypse of John." *Semeia 36: 'Early Christian Apocalypticism, Genre and Social Setting.'* Decatur, Georgia: SBL/Scholars Press.

Henderson, I. H., 1996. *Jesus, Rhetoric and Law*. BINS 20. Leiden: Brill.

Hendriksen, W., 1954. *Exposition of the Gospel according to John*. New Testament Commentary. Grand Rapids: Baker.

Herman, V., 1995. *Dramatic Discourse: Dialogue as Interaction in Plays*. London/New York: Routledge.

Hernando, J.D., 2014. "Episodes of Personal Encounter: Inquiry into John's Christology." *But These are Written . . . Essays on Johannine Literature in Honor of Professor Benny C. Aker*. Eds. Keener, C. S., Crenshaw, J. S., and Daniel May, J. Eugene, Oregon: Pickwick Publications.

Hezser, C., 2016. "The Torah Versus Homer: Jewish and Greco-Roman Education in Late Roman Palestine." *Ancient Education and Early*

Christianity. Library of New Testament Studies 533. Eds. Hauge, M. R., and Pitts. London/New York: Bloomsbury T & T Clark.

Hiebert, D. E., 2003. *An Introduction to the New Testament*. Three Volume Collection. Waynesboro: Gabriel Publishing.

Hill, B. R., Knitter, P., and Madges, W., 2004. *Faith, Religion, and Theology: A Contemporary Introduction*. Mystic: Twenty-Third Publications.

Hochman, B., 1985. *Character in Literature*. Ithaca: Cornell University Press.

Hock, R. F., and O'Neil, E. N., eds., 1986. *The Chreia in Ancient Rhetoric*. Vol. 1: The Progymnasmata, Text and Translations 27. Atlanta: Scholars Press.

Hoeck, A., 2012. "The Johannine Paraklete: Herald of the Eschaton." *J. Biblic. Pneumatological Res. 4*.

Holquist, M., 1990. *Dialogism: Bakhtin and His World*. London: Routledge.

Hornby, A. S., 1948/2000. *Oxford Advanced Learner's Dictionary*. Sixth Edition. Oxford: University Press.

Howard-Brook, W., 1997. *John's Gospel and the Renewal of the Church*. Maryknoll: Orbis.

Howard, W. F., 1952. *The Gospel according to St. John*. The Interpreter's Bible. Vol. VIII. New York/Nashville: Abingdon Cokesbury Press.

Howarth, D., 2000. *Discourse, Concepts in Social Sciences*. Buckingham/ Philadelphia: Open University Press.

Huie-Jolly, M., 2002. "Maori 'Jews' and a Resistant Reading of John 5:10-47." *John and Postcolonialism: Travel, Space and Power*. Eds. Dube, M.W., and Staley, J.L. London/New York: Sheffield Academic Press.

Hurtado, L. W., 1992. "Christ." *DJG*. Downers Grove: InterVarsity Press.

________, 1992. "God." *DJG*. Downers Grove: InterVarsity Press.

I

Ibrahim, M., 2002. *Providing Education for Out-of-School Youth in Bangladesh*. London: Commonwealth Secretariat.

Ihenacho, D. A., 2001. *The Community of Eternal Life: The Study of the Meaning of Life for the Johannine Community*. Lanham/New York/ Oxford: University Press of America.

Inbody, T., 2005. *The Faith of the Christian Church: An Introduction to Theology*. Grand Rapids/Cambridge: Eerdmans.

International Monetary Fund Staff Council Reports., 2005. Bangladesh: Poverty Reduction Strategy Paper. IMF Country Report.

Irudaya, R., 2003. "Attitudes and Approaches Employed in the Dialogue of Jesus with the Samaritan Woman II: Their Relevance to Interreligious Dialogue Today." *VJTR 67*.

J

Jackelén, A., 2016. "Justification and Justice: The Relevance of Lutheran Distinctions in Church and Society." *Global Perspectives on the Reformation: Interactions between Theology, Politics and Economics*. The Lutheran World Federation 61. Eds. Burghardt, A., and Sinn, S. Leipzig: Evangelische Verlagsanstalt.

Jaffe, A., ed., 2009. *Stance: Sociolinguistic Perspective*. Oxford: Oxford University Press.

Jahan, R., 1975. "Women in Bangladesh." *Women for women, Bangladesh 1975*. Dhaka: Women for Women Research and Study Group.

Jeyaraj, D., 2009. "Indian Participation in Enabling, Sustaining, and Promoting Christian Mission in India." *India and the Indianness of Christianity*. Ed. Young, R. F. Grand Rapids: Eerdmans.

________, 2006. *Bartholomäus Ziegenbalg, the Father of Modern Protestant Mission: An Indian Assessment*. Delhi: ISPCK; Chennai: Gurukul.

Johnson, D. H., 1992. "Life." *DJG*. Ed. Green, J. B. Downers Grove: IVP.

________, 1992. "Logos." *DJG*. Eds. Green, J. B., and McKnight, S. Illinois: IVP.

Jones, E. S., 2006. *The Word Became Flesh*. Abingdon Press.

________, 2005. *The Christ of the Indian Road*. Kessinger Publishing.

________, 1946. *Abundant Living*. Hodder & Stoughton.

Jones, J. K., 2008. *The Women in the Gospel of John: The Divine Feminine*. St. Louise: Chalice Press.

Jongeneel, J. A. B., 1995/2006. *Philosophy, Science, and Theology of Mission in the 19th and 20th Centuries: A Missiological Encyclopedia I: Philosophy and Science of Mission*. Frankfurt: Peter Lang.

Joubert, J., 2007. "Johannine Metaphors/Symbols Linked to the Paraclete-Spirit and Their Theological Implications." *Acta Theologica* 27/1. South Africa: The University of the Free State.

Junge, M., 2016. "Global Perspective on the Reformation." *Global Perspectives on the Reformation: Interactions between Theology, Politics and Economics*. The Lutheran World Federation 61. Eds. Burghardt, A., and Sinn, S. Leipzig: Evangelische Verlagsanstalt.

K

Kabir, R., 1997. "Cyclones: The Days After." *DHA News*. Geneva: Department of Humanitarian Affairs.

Kanagaraj, J. J., 2006. "Use of New Testament Metaphors in Mission." *Transformation* 23/2.

________, 2005. *The Gospel of John: A Commentary*. Secunderabad: OM Books.

________, 2001. "The Profiles of Women in John: House-Bound or Christ-Bound." *Bangalore Theological Forum*. Vol. 33/2. Bangalore: United Theological College.

Kapoor, K., 2005. *Dimensions of Pānini Grammar: The Indian Grammatical System*. D. K. Printworld.

Kappen, K., 2002. *Jesus and Culture*. Delhi: ISPCK.

________, 2002. *Jesus and Society*. Delhi: ISPCK.

Kärkkäinen, V-M., 2003. *An Introduction to the Theology of Religions: Biblical, Historical and Contemporary Perspectives*. Downers Grove: IVP Academic.

Käsemann, E., 1969. "The Structure and Purpose of the Prologue to John's Gospel." *New Testament Questions of Today*. Philadelphia: Fortress.

Keener, C. S., 2003. *The Gospel of John: A Commentary*. Vol. 2. Peabody: Hendricksen Publishers.

________, 2003. *The Gospel of John: A Commentary*. Vol. 1. Peabody: Hendricksen Publishers.

________, 1993. *The IVP Bible Background Commentary: New Testament*. Downers Grove, Illinois: InterVarsity Press.

Kelly, A. J., and Moloney, F. J., 2003. *Experiencing God in the Gospel of John*. New York/Mahwah: Paulist Press.

Kennedy, G. A., 1984. *New Testament Interpretation through Rhetorical Interpretation*. Chapel Hill: The University of North Carolina Press.

Kermode, F., 1987. "John." *The Literary Guide to Bible*. Eds. Alter, R., and Kermode, F. Harvard: University Press.

________,1986. "St. John as Poet." .....

________,1979. The Genesis of Secrecy: ......

Koester, C. R., 2013. "Theological Complexity and the Characterization of Nicodemus in John's Gospel." *Characters and Characterization in the Gospel of John*. London/New York: Bloomsbury.

________, 2008. "Jesus' Resurrection, the Signs, and the Dynamics of Faith in the Gospel of John." *The Resurrection of Jesus in the Gospel of John*. WUNT 222. Eds. Koester, C. R., and Bieringer, R. Tübingen: Mohr Siebeck.

________, 1995. *Symbolism in the Fourth Gospel: Meaning, Mystery, Community*. Minneapolis: Fortress Press.

________, 1990. "'The Savior of the World' (John 4:42)." *Journal of Biblical Literature*. Vol. 109/4: 665-680.

Koester, H., 1980. *Introduction to the New Testament: History and Literature of Early Christianity*. Vol. 2. Philadelphia: Fortress Press.

Kok, K., 2010. "As the Father has sent me, I send you: Towards a missional-incarnational ethos in John 4." *Moral Language in the New Testament: The Interrelatedness of Language and Ethics in Early Christian Writings*. Tübingen: Mohr Siebeck.

Köstenberger, A. J., 2004. *John*. BECNT. Grand Rapids: Baker Academic Press.

________, 2001. *Studies on John and Gender: A Decade of Scholarship*. Studies in Biblical Literature 38. New York/Oxford: Peter Lang.

________, 1999. *Encountering John: The Gospel in Historical, Literary, and Theological Perspective*. Grand Rapids, Michigan: Baker Book House.

________, 1998. *The Mission of Jesus and the Disciples: According to the Fourth Gospel*. Grand Rapids, Michigan: Eerdmans.

Kutscher, S., and Werning, D. A., eds., 2014. *On Ancient Grammars of Space: Linguistic Research on the Expression of Spatial Relations and Motion in Ancient Languages*. Berlin/Boston: Walter de Gruyter.

Kynes, W. L., 1992. "New Birth." *Dictionary of Jesus and the Gospels*. Leicester: InterVarsity Press.

Kysar, R., 2007. *John the Maverick Gospel*. Third Edition. Louisville/London: Westminster John Knox Press.

________, 2005. "The Whence and Whither of the Johannine Community." *Life in Abundance: Studies of John's Gospel in Tribute to Raymond E. Brown*. Ed. Donahue, J. R. Collegeville, Minnesota: Liturgical Press: 65-81.

________, 1992. "John, the Gospel of." *ABD*. Freedman, D. N. Vol. 3. New York: Doubleday.

L

Ladd, G. E., 1974. *A Theology of the New Testament*. Grand Rapids: Eerdmans.

Lamb, D. A., 2014. *Text, Context, and the Johannine Community: A Sociolinguistic Analysis of the Johannine Writings*. New York/London: Bloomsbury T & T Clark.

Larsen, K. B., 2008. *Recognizing the Stranger: Recognition Scenes in the Gospel of John*. Vol. 93. Leiden/Boston: Brill.

Larsson, T., 2001. *God in the Fourth Gospel: A Hermeneutical Study of the History of Interpretation*. Coniectanea Biblica: New Testament Series 35. Stockholm, Sweden: Almqvist and Wiksell International.

Lausberg, H., 1998. *Handbook of Literary Rhetoric: A Foundation for Literary Study*. Leiden/Boston/Köln: Brill.

Law, V., 2003. *The History of Linguistics in Europe: From Plato to 1600*. Cambridge: Cambridge University Press.

Lehmann, E. A., 1956. *It Began at Tranquebar*. Madras: CLS.

Leidig, E., 1979. *Jesu Gespräch mit der Samaritanerin und Weitere Gespräche im Johannesevangelium*. Band XV der Theologischen Dissertationen, herausgegeben von Bo Reicke. Basel: Friedrich Reinhardt Kommissionsverlag.

Liebau, H., 2018. *Cultural Encounters in India: The Local Co-workers of Tranquebar Mission, 18th to 19th Centuries*. London/New York: Routledge.

Lincoln, A. T., 2005. *The Gospel according to Saint John*. BNTC. London: Continuum.

Lindars, B., Edwards, B. R., and Court, J. M., *The Johannine Literature: With an Introduction by R. Alan Culpepper*. Sheffield: Sheffield Academic Press.

Lindars, B., 1972. *The Gospel of John*. New Century Bible. London: Oliphants.

"Linguistics," 1963. *Encyclopaedia Britannica*. Vol. 14. Chicago: William Benton.

Loader, W., 2019. "Competing Spiritualities: Reflections on John 6 in Global Perspective." *Matthew, Paul and Others: Asian Perspectives on New Testament Themes*. Innsbruck: University Press.

________, 2017. *Jesus in John's Gospel: Structure and Issues in Johannine Christology*. Grand Rapids: Eerdmans.

Louw, J. P., 1992. "Reading a Text as Discourse." *Linguistics and New Testament Interpretation: Essays on Discourse Analysis*. Ed. Black, D. A. Nashville, Tennessee: Broadman Press.

Lührmann, D., 1992. "Faith." *The Anchor Bible Dictionary*. Vol. 2. New York/London: Doubleday.

M

MacDonald, G., 2012. *The Evangelical Universalist*. Second Edition. Eugene, Oregon: Cascade Books, 2012).

Malbon, E. S., 1991. "Ending at the Beginning." *Semeia 52*.

Malina, B. J., and Rohrbaugh, R. L., 1998. *Social-Science Commentary on the Gospel of John*. Minneapolis: Fortress Press.

Mangalwadi, V and R., 1993/1999. *The Legacy of William Carey: A Model for the Transformation of a Culture*. Wheaton: Crossway Books.

Maniparampil, J., 2004. *Reading the Fourth Gospel: A Text Book for Students of Gospel according to John*. Bangalore: Claretian Publications.

Manns, F., 1988. *John and Jamnia: How the Break Occurred between Jews and Christians c. 80-100 CE*. Jerusalem: Franciscan Printing Press.

Marak, K.C., and Jacob, P.S., ed., 2000. *Conversion in a Pluralistic Context: Perspectives and Perceptions*. Pune/Delhi: CMS/ISPCK.

Maranhão, T., 1990. *The Interpretation of Dialogue*. Chicago: University of Chicago.

Martin, R. P., 1975. *New Testament Foundations: A Guide for Christian Studies*. Vol 1: The Four Gospels. Exeter: The Paternoster Press.

Martin, T. J., 1976/1988. *Living Words: Studies in Dialogues about Religion*. Atlanta, Georgia: Scholars Press/Oxford: Oxford University Press.

Martyn, J. L., 1968. *History and Theology in the Fourth Gospel*. Nashville: Abingdon.

Marxsen, W., 1959/1969. *Der Evangelist Markus* (Eng. Tr. *Mark the Evangelist*).

Massey, J., 1996. *Roots of Dalit History, Christianity, Theology, and Spirituality*. Delhi: ISPCK.

McKim, D. K., 1996. *Westminster Dictionary of Theological Terms*. Louisville/London: Westminster John Knox Press.

McKinzie, G., 2017. "The Hermeneutics of Incarnational Evangelism: Reading the Gospel with Peruvians." *Fuller Magazine: Reading Scripture Globally* 8.

McReynolds, K., 1995. "Mary, the Mother of Jesus." *New International Encyclopedia of Bible Characters*. Ed. Gardner, P. D. Grand Rapids: Zondervan: 444-447.

Meeks, W. A., 1972. "The Man from Heaven in Johannine Sectarianism." *JBL* 91.

Merenlahti, P., 2016. "You Cannot Serve God and Wealth." *Global Perspectives on the Reformation*. Leipzig: Evangelische Verlagsanstalt.

Merkle, B. L., 2009. *Why Elders? A Biblical and Practical Guide for Church Members*. Grand Rapids: Kregel Publications.

Michael, S. M., 2014. *Challenges to Christian Mission: Problems and Prospects*. Pune: Ishvani Kendra.

Michaels, J. R., 2010. *The Gospel of John*. NICNT. Grand Rapids: Eerdmans.

________, 1992. "Commandment." *Dictionary of Jesus and the Gospels*. Downers Grove: InterVarsity Press.

Millard, A., 2000/2001. *Reading and Writing in the Time of Jesus*. The Biblical Seminar 69. Sheffield: Sheffield Academic Press.

Milne, B., 1993. *The Message of John*. The Bible Speaks Today Series. Vol. 4. Nottingham: InterVarsity Press.

Mittra, S., and Kumar, B., eds., 2004. *Encyclopedia of Women in South Asia*. Vol. 3. Delhi: Kalpaz Publications.

Mlakuzhyil, G., 1987. *The Christocentric Literary Structure of the Fourth Gospel*. AnBib 117. Rome: Pontificio Instituto Biblico.

Modrak, D. K., 2001. W. *Aristotle's Theory of Language and Meaning*. Cambridge: Cambridge University Press.

Moloney, F. J., 2013. *Love in the Gospel of John: An Exegetical, Theological, and Literary Study*. Grand Rapids: Baker Academic.

________, 1989/1998. *The Gospel of John*. Sacra Pagina Series 4. Collegeville, Minnesota: Liturgical Press.

________, 1996. *Signs and Shadows: Reading John 5-12*. Minneapolis: Fortress Press.

Moore, S. D., 1989. *Literary Criticism and the Gospels: The Theoretical Challenge*. New Haven/London: Yale University Press.

Mopsuestia, T., 2010. *Commentary on the Gospel of John*. ACT. Downers Grove, IVP.

Morris, L., 1995. *The Gospel according to John*. NICNT. Revised Edition. Grand Rapids: Eerdmans.

________, 1992. "Love." *Dictionary of Jesus and the Gospels*. Downers Grove: InterVarsity Press.

________, 1971. *The Gospel according to John*. Grand Rapids: Eerdmans.

Motyer, S., 1997. *Your Father the Devil? A New Approach to John and 'the Jews.'* Paternoster Biblical and Theological Studies. UK: Paternoster Press.

Mukherjee, S., 1998/1999. *A Dictionary of Indian Literature*. Vol. 1. Hyderabad: Orient Longman.

Mukhopadhayay, I., 1993. "William Carey's Contributions for the Promotion of Sanskritic Studies." *Carey's Obligation and India's Renaissance*. Eds. Daniel, J. T. K., and Hedlund, R. E. Serampore: Council of Serampore College.

Murshid, G., 1992. *Kalantare Bangla Gadya*. Calcutta: Ananda Publishers.

N

Namita., 2000. *A New Paradigm for Evangelization in the Third Millennium: In the Light of Mission in the Gospel according to St. John and Early Upanishads*. Bangalore: St. Peter's Pontifical Institute Publications.

Newbigin, L., 1989. *The Gospel in a Pluralist Society*. Grand Rapids: Eerdmans.

Neyrey, J. H., 2009. *The Gospel of John in Cultural and Rhetorical Perspective*. Grand Rapids, Michigan: Eerdmans.

________, 2007. *The Gospel of John*. The New Cambridge Bible Commentary. Cambridge: Cambridge University Press.

________, 2003. "What's Wrong with This Picture? John 4, Cultural Stereotypes of Women, and Public and Private Space." *A Feminist Companion to Bible*. Ed. Levine, A-J. Vol. 1. Cleveland: The Pilgrim Press.

Nicklin, T., 1906. *Book Review: Abbott's Johannine Vocabulary*. The Classical Review. Vol. 20/3: 172-175.

Nida, E. A., 1980. *A Handbook on the Gospel of John*. New York: United Bible Societies.

O

Oberdorfer, B., 2016. "Law and Gospel and Two Realms: Lutheran Distinctions Revisited." *Global Perspectives on the Reformation: Interactions between Theology, Politics and Economics*. The Lutheran World Federation 61. Burghardt, A., and Sinn, S. Leipzig: Evangelische Verlagsanstalt.

O'Day, G. R., 1986. *Irony and the Johannine Theology of Revelation: An Investigation of John 4*. Ann Arbor, Michigan: University Microfilms International.

Ong, H. T., 2016. *The Multilingual Jesus and the Sociolinguistic World of the New Testament*. Leiden/Boston: Brill.

Ormerod, N. J., and Clifton, S., 2009. *Globalization and the Mission of the Church: Ecclesiastical Investigations* 6. England: T & T Clark.

Østenstad, G., 1998. *Patterns of Redemption in the Fourth Gospel*. Studies in the Bible and Early Christianity. Vol. 38. Lewiston/Queenston/Lampeter: The Edwin Mellen Press.

P

Painter, J. P., 1993. *The Quest for the Messiah: The History, Literature and Theology of the Johannine Community*. Nashville: Abingdon.

Painter, R. J., 2011. *The Gospel of John: A Thematic Approach*. Eugene: Wipf & Stock.

Pamment, M., 1983. "The Fourth Gospel's Beloved Disciple." *ExpTim* 94.

Pandey, S., 2003. *Christianity in Nepal: Unity in Diversity*. Kathmandu: National Churches Fellowship of Nepal.

Parsenios, G. L., 2010. *Rhetoric and Drama in the Johannine Lawsuit Motif.* WUNT 258. Tübingen, Germany: Mohr Siebeck.

________, 2005. *Departure and Consolation: The Johannine Farewell Discourses in Light of Greco-Roman Literature*. Leiden/Boston: Brill.

Paschal, R. W., 1992. "Service." *Dictionary of Jesus and the Gospels*. Eds. Green, J. B., and McKnight, S. Downers Grove: InterVarsity Press: 747-751.

Peace, R.V., 1999. *Conversion in the New Testament: Paul and the Twelve*. Grand Rapids, Michigan/Cambridge, UK: Eerdmans.

Pepin, J., 1987. "Logos." *The Encyclopedia of Religion*. Vol. 9. Ed. Eliade, M. New York: McMillan Publishing Company.

Perry, C., 2000. *A Bibliographical History of the Church in Nepal*. Third Edition. Kathmandu: Nepal Church History Project.

Petersen, N. R., 1993. *The Gospel of John and the Sociology of Light: Language and Characterization in the Fourth Gospel*. Eugene, Oregon: Wipf & Stock.

Popp, T., 2013. "Thomas: Question Marks and Exclamation Marks." *Character Studies in the Fourth Gospel: Narrative Approaches to Seventy Figures in John*. WUNT. Tübingen: Mohr Siebeck.

Porter, S. E., 2015. *Linguistic Analysis of the Greek New Testament: Studies in Tools, Methods, and Practice*. Grand Rapids: Baker Academic Press.

________, 2000. "Greek of the New Testament." *Dictionary of New Testament Background*. Eds. Evans, C. A., and Porter, S. E. Downers Grove: InterVarsity Press.

________, 1992. "Joseph, Husband of Mary." *The Anchor Bible Dictionary*. Vol. 3. New York: Doubleday.

Powell, M. A., 1990. *What Is Narrative Criticism?* Minneapolis: Fortress Press.

Press, G. A., 2007. *Plato: A Guide for the Perplexed*. London: Continuum.

Purvis, J. D., 1992. "Samaria (City)." *The Anchor Bible Dictionary*. Vol. 5. New York: Doubleday: 914-921.

Q

Quast, K., 1991/1996. *Reading the Gospel of John: An Introduction*. New York/Mahwah: Paulist Press.

R

Ralte, R., 2014. *Hindus and Hindutva: Hindu Tolerance, Hindutva Exclusivism, Emergence of Assertive Hinduism*. Taiwan: PTCA.

Ray, N. R., 1993. "William Carey—A Linguist with a Difference." *Carey's Obligation and India's Renaissance*. Eds. Daniel, J. T. K., and Hedlund, R. E. Serampore: Council of Serampore College: 155-158.

Redman, J. C. S., 2012/2013. "Eyewitness Testimony and the Characters in the Fourth Gospel." *Character and Characterization in the Gospel of John*. Ed. Skinner, C. W. London/New Delhi/New York/Sydney: Bloomsbury: 59-78.

Reed, W. L., 1993. *Dialogues of the Word: The Bible as Literature According to Bakhtin*. Oxford/New York: Oxford University Press.

Reinhartz, A., 2003. "Women in the Johannine Community: An Exercise in Historical Imagination." *A Feminist Companion to John*. Vol. 2. London/New York: Sheffield Academic Press.

________, 1992. *The Word in the World: The Cosmological Tale in the Fourth Gospel*. SBLMS 45. Atlanta: Scholars Press.

Renn, S. D., 2005. *Expository Dictionary of Bible Words*. Peabody: Hendrickson Publishers.

Rensberger, D. K., 1988. *Johannine Faith and Liberating Community*. Philadelphia: Westminster.

Resseguie, J. L., 2005. *Narrative Criticism of the New Testament: An Introduction*. Grand Rapids: Baker Academic.

________, 2001. *The Strange Gospel: Narrative Design and Point of View in John*. Biblical Interpretation Series 56. Leiden/Boston/Köln: Brill.

Ricoeur, P., 1988. *Time and Narrative*. Chicago/London: The University of Chicago Press.

________, 1976. *Interpretation Theory: Discourse and the Surplus of Meaning*. Fort Worth: Texas Christian University Press.

Ridderbos, H., 1987/1997. *The Gospel of John: A Theological Commentary*. Grand Rapids, Michigan: Eerdmans Publishing Company.

Ringe, S. H., 1999. *Wisdom's Friends: Community and Christology in the Fourth Gospel*. Louisville, Kentucky: Westminster John Knox Press.

Ritzer, G., 2010. *Globalization: The Essentials*. UK: Wiley-Blackwell.

Robbins, V. K., 1988. "The Chreia." *Greco-Roman Literature and the NT*. Ed. Aune, D. E. Atlanta, Georgia: Scholars Press/SBL.

Robertson, R., 2017. *John: The Jewish Gospel*. Blommington: Thomas Nelson & Zondervan.

Robertson, S., 2009. *Approaching Religion in a Pluralistic Context*. Bangalore: BTESSC/SATHRI.

Robinson, J. A. T., 1962/1963. "The Relation of the Prologue to the Gospel of St. John." *NTS* 9.

________, 1962. *Twelve New Testament Studies*. Naperville, Illinois: Alec R. Allenson.

Robinson, R., and Clarke, S., eds., 2003. *Religious Conversion in India: Modes; Motivations, and Meanings*. New Delhi: Oxford University Press.

Roth, J. D., 2016. "Just Peacemaking: Christian Pacifism as a Form of Political Responsibility." *Global Perspectives on the Reformation: Interactions between Theology, Politics and Economics*. The Lutheran World Federation 61. Eds. Burghardt, A., and Sinn, S. Leipzig: Evangelische Verlagsanstalt.

Roy, J. M., 2002. *Love to Hate: America's Obsession with Hatred and Violence*. New York: Colombia University Press.

S

Sadananda, D. R., 2004. *The Johannine Exegesis of God: An Exploration into the Johannine Understanding of God*. Berlin/New York: Walter de Gruyter.

Samartha, S. J., 1991. *One Christ, Many Religions*. Maryknoll: Orbis Books.

Schaeffer, J. D., 1988. "Dialogue." *Dictionary of Literary Themes and Motifs, A-J*. New York: Greenwood Press.

Schnackenburg, R., 1980. *The Gospel according to Saint John*. 3 Vols. London: Burns & Oates.

Schneiders, S. M., 2002. "To See or Not to See: John 9 as a Synthesis of the Theology and Spirituality of Discipleship." *Word, Theology and Community in John*. St. Louise, Missouri: Chalice Press.

________, 1999. *Written That You May Believe: Encountering Jesus in the Fourth Gospel*. New York: A Herder & Herder Book.

Schnelle, U., 2008. "Cross and Resurrection in the Gospel of John." *The Resurrection of Jesus in the Gospel of John*. WUNT 222. Eds. Koester, C. R., and Bieringer, R. Tübingen: Mohr Siebeck.

________, 2007. *Theology of the New Testament*. Grand Rapids: Baker Academic.

Scholer, D. M., 1992. "Women." *DJG*. Downers Grove: InterVarsity Press: 880-887.

Schoneveld, J., 1990. "Torah in the Flesh: A New Reading of the Prologue of the Gospel of John as a Contribution to a Christology without Anti-Judaism." *The New Testament and Christian-Jewish Dialogue: Studies in Honor of Daniel Flusser*, *Immanuel* 24/25.

Schweizer, A., 1841. *Das Evangelium Johannes nach seinem innern Werthe und seiner Bedeutung für das Leben Jesu kritisch untersucht*. Leipzig.

Segovia, F. F., 1991. *The Farewell of the Word: The Johannine Call to Abide*. Minneapolis: Fortress Press.

Sen, A. K., 2002. "Bengali Language, Literature and William Carey." *Carey Day Souvenir*. Serampore: Serampore College.

Senior, D., 1991. *The Passion of Jesus in the Gospel of John*. Collegeville: Liturgical Press.

Shillington, V. G., 2012. "The Spirit-Paraclete as Jesus' Alter Ego in the Fourth Gospel (John 14-16)." *Vis. Winn. Man 13.1*.

Simhadri, Y. C., 1989. Development of Emerging World Youth. Delhi: Mittal Publications.

Skinner, C. W., 2012. "Introduction." *Characters and Characterization in the Gospel of John*. London: Bloomsbury T & T Clark.

________, 2009. *John and Thomas—Gospels in Conflict? Johannine Characterization and the Thomas Question*. PTMS. Eugene: Pickwick Publications.

Smalley, S., 1998. *John: Evangelist & Interpreter*. Second Edition. Carlisle: Paternoster Press.

Smith, A. C., 1999. "Carey, William." *Bibliographical Dictionary of Christian Missions*. Ed. Anderson, G. H. Grand Rapids: Eerdmans.

Smith, D. M., 1999. *John*. Abingdon New Testament Commentary. Nashville: Abingdon Press.

Soja, E. W., 1996. *Third Space: Journeys to Los Angeles and Other Real-and-Imagined Places*. Malden, Mass.: Wiley.

Spivey, J. T., 2002. "The Hermeneutics of the Medieval and Reformation Era." *Biblical Hermeneutics: A Comprehensive Introduction to Interpreting Scripture*. Eds. Corley, B., Lemke, S. W., and Lovejoy, G. I. Second Edition. Nashville: B & H Publishing Group.

Spivey, R. A., and Smith, D. M., 1969. *Anatomy of the New Testament: A Guide to Its Structure and Meaning*. London: The Macmillan Company.

Stagg, E & F., 1978. *Woman in the World of Jesus*. Philadelphia: The Westminster Press.

Stambaugh, J. E., and Balch, D. L., 1986. *The New Testament in Its Social Environment*. Philadelphia: The Westminster Press.

Stanton, G., 2002. *The Gospels and Jesus*. Oxford Bible Series. Second Edition. Oxford: Oxford University Press.

Stegall, T. L., 2009. *The Gospel of Christ: A Biblical Response to the Crossless Gospel Regarding the Contents of Saving Faith*. Milwaukee: Grace Gospel Press.

Stein, R. H., 2008. *Mark*. Baker Exegetical Commentary on the New Testament. Grand Rapids: Baker Academic Press.

Stibbe, M. W. G., 1994. *John's Gospel*. New Testament Readings. London/New York: Routledge.

________, 1993. *John*. Readings: A New Biblical Commentary. Sheffield: Sheffield Academic Press.

Stockhammer, M., ed., 1963. *Plato Dictionary*. London: Vision Press.

Story, C. I. K., 1997. *The Fourth Gospel: Its Purpose, Pattern, and Power*. Shippenburg: Ragged Edge Publication.

Stube, J. C., 2006. *A Greco-Roman Rhetorical Reading of the Farewell Discourse*. LNTS 309. London/New York: T & T Clark International.

Swain, S. R., 2008. *Father, Son, and Spirit: The Trinity and John's Gospel*. New Studies in Biblical Theology. Downers Grove: InterVarsity Press.

Swartley, W. M., 2013. *John*. BCBC. Harrisonburg and Waterloo: Herald Press.

Sylva, D., 2013. *Thomas—Love as Strong as Death: Faith and Commitment in the Fourth Gospel*. London/New York: Bloomsbury T & T Clark.

T

Talbert, C. H., 1992. *Reading John: A Literary and Theological Commentary on the Fourth Gospel and the Johannine Epistles*. New York: Crossroad.

Tasker, R. V. G., 1960/1988. *The Gospel according to St. John: An Introduction and Commentary*. Leicester, England: InterVarsity Press/Grand Rapids, Michigan: Eerdmans Publishing Company.

Terry, M. S., 1999. *Biblical Hermeneutics*. Eugene: Wipf & Stock.

Thielman, F., 1991. "The Style of the Fourth Gospel and Ancient Literary Critical Concepts of Religious Discourse." *Persuasive Artistry: Studies in New Testament Rhetoric in Honor of George A. Kennedy: Journal for the Study of the New Testament Supplement Series 50*. Ed. Watson, D. F. Sheffield: JSOT Press.

Thiselton, A. C., 1992. *New Horizons in Hermeneutics: The Theory and Practice of Transforming Biblical Reading*. Grand Rapids: Zondervan Publishing House.

Thomas, M. C., 2018. "Orientalism," published in https://www.britannica.com/science/Orientalism-cultural-field-of-study. Accessed on 14th Oct. 2018.

Thomas, M. M., and Devanandan, P. D., eds., 1960. *Christian Participation in Nation Building: The Summing Up of a Corporate Study on Rapid Social Change*. Bangalore: NCCI and CISRS.

Thomas, V. V., 2017. "The Impact of Reformation on Indian Church and Mission: A Historical Perspective." *SATHRI Journal*. Vol. 11/1.

Thomaskutty, J., 2019. "A Dialogue between 'the Eastern' and 'the Western' in New Testament Scholarship: A Proposal." *Bangalore Theological Forum* LI/1.

________, 2019. "The Spirit's Witness in John and the Apocalypse." *Mission After Pentecost: The Witness of the Spirit from Genesis to Revelation*. Ed. Yong, A. Grand Rapids: Baker Academic Press.

________, 2019. "Re-reading the Gospel of John in the light of William Carey's Linguistic Methods." *Serampore Mission: Perspectives in Contexts*. Delhi: ISPCK.

________, 2018. *Saint Thomas the Apostle: New Testament, Apocrypha, and Historical Traditions*. Jewish and Christian Texts Series 25. London/ New York: Bloomsbury T&T Clark.

________, 2017. "Reading John's Gospel as a Jewish-Christian Conflict Narrative: A Paradigm for Contemporary India." *Religious Freedom and Conversion in India*. Eds. John, A. V., Longkumer, A., and Kumar, N. A. Bengaluru: SAIACS Press.

________, 2017. "Biblical Interpretation in the Global-Indian Context." *Fuller Magazine*. Issue 8. Pasadena: Fuller Theological Seminary: 64-68.

________, 2017. "Reading John's Gospel in the Bangladeshi Context." *Journal of Asian Evangelical Theology*. Vol. 21/1-2. March-September 2017: 53-72.

________, 2016. "Reading John's Gospel in the Nepali Context." *Journal of Asian Evangelical Theology*. Vol. 20. No. 1. March 2016: 5-21.

________, 2015/1. *Dialogue in the Book of Signs: A Polyvalent Analysis of John 1:19-12:50*. Biblical Interpretation Series 136. Leiden/Boston: Brill.

________, Sep. 2013-Mar. 2015/2. "Dialogical Nature of John's Prologue." *Union Biblical Seminary Journal*. Vol. 8.2-9.1:1-17.

________, 2015/3. "Reading John's Gospel to the Nepali Context." *Nepali Theological Journal*. South Korea: ACTS College: 63-82.

________, Jan.-June 2015/4. "Glo[b/c]alization and Mission[s]: Reading John's Gospel." *New Life Theological Journal*. Vol. 5.1: 56-77.

________, 2014. Proefschrift: *The Nature and Function of Dialogue in the Book of Signs*. Nijmegen: Radboud Universiteit Nijmegen.

Thompson, M. M., 2015. *John: A Commentary*. The New Testament Library. Louisville: Westminster John Knox Press.

________, 2008. "Children in the Gospel of John." *The Child in the Bible*. Grand Rapids: Eerdmans.

________, 1992. "John, Gospel of." *Dictionary of Jesus and the Gospels*. Eds. Green, J. B., and McKnight, S. Downers Grove: InterVarsity Press: 368-383.

Tobin, T. H., 1992. "Logos." *The Anchor Bible Dictionary*. Vol. 4. Ed. Freedman, D. N. New York: Doubleday.

Tolmie, D. F., 1999. *Narratology and Biblical Narratives: A Practical Guide*. San Francisco/London: International Scholars Publications.

Torrey, C. C., 1993. *The Four Gospels: A New Translation*. New York: Harper.

Tovey, D., 2007. *Jesus, Story of God: John's Story of Jesus*. Adelaide: ATF Press.

Trebilco, P., 2012. *Self-designations and Group Identity in the New Testament*. Cambridge: University Press.

Tsoukas, H., and Knudsen, C., eds., 2003. *The Oxford Handbook of Organizational Theory: Meta-Theoretical Perspectives*. Oxford: Oxford University Press.

Turner, M. M. B., 1992. "Holy Spirit." *Dictionary of Jesus and the Gospels*.

Turner, N., 1963-1976. *A Grammar of New Testament Greek*. Vol. 3: Syntax; Vol. 4: Style. Edinburgh: T & T Clark.

V

Valentine, S. R., 1996. "The Johannine Prologue—a Microcosm of the Gospel." *Evangelical Quarterly* 68.

Van Aarde, A. G., 2009. "Narrative Criticism." *Focusing on the Message: New Testament Hermeneutics, Exegesis, and Methods*. Pretoria: Protea: 381-418.

Van Belle, G., 1994. *The Signs Source in the Fourth Gospel: Historical Survey and Critical Evaluation of the Semeia Hypothesis*. Bibliotheca Ephemeridum Theologicarum Lovaniensium CXVI. Leuven: University Press.

Van der Watt, J. G., 2012. "Narrative Analysis and Ethics." *Unpublished Document.* Nijmegen: Radboud Universiteit.

________, 2010. "Ethics through the Power of Language: Some Explorations in the Gospel according to John." *Moral Language in the New Testament*. Eds. Zimmermann, R., and Van der Watt, J. G. Vol. 2. Tübingen: Mohr Siebeck: 139-167.

________, 2009. "Repetition and Functionality in the Gospel according to John." *Repetitions and Variations in the Fourth Gospel: Style, Text, Interpretation*. Eds. Van Belle, G., Labahn, M., and Maritz, P. Leuven: Uitgeverij Peeters: 87-108.

________, 2007. *An Introduction to the Johannine Gospel and Letters*. T&T Clark Approaches to Biblical Studies. New York: T&T Clark.

________, 2007. "I Am the Bread of Life: Imagery in John 6:32-51." *Acta Theologica* 27/2.

________, 2000. *Family of the King: Dynamics of Metaphor in the Gospel according to John*. Boston: Brill.

________, 1995. "The Composition of the Prologue of John's Gospel: The Historical Jesus Introducing Divine Grace." *Westminster Theological Journal* 57.

Vanhoozer, K. J., 1998. *Is There a Meaning in this Text? The Bible, the Reader and the Morality of Literary Knowledge*. Leicester: Apollos.

Van Kooten, G. H., 2005. *The Creation of Heaven and Earth: Re-Interpretations of Genesis 1 in the Context of Judaism, Ancient Philosophy, Christianity, and Modern Physics*. Leiden/Boston: Brill.

Varghese, J., 2009. *The Imagery of Love in the Gospel of John*. Roma: Gregorian & Biblical Press.

Vashum, Y., 2011. *Tribal Theology and the Bible: A Search for Contextual Relevance*. Jorhat: Tribal Study Center/Eastern Theological College.

Vellanickal, M., 1977. *The Divine Sonship of Christians in the Johannine Writings*. Rome: Biblical Institute Press.

Verghese, B. K., 2014. *Let There be India! Impact of the Bible on Nation Building*. Chennai: WOC Publishing/Mumbai: Media Concerns.

Visotzky, B. L., 2005. "Methodological Considerations in the Study of John's Interaction with First Century Judaism." *Life in Abundance: Studies of John's Gospel in Tribute to Raymond E. Brown, S. S.* Collegeville, Minnesota: Liturgical Press.

Voigt, G., 1991. *Licht-Lieve-Leben: Das Evangelicum nach Johannes*. Gottingen: Vandenhoeck & Ruprecht.

Von Wahlde, U. C., 2010. *The Gospel and Letters of John*. Vol. 2. Grand Rapids: Eerdmans.

W

Waetjen, H. C., 2005. *The Gospel of the Beloved Disciple: A Work in Two Editions*. London: T & T Clark.

Wallace, D. B., 1996. *Greek Grammar Beyond the Basics*. Grand Rapids: Zondervan.

Walters, M., 1995. *Globalization*. UK: Routledge.

Warren, A., and Wellek, R., 1955. *Theory of Literature*. London: Jonathan Cape.

Watson, D. F., 1992. "Chreia/Aphorism." *Dictionary of Jesus and the Gospels*. Eds. Green, J. B., McKnight, S., and Marshall, I. H. Illinois: InterVarsity Press.

Wead, D. W., 1970. *The Literary Devices in John's Gospel*. Basel: Friedrich Reinhardt Kommissionsverlag.

Webb, S. H., 2012. *Jesus Christ, Eternal God: Heavenly Flesh and the Metaphysics of Matter*. Oxford/New York: Oxford University Press.

Wenham, J. W., 1965. *The Elements of New Testament Greek*. Cambridge: University Press.

White, J. L., 1988. "Ancient Greek Letters." *Greco-Roman Literature and the New Testament*. Ed. Aune, D. E. Atlanta: Scholars Press: 85-105.

Wilkins, M. J., 1992. "Disciples." *Dictionary of Jesus and the Gospels*. Eds. Green, J. B., and McKnight, S. Downers Grove: InterVarsity Press: 176-182.

Williamson, H. G. M., 1992. "Sanhedrin." *DJG*. Downers Grove: InterVarsity Press: 724-728.

Windham, J. P., 1995. *At the Top of the World: Let's Travel to Nepal Together*. Windows on the World Series 3. Tampa: Global Age Publishing.

Windisch, H., 1968. *The Spirit-Paraclete in the Fourth Gospel*. Minneapolis: Fortress Press.

Wingate, A., 1997/1999. *The Church and Conversion: A Study of Recent Conversions to and from Christianity in the Tamil Area of South India*. Delhi: ISPCK.

Wise, M. O., 1992. "Languages of Palestine." *Dictionary of Jesus and the Gospels*. Eds. Green, J. B., and McKnight, S. Downers Grove: InterVarsity Press: 434-444.

Witherington, B., 1995. *John's Wisdom: A Commentary on the Fourth Gospel*. Louisville: Westminster John Knox Press.

________, 1992. "Lord." *Dictionary of Jesus and the Gospels*. Eds. Green, J. B., and McKnight, S. Downers Grove: InterVarsity Press: 484-492.

________, 1988. *Women in the Earliest Churches*. Cambridge: Cambridge University Press.

Wright, C. J. H., 2006. *The Mission of God: Unlocking the Bible's Grand Narrative*. Downers Grove: InterVarsity Press.

Y

Yong, T. T., and Rahman, M. M., 2013. "Introduction: Diaspora Engagement and Development in South Asia." *Diaspora Engagement and Development in South Asia*. Eds. Yong, T. T., and Rahman, M. M.

Index of Ancient Sources

Old Testament

Genesis

1 59, 287
1:1 46
2:7 108
8:8-12 98
24:34-67 9
49 192

Exodus

3:14 83
12:46 136
16:4 30

Numbers

9:12 136
21:9 30

Deuteronomy

6:4-9 104
18:18 179

Joshua

22-24 192

1 Samuel

2:8 78

2 Kings

17:27-31 179

1 Chronicles

28-29

Job

18:18 78

Psalms

9:8 78
18:15 78
22:18 30
24:1 78
33:8 78
34:20 136
50:12 78
77:16 102
77:20 102
96:13 78

Proverbs

5:15-18 99
8:31 78

Song of Songs

4:12-15 99

Isaiah

5 161
6:10 30
9:2 98
13:11 78
24:4 78
27:6 78
32:15-18 98
40-55 199, 264
44:3-5 98, 99
52:13-53:12 199
61:1 98

Jeremiah

10:12 78

Ezekiel

36:25-27 98
36:26-27 99

Joel

2:28-32 99

Nahum

1:5 78

Zechariah

12:10 99, 136
13:7 30
14:8 102

New Testament

Matthew

1-2 174
8:5-13 32
10:1-42 192
10:24 203
12:42 176
13:56 176
16:26 78
18:7 78
20:20-28 203
24-25 192
26:15 183
27:11-14 32

Mark

1-8 199
3:31-32 176
4:10-20 192
6:3 174, 176
6:7-13 192
8:14-21 192
8:27-33 192
8:36 78
9:1-13 192
9:33-41 192
10:23-45 192
10:35-45 203
10:45 199, 204
13 192, 193
14-15 193
14:3-42 192
14:12 193
15:2-5 32

Luke

1-2 174
8:19-20 176
10:38-42 180
10:39 181
10:40 183
10:41 181
22:15 193
22:24-28 203
23:2-4 32

John

1-12 44, 241, 257, 259
1:1-18 xii, 7, 39, 42, 45, 47, 50, 51, 56, 82, 111, 161
1:1-13 48
1:1-5 xii, 10, 42
1:1-3 111
1:1-2 44, 46, 49
1:1 xvi, 6, 10, 52, 80, 87, 137, 141
1:2 52
1:3-5 44, 46
1:3 44, 49, 82, 111
1:4-5 6, 10, 49
1:4 6, 10, 46
1:5 5, 33, 47
1:6-9 46, 119
1:6-8 44, 49
1:6 230
1:7 46, 112
1:9-18 49
1:9-11 10
1:9-10 44, 51
1:9 vii, 13, 46, 111
1:10-11 46, 47, 94, 114
1:10 46
1:11 44, 82, 116
1:12-16 47
1:12 5, 6, 13, 44, 111, 112, 212
1:13 33, 44
1:14 6, 10, 44, 46, 48, 80, 82, 246
1:15 44, 119
1:16-17 111
1:16 44
1:17 26, 44, 105
1:18 10, 13, 44, 80, 87
1:19-12:50 xiv, 53, 102, 103, 109, 165
1:19-2:12 xii, 8, 56, 58, 59, 63, 64, 119
1:19-34 56, 246
1:19-28 33, 55
1:19-21 26

1:19 8, 33
1:23 30, 67
1:26-27 119
1:26 10, 116
1:29-34 119
1:29 7, 99
1:31 99
1:32-35 98
1:32 99
1:33 7, 99
1:34 98, 99
1:37 230
1:38 7
1:39 26
1:40-42 140
1:41 99, 120, 158, 247
1:42 120, 230
1:43 230
1:45 67, 87, 99, 120, 177, 230, 247
1:47 33
1:49 7, 99, 120, 247
2:1-12 63, 64, 87, 259
2:1-11 10, 11, 12, 50, 55, 56, 63, 83, 99, 121, 155, 161, 176, 234, 236, 237, 250, 255, 256
2:1-5 173, 174, 175, 176, 186
2:6-7 26
2:6 67
2:8 26
2:9 26
2:10 7
2:11 67, 121, 211, 213, 214, 215
2:12-25 50, 57, 174
2:13-22 xii, 8, 56, 58, 99, 121, 122, 242, 258
2:16-18 26, 67
2:17 26, 30
2:19-22 161
2:19 67
2:21 10
2:22 67, 80, 112, 113, 214
2:23 212, 213, 214, 215
3:1-21 xii, 8, 56, 57, 58, 59, 230, 259
3:1-10 56, 57, 120
3:3-5 100, 242, 258
3:3 13, 99, 161
3:5 10, 13, 99
3:6 33, 100
3:8 7, 100
3:10-15 116, 117
3:11-21 57
3:11 34, 212
3:13-14 254
3:14 30
3:15-18 118
3:15-16 6, 215
3:15 10, 211
3:16-17 51, 104, 211
3:16 7, 10, 13, 80, 114, 216, 254
3:17-21 80
3:17 87
3:18 10, 34, 80, 112, 211, 212, 215, 216
3:19-20 6
3:19 51, 114
3:20-21 34
3:22-36 8, 56, 57, 58, 119
3:23-25 26
3:28 67
3:30 119
3:31-36 7
3:31-32 34
3:31 33
3:33 80
3:34 87
3:35 80
3:36 33, 118, 211, 215
4:1-42 xii, xvi, 8, 50, 57, 58, 59, 89, 145, 146, 155, 173, 186, 230, 234, 249, 251
4:4-26 32, 177, 178
4:7-26 7, 9
4:7-15 10, 56, 146, 150, 179
4:8-9 26, 120, 259
4:10 10, 259
4:12 148
4:13-14 67, 178
4:13 13
4:14-15 10, 120
4:14 7, 118
4:16-26 56, 57, 178, 179
4:16-18 146, 150, 178, 179
4:19-26 67, 146, 150, 179
4:19 84, 120
4:20 230
4:21-24 102
4:22 26
4:23 100, 117

4:24 7, 85, 100
4:25-26 84, 120, 158, 179
4:26 10, 179
4:29-30 180
4:31-38 56
4:31-34 10
4:34 83
4:36 118
4:38 87
4:39-42 177
4:39 10, 211, 212
4:41-42 112, 180
4:41 67, 212
4:42 10, 40, 84, 117, 120
4:43-54 8, 50, 55-56, 58, 64, 113
4:43 87
4:46-54 32, 63, 67, 83, 155, 161, 214, 230, 234, 237, 242, 249, 256, 258
4:53-54 213
4:53 67, 113, 120, 230, 214, 215
5:1-47 xii, 8, 58, 59, 64, 242, 259
5:1-18 63, 83, 165, 230, 234, 237, 249, 256, 259
5:1-9 10, 64, 237
5:9-13 56
5:10-47 56
5:16 47
5:18 47, 69, 166
5:19-29 80
5:23 87
5:24 118, 214, 215
5:26 80
5:37 80, 112
5:38 214
5:39 118
5:42 114
5:43 104, 114, 212
5:44 80
5:46-47 113, 214
5:47-49 214
6:1-71 8, 50, 57, 58, 60, 249
6:1-21 60
6:1-15 xii, 10, 55, 63, 64, 65, 83, 122, 234, 235, 237, 255, 256
6:3-5 26
6:5-14 56
6:14 51, 67, 215
6:16-21 10, 56, 63, 64, 83, 161, 237, 256
6:22-71 xii, 60, 64, 233
6:22-59 55, 155, 161, 165, 236, 242, 255, 259
6:27 10, 118
6:28-29 211
6:29 112, 211
6:30-33 67, 214
6:31 30
6:33 6, 10
6:35-51 259
6:35 10, 65, 118, 166, 211
6:38 87
6:40 118, 211, 212, 215
6:41-59 10, 167
6:41 47
6:42 87, 165, 177
6:45 30
6:47 118, 212, 215
6:48 6, 10, 65, 166
6:51 10, 87
6:52 165
6:53-58 101, 118
6:55 87
6:57 80
6:59 26
6:60-66 165
6:63 101, 118
6:64 89
6:67-71 55, 56, 57, 120
6:68 118
6:69 113, 117, 119, 211, 213
6:70-71 89
6:71 26
7:1-8:59 57, 59, 164, 242, 249, 259
7:1-52 58
7:1-9 69, 175, 176, 177, 230
7:1 47
7:3 87
7:10-8:59 xii, 87, 165
7:11-24 167
7:14-36 56, 57, 165
7:14 xii
7:19-24 67, 165, 166
7:25 166
7:26-28 162
7:28-29 117
7:29 87

7:31 67, 211, 214, 215
7:35 28
7:37-39 102, 103, 109, 113, 118
7:37-38 10, 67, 165
7:38 10
7:40-44 60, 162, 165
7:45-52 69, 120, 211
7:45-42 60
8:12-59 58
8:12-20 56, 57, 165
8:12 6, 10, 51, 65, 161, 166, 236, 255, 259
8:13-47 167
8:14 116
8:16 83
8:17 30
8:19 116
8:21-30 56, 67, 113, 165, 211, 212, 213
8:23 33, 79
8:26 80
8:29 83
8:31-59 60, 80, 117, 165, 169, 214, 215
8:32 viii, 117
8:33-58 67
8:40 80
8:42 86, 114
8:44-45 33, 214
8:44 10
8:45 214
8:48 165
8:55 116
8:57-59 69
8:58 52, 165
9:1-10:21 58, 59, 63
9:1-41 xii, 11, 50, 64, 65, 83, 89, 159, 164, 165, 230, 233, 234, 236, 237, 242, 249, 255, 257, 259
9:1-12 10
9:1-7 55, 56, 57
9:4-6 26
9:5 6, 10, 51, 65, 161, 166, 236, 255, 259
9:8-12 55, 60, 165
9:9 26
9:11 121, 159
9:12-13 113
9:13-17 55, 113, 121, 159, 165
9:18-23 55, 165, 211
9:22 28, 157, 162, 232, 252
9:24-34 165
9:25 117
9:31-33 81, 113, 159
9:34 11, 28, 166, 232, 236, 252, 255
9:35-41 69, 113, 121, 212, 215
9:38 159
9:39-41 56, 165
9:39 6, 79
9:40-10:18 167
10:1-21 5
10:1-18 xii, 65, 230
10:1-11 9
10:1-7 233
10:4 117
10:7 10, 11, 65, 166, 236, 255
10:9 10, 11, 65, 166
10:10 119
10:11 10, 11, 65, 166, 233, 236, 255
10:14 11, 86, 117
10:15 86, 119
10:17 119, 254
10:19-42 69
10:19-21 60, 67, 165
10:22-42 58
10:22-39 55, 56, 57, 165, 167
10:22-23 xii
10:25 214
10:26-28 113
10:27 117
10:28 119
10:29 80
10:31 47
10:34 30
10:36 51
10:37-39 214
10:37 214
10:38 86, 214
10:40-42 215
10:42 212
11:1-12:11 126, 141
11:1-54 xii, 56, 58, 63, 64, 70, 161, 184, 249, 251
11:1-44 50, 83, 115, 155, 167, 173, 180, 184, 185, 186, 215, 234, 237, 257
11:7-16 56, 165

11:8	47
11:12-14	26
11:15	214
11:16	xvi, 121, 125, 126, 127, 128, 129, 130, 131, 132, 133, 138, 140
11:17-44	127
11:17-27	56, 128, 165, 181
11:21-27	67, 119, 126, 181, 182, 215
11:25	6, 10, 11, 65, 129, 166, 181, 233, 236, 255
11:27	51, 113, 211, 213, 215
11:28	119, 181
11:30-37	55, 128, 182, 184
11:38-44	56, 113, 182, 211
11:41	80
11:42	213, 214
11:45-53	157, 166, 212, 232, 252, 214
11:45-46	26, 69, 70, 128
11:47-50	64
11:54-57	55, 60
11:54-55	26
11:55-12:50	57, 58
11:57-12:1	26
12:1-11	50, 55, 56, 57, 212, 215
12:1-8	89, 121, 129, 173, 180, 181, 182, 183, 186, 230, 234, 235, 251
12:9-11	166
12:12-19:42	81
12:12-36	56, 165
12:13-15	67
12:12	26
12:13	30
12:19	79
12:20-36	81, 181, 241
12:20-22	84
12:22	26
12:23	70
12:25	119
12:27-36	167
12:31	78, 81
12:34	162
12:35	117
12:36-50	56, 69
12:37-38	113, 213, 214
12:38	30
12:40	30
12:42	28, 157, 162, 212
12:44-46	112, 119
12:46	10, 51
12:48	212
12:50	8, 119
13:1-20:31	125
13:1-17:26	xii, 102, 130, 141, 192, 241, 257, 259
13:1-30	50
13:1-20	xvii, 10, 130, 191, 192, 193-207, 231
13:1	115, 132, 254
13:2	89, 133
13:7	131
13:13-14	231
13:15-17	231, 232
13:16	87
13:17	117
13:18-30	12, 211, 213
13:18	30, 133
13:20	212
13:21	133
13:26-30	133
13:27	33
13:34-35	117
13:34	114
13:35	114
13:36	132
14-16	258
14:1	212
14:3	132
14:4	133
14:5	xvi, 121, 125, 130, 131, 132, 133, 138
14:6	vii, 6, 10, 11, 65, 105, 119, 125, 133, 166, 233, 255
14:7-8	86
14:8-14	133
14:9	131
14:10-11	86, 112, 211, 213, 214
14:12	213
14:15-31	215, 236, 238, 255, 258
14:15-17	85, 103, 104, 108, 115, 133, 218, 257
14:16	85, 104, 232
14:17-20	106
14:17	7, 117, 132
14:18-24	232
14:20	86
14:21	115

14:23	115
14:24	115, 236, 256
14:26	85, 87, 103, 105, 106, 133, 218, 232, 257
14:27	106
14:30-31	81
14:30	78, 81, 133
14:31	115, 131
15:1-15	9
15:1-11	5, 63, 232, 238, 255, 258
15:1-5	11, 236
15:1	10, 65, 166
15:4	215
15:5	10, 65, 166
15:7	215
15:9-10	115, 215
15:12-13	115, 119
15:14	115
15:15-20	130
15:17	115
15:18-25	133
15:21	118
15:25	30
15:26-27	85, 86, 103, 106, 108, 133, 257
15:26	87, 106, 218, 232, 236, 238, 255, 258
16:2-4	133
16:2	28, 157, 164, 232, 252
16:5	132
16:7-11	85, 86, 133, 218, 257
16:7	87, 232
16:8-11	81, 106
16:11	78, 133
16:12-15	103, 106, 133, 236, 238, 255, 257, 258
16:27-28	104, 116, 211, 213
16:28	51
16:30-31	112-113, 211, 213, 215
16:32	30, 83
16:33	47, 79
17:1-26	232, 238, 258
17:1-13	80
17:1-8	83
17:1-2	103
17:1	33, 132
17:2	119
17:3	119, 215
17:4	83
17:8	211, 212, 213
17:12	133
17:14	79
17:15	80, 133
17:17-18	86
17:18	51, 87, 94
17:20	212
17:21	51, 79, 86, 108, 113, 211, 213
17:23	51, 108, 116, 117, 232
17:24-25	254
17:24	116
17:26	116, 131, 215
18:1-19:42	xii, 166
18:1-8	89, 215
18:1-3	26
18:5-6	26
18:15-18	12
18:19-24	164
18:28-19:16	50, 157, 164
18:29-38	32
18:37	51, 104
19:11	81
19:17-22	157
19:24	30
19:25-27	12, 173, 174, 176, 186
19:25	183
19:26	87
19:28	30
19:31-37	136
19:34	10, 87
19:35	114
19:37	30
19:39	120
20-21	xvi
20:1-31	134, 138, 141, 251
20:1-29	xii
20:1-2	89, 173, 183, 186
20:3-10	12
20:8	114, 215
20:11-18	89, 120, 173, 183, 186
20:19	157
20:21-23	102, 107, 109
20:21	85, 87
20:24-28	xvi, 114, 120, 125, 134, 138, 139, 140, 141, 215
20:25	134, 135, 136, 137, 138
20:27	135, 136
20:28	xvi, 52, 87, 121, 134, 136, 138, 140, 141, 247

20:29 114, 125, 135, 215
20:30-31 xiii, 89, 213
20:31 113, 118, 211, 213, 214, 260
21:1-25 xii, 138, 139, 140, 141
21:1-3 10, 121
21:2 125, 138, 139, 141
21:5 139
21:6 139
21:7-8 139
21:15-17 116, 139
21:20-23 12
21:24-25 89
21:25 xiii

Acts

1:8 84, 107
1:14 174, 177
2:1-4 107

1 Corinthians

12:7-11 100
14:14-16 100

Ephesians

5:19-20 100

Colossians

1:16 111
3:16 100-101

Hebrews

11:7 78

1 John

2:1 85, 257
2:2 78
2:3-5 215
2:6 215
2:28 215
3:6 215
3:23 215
3:24 213, 215
4:12 80
4:16 214, 215
4:20 80
5:1 213, 215
5:4 211
5:5 213, 215
5:8 87
5:10 215
5:19 81
5:20 87

3 John

11 81

Revelation

2-3 140

Other Sources

Plato

Phaedrus
276c 62

Aristotle

Rhet
1.2.18, 1357b 63
1.2.1356a 68

Poet
6.24 72
11 69
1425b.13-14 69
1449b 73
1450a.34-35 166
1450b-1451b 73
1452b.8 166

Qumran Writings

1QH 3:9-10 99
1QS 3:18-25 104

Rabbinical Writings

b. Nid 31b 178
m. Abot 3:1 99
t. Jud 20:1-5 104

Apocryphal Writings

3 Enoch 6:3 99
Jub 25:14 104

Dionysius of Halicarnassus

Lysias 24 50
Thucyd 19 50

Eusebius

HE. 6:17.7 123

Quintilian

Inst
10.1.19-27 xiii
10.2.1-2 xiii, 73
10.2.18 61
10.2.27 xiii, 61

Index of Authors

A

Abbott, E. A. 25, 26
Allison, D. C. 217
Anderson, P. N. ix, x, 9, 10, 45, 55, 62, 68, 163, 164
Anderson, R. T. 177, 180
Arangadan, C. 20, 22
Ashton, J. 104
Asiedu-Peprah. 167
Athithan, A. 17
Attridge, H. W. 254
Aune, D. E. 33, 37, 38, 55

B

Bailey, J. L., and Vander Broek, L. D. 69
Bakhtin, M. M. 39, 45, 55, 68
Baldick, C. 69, 70, 72, 153, 154, 165
Ball, D. M. 233, 255, 256
Banerjee, T. 19
Barr, J. 27
Barrett, C. K. 25, 32, 53, 54, 86, 113, 131, 132, 135, 140, 230, 231, 237, 256, 257
Barry, J. G. 63
Barth, G. 211, 212, 213, 214, 215
Bartholomä, P. F. 60, 79
Barus, A. 57, 92
Bauckham, R. 38, 83, 180, 184
Beasley-Murray, G. R. 6, 7, 10, 28, 46, 53, 72, 81, 112, 116, 117, 118, 119, 120, 121, 157, 174, 177, 192, 193, 196, 200, 203, 204, 232, 237, 243, 246, 248, 256
Beets, M. G. J. 64
Behm. 103
Beirne, M. M. 185, 251
Belal, A. R. 250
Bennema, C. 13, 46, 49, 79, 87, 88, 113, 119, 120, 128, 135, 157, 161, 162, 175, 178, 185, 192, 199, 201, 202, 204
Bernard, J. H. 137, 199
Bhattacharya, K. 20
Bird, M. F., Evans, C. A., and Gathercole, S. J. 195
Blenkinsopp, J. 199
Blomberg, C. L. 24, 25, 27, 131, 139, 148, 157, 158, 174, 183, 201, 203, 232, 240, 241, 252
Bloomfield, L. 17
Blount, B. K. 93
Bodine, W. R. 16
Boismard, M. E. 44, 195
Bonney, W. 128, 129, 132, 134, 140
Booser, K. D. 49
Borchert, G. L. 101, 102, 103, 105, 106, 107, 158, 162, 163, 174, 176, 179, 181, 182, 192, 194, 197, 198, 205
Bosch, D. J. 80, 91, 222, 233
Bowman, J. 127
Boyd, R. M. 93, 222, 223, 225
Brant, J. A. 29, 48, 56, 69, 73, 74, 81, 98, 99, 100, 101, 103, 104, 105, 106, 113, 115, 116, 117, 121, 122, 132, 133, 135, 139, 166, 167, 181, 182, 183, 184, 185

Brashler, J. A. 176, 177
Brodie, T. L. 54, 167
Brouwer, W. 131
Brown, R. E. 28, 31, 38, 40, 44, 53, 59, 83, 85, 98, 99, 156, 157, 159, 161, 162, 169, 174, 176, 178, 179, 181, 182, 193, 195, 197, 210
Bruce, F. F. 104, 130, 134, 174, 175, 181, 182, 184, 192, 199, 200, 202, 205, 248
Bruner, F. D. 130, 136, 137
Bultmann, R. 53, 88, 93, 127, 132, 135, 195, 211, 215
Burge, G. M. 196, 235, 241, 255
Burnett, F. W. 13
Burridge, R. 37, 49, 77, 229
Buss, M. J. 55
Buth, R. 26, 27
Byrne, B. 126, 127, 128

C

Cabezón, J. I. 9
Caird, G. B. 32
Calvin, J. 176, 235, 236, 238, 251, 255, 257
Caragounis, C. C. 239, 242, 258
Carey, S. P. 20, 22
Carson, D. A. 41, 42, 46, 93, 104, 113, 132, 138, 166, 179, 193, 248
Carter, W. 46, 50, 65, 127, 211, 232
Chakkuvarackal, J. 17, 18, 19, 20, 22, 23, 24, 27, 33, 86, 180, 183, 185, 187
Charlesworth, J. H. ix, 129, 130
Chatman, S. 55, 63, 68, 154, 175
Chatterjee, S. K. 18, 20, 21, 22
Chennattu, R. M. 188
Chow, E. N., and Berheide, C. W. 94
Claassens, L. J. M. 39
Clements, K. 219
Collins, P. M. 225
Collins, R. F. 12, 126, 192
Coloe, M. L. 70, 174, 175, 176, 206
Cone, J. 93
Conzelmann, H. 214, 215
Cotterell, P., and Turner, M. 25
Culpepper, R. A. 13, 38, 40, 44, 47, 70, 72, 81, 113, 114, 115, 116, 118, 120, 159, 164, 175, 177, 180, 182, 184, 193, 251

D

Das, S. 21, 187
Davids, P. H. 242
Davies, M. 70
De, S. K. 21
DeConick, A. D. 132, 133
De Jonge, M., and Van Duyne, H. M. J. 56
De Klerk, J. C., and Schnell, S. W. 65
Delon, M. 17
Denning-Bolle, S. 29, 61, 62
deSilva, D.A. 155
Devasahayam, V. 93
Dodd, C. H. 28, 53, 54, 56, 57, 59, 60, 64, 70, 87, 161, 164, 165, 166, 183, 211, 215, 216
Domeris, W. R. 13
Dorner, I. A. 218
Duke, P. 49, 82, 127
Dunn, J. D. G. 213, 214, 215

E

Eco, U. 71, 72
Elam, K. 58
Ellis, P. F. 56, 70
Engberg-Pedersen, T. 192
Esler, P. F., and Piper, R. A. 13, 115, 181

F

Fitzmyer, J. A. 26, 29, 30, 33, 34, 130
Flemming, D. 37, 38
France, R. T. 112, 114, 211, 212, 214, 216, 217
Funk, R. F. 55

G

Gangopadhyay, U. 20
Gardner-Chloros, P. 22
Garver, E. 66
Gaventa, B. R. 174
Gench, F. T. 74, 82
Genette, G. 159
George, K. M. 20
George, T. 220
Gillman, F. M. 177
Gine, P. C. 23
Green, J. B. 201

Greimas, A. J., and Courtés, J. 29, 71, 154
Grelot, P. 25
Gromacki, R. G. 28, 31, 34
Gundry, R. H. 31
Gupta, R. K. D. 16, 17, 18, 20
Guthrie, D. 24, 25, 26, 27, 28, 33, 123, 168, 199
Guthrie, W. K. C. 62
Gutiérrez, G. 93

H

Haenchen, E. 128, 134, 140
Hahn, F. 91
Halliday, M. A. K. 32, 33
Harnack, A. V. 49, 50
Harris, E. 46
Harris, M. J. 196
Haskins, S. 121, 185
Hays, R. B. 85
Heever, V. D. 9
Hellholm, D. 66
Henderson, I. H. 5
Hendriksen, W. 127
Herman, V. 55
Hernando, J.D. 165, 167
Hezser, C. 34
Hiebert, D. E. 31, 34
Hill, B. R., Knitter, P., and Madges, W. 221
Hochman, B. 72
Hock, R. F., and O'Neil, E. N. 41
Hoeck, A. 105
Holquist, M. 39
Howard-Brook, W. 127
Howard, W. F. 25, 161, 163
Howarth, D. 60
Huie-Jolly, M. 158
Hurtado, L. W. 80, 213

I

Ibrahim, M. 250
Ihenacho, D. A. 92
Inbody, T. 220, 221
Irudaya, R. 84

J

Jackelén, A. 227, 228
Jacob, P. S. 147
Jaffe, A. 22
Jahan, R. 252
Jeyaraj, D. 222
Johnson, D. H. 40, 118, 119, 217, 233, 234
Jones, E. S. 185, 225
Jongeneel, J. A. B. 91
Joubert, J. 85, 86, 238, 239, 258
Junge, M. 220

K

Kabir, R. 250
Kanagaraj, J. J. viii, 10, 41, 47, 106, 175, 177, 178, 180, 183, 184, 185, 186, 231, 235, 251, 252
Kapoor, K. 17
Kappen, S. 93
Kärkkäinen, V-M. 225
Käsemann, E. 50
Keener, C. S. 49, 50, 63, 64, 67, 138, 155, 157, 161, 163, 179, 180, 193, 194, 198, 199
Kelly, A. J., and Moloney, F. J. 88, 158, 161
Kennedy, G. A. 37, 62, 63, 255
Kermode, F. xii, 42, 66, 72
Koester, C. R. 9, 11, 84, 120, 180, 254
Koester, H. 38
Kok, K. 89, 178, 237, 257
Köstenberger, A. J. 49, 56, 63, 65, 87, 90, 98, 127, 136, 137, 155, 156, 157, 159, 161, 174, 175, 178, 180, 181, 182, 192, 195, 197, 200, 201, 238, 258
Kutscher, S., and Werning, D. A. 16
Kynes, W. L. 242, 258
Kysar, R. 49, 50, 74, 160, 210, 211

L

Ladd, G. E. 212, 213, 214
Lamb, D. A. 28
Larsen, K. B. 69
Larsson, T. 138
Lausberg, H. 55
Law, V. 16, 17
Lehmann, E. A. 222
Leidig, E. 59
Liebau, H. 222
Lincoln, A. T. 129

Lindars, B., Edwards, R. B., and Court, J. M. 48
Lindars, B. 46, 49
Loader, W. 203, 204
Louw, J. P. 32, 59
Lubbock, P. 38
Lührmann, D. 216

M

MacDonald, G. 52
Malbon, E. S. 45
Malina, B. J., and Rohrbaugh, R. L. 25, 26, 32, 33, 91, 153, 237, 239, 241
Mangalwadi, V and R. 18, 20, 22
Maniparampil, J. 64, 65, 85, 86
Manns, F. 162
Maranhão, T. 55
Martin, R. P. 26, 30, 34
Martin, T. J. 55
Martyn, J. L. 29, 38, 60, 80, 90, 156, 159, 162, 163, 165, 168, 169, 186, 206, 210, 248
Marxsen, W. 154, 156, 157, 168, 186
McKim, D. K. 17
McKinzie, G. 247
McReynolds, K. 176
Meeks, W. A. 38, 210
Merenlahti, P. 224
Merkle, B. L. 201
Michael, S. M. 168
Michaels, J. R. 99, 100, 115, 199, 200, 201, 202
Millard, A. 38
Milne, B. 158, 174, 175, 176
Mittra, S., and Kumar, B. 250
Mlakuzhyil, G. 48, 138
Modrak, D. K. 17
Moloney, F. J. 6, 7, 10, 50, 53, 59, 86, 107, 108, 113, 116, 118, 119, 121, 122, 129, 132, 133, 135, 157, 159, 160, 163, 174, 175, 177, 179, 184, 185, 193, 195, 196, 197, 198, 203, 205, 206, 231, 236, 240, 243, 256
Moore, S. D. 72
Mopsuestia, T. 135, 136, 137
Morris, L. 114, 136, 158, 161, 174, 175, 177, 179, 193, 194, 195, 197, 198, 200, 205, 231, 232, 234, 236, 250, 252, 256
Motyer, S. 88
Mukherjee, S. 21
Mukhopadhayay, I. 18, 19
Murshid, G. 19

N

Namita. 158
Newbigin, L. 225
Newman, B. M., and Nida, E. A. 127
Neyrey, J. H. 44, 46, 56, 99, 101, 103, 130, 154, 157, 165, 166, 175, 176, 178, 180, 181, 182, 194
Nicklin, T. 26

O

Oberdorfer, B. 224
O'Day, G. R. 59
Ong, H. T. 31
Oniga. 17
Ormerod, N. J., and Clifton, S. 77, 88, 94
Østenstad, G. 68

P

Painter, J. P. 51, 78, 79, 82, 87, 162, 167
Painter, R. J. 87
Pamment, M. 13
Pandey, S. 205, 206, 234
Parsenios, G. L. 48, 167
Paschal, R. W. 195, 199, 201, 202, 203, 205
Peace, R.V. 154
Pepin, J. 40
Perry, C. 205, 206, 232, 235, 237, 252, 257
Petersen, N. R. 25, 34, 86, 128, 154, 160, 161
Popp, T. 126, 127, 128, 131
Porter, S. E. 31, 32, 34, 35, 177
Powell, M. A. 60, 70
Press, G. A. 55, 56, 61, 63, 66
Purvis, J. D. 177

Q

Quast, K. 148, 158, 162, 164, 165, 166, 167, 194

R

Ray, N. R. 18, 19, 20, 21
Redman, J. C. S. 157
Reed, W. L. 39
Reinhartz, A. 84
Renn, S. D. 10, 112, 119
Rensberger, D. K. 92, 129
Resseguie, J. L. 67, 69, 72, 79, 90, 194, 204, 206
Ricoeur, P. 70, 148
Ridderbos, H. 139, 247
Ringe, S. H. 88
Ritzer, G. 77
Robbins, V. K. 41
Robertson, R. 27
Robertson, S. 151
Robinson, J. A. T. 46, 50, 51
Robinson, R., and Clarke, S. 169
Roth, J. D. 224
Roy, J. M. 165

S

Sadananda, D. R. 58
Samartha, S. J. 93
Schaeffer, J. D. 67, 68
Schnackenburg, R. 64, 65, 80, 98, 99, 100, 101, 102, 103, 104, 112, 113, 114, 115, 117, 131, 133, 135, 139, 140, 183, 184
Schneiders, S. M. 11, 13, 57, 59, 84, 89, 92
Schnelle, U. 211, 212, 214, 215, 217, 220, 254
Scholer, D. M. 174, 180, 235, 251
Schoneveld, J. 42
Schreiner, T. 219
Schweizer, A. 53
Segovia, F. F. 195
Sen, A. K. 19
Senior, D. 194
Shillington, V. G. 105, 106
Skinner, C. W. 12, 125, 126, 137, 157
Smalley, S. 48
Smith, A. C. 222
Smith, D. M. 79, 167
Soja, E. W. 150, 246, 260
Spivey, J. T. 219
Spivey, R. A., and Smith, D. M. 49
Stagg, E and F. 174, 177, 180, 182, 184
Stambaugh, J. E., and Balch, D. L. 33, 34
Stanton, G. 25
Stegall, T. L. 212
Stein, R. H. 199
Stibbe, M. W. G. xii, 29, 45, 46, 69, 70, 79, 80, 83, 88, 92, 113, 129, 139, 157, 158, 160, 166, 167, 174, 176, 177, 181, 182, 184, 229, 240, 246
Story, C. I. K. 129
Stube, J. C. 192
Swartley, W. M. 136, 137
Sylva, D. 126, 128, 130, 131, 134, 139, 206

T

Tagore, R. 20
Talbert, C. H. 56, 136
Tasker, R. V. G. 231, 236, 238, 255, 258
Tavare, B. 170
Terry, M. S. 5
Thielman, F. 41
Thomas, M. M., Devanandan, P. D. 205, 225
Thomas, V. V. 222, 226
Thomaskutty, J. viii, xiii, xv, 8, 9, 11, 28-30, 54, 113-117, 120-122, 134, 145, 148, 158-166, 170, 175, 177-180, 182, 185-187, 196, 197, 204-206, 210, 216-219, 221, 227, 229, 231-236, 238, 240, 241, 243, 246, 250-253, 255-260
Thompson, M. M. 27, 28, 47, 126, 134, 135, 137, 138, 139, 140, 163, 196, 247, 248
Tobin, T. H. 40
Tolmie, D. F. 55
Torrey, C. C. 31, 33
Tovey, D. 55, 157, 162
Trebilco, P. 253
Turner, M. M. B. 26, 85, 86, 87, 98, 99, 100, 104, 218

V

Valentine, S. R. 49
Van Aarde, A. G. 29, 72
Van Belle, G. 53
Van der Watt, J. G. ix, 9, 10, 25, 26, 49, 60, 66, 80, 81, 85, 89, 92, 159, 162, 233, 234, 236, 237, 238, 240, 247, 255, 256
Vanhoozer, K. J. 67

Van Kooten, G. H. 29, 59, 61, 62
Varghese, J.. 206
Vashum, Y. 93
Vellanickal, M. 84
Visotzky, B. L. 90
Voigt, G. 70, 82, 160
Von Wahlde, U. C. 128

W

Waetjen, H. C. 129
Wallace, D. B. 5, 7, 146, 175, 240
Walters, M. 77, 241
Warren, A., and Wellek, R. 11, 66, 70
Watson, D. F. 41
Wead, D. W. 38
Webb, S. H. 195
Wenham, J. W. 33, 201
White, J. L. 34
Wilkins, M. J. 197
Williamson, H. G. M. 178
Windham, J. P. 230
Windisch, H. 88
Wingate, A. 169
Wise, M. O. 27, 30, 31
Witherington, B. 8, 48, 99, 100, 101, 104, 105, 106, 113, 114, 115, 116, 117, 122, 137, 139, 182, 183, 184, 185, 186, 197
Wright, C. J. H. 80, 91

Y

Yong, T. T., and Rahman, M. M. 230